"With research syntheses on topics including labour markets, care, macroeconomic issues, and social norms, along with diverse case studies from many countries, *Women's Economic Empowerment: Insights from Africa and South Asia* represents a vital new contribution to our understanding of the relationship between gender inequality and the dynamics of economies in low-resource settings."

– Ruth Levine, CEO, IDinsight, USA

"This edited volume presents cutting-edge research on women's economic empowerment from diverse settings in the Global South. Through an examination of the gendered continuities, disruptions, and contradictions in the social and economic status of women in developing countries, it demonstrates why structural gender inequalities may persist despite individualised advancement of some women and what can be done about it."

– Bipasha Baruah, Professor and Canada Research Chair in Global Women's Issues, Western University, Canada

"Does economic growth promote gender equality? Based on rigorous primary research in 50 countries in the developing world, the answers from this ambitious research program reflect the context-specificity of gender relations and the complex relationships among labor markets, social norms, and care work to identify options for programs and policy."

– Agnes Quisumbing, Senior Research Fellow, International Food Policy Research Institute, USA

WOMEN'S ECONOMIC EMPOWERMENT

This book investigates the barriers to women's economic empowerment in the Global South. Drawing on evidence from a wide range of countries, the book outlines important lessons and practical solutions for promoting gender equality.

Despite global progress in closing gender gaps in education and health, women's economic empowerment has lagged behind, with little evidence that economic growth promotes gender equality. The International Development Research Centre's (IDRC) Growth and Economic Opportunities for Women (GrOW) programme was set up to provide policy lessons, insights, and concrete solutions that could lead to advances in gender equality, particularly on the role of institutions and macroeconomic growth, barriers to labour market access for women, and the impact of women's care responsibilities. This book showcases rigorous and multi-disciplinary research emerging from this ground-breaking programme, covering topics such as the school-to-work transition, child marriage, unpaid domestic work and childcare, labour market segregation, and the power of social and cultural norms that prevent women from fully participating in better paid sectors of the economy.

With a range of rich case studies from Burkina Faso, Democratic Republic of the Congo, Ethiopia, Ghana, India, Kenya, Nepal, Rwanda, Sri Lanka, Tanzania, and Uganda, this book is perfect for students, researchers, practitioners, and policymakers working on women's economic empowerment and gender equality in the Global South.

Kate Grantham is an international development researcher, educator, and consultant focused on gender equality and women's empowerment issues.

Gillian Dowie is a senior programme officer in the Sustainable Inclusive Economies programme at IDRC, currently based in New Delhi, India.

Arjan de Haan is a senior programme specialist with IDRC's Sustainable Inclusive Economies programme.

ROUTLEDGE STUDIES IN DEVELOPMENT AND SOCIETY

Feminist Advocacy, Family Law and Violence against Women
International Perspectives
Edited by Mahnaz Afkhami, Yakın Ertürk, and Ann Elizabeth Mayer

Civil Society in the Global South
Edited by Palash Kamruzzaman

Quality in Higher Education as a Tool for Human Development
Enhancing Teaching and Learning in Zimbabwe
Patience Mukwambo

Cultural Resistance and Security from Below
Power and Escape through Capoeira
Zoë Marriage

The Prior Consultation of Indigenous Peoples in Latin America
Inside the Implementation Gap
Edited by Claire Wright and Alexandra Tomaselli

Transnational Social Mobilisation and Minority Rights
Identity, Advocacy and Norms
Corinne Lennox

Women's Economic Empowerment
Insights from Africa and South Asia
Edited by Kate Grantham, Gillian Dowie, and Arjan de Haan

For more information about this series, please visit: www.routledge.com/Routledge-Studies-in-Development-and-Society/book-series/SE0317

WOMEN'S ECONOMIC EMPOWERMENT

Insights from Africa and South Asia

Edited by Kate Grantham, Gillian Dowie, and Arjan de Haan

Routledge
Taylor & Francis Group
LONDON AND NEW YORK

International Development Research Centre
Ottawa • Amman • Montevideo • Nairobi • New Delhi

First published 2021
by Routledge
2 Park Square, Milton Park, Abingdon, Oxon OX14 4RN

and by Routledge
52 Vanderbilt Avenue, New York, NY 10017

Routledge is an imprint of the Taylor & Francis Group, an informa business

Co-published with the

International Development Research Centre
PO Box 8500, Ottawa, ON K1G 3H9 Canada
info@idrc.ca / www.idrc.ca

The research presented in this publication was carried out with the financial assistance of Canada's International Development Research Centre; the Foreign, Commonwealth and Development Office; and the William and Flora Hewlett Foundation. The views expressed herein do not necessarily represent those of the funders.

British Library Cataloguing-in-Publication Data
A catalogue record for this book is available from the British Library

Library of Congress Cataloging-in-Publication Data
Names: Grantham, Kate E., editor. | Dowie, Gillian, editor. | Haan, Arjan de, editor. | International Development Research Centre (Canada), issuing body.
Title: Women's economic empowerment : insights from Africa and South Asia / edited by Kate Grantham, Gillian Dowie, and Arjan de Haan.
Description: Abingdon, Oxon ; New York, NY : Routledge ; Ottawa : International Development Research Centre, 2021. |
Series: Routledge studies in development and society | Includes bibliographical references and index.
Identifiers: LCCN 2020039902 (print) | LCCN 2020039903 (ebook) | ISBN 9780367693794 (hardback) | ISBN 9780367694791 (paperback) | ISBN 9781003141938 (ebook) | ISBN 9781552506172 (IDRC ebook)
Subjects: LCSH: Growth and Economic Opportunities for Women. | Women in economic development--Africa. | Women--Africa–Economic conditions. | Women in economic development–South Asia. | Women–South Asia--Economic conditions. | Non-governmental organizations--Africa. | Non-governmental organizations--South Asia.
Classification: LCC HQ1240.5.A35 W663 2021 (print) | LCC HQ1240.5.A35 (ebook) | DDC 305.4096--dc23
LC record available at https://lccn.loc.gov/2020039902
LC ebook record available at https://lccn.loc.gov/2020039903

ISBN: 978-0-367-69379-4 (hbk)
ISBN: 978-0-367-69479-1 (pbk)
ISBN: 978-1-003-14193-8 (ebk)
ISBN: 978-1-55250-617-2 (IDRC ebk)

Typeset in Bembo
by Taylor & Francis Books

In memory of our colleague Stephan Klasen (1966–2020), a mentor and an inspiration to many.

CONTENTS

ILLUSTRATIONS

Figures

Tables

CONTRIBUTORS

Doris Buss is a professor of Law and Legal Studies at Carleton University in Canada, cross-appointed to Carleton's Institute of African Studies. Her research examines the socio-legal dimensions of international law and politics on women's rights, resource extraction, armed conflict, and its aftermath.

Deepta Chopra is a feminist social scientist and Research Fellow at the Institute of Development Studies in the UK, leading the Institute's work on women's empowerment and unpaid care. Deepta's research interests include the gendered political economy, empowerment of women and girls, and their links with unpaid care. She has developed and implemented several research projects on social protection and economic empowerment of women and girls in South Asia and sub-Saharan Africa.

Gisèle Eva Côté is senior gender and social inclusion specialist with IMPACT, leading their work on gender and natural resource management. Gisèle has over 25 years of international experience on human rights, women's rights, and Indigenous rights, as well as rights to land and natural resources in Latin America and Africa (in particular, in the Democratic Republic of Congo).

Arjan de Haan is a senior programme specialist with the International Development Research Centre's (IDRC) Sustainable Inclusive Economies programme. Before joining IDRC, Arjan was the social development advisor at the UK's Department for International Development (now the Foreign, Commonwealth and Development Office) for ten years and taught international development at the Institute of Social Studies in the Netherlands, Guelph University in Canada, and University of Sussex in the UK. Arjan holds a PhD in social history from Erasmus University Rotterdam.

Gillian Dowie is a senior programme officer on the Employment and Growth team at IDRC, currently based in the Asia regional office in New Delhi, India. She manages a portfolio of research on innovative social and economic development interventions with a focus on women's economic empowerment, including the first phase of the GrOW programme.

Nancy Folbre is professor emerita of Economics and director of the Program on Gender and Care Work at the Political Economy Research Institute at the University of Massachusetts Amherst in the US. In addition to numerous articles published in academic journals, she is the author of *The Rise and Decline of Patriarchal Systems* (forthcoming in 2021 from Verso). You can learn more about her at her website and blog, *Care Talk*.

Kate Grantham is an international development researcher, educator, and consultant focused on gender equality and women's empowerment issues ranging from education and decent employment, to health and gender-based violence, to social norms and care work. She is founder and principal consultant at FemDev, a global development consulting firm passionate about feminist approaches to research, evaluation, and analysis. Kate has a PhD in Women's Studies and Feminist Research from the University of Western Ontario in Canada.

Ramani Gunatilaka is a research associate at the International Centre for Ethnic Studies in Sri Lanka and an independent consultant analysing labour markets and subjective wellbeing. Her recent work focused on women's employment, skills deficits in the manufacturing sector, migration, and the distribution of consumption in fishing communities in Cambodia, India, and Sri Lanka. She is currently working on a study of the factors associated with the demand for women workers in Sri Lanka.

James Heintz is the Andrew Glyn Professor of Economics at the University of Massachusetts Amherst. His research and writing have focused on labour markets and employment policies, the distributive consequences of macroeconomic policies, gender and feminist economics, and the intersection between economics and human rights. He has worked on collaborative projects with numerous national and international institutions, including the Office of the High Commissioner for Human Rights, the International Labour Organization, and UN Women.

Jennifer Hinton is a leading scholar and consultant on artisanal and small-scale mining (ASM) with extensive local experience in Central and East Africa. She has a PhD in Mining Engineering from the University of British Colombia, is an adjunct professor at Carleton University in Canada, director of a number of Canadian mineral exploration companies, and co-owner of a small-scale mine. She has published widely on ASM, formalisation, gender, and mercury reduction.

Naila Kabeer is joint professor at the Departments of International Development and Gender Studies at the London School of Economics. She has extensive experience in research, teaching, and advisory work on gender, labour markets, social protection, and collective action. Her publications include *Mainstreaming Gender and Social Protection in the Informal Economy* (2008) and *Organizing Women Workers in the Informal Economy: Beyond the Weapons of the Weak* (2013).

Jane Kabubo-Mariara is a professor of Economics at the University of Nairobi, where she served as the director of the School of Economics from 2010 to 2016. She has been the executive director of the Partnership for Economic Policy since 2016. Her research interests include multidimensional and child poverty, youth and female labour market outcomes, among others. She co-led the GrOW-funded project on school-to-work transitions in six sub-Saharan African countries with Andy McKay.

Adalbertus Kamanzi is currently senior lecturer with the Master's Programme of Development Studies at the University of Namibia, Oshakati Campus. He has experience working professionally with the governments of Tanzania and Uganda, civil society, private companies, international development partners, academia, and research institutions. He has been involved in collaborative research worldwide and co-led multidisciplinary research projects in the areas of gender studies and agricultural economics with the University of Sussex and Washington University, respectively.

Sophia Kan is a postdoctoral research associate at the University of Göttingen Development Economics Group in Germany. Her research interests include migration, remittances, and female labour force participation.

Richard Kibombo is senior research fellow and an evaluation specialist at the Development Research and Social Policy Analysis Centre in Uganda. He holds a Master of Science degree in Statistics from the University of Wisconsin and a Bachelors of Statistics from Makerere University in Uganda. He has extensive experience in research, evaluations, and data processing, including in the areas of education, health, and natural resource management.

Stephan Klasen sadly passed away on 28 October 2020 after a long illness through which he remained fully committed to his work promoting gender equality. The editorial team for this book was privileged to benefit from his contributions. He was professor of Development Economics at the University of Göttingen in Germany. He obtained a PhD from Harvard University and held positions at the World Bank, King's College, and the University of Munich. His research focused on issues of poverty, inequality, environment, and gender. He was a member of the UN Committee on Development Policy and president of the European Development Research Network.

Sonia Laszlo is associate professor of Economics at McGill University and former director of McGill's Institute for the Study of International Development. Her expertise covers several aspects of applied microeconomic analysis in economic development. She has conducted research in Peru, Kenya, and in the Caribbean, using laboratory experiments, surveys, and randomised controlled trials. Her current research includes investigating the effects of social policies and conditions, with a focus on women and women's empowerment.

Joanne Lebert is the executive director of IMPACT (formerly Partnership Africa Canada). Joanne joined IMPACT in 2011 after years working in the non-governmental sector on gender-based violence and armed conflict, and as a researcher on global dimensions and the cultural politics of human rights. She is a leading expert on gender, artisanal, and small-scale mining, natural resource governance, and responsible supply chains of conflict-free minerals.

Rachel Marcus is senior research fellow at the Overseas Development Institute. Rachel has 25 years' experience as a social development researcher and practitioner. Her main areas of thematic interest are social and gender norm change, education, skills, and economic empowerment. She has also worked on social aspects of climate change and child protection. She is a lead technical advisor for the Advancing Learning and Innovation on Gender Norms platform.

Andy McKay is professor of Development Economics at the University of Sussex in the UK. He researches issues of poverty and living standards, labour, and gender among other areas, especially in sub-Saharan Africa and Asia. He acts as managing editor of the *Review of Development Economics* and is a regular resource person with the African Economic Research Consortium. He is director of the Young Lives research programme at the University of Oxford from 2020–2025.

Claudia Mitchell is a Distinguished James McGill Professor in the Department of Integrated Studies at McGill University in Canada. She is the director of the Institute of Human Development and Well-being and leads the Participatory Cultures Lab, a Canada Foundation for Innovation-funded unit focusing on research and training in the area of participatory visual methodologies. She is the co-founder and editor of *Girlhood Studies: An Interdisciplinary Journal.*

Stella Muthuri is currently a research specialist with the East Africa Research Hub of the UK's Foreign, Commonwealth and Development Office (FCDO). Previously, she was at the African Population and Health Research Center, investigating growth and economic opportunities for women with young children living in urban informal settlements through provision of childcare, and exploring what works to prevent and respond to violence against women and girls in humanitarian settings, among other projects.

Milka Njeri is a research officer at the African Population and Health Research Center, where she has been coordinating research projects for eight years. She holds a Master's degree in food, nutrition, and dietetics. Her research interests are maternal and child health and nutrition, especially interventions to promote optimal child and adolescent health, growth, and development in sub-Saharan Africa.

Milka Nyariro is an FRQSC-funded PhD candidate in the Faculty of Education at McGill University in Canada, and a 2018 International Development Research Centre doctoral research fellow. Her research interests include girlhood studies, women's economic empowerment, and addressing sexual and gender-based violence in schools and communities. Her PhD examines barriers to education for out-of-school pregnant teenagers and young mothers in low-resourced urban settings in Nairobi, Kenya.

Blair Rutherford is a professor of Anthropology at Carleton University and a research associate at the African Centre for Migration & Society at the University of the Witwatersrand. For more than 25 years, he has conducted ethnographic research in four African countries on the cultural politics of rural livelihoods and rural development initiatives. Among other publications, he is the author of two monographs concerning farm workers in Zimbabwe.

S.M. Hani Sadati is an FRQSC-funded PhD candidate in the Department of Integrated Studies in Education at McGill University. His PhD research is on participatory digital game development to address sexual and gender-based violence in agriculture colleges in Ethiopia. He is the co-founder and coordinator of the Games and Gamification for Human Development & Well-being Working Group of the McGill Institute for Human Development and Well-being.

Abby Sebina-Zziwa is senior research associate at the Development Research and Social Policy Analysis Centre and a private consultant on land, gender, and property rights, following a 25-year research career at Makerere Institute of Social Research at Makerere University in Uganda. She has a PhD in Anthropology from the University of Copenhagen. She currently chairs the Technical Committee on Systematic Land Adjudication and Certification with the Ministry of Lands and Housing in Uganda.

Jennifer Stewart is an associate professor with the School of Public Policy and Administration at Carleton University in Canada. Her research examines the relationship between the labour market and individual wellbeing with a specific focus on how this relationship works for women.

Ranmini Vithanagama is a researcher with the International Centre for Ethnic Studies in Sri Lanka. She is an economist with research interests in women's empowerment, women's livelihoods, forced migration, and disability. Ranmini holds Bachelor's and Master's degrees in Economics from the University of Colombo in Sri Lanka.

ACKNOWLEDGEMENTS

Developing this volume was only possible because of the collective effort of many friends and colleagues. We first need to thank all the authors in this volume, who have patiently dedicated their time to writing, revising, and editing. Many hours of work from everyone involved has gone into this, and we are lucky to have had such a stellar pool of researchers and thought leaders to draw from.

This book would not exist without the success of the Growth and Economic Opportunities for Women (GrOW) programme, which was made possible with support from the UK's Foreign, Commonwealth and Development Office (FCDO), the William and Flora Hewlett Foundation, and Canada's International Development Research Centre (IDRC). Specific thanks go to Katie Chapman, Benedetta Musillo, Chloe O'Gara, Althea Anderson, Ruth Levine, Helena Choi, Kim Brehm, Steven Lee, Tim Hatton, Lina Payne, Stephen Coyle, and Tim Green, among others. GrOW was the result of the dedication of a large IDRC team who provided support in various critical ways: Martha Melesse, Tiffany Barnes-Huggins, Mylène Bordeleau, Alejandra Vargas Garcia, Madiha Ahmed, Edgard Rodriguez, Flaubert Mbiekop, Paul Okwi, Bouba Housseini, Carolina Robino, Francisco Cos-Montiel, Thanya Bastien, Wilfredo Jirón, Louise Guénette, and Margaret Male are just a few whose role needs to be acknowledged. Nanci Lee, the poet-educator who led the external evaluation of the GrOW programme, has contributed much and inspired many of us.

Countless others have contributed to GrOW, particularly the many members of 14 research teams spread across the globe, roughly 225 of whom are from countries in the Global South, as well as numerous advisors and contributors, some of whom are included in this volume. Professor Naila Kabeer wrote the foundational evidence review, which informed the focus and design of the GrOW programme, and she has contributed to this volume. Her intellectual leadership was critical from the outset. Professor Sonia Laszlo, who co-authored the introduction with us, has provided valuable guidance to the GrOW programme, to the field of measuring women's economic empowerment, and to the development of this volume. We are grateful to her for her many contributions.

We thank IDRC's publisher, Nola Haddadian, for guiding us through this process, editing each chapter, answering our questions, and pushing us to develop the best version of this book possible. From Routledge, we wish to thank Helena Hurd and Matthew Shobbrook for their guidance and advice, as well as the anonymous reviewers who provided valuable comments on the book proposal and chapters.

We hope that this book will contribute to understanding the many and dynamic barriers to economic equality that women face throughout the world, drawing attention to the systemic and social challenges that are so difficult to overcome. True equality is an uphill battle, and this volume is the product of a collective commitment to constantly push for change.

The opinions expressed in this work do not necessarily reflect those of any funding organisations. Responsibility for omissions of fact or judgment rests solely with us.

Kate Grantham, Arjan de Haan, and Gillian Dowie

ACRONYMS AND ABBREVIATIONS

AAR	ActionAid Rwanda
AFM	Administrateurs de Foyer Minier (Directors of the Mine)
ASM	Artisanal and small-scale mining
BEE	Black Economic Empowerment
DCS	Department of Census and Statistics (Sri Lanka)
DHS	Demographic and Health Surveys
DRC	Democratic Republic of the Congo
ESI	Empowerment in Slums Index
FLFP	female labour force participation
GBV	gender-based violence
GDP	gross domestic product
GMM	Generalized Method of Moments
GrOW	Growth and Economic Opportunities for Women
IDRC	International Development Research Centre
IDS	Institute of Development Studies
IPV	intimate partner violence
ISST	Institute of Social Studies Trust
LMIC	low- and middle-income country
LRI	Likelihood Ratio Index
LTTE	Liberation Tigers of Tamil Eelam (Sri Lanka)
MENA	Middle East and North Africa
MGNREGA	Mahatma Gandhi National Rural Employment Guarantee Act (India)
MLE	Maximum Likelihood Estimation
MS	Mahila Samakhya (India)
NGO	Non-governmental organisation
OECD	Organisation for Economic Co-operation and Development

PDG	Président Directeur Général (Chief Executive Officer)
PSDF	Punjab Skills Development Fund
RCT	randomised control trial
SDGs	Sustainable Development Goals
WEE	women's economic empowerment
WEAI	Women's Empowerment in Agriculture Index
WESI	Women's Empowerment in Slums Index
WIEGO	Women in Informal Employment Globalizing and Organizing

INTRODUCTION

The Growth and Economic Opportunities for Women programme

Gillian Dowie, Arjan de Haan, Sonia Laszlo, and Kate Grantham

Introduction

Women's economic empowerment (WEE) is increasingly at the centre of international development policy—not just as a means to an end, but as an end in itself. In order to reach several development objectives, such as those set out in the UN Sustainable Development Goals, empowering women is seen as key to reducing poverty and improving the health and wellbeing of future generations. Women make up one half of the human population, yet they suffer gross inequalities: gender gaps in income and human capital persist despite rapid improvement in global living standards and educational attainment, and women continue to disproportionately bear the burden of unpaid care work and be subject to gender-based discrimination and violence.

The Growth and Economic Opportunities for Women (GrOW) programme set out to provide cutting-edge evidence to inform social and economic policies that improve poor women's opportunities and lives while promoting economic growth. Launched in 2013, GrOW was a unique, multi-funder partnership between the UK's Foreign, Commonwealth and Development Office, the William and Flora Hewlett Foundation, and Canada's International Development Research Centre. It focused on the barriers that women face in low-income contexts, how economic growth promotes or hinders women's empowerment, and the ways women's empowerment can promote growth.

At the outset, the design of the GrOW programme was motivated by the call to build an evidence base on the economic dimensions of gender inequalities (Buvinic and Furst-Nichols 2014; Grown, Addison, and Tarp 2016) and to assess whether a global reduction in gender gaps in health and education translate into economic gains. This theme was informed by a background conceptual paper by Naila Kabeer (2017)—an updated version of which is included in part one of this volume—which provided a detailed review of the evidence on the relationship between economic growth and gender equality, demonstrating that the former does not always promote the latter or not sufficiently so. This paper also identified the definition of WEE used at the inception of the programme as the "capacity of women to participate in, contribute to, and benefit from growth processes in ways that recognise the value of their contribution, respect their dignity, and make it possible to negotiate a fairer distribution of the benefits of growth" (OECD-DAC Gender Equality Network 2011).

GrOW promoted, simultaneously, a strengthened evidence base on barriers to women's economic opportunities and its relationship with economic growth, local capacities for innovative analysis on women's empowerment, and the uptake of research to inform policy and practice at national and international levels. It supported 14 projects in 50 countries, with primary research conducted in 18 countries initiated through a global call for proposals. GrOW supported over 85 southern-based policy-oriented researchers, 60% being women, who produced 60 high quality papers and policy briefs and over 30 recorded cases of impactful policy engagement. GrOW also produced five synthesis pieces that draw out overarching lessons from the programme, four of which are included in part two of this volume.

The portfolio of GrOW-supported research includes a diversity of methods and tools, providing innovative and cutting-edge evidence. This diversity, which included both quantitative and qualitative methods and is reflected in the case studies in Part III of this volume, proved to be a key strength of this research. Qualitative studies added to the depth and contextual relevance of some key takeaways from the quantitative work. Often, projects themselves built on multiple methods. Rigorous experimental or non-experimental tools provided the possibility to delve into causal relationships, while the qualitative work added the rich texture to speak to underlying mechanisms. We see examples of this combination of tools in projects that document the interplay between women's paid and unpaid work, and those that explore role of social norms in women's labour market decisions.

For example, in Kenya and India, researchers implemented randomised control trials (RCTs) that they combined with qualitative methods to test whether and how the provision of daycare can unlock the potential of women in the labour market (Richardson et al. 2018; Clark et al. 2019). A deeper exploration of one of the innovative mixed-methods approaches is included in Chapter 7 of this volume by Milka Nyariro and colleagues. In India, Nepal, Tanzania, and Rwanda, researchers combined survey data with an in-depth case study to assess how women and families in low-income households balance unpaid care work with income-earning activities (Chopra and Zambelli 2017; see Chapter 8 in this volume by Deepta Chopra for more details). These studies explored how WEE programmes and policies can be improved to help women achieve a better balance between income-generating and caring roles in contexts where women disproportionately bear the burden of care for their children and households. The solutions- and policy-oriented approaches adopted by these and other GrOW researchers successfully combined different methods, including demonstrating the 'why' as well as the 'what' of WEE programming with positive results (de Haan, Dowie, and Mariara 2020).

Key themes from GrOW-supported studies

Together, GrOW-supported research documents the deep, systemic nature of the challenges that women face in achieving equality in economic and social spheres, and in finding and keeping decent work opportunities. Given the policy orientation of this research, the studies point to effective solutions that bring women into the labour force, while remaining conscious of the need for decent work and better work-life balance.

One of the key questions the programme addressed related to the links between economic growth and empowerment. Chapter 3 in this volume by Sophia Kan and Stephan Klasen provides an overview of evidence from GrOW research that finds reducing certain types of gender inequalities, such as in education, can lead to economic growth, but there is little strong evidence that the same is true of other inequalities, such as employment opportunities or access to credit.

Research across GrOW demonstrates that economic growth alone is not sufficient to bring about progress on gender equality, even in the labour market. Rates of women's labour force participation vary across regions, and there is little evidence of a narrowing in the gender gap. Klasen et al. (2019) demonstrate that women still often participate in the labour force out of distress in contexts where economic growth is creating too few decent job opportunities overall. In poorer countries, they found that women often leave the labour market as soon as it is affordable to do so. Even in the context of programmes that aim to be empowering, women often still work out of necessity and many of these jobs are of low quality, disempowering, or reinforce traditional gender roles. Indeed, for many women who face such labour market conditions, withdrawal may very well enhance their wellbeing.

Reasons why recent progress in narrowing gender gaps in education, health, and political representation is not matched by similar improvements in labour market outcomes for women are further explored in Chapter 2 by James Heintz. While more research is necessary to flesh out these discrepancies, including on the role of norms and discrimination, gender-based violence, and unpaid care, existing evidence shows that interventions designed to enhance WEE have been effective at improving income and subjective wellbeing. Whether such interventions would affect economic growth if implemented at scale remains a question for future research.

Moreover, there is no clear trend in occupational and sectoral segregation among women. There are very few cases in which women enter occupations 'traditionally' considered male, a form of segregation that has increased on average (Borrowman and Klasen 2019). In countries that have seen growth in natural resources, for example, many of the new formal sector opportunities have been filled by men, as illustrated in the case of the mining sector in Chapter 6 of this volume by Doris Buss and colleagues. Researchers demonstrate that occupational segregation exists even in the lowest ranks of job ladders. Globally, women's participation in the services sector has been increasing, though these opportunities are often informal, precarious, and low-paying.

Occupational segregation is thus a likely candidate to explain why economic growth does not lead to increases in gender equality. Particularly in contexts where few jobs are created, women continue to remain in lower paid and insecure jobs. It also means that economic policies, by themselves, have limited impact on gender equality if female labour is absorbed by the informal sector. Furthermore, policies promoting industrial growth, including trade, will have mixed effects on women's employment depending on existing occupational segregation.

Another key theme from GrOW-supported studies is that underlying these macroeconomic trends, spoken and unspoken expectations about women's roles continue to dictate and constrain their behaviour and their choices. Unequal and often entrenched gender norms—embedded in institutions and even laws—continue to create significant barriers to women's engagement in the labour market, and these can play out both on the demand and supply sides. On the demand side, norms about suitable jobs for women can be very strong and lead to discriminatory practices. On the supply side, gender norms around unpaid household reproductive work mean that, even as women become more active in the workforce, they bear the double burden of caring for children and the elderly, and the bulk of household chores. These norms may also inhibit a family's willingness to invest in their daughters' education and human capital. Whether they work through demand or supply channels, such norms create inequities as well as inefficiencies in labour markets.

Findings from GrOW-supported research on the relationship of WEE to gender relations, social norms, and unpaid care work are synthesised by Nancy Folbre (Chapter 4 in this volume). Folbre highlights that unpaid care continues to be undervalued and poorly measured, contributing to a bias in public policy and investment that are key to addressing constraints on women's time use, income, and labour force participation. Scarce, expensive, and low-quality provision of childcare is a continued barrier to women's employment opportunities globally, and inadequate investment in social infrastructure limits improvements in productivity of women's paid and unpaid work.

Rachel Marcus' contribution in Chapter 5 describes in detail the ways in which discriminatory gender norms affect women's work experiences and economic opportunities. Marcus summarises the GrOW evidence on how these social norms contribute to stagnation in access to decent job opportunities in manifold ways: ambivalence about women working outside the home plays a very important role, particularly in Asia; norms limiting or even prohibiting women from carrying out specific activities; norms around masculinity that reduce men's contribution to unpaid care and household work; norms about early marriage and child-bearing that limit girls' education; and women's fear of sexual violence at, and on the way to, work.

In Chapter 9, the case study by Ramani Gunatilaka and Ranmini Vithanagama in the post-conflict context of Sri Lanka's Northern Province illustrates the factors determining women's economic opportunities. Women's labour force participation is impacted by household composition and tends to be driven by distress. There is no indication that norms around women's work were eased after the conflict, and women pushed into the labour market remain in low quality, informal work under considerable financial stress. Income support may alleviate this pressure, but a range of policies are needed to address the disadvantages that women face.

Chapter 10 by Jane Kabubo-Mariara, Adalbertus Kamanzi, and Andy McKay focuses on the school-to-work-transition of girls in six African countries, highlighting the multiple and reinforcing labour market constraints women face in contexts of poverty, including limited educational prospects, responsibility for unpaid care and household work, and early marriage and pregnancy. Policies to address these constraints, similarly, need to be multi-faceted, including improvements in education quality and incentives to stay in school, eliminating discriminatory social and legal norms, broadening opportunities for skills training and decent employment, and reducing the burden of unpaid care that falls disproportionately on women and girls.

A recurring theme in GrOW-supported research relates to women's 'double burden' of paid work and unpaid care that constrains poor women's labour market choices and opportunities. Studies in Kenya, India, Nepal, Tanzania, and Rwanda, explored in Chapters 7 and 8 in this volume, looked at how women balance unpaid care work and income-earning activities, and found that the double burden exhausts poor women, leaving them very little time to rest, and this also negatively impacts their children. Importantly, Chapter 8 explores the ways that women's employment and empowerment programmes have also neglected women's double burden, contributing to their mental and physical depletion.

One key takeaway for policy interventions targeting labour force participation is the need to consider this double burden. Indeed, programmes that promote employment will fail to translate into increased and sustained women's labour force participation if they ultimately need to withdraw from the labour market to care for children. If they do return to work when their children are old enough to go to school, it is well known that women pay a higher child wage penalty than men, globally. The GrOW-supported research in Kenya (Clark et al. 2019) showed that publicly provided childcare can be an effective policy option. It demonstrated that having access to childcare can sharply narrow the gender gap in labour force participation and reduce excessive workloads for those already working. With safe and affordable care, women can find better jobs and better hours.

Each of these themes—labour markets, macroeconomics, unpaid care, and social norms—are explored in more depth throughout this volume. A central thread in all this work is how interconnected these themes are. For women, and poor women in particular, employment opportunities and women's double burden are deeply interlinked. The key to understanding women's roles and experiences in the labour market is to understand the interplay between these barriers and constraints. To move toward gender equality, policies and programmes need to target and address the deeper structural issues that prevent women from achieving economic and social equality.

Measurement of WEE in GrOW-supported research

One key challenge in managing a large portfolio of diverse research projects that aim to understand how to improve women's economic opportunities lies in how to measure its impacts. The question of how to measure WEE is neither new nor resolved. The concept itself is complex, multi-dimensional, and sensitive to culture and context, meaning that its measurement is likely to be equally so (Kabeer 1999; Buvinic and Furst-Nichols 2015; Donald et al. 2020; Laszlo et al. 2020). While there is no consensus in the literature on a definitive instrument that captures this complexity, many instruments do build on Kabeer's (1999) conceptual contribution. Namely, that women's empowerment is a combination of three interconnected concepts: agency, resources, and achievements. Part of the additional challenge in measuring WEE is the fact that these three concepts are not additive components, rather they operate as a process.

GrOW-supported projects adopted the measurement approach that best suited their research needs and methods. Laszlo and Grantham (2017) conducted a review of the 14 GrOW projects and found a great degree of heterogeneity of measurement efforts. Out of the 32 project documents reviewed by the authors, they found that these documents included up to 40 different indicators related to WEE. While not all projects or documents set out to measure WEE explicitly, most included some indicator or index related to economic empowerment. Several studies employed existing surveys in their data collection and analysis, like USAID's Demographic and Health Surveys (DHS) or the International Food Policy Research Institute's Women's Empowerment in Agriculture Index (WEAI).

Not surprisingly, given the "economic opportunity" focus of the GrOW projects, a large majority of these projects (27 out of the 32 documents) reported some measure related to labour force participation—employment status, occupation, or sector. Twenty-one of the 32 documents reported some measure of human capital—namely literacy, educational attainment, or gender gap in schooling. Meanwhile, 18 of the 32 documents used some measure of women's autonomy in household decisions in their analysis. Examples of these types of indicators include the widely used measures identifying who (the woman, her spouse, jointly with spouse, someone else) makes key household decisions such as over major expenses, how to spend the woman's income, or about child health or education matters. These indicators relate to the dimension of agency related to control over resources. Finally, nine documents are associated with some measure of gender inequality in social norms (such as freedom of movement or attitudes toward violence against women) and another nine with some measure of gender inequality in legal institutions (civil liberties, requiring permission to work or have a bank account, restrictions on land ownership).

GrOW also supported a multidisciplinary review of the literature on measurement of WEE in intrahousehold settings. Using intrahousehold models of decision-making developed by economists (Haddad, Hoddinott, and Alderman 1997; Browning and Chiappori 1998) as a point of departure, Laszlo et al. (2020) show that most existing measures can be mapped into a constrained optimisation problem. Many indicators of agency tie directly into a bargaining power parameter which weights household members' preferences. If women obtain (through external or internal means) more bargaining power, they are more able to assert and act on their own preferences. A higher income as a share of the household budget is the natural way economists have considered an increased bargaining power (e.g. Browning and Chiappori 1998; Basu, Narayan, and Ravallion 2001). However, both norms and psychological factors may influence the degree to which a woman can negotiate and assert these preferences. More gender equal norms around intra-household decision-making and psycho-social factors (e.g. goal setting, self-esteem, self-confidence) can influence her bargaining power. The authors propose these sorts of measures to be *direct* and they map well with notions of both individual and relational agency (relational with respect to other household decision-makers).

Ultimately, the portfolio of GrOW-supported research points to the limits of attempting to measure WEE with a single cross-cutting instrument. Despite recent advances in developing such instruments, researchers tend to apply definitions and instruments that fit their context and conceptual framework. Context matters, both cultural and topical, and thus selection of measurement tools must reflect that complexity.

Organisation of the volume

This volume brings together state-of-the-art research on WEE in developing country contexts, based on evidence emerging from the GrOW programme. It showcases advances in research on WEE and highlights where the field has moved over the last five to ten years.

The contributors featured in this volume are researchers who led GrOW-funded studies, as well as WEE experts and thought leaders who helped conceptualise the programme in its beginning stages and who later synthesised programme findings and situated them within the wider body of global evidence. Their work encourages readers to examine the societal structures and norms that keep women from achieving equality in the economic spheres of their lives, as well as the political and social, and how these are all connected. Issues covered include the school-to-work transition, early marriage and pregnancy, unpaid care and household work, labour market segregation, and the power of discriminatory social and cultural norms that prevent women from fully participating in better paid sectors of the economy. Additionally, the book examines the importance of addressing economic empowerment in a holistic manner—i.e., providing better access to basic services, better economic opportunities, a supportive legal framework, and securing a strong commitment from policymakers to address gender inequality and promote WEE.

The book is divided into three parts with Part I conceptualising the relationship between economic growth and gender equality (which provided the foundation for the GrOW programme). Part II synthesises research coming out of GrOW on different topics (i.e. labour markets, macroeconomics, unpaid care, and social norms) and positions this new knowledge within the larger body of global research. Finally, Part III presents GrOW-supported case studies from developing country contexts, including Burkina Faso, Democratic Republic of the Congo, Ethiopia, Ghana, India, Kenya, Nepal, Pakistan, Rwanda, Sri Lanka, Tanzania, and Uganda. Organised in this way, the collection moves from broad discussions of different WEE topics to specific case studies that provide more contextual evidence and analysis, including on the kinds of methods that allow for this depth of insight. The concluding chapter revisits the main themes of the book, focusing on implications for research, policy, and practice on WEE.

The case studies in this volume are representative of GrOW topic areas and focus regions of South Asia and sub-Saharan Africa. The first case study presented in Part III by Doris Buss and colleagues (Chapter 6) examines authority structures and institutions as contexts shaping gender norms and their navigation by women working in artisanal and small-scale mining. The research for this chapter comes from a mixed-methods study of women's livelihoods at six artisanal and small-scale mine sites, two in each of Democratic Republic of Congo, Rwanda, and Uganda. In Chapter 7, Milka Nyariro and colleagues discuss the methodology and results of a PhotoVoice participatory evaluation conducted as part of a larger randomised study in which mothers living in an urban settlement in Kenya received vouchers for access to subsidised daycare. In Chapter 8, Deepta Chopra presents the results of mixed-methods research with low-income women living in India, Nepal, Tanzania, and Rwanda to examine the relationship between paid work and unpaid care work. Further, this chapter highlights the physical and mental impacts of entering the paid labour market on women and their families. Chapter 9 by Ramani Gunatilaka and Ranmini Vithanagama explores the various demographic, socio-economic, institutional, and conflict-related factors influencing women's labour force participation in Sri Lanka's Northern Province. The final case study by Jane Kabubo-Mariara and colleagues (Chapter 10) provides a cross-country examination of the school-to-work transition of young women, looking at issues of family formation and the challenge of addressing interacting factors including education, workforce transition, marriage, pregnancy, and childcare. This research includes evidence from Burkina Faso, Ethiopia, Ghana, Kenya, Tanzania, and Uganda.

The collection of research in this volume is intended to provide insights, policy lessons, new research directions, and concrete solutions that can lead to advances in gender equality and WEE. By exploring the role of institutions and macro-economic growth, unpacking the barriers to labour market engagement for women, and examining the impact of social norms and women's care responsibilities, the volume demonstrates the interlinked and systemic nature of barriers to gender equality in women's economic and social lives in developing country contexts. The evidence is intended to contribute to the development of policies and programmes that are gender transformative and that affect real change for women, as we celebrate the 25th anniversary of the Beijing Declaration and Platform for Action on gender equality and enter the final decade for delivering on SDG 5: achieving gender equality and empowering women and girls.

References

Basu, Kaushik, Ambar Narayan, and Martin Ravallion (2001). Is literacy shared within households? Theory and evidence for Bangladesh. *Labour Economics* 8(6): 649–665.

Borrowman, Mary, and Stephan Klasen (2019). Drivers of gender sectoral and occupational segregation in developing countries. *Feminist Economics* 26(2): 62–94.

Browning, Martin, and Pierre Chiappori (1998). Efficient intra-household allocations: A general characterization and empirical tests. *Econometrica* 66(6): 1241–1278.

Buvinic, Mayra, and Rebecca Furst-Nichols (2014). Promoting women's economic empowerment: What works? Policy Research Working Paper 7087. Washington, DC: World Bank Group. http://documents.worldbank.org/curated/en/864621468337180679/Promoting-womens-economic-empowerment-what-works.

Buvinic, Mayra, and Rebecca Furst-Nichols (2015). Measuring women's economic empowerment: Companion to a roadmap for promoting women's economic empowerment. Washington, DC: United Nations Foundation. www.fsnnetwork.org/sites/default/files/measuring_womens_econ_emp_final_06_09_15.pdf.

Chopra, Deepta, with Elena Zambelli (2017). No time to rest: Women's lived experiences of balancing paid work and unpaid care work. Global Synthesis Report for Women's Economic Empowerment Policy and Programming. Brighton: Institute of Development Studies. www.ids.ac.uk/publications/no-time-to-rest-womens-lived-experiences-of-balancing-paid-work-and-unpaid-care-work/.

Clark, Shelley, Caroline W. Kabiru, Sonia Laszlo, and Stella Muthuri (2019). The impact of childcare on poor urban women's economic empowerment in Africa. *Demography* 56: 1247–1272.

de Haan, Arjan, Gillian Dowie, and Jane Mariara (2020). To RCT or not, is not the question: Methods for policy-relevant research on gender equality. *World Development* 127.

Donald, Aletheia, Gayatry Koolwal, Jeannie Annan, Kathryn Falb, and Markus Goldstein (2020). Measuring women's agency. *Feminist Economics* 26(3): 200–226.

Grown, Caren, Tony Addison, and Finn Tarp (2016). Aid for gender equality and development: Lessons and challenges. *Journal of International Development* 28(3): 311–319. https://onlinelibrary.wiley.com/doi/full/10.1002/jid.3211.

Haddad, Lawrence, John Hoddinott, and Harold Alderman (Eds.) (1997). *Intra-household resource allocation in developing countries: Models, methods, and policy*. Baltimore: Johns Hopkins University Press.

Kabeer, Naila (1999). Resources, agency, achievements: Reflections on the measurement of women's empowerment. *Development and Change* 30(3): 435–464. www.utsc.utoronto.ca/~kmacd/IDSC10/Readings/research%20design/empowerment.pdf.

Kabeer, Naila (2017). Women's economic empowerment and inclusive growth: Labour markets and enterprise development. GrOW Research Working Paper Series, GWP-2017–01. Montreal: Institute for the Study of International Development, McGill University. http://grow.research.mcgill.ca/pubs/GWP-01-2017.pdf.

Klasen, Stephan, Janneke Pieters, Manuel Santos Silva, and Le Thi Ngoc Tu (2019). What drives female labour force participation? Comparable micro-level evidence from eight developing and emerging economies. IZA Discussion Paper Series No. 12067. Bonn: Institute of Labor Economics (IZA). http://ftp.iza.org/dp12067.pdf.

Laszlo, Sonia, and Kate Grantham (2017). Measurement of women's economic empowerment in GrOW projects. GrOW Research Working Paper Series, GWP-2017–08. Montreal: Institute for the Study of International Development, McGill University. http://grow.research.mcgill.ca/publications/working-papers/gwp-2017-08.pdf.

Laszlo, Sonia, Kate Grantham, Ecem Oskay, and Tingting Zhang (2020). Grappling with the challenges of measuring women's economic empowerment in intrahousehold settings. *World Development* 132: 1–13.

OECD-DAC Gender Equality Network (2011). Women's economic empowerment. Issues paper. Paris: OECD-DAC Gender Equality Network (GENDERNET). https://www.oecd.org/dac/gender-development/47561694.pdf.

Richardson, Robin A., Sam Harper, Norbert Schmitz, and Arijit Nandi (2018). The effect of affordable daycare on women's mental health: evidence from a cluster randomized trial in rural India. *Social Science & Medicine* 217: 32–41.

PART I

Conceptualising the relationship between economic growth and gender equality

1

GENDER EQUALITY, INCLUSIVE GROWTH, AND LABOUR MARKETS

Naila Kabeer

Introduction: markets as sites of gender subordination

Growth is inclusive when it ensures livelihood opportunities for all sections of the population. An inclusive growth agenda is thus concerned not only with the quantity of employment but also with its distribution. Recent research suggests both an instrumental and an intrinsic rationale for an explicit focus on gender equality within such an agenda. The instrumental rationale reflects a strong and growing body of research suggesting that gender equality has a positive impact on economic growth. This relationship appears most consistent regarding education (more widely studied) and employment (less widely studied) and holds for a variety of different countries and across differing time periods over the past half century (Kabeer and Natali 2013).

These positive macro-level findings are supported by both macro-level evidence (Klasen 1999, 2002; Seguino 2007a) and a wealth of micro-level studies (Quisumbing 2003; Doepke and Tertilt 2011; World Bank 2012) showing that women's access to valued economic resources can have a range of positive outcomes for their voice and influence within the household, including their ability to invest in the human capital and capabilities of their children. Women's increased participation in the labour market can also have a positive effect on gender-related norms and attitudes in countries (Seguino 2007b). Such findings provide a strong intrinsic rationale for ensuring women's participation in processes of growth—it contributes to the inclusiveness of growth merely by the fact that women make up half of the world's population, but it is also likely to improve the distributional pattern of the growth process.

However, evidence on the converse relationship—the implications of growth for gender equality as measured by a range of indicators—is far more mixed (Kabeer and Natali 2013). Indeed, some of the fastest growing low- and middle-income countries (LMICs) show the least signs of progress on gender equality in terms of economic and political access (World Economic Forum 2018). Economic growth *per se* clearly cannot be relied on to promote gender equality. At the same time, the findings noted above suggest that growth is far more likely to promote women's bargaining power and household wellbeing when it is accompanied by an expansion of women's education and employment.[1]

These findings highlight the pivotal importance of women's access to economic resources, both contributing to growth as well as promoting the equity of growth outcomes. They help to explain some of the growing interest in the economic dimensions of gender equality within the international development community, epitomised by the emergence of the concept of women's economic empowerment (WEE).

Conceptualisations of women's empowerment have always included a material dimension. The new focus on their *economic* empowerment has had a double-edged impact. On the one hand, it has narrowed the empowerment agenda for many policymakers to a largely market phenomenon. On the other, it has allowed feminist researchers to draw attention to the market as a site of women's subordination rather than as the competitive mechanism for welfare maximisation that is assumed in a great deal of mainstream economics.

The aim of this chapter is to demonstrate how gender inequalities in wider society are perpetuated and reinforced by market forces in ways that block women's capacity to contribute to more inclusive forms of economic progress. The chapter begins by exploring how mainstream and feminist economics have understood labour market inequalities and outlines a conceptual framework to guide an empirical analysis of the constraints on women's efforts to earn a livelihood. It then provides an empirical overview of the intersectional stratification of market opportunities, how gender overlaps with other socioeconomic inequalities in determining the position of men and women within the occupational hierarchies of the market. Next, it turns to explore the ways that gender inequalities within and beyond the household operate to constrain women's ability to take up paid work and restrict the kinds of work they can do. Following this, the text draws on studies of waged workers and self-employment to provide a more detailed illustration of these constraints as they play out in the labour market. The chapter concludes by drawing out the policy implications of the analysis.

Gender inequalities in the labour market: theoretical approaches and an analytical framework

Theoretical approaches to labour market analysis can be broadly divided into neoclassical theories, which focus on individual choice, and sociological theories, which focus on structural constraints. There has been some convergence of these approaches over time as social norms and legal constraints have been incorporated into choice-theoretic frameworks and as greater attention is paid to issues of choice and agency within structuralist explanations—but important differences remain.

Individual choice is, of course, at the heart of neoclassical economics and has dominated much of its analysis of gender and labour markets. It conceptualises workers' decisions to sell their labour in terms of their efforts to maximise utility and employers' decisions to hire labour in terms of their efforts to maximise profits. Differences in how men and women fare in the labour market are explained in several ways.

One explanation suggests that gender-differentiated labour market outcomes reflect gender differential investments in human capital endowments, a rational response to women's role in biological reproduction and family care and, by extension, their weaker attachment to the labour market (Polachek 1981). A second argues that gender inequalities in labour market outcomes reflect a 'taste for discrimination' on the part of individual employers but maintains that such tastes can only be sustained in the absence of competitive markets (Becker 1971). A third puts forward the idea of 'statistical discrimination', suggesting that, given imperfect information, employers use aggregate group characteristics, such as group averages of education levels, to make judgements about the suitability of all members of that group for particular jobs. This means individuals belonging to different social groups can be treated very differently even if they are identical in every other way (Arrow 1973). More recently, women's lesser ability to adjust to market signals as easily as men, as a result of their family responsibilities, has been described as giving employers the monopsony-like power to hire women on less favourable terms than men (Manning 2003).

Neoclassical economic analysis of labour markets relies almost exclusively on variable-centred econometric techniques to translate its theoretical models into empirical estimates. This has helped to identify and measure gender differences and discrimination but throws very little light on the underlying causes. These are generally assumed to reflect the theoretical model adopted rather than being considered a matter for empirical investigation. For feminist economists, on the other hand, gender is "more than a dummy variable" (Figart 2005). Figart uses econometric approaches to the gender wage gap to illustrate the limitations of such an approach. She notes that an unexplained residual in these estimates, once gender differences in education, experience, skills, size of firm, and other likely influences on wages have been controlled for, is taken by economists to be a measure of gender discrimination. In fact, some economists believe that this residual would converge to zero if the model was correctly specified. However, as Figart points out, decreasing the size of the residual by adding explanatory variables does not necessarily imply a reduction in gender discrimination. It merely shifts the analysis of discrimination to the processes that explain gender differences in education, experience, skills, size of firm, and other likely influences on wages.

Feminist economists have paid greater attention to the causal processes that underlie gender inequality in labour market outcomes. Some of this work relates to the social construction of apparently objective market phenomena such as skills and wages. Treiman and Hartmann (1981) were among the first to point out that the higher the female-intensity of an occupation in the US, the lower were the wages associated with it. Phillips and Taylor (1980) drew on empirical evidence to suggest that definitions of skill in the workplace, and the associated wages, were often based on the identity of the person carrying out the jobs rather than on the technical demands of the job. In other words, "women workers carry into the work place their status as subordinate individuals, and this status comes to define the work they do" (Phillips and Taylor 1980: 79). Far from being an objective economic fact, skill was often an ideological category imposed on certain types of work by virtue of the sex and the bargaining power of the workers who performed it.

Other insights relate to the factors which give rise to the systematic social stratification observed in the occupational structure. An early explanation for the phenomenon of 'crowding', the over-representation of marginalised groups in a limited range of occupations, was put forward by Edgeworth (1922) who focused on the collective action of male-dominated unions in excluding women from 'men's work', causing an oversupply of women and the reduction of their wages. A later explanation by Bergmann (1974) suggested that women and black people had been historically confined to a narrow range of occupations on the margins of the labour market by social stereotyping and employer discrimination. Whatever the precise combination of mechanisms, 'crowding' can be observed in labour markets across the world, increasing the monopsony power of employers over marginalised groups of workers and preserving better jobs in the economy for privileged sections of the workforce.

For feminist economists, therefore, gender inequality in the marketplace cannot be explained away in terms of choices and preferences of individual workers and employers. Rather it is structured into market forces by discriminatory practices inherited from the past, as well as by the bargaining power exercised in the present by different groups of market actors pursuing their own self-interest. Employers and workers may well be engaged in a struggle over wages and working conditions, but they may also gain collective benefit from colluding to exclude particular groups of workers. For instance, employers have benefitted from exploiting gender divisions within the workforce as a means of weakening class solidarity or constructing some of the workforce as secondary earners, a 'reserve army' of labour, to be drawn in at the height of the business cycle and laid off during recessions. Organised male workers have been able to use collective action to constitute themselves as the core workforce, with access to permanent jobs, a 'family wage', and both legal and social protection, creating barriers which insulate them from competition with the rest of the workforce.

Feminist economists thus acknowledge that individuals and groups make choices and exercise agency but suggest that they do so within the limits imposed by the structural distribution of rules, norms, assets, and identities between different groups in their society. Gender disadvantage in the labour market is a product of these 'structures of constraint' (Folbre 1994), which operate over the life course of men and women, although somewhat differently for different social groups in different social contexts. These structures may be captured for analytical purposes by a stylised categorisation which helps to highlight their institutional, rather than purely individual, character. Drawing on Whitehead's distinction between relationships that are 'intrinsically' gendered and those that are 'bearers of gender', we can usefully distinguish between two broad categories of structural constraint (Whitehead 1979; Kabeer 2008).

The first set of constraints derives from the customary norms, beliefs, and values that characterise social relationships within the institutions of family and kinship, relationships which are 'intrinsically gendered' (Whitehead 1979). These norms, beliefs, and values define the dominant models of masculinity and femininity which prevail in different societies and which assign men and women, and boys and girls, to different roles and responsibilities on the basis of these definitions, generally ascribing a lower value to those aptitudes, abilities, and activities conventionally defined as 'feminine' relative to those conventionally defined as 'masculine'. They thus define constraints which apply to women and men by virtue of their gender.

Intrinsically gendered constraints contribute to the gendered pattern of labour market outcomes observed in different regions of the world. Men's higher labour force participation relative to that of women across the world reflects the breadwinning responsibilities ascribed to them in most cultures. Women's labour force participation around the world, on the other hand, varies considerably. While most societies ascribe primary responsibility for unpaid work within the domestic domain to women and girls, they vary considerably in their expectations of women's economic contributions. In some regions, including much of sub-Saharan Africa and parts of South East Asia, women are expected to share in breadwinning responsibilities and may inherit property and manage their own farms and enterprises in order to fulfil these responsibilities. In others, not only are they expected to confine themselves to unpaid domestic work, but there are strong cultural restrictions on their mobility in the public domain. Such restrictions contribute to the much lower rates of female labour force participation (FLFP) in the Middle East and North Africa (MENA) and in South Asia compared to the rest of the world (UN Women 2015).

Intrinsically gendered constraints may also structure the kinds of productive activity considered suitable for men and women. For instance, there are long-standing taboos about women touching the plough in South Asia which serves to restrict such work to men. In West Africa, where women have traditionally been active as farmers in their own right, there are frequent references in the literature to 'male' and 'female' crops—although what constitutes a male or female crop may vary considerably. These customary constraints can be seen as containing the seeds of gender-segmentation of the occupational structure.

The norms, values, and practices associated with the intrinsically gendered relations of family, kinship, and community are further reinforced through a second category of constraints that are associated with the public domains of states, markets, and civil society. Unlike the relations of family and kinship, the institutions of states and markets are purportedly impersonal. They become 'bearers of gender' (Whitehead 1979) when they reflect and reproduce preconceived notions about masculinity and femininity as routine aspects of their rules, procedures, and practices.

For instance, many countries in the world have statutory laws which explicitly discriminate against women. The World Bank's 2019 review of laws pertaining to women's entrepreneurship and employment in 189 countries found widespread evidence of legal differences between men and women which differentiated their rights to property and their capacity for economic agency: 18 countries gave husbands the legal right to prevent their wives from working, 37 countries restricted women's right to travel, and 104 countries had laws preventing women from working in specific jobs (World Bank 2019a). The report noted that countries with higher levels of legal discrimination against women also reported lower levels of FLFP.

Along with this formalised gender discrimination, the attitudes and behaviour on the part of actors in the public arena can further curtail women's capacity to take advantage of economic opportunities. For instance, as the World Bank (2019b) recently noted, women in over half of the countries of the world are unable to assert their land and property rights, despite legal provision, demonstrating the gap that exists between the law and its enforcement. Anker and Hein (1985) point out that many employers expressed a preference for male workers on the grounds that women were seen to have a weaker attachment to the labour market, with higher rates of absenteeism and turnover. For some jobs, however, particularly in highly competitive, labour-intensive export sectors, the preference was for female labour because they made less trouble (Kabeer 2000) or because they could be paid less on the grounds that they were secondary earners, merely earning pin money ('working for lipstick') (Joekes 1985).

Hampel-Milagrosa (2011) reports examples of woman entrepreneurs in Ghana who were denied business by male customers and purchasing agents on grounds of their gender. While in India, Chhachhi and Pittin (1996) described how male workers within a factory they studied rejected the demands of women workers for company transport to and from work as being irrelevant to the 'real' issue of wages—despite the fact that the women's demands reflected the very real sexual harassment they faced on public transport.

Gender-related constraints, within both domestic and public arenas, thus underpin many of the inequalities we observe in relation to labour market processes and outcomes, including disparities in wages and segregation of jobs. They may operate invisibly and routinely through institutionalised forms of discrimination or more overtly through the actions of powerful individuals and groups. In addition, they may operate as indirect feedback mechanisms that represent rational responses to pre-existing constraints.

For instance, customs and laws cannot be held directly responsible for the fact that women farmers received only 3% of contracts issued by agro-processing firms for growing snow peas and broccoli, the most important export crops in the Central Guatemala (World Bank 2012); that less than 10% of women farmers benefitted from the smallholder contract-farming schemes in the Kenyan export-oriented horticultural sector (Dolan 2001); and that contract-farming schemes in China issued contracts exclusively to men (Eaton and Shepherd 2001). Instead, as Dolan (2001) points out, companies pursued such behaviour because of their need to secure access to land and labour for a guaranteed supply of primary produce—women do not generally have statutory rights over land nor do they exercise the same authority over family labour as their husbands or brothers. Equally there is nothing in custom or law that requires girls to be given less education than boys but if women face poorer job prospects in the labour market relative to men, it is understandable that parents will invest more resources in their sons' health and education than that of their daughters, particularly among poorer households with severe resource constraints. Feedback mechanisms thus reinforce and perpetuate gender inequality over time.

There are two final points to add to our conceptual framework. The first relates to the fact that gender is not the only form of inequality in a society. Many of the disadvantages faced by women from low income or socially marginalised groups in their struggle to make a living are shared by men from such groups, but gender generally (though not always) intensifies the implications of class and other forms of disadvantage in ways that will be touched on in the chapter.

Second, while the institutionalised nature of gender disadvantage discussed in this section is intended to emphasise its resilience in the face of change, gender disadvantages are not immutable. Both endogenous social change as well as purposive forms of public action have made important inroads into long-standing gender inequalities of various kinds. The discussion in the rest of this book of public policies and collective actions that have helped to promote WEE are evidence that change is possible.

Gender inequalities in paid and unpaid work: empirical trends and patterns

A brief empirical description of the gender distribution of both paid and unpaid work across the world will help to provide an overview of how gender structures labour market opportunities in the present era. According to the International Labour Organization (ILO 2018), women's global labour force participation rate was 48.5% in 2018 compared to 75% for men—a gap of 26.5 percentage points. This gap has narrowed by just two percentage points since 1990, with the bulk of the reduction occurring in the years up to 2009. While male labour force participation rates exceed those of women across the world, the gap varies considerably by region. The greater restrictions, both legal and customary, on women's mobility in the public domain probably explain why the gap is largest in the MENA and South Asia regions (over 50 percentage points compared to nine percentage points in sub-Saharan Africa).

Women have been moving out of agriculture and into services and manufacturing—although at a different pace in different regions and generally more slowly than men. Agriculture continues to account for 71% of women's employment in South Asia compared to 47% for males while it accounts for around 59% and 56% of female and male employment respectively in sub-Saharan Africa (UN Women 2015). Much of the growth in female employment has been in the service sector where it has risen from 35% in 1992 to 47% in 2012 (ILO 2012). The equivalent rates for the male labour force were 34% and 41%. Industry accounted for just 16% of female employment and 26% of male employment in 2012, largely unchanged from 1992.

However, the movement out of agriculture has not necessarily signified a movement into the kind of 'decent work and productive employment' highlighted, for instance, by the ILO and, more recently, by the UN Sustainable Development Goals. First, according to the ILO (2018), many more women are unemployed than men, with a much higher ratio of female to male unemployment in developing countries (1:1.3), compared to near parity in developed countries (1:1.1).

Second, the rise in FLFP has been occurring at a time when employment more generally has become more precarious and insecure. While working women have always been disproportionately represented in informal employment at the lower end of the occupational hierarchy, evidence from a wide range of developing countries shows the widespread and increasing entry of both men women into what the ILO terms 'atypical' work: temporary, casual, seasonal, or part-time work, often in home-based activities or subcontracted by intermediaries, as part of global value chains (Zammit 2010).

Third, these changes mean that the rise in FLFP has had very little effect on the gender stratification of economic opportunities. There has been a very modest decline in horizontal segregation of the occupational structure, the distribution of men and women across different occupations. According to UN Women (2015), the last two decades have seen some movement by women into certain job categories that were already quite 'mixed' and very few inroads into occupations that were dominated by men to start with, while predominantly female occupations, which tend to have lower status and pay, have remained feminised or have become more so. There has also been very little change in vertical segregation, the distribution of men and women across the occupational hierarchy. According to the ILO (2016), women continue to be under-represented in management and executive positions across the world, with their share declining in several countries.

The informal economy has its own occupational hierarchies which are not necessarily captured by ILO data. Chen et al. (2005) suggest that employers rank at the top of the informal hierarchy, followed by informal employees, own-account operators, and casual wage workers with predominantly home-based pieceworkers at the bottom. There is a close association between the quality of jobs and social identity with men dominating the upper echelons of the hierarchy and women from the poorest and most socially marginalised groups in terms of caste, race, ethnicity, and legal status concentrated at the bottom (Kabeer 2010).

Fourth, the persistence of women's disadvantage in the labour market is evident in continued gender disparity in earnings. Global estimates suggest that the gender pay gap stands at around 23%—in other words, women earned 77% of male wages—although this figure varied considerably by region, with the highest gaps recorded for South Asia (ILO 2016; UN Women 2015). While there had been a decline from 26.2% in 1995, the ILO (2016) noted that, at this rate of progress, pay equity between men and women would not be achieved before 2086.

One limitation of these estimates is that they fail to capture inequalities in earnings from wage and self-employment in the informal economy because of the lack of comparable data. Yet this is where most working women are located and where, according to existing evidence, gender wage gaps appear to be largest (Avirgan , Bivens, and Gammage 2005; Chen et al. 2005; UN Women 2015). For instance, regional data suggests that women's earnings in the informal economy in Latin America were about 53% of men's in 1998 (Barrientos 2002). In sub-Saharan Africa, the gender pay gap was 28% in informal employment compared to 6% for formal workers (UN Women 2015).

According to more micro-level data, women agricultural wage labourers were paid between a third to a half of male rates for a day's work in North East Ghana, while the Benin poverty assessment reported rural women being paid about half as much as men "because the work given to them is considered less arduous" (Whitehead 2009: 49). In Costa Rica, women's hourly earnings varied from 85% of men's earnings in the formal sector to 57% in domestic wage labour (Chen et al. 2005). In Vietnam, men earned nearly 50% more than women in informal employment despite there being no significant difference in working hours, education, and seniority (Cling, Razafindrakoto, and Roubaud 2011). And in India, Das (2006) found that casual female wage workers earned half the wages of casual male workers, even after controlling for differences in their individual characteristics.

A final indicator of the persistence of gender disadvantage is evidence that women's increasing entry into paid work has not been accompanied by a commensurate change in the gender division of unpaid labour in the domestic economy. By and large, women remain responsible for a great deal of the unpaid work that ensures the survival and care of their families over time. This unpaid work encompasses the care of children, the elderly, and the sick; domestic activities such as preparation of food and collection of fuel and water; as well as expenditure saving activities such as food production, livestock care, homestead farming, and so on. The available evidence overwhelmingly suggests that women tend to take greater responsibility for these activities than men (ILO 2016). The fact that they continue to do so even if they take up paid employment means that working women tend to work longer hours each day than working men, giving rise to the phenomenon of 'time poverty'.

The resilience of the gender division of unpaid domestic labour introduces considerable variations in women's labour force participation over their life course with much lower rates of participation in their reproductive years (UN Women 2015). It also introduces life course variations in the kinds of work that women do. One generalisation that appears to be emerging from a review of the empirical literature from a variety of different contexts is that women with young children are more likely to be self-employed, often in household-based activity, than single women or women without children (Kabeer 2008). There appear to be two main exceptions to this generalisation which embody the intersection between class and gender at two ends of the income distribution.

The first exception relates to better-off, usually married, women with children. They are more likely to be found in salaried forms of work which provide maternity leave and childcare support as they can better afford to pay for help with childcare and domestic chores, and they are more likely to have access to time-saving infrastructure (e.g. electricity, running water, sanitation). This is supported by analysis of time-use data in six LMICs which found that time spent in unpaid care work declined with rising levels of household income (Budlender 2008).

The second exception relates to very poor women with children, particularly those who are household heads and hence primary earners (Sender 2003). Such women take up waged work either because it offers higher returns than the forms of self-employment available to them or because they lack start-up capital, skills, and networks to run their own enterprise. These women have to manage their childcare responsibilities in ways that can often have adverse consequences for themselves and their children—taking young children to work with them, leaving them in the care of older female siblings (whose education thereby suffers), or leaving them at home unattended.

Evidence of the persistence of gender inequalities in relation to labour market outcomes raises important questions in relation to WEE. First, given the resilience of the gender division of unpaid labour, and women's continuing responsibility for this work, can we assume that all women will want to undertake paid work with the additional burdens it will involve? And second, given that the majority of working women only have access to a limited range of generally poorly paid work, can we assume that paid work for women is necessarily empowering, an implicit assumption in much of the economic empowerment agenda?

In terms of the first question, the position taken by this paper is captured by the following quote from the ILO (2008: 2):

> While one should not assume that all women want to work, it is safe to say that women want to be given the same freedom as men to choose work if they want to; and if they choose to work, they should have the same chance of finding decent jobs as men.

In other words, we believe that all women should have the freedom to work if they want to and that their choice of work should not be determined by their gender.

The second question is a matter for empirical investigation. However, a useful entry point into this discussion is provided by the findings of a research project which explored the empowerment potential of different forms of activity for women in Ghana, Egypt, and Bangladesh (Kabeer et al. 2013). Surveys of women were carried out on a coordinated basis in each country, using a common core of questions and common indicators of empowerment. The indicators ranged from the conventional concern with the role in decision-making found in the empowerment literature; to subjective indicators capturing a 'sense of agency' and the value given by women themselves, their families, and their communities to their productive activity; and finally, community-based indicators, including mobility in the public domain, involvement in the life of the community, and participation in politics.

In all three countries, women in market-oriented work were more likely to report positive impacts in terms of these indictors than economically inactive women. At the same time, these positive impacts varied across different categories of market-oriented work, suggesting that while engagement in paid activity did hold out greater potential for women's empowerment, the kind of work they did was also important. Of particular significance was the fact that, in all three countries, women in formal wage employment were most likely to report positive impacts. This was generally work in the public sector. It offered higher wages than most other forms of work available to women, but, more importantly, it also offered stability of employment, legal protection, social security, and a measure of social acceptability. As Sholkamy noted in relation to the Egyptian study, the state in Egypt could be described as the only "genuine equal opportunity employer" in the country (2012: 124).

The relative impacts of other forms of work varied across countries. The likelihood of positive impacts was generally greater for paid work outside the home than market-oriented work within the home in both Egypt and Bangladesh. In Ghana, on the other hand, where there are fewer restrictions on women's mobility in the public domain and a longer tradition of independent female enterprise, the inside/outside distinction was less important. Instead women in off-farm self-employment were more likely to report positive impacts than those in informal waged work and farm-based self-employment.

Our response to the second question would therefore be that the empowerment potential of women's employment will depend on various factors, but work that comes closest to the conditions associated with formal employment—security of employment, regularity of income, and some degree of protection against exploitation by self or others—is likely to have the greatest transformative potential. Our concern in this chapter is with the challenges that women face in moving into these kinds of employment.

Choice without options: the distress sale of labour

We begin our analysis of the operation of gendered structures of constraint within labour markets by exploring the factors that lead women to take up paid work. We can probably assume that most men undertake economic activity in response to their socially ascribed roles as breadwinners. To that extent, they have little choice about the matter. However, as we noted, there is remarkably little evidence to suggest that they would prefer to stay at home and specialise in unpaid work or even assume a fairer responsibility for it. For women, on the other hand, their ascribed responsibilities for unpaid care work and household chores are likely to constitute an important consideration as to whether they take up paid work and the kind of paid work they accept.

As we noted, poverty is an important factor driving women's labour force participation rates. While there is some regional variation in the labour force participation rates of women from more affluent households, women from poorer households in most regions are either economically active or seeking to become so. In cultures like that in South Asia, where there are strict norms of female seclusion, there is in fact a strong association between household poverty and women's labour force participation (Hossain and Sen 1991; Sathar and Desai 1996; Das 2006; Bridges, Lawson, and Begum 2011). Indeed, in India, women from lower caste and tribal groups have 'always' worked.

In Latin America, there is a positive relationship between household income and FLFP rates, but poorer women are more likely than men from similar households, as well as women from better off households, to report unemployment (Sedlacek, Gutierrez, and Mohindra 1993; Espino and Aznar 2006). In post-apartheid South Africa, high levels of male unemployment among poorer households led to rising labour force participation by women but, given the dearth of economic opportunities, also to higher rates of unemployment (Casale and Posel 2005). We can therefore assume that poorer sections of the female workforce across the world are working under conditions of economic distress out of necessity rather than choice.

Research from developing country contexts also suggest that the distress sale of female labour tends to increase during periods of economic crisis as households seek to compensate for their declining incomes by mobilising additional workers, usually women and children who had not previously been working.[2] This is demonstrated by Bhalotra and Umaña-Aponte (2010) who analysed micro-data from 154 Demographic and Health Surveys from 63 developing countries between 1986 and 2006 to study the impact of fluctuations in per capita GDP on women's current employment status at the time of the survey. They found evidence of a strong counter-cyclical pattern in Asia and Latin America, with less educated women dominating this 'added worker' effect, supporting the 'distress sale' interpretation of their entry into paid work. The employment of married women and women with at least one child under five was also more sensitive to the business cycle—evidence of their secondary worker status. Most of these women had not been working before and most went into self-employment, presumably in the informal economy. The added worker effect was weaker among women from wealthier households or with husbands who had at least secondary education. Weaker cyclicality was displayed by more educated women, suggesting steadier labour market attachment.

In contrast to other regions, women's employment patterns were significantly pro-cyclical in sub-Saharan Africa. This pattern was strongest among women who were currently married, had well-educated husbands, and were in the upper income quartiles. It was weakest among poorer rural women and women with young children. The authors concluded that to the extent that income pooling was not the norm in African households, African women tend to behave like primary workers. Their pro-cyclical pattern reflected the loss of paid jobs in recessions, only some of which was compensated by a rise in self-employment.

Other studies also support the idea that women's labour force participation rises in response to economic distress. For instance, studies from Argentina by Cerrutti

(2000) and from Mexico by Parrado and Zenteno (2001) found evidence of a gender-specific added worker effect, particularly among poorer households, and among households with unstable male employment in the case of Argentina.

Further insights into this phenomenon are provided by Posadas and Sinha (2010) who used Indonesian panel data from between 1993 and 2007 to examine the effects of the 1997–1998 financial crisis. They also found evidence of the added worker effect, largely on the part of wives, in response to a shock to the husbands' earnings during the crisis. Forty-one per cent of these women went into self-employment while 23% took up private wage employment. What was interesting was that this effect appeared to persist for several years after the crisis. Between 87 and 94% of these added workers continued to work, and each additional year in the labour market reduced the probability of women leaving the labour market by 1.5 percentage points. As the authors point out, the persistence of this added worker effect needs further investigation. It may be that shocks have a more lasting effect than assumed in the literature or it may be that once women have overcome barriers to their labour market participation, they opt to stay on.

While quantitative evidence has been able to pick up the 'added worker' effect in explaining women's entry into the labour market, qualitative research suggests that part of the rise in FLFP may be a response to long-term processes of impoverishment rather than confined to economic shocks. Reviewing the African literature, Whitehead (2009: 48) states that falling and/or insecure incomes from farming have pushed many women and men into own-account activities in rural economies as part of diversification strategies where "limited access to start-up capital and other resources combine with gender biases in the market to cluster women in low-entry, low-return activities". In Latin America too, Deere (2009) points out that neo-liberal restructuring and the growth of rural poverty rates have led to increasing numbers of rural households seeking off-farm employment in both own-account and waged work. She notes a greater trend for women relative to men to diversify into 'safety net' or 'last resort' non-agricultural activities, generally characterised by low productivity and low remuneration, in order to keep their households from destitution.

In summary, evidence of the kind discussed in this section suggests that there is a sizeable segment of economically active women at any one time who are working to meet the daily survival needs of their families, to offset the impact of idiosyncratic or generalised shocks, or to cope with intensified processes of impoverishment. These women may be married, divorced, widowed, or single, they may or may not have dependents to support, but they are largely women with low levels of education who come from the poorest households in their society. The supply of labour by these women is not only unlikely to reflect an active choice on their part, it is also least likely to be in forms of work that could be considered empowering.

Suppression of choice: constraints on women's labour market options

While economic distress may have forced many women into paid work, there are also factors at play that prevent other women from working at all or restrict the kinds of work they do. Women's primary responsibility for various forms of unpaid work within the home clearly play a role in explaining their lower rates of labour force participation relative to men. They also explain their greater concentration in forms of work that are compatible with discharging these responsibilities but frequently carry poorer remuneration—easy-entry, part-time, casual, irregular, seasonal, and often home-based.

For some authors, these patterns are construed in terms of choice on the part of women. For instance, Maloney (2004) interprets the fact that the majority of women in his review of the literature on informal work said that they had opted for informal work because it accommodated their household chores as clear evidence that they 'chose' this form of work. In a handbook on women-owned enterprises, Welter and Andersson (2007: 9, my italics) claim that "the sectors women generally *prefer* for starting a business are mostly characterised by high turbulence rates, thus providing relatively few opportunities for rapid business growth".

This stress on choice and preferences as the sole explanation for women's labour market choices needs to be problematised. While economists tend to view preferences as 'given', and hence not worth further investigation, there are grounds for arguing that a power-theoretic framework may be more appropriate for explaining gendered patterns of labour force participation than one that revolves around choice. We have already noted the existence of legal formal constraints on women's capacity for choice in the labour market, including the need to seek their husbands' permission before they open a bank account, travel, start an enterprise, or take up particular kinds of waged work.

However, the impact of informal norms and customs are likely to be more widespread than law. These invest dominant household members, usually men, with the authority to determine how women use their time. For instance, my own study of female labour supply decision-making among Bangladeshi households in London and Dhaka reported on several women who were forbidden to take up paid work outside the home by their husbands and in-laws as well as noting the prolonged negotiations through which other women obtained permission to do such work (Kabeer 2000).

In both Mozambique and Tanzania, research has shown how husbands and fathers prevent women from engaging in outside paid work, particularly forms of paid work where they were likely to come into contact with other men (Oya 2010). In Mexico, women confirmed that husbands were openly against, or at best dubious about, having spouses work outside the home: "The need to ask 'permission' to work and abide by the husband's opinion was a serious issue for young and middle-aged women" (Appendini 2010: 134).

Constraints apply in less explicit ways as well—as part of various socially ascribed obligations associated with household gender relations. In West Africa, where there is a long-established tradition of women cultivating their own fields, Dey Abbas (1997) found that women's obligations to work on their husbands' fields meant that they were often unable to give sufficient or timely labour to their own fields and enterprises. In rural Tanzania, while men identified transport, marketing constraints, and lack of credit as the main reasons for their lack of success in expanding agricultural production, women mentioned the time needed to look after their families, food preparation, and work on their husbands' gardens (Fontana and Paciello 2010).

Ghosh (2009) reports that successive National Sample Surveys in India report increasing proportions of women saying that they perform unpaid domestic work out of compulsion rather than choice. According to Das (2006), over 93% of women currently not in the labour force give this response. Of these, 65% say it is because there is no other member of the household who will take on these duties. About a third of these women would like to be employed, around 25% in regular full-time work, and nearly 70% in regular part-time work. The percentages wanting regular full-time work were higher for women with post-primary education.

In urban Brazil, the absence of support for their childcare responsibilities was found to restrict the capacity of women to look for work outside the home as well as reducing the income earned by those who did (Deutsch 1998). Two-thirds of the mothers who were not already working full-time said that they would either seek outside employment or increase the number of hours they worked outside the home if childcare services were made available. Strong correlations were found between utilisation of full-time childcare outside the house and formal sector occupation.

Brickell's study (2011) in Cambodia offers some qualitative insights into why women's primary responsibilities for unpaid domestic work remain intact even when they take up paid work. Brickell found that men justified their refusal to help working wives within the home by invoking Khmer notions of masculinity. Women accepted the status quo partly in order to avoid conflict with their husbands with the attendant possibility of marital breakdown, and partly because they knew that if they did not do it, nobody else would. Brickell concluded that the Cambodian women she interviewed remained responsible for housework not out of positive feelings about their roles but rather "from a coercive situation of paternal irresponsibility" (Brickell 2011: 1362).

One other study that questions the element of choice entailed in women's concentration in 'atypical' work comes from Honduras and explores how men and women evaluate full- and part-time jobs (Lopez Boo, Madrigal, and Pages 2010). It points out that if individuals were making optimal choices, they would choose to work full- or part-time according to their preferences and those working full-time would, other things being equal, be as satisfied with their jobs as those who were either working part-time or were economically inactive. However, those operating under various constraints were likely to be forced to accept or remain in less desirable jobs. Comparing job satisfaction, as a measure of welfare at work, across gender and categories of work provided an insight into gender differences in preferences and constraints (Lopez Boo, Madrigal, and Pages 2010: 1545).

They found a significant gender differential in the relationship between job satisfaction and type of work. Unlike results for many European countries, they found women working full-time (more than 30 hours a week) reported greater satisfaction in their work than those working part-time. Furthermore, contrary to the view that married women preferred part-time jobs which allowed them to combine work and family responsibilities, the study found that married women with children reported higher levels of satisfaction with full-time work than single women or married women without children. The likelihood that full-time work was valued for its larger contribution to household income was reinforced by the finding that poor women valued full-time work more than women who were not poor. Many of these poorer women worked in small firms in the informal economy where working conditions tend to be worse than full-time jobs in large firms—yet those in full-time jobs expressed greater job satisfaction than did better-off women in full-time jobs in large firms. Given their poverty, part-time jobs clearly carried too high an income penalty. The study concluded that "many women are labour supply constrained, working part-time not by choice but rather because of lack of more work" (Lopez Boo, Madrigal, and Pages 2010: 1567).

In summary, such evidence, scattered as it is, suggests that we cannot assume that a uniform, rational choice framework will explain why women work and what determines the kinds of work they do. Gendered patterns of labour force participation are likely to reflect varying degrees of choice and constraint on the part of different groups of women, reflecting not only their individual and household characteristics, such as age, education, wealth, husband's education, and so on, but also the acceptability of different forms of work for men and women within the local culture as well as the amount and kinds of work available. However, a reasonable generalisation to draw from the discussion in this section, one which supports the concluding comments in the previous section, is that the empowerment potential of paid work is likely to be greater when the decision to work, as well as the kind of work taken up, is the result of active choice on the part of women rather than driven by distress or authorised by dominant household members. In the next section, we draw on the literature on own-account work and waged work to examine in greater detail how choice and constraint interact in segmenting labour market choices for women.

From survival to accumulation: gender and entrepreneurship continuum

A substantial proportion of working men, and the majority of working women, in LMICs are self-employed. They are either own-account workers or in unpaid family labour; there are very few employers. Women are generally more likely than men to be found in unpaid family labour and less likely to be own-account workers. The ILO classifies both these categories as 'vulnerable' work because they offer little or no remuneration and are generally outside the remit of legal and social protection. However, in terms of their transformative potential, it is important to distinguish between them. While unpaid family labour contributes to the productive efforts of the household, it does not offer women any remuneration and does little to challenge their subordinate position within the family or to expand their social networks beyond it. We therefore turn to own-account work, which does offer some direct remuneration, and examine the interplay of choice and constraint in stratifying access to this form of work.

The literature on own-account activity, whether in micro-, small-, or medium-sized enterprises, makes a broad distinction between entrepreneurs on the basis of their motivation for taking up these activities, distinguishing between those who are necessity-driven or those who are opportunity-led. This suggests that while many own-account activities reflect household distress and are characterised by high levels of self-exploitation, not all enterprises can be characterised as 'vulnerable work'. Instead, own-account enterprises need to be conceptualised as a continuum, with small, self-managed, survival-oriented enterprises at one end, and larger, accumulation-oriented enterprises, with one or more employees, at the other. While women are more likely than men to be crowded into the survival end of the continuum, they can also be found at different points of the continuum with the percentages in accumulation-oriented enterprises varying by region (Minniti and Naudé 2010; ILO 2019).

This pattern poses two questions: first, why are women more likely than men to be concentrated at the survival-oriented, informal end of the enterprise spectrum, where there is unlikely to be much evidence of active choice; and second, what differentiates these women from those in more formal, accumulation-oriented enterprise. These questions relate to differences between male and female entrepreneurs as well as to differences between female entrepreneurs occupying different positions in the enterprise continuum.

Efforts to explain gender differences in the likelihood of entrepreneurial success have focused on standard economic variables, such as education, skills, work experience, and access to capital; on various 'perceptual' factors, such as attitude to risk, problem solving capacity, and self-confidence, believed to define the entrepreneurial personality; and, in many cases, measures of women's familial responsibilities. Economic variables, along with the gender division of unpaid care work, have been found to play an important role in explaining gender differences in entrepreneurial trajectories. In fact, Barrientos (2002) suggests that one reason why more women than men appear to be concentrated in informal self-employment in Latin America is that they face fewer penalties for their lack of education. Educational qualifications are less important for self-employment than waged employment, particularly formal waged employment. The findings for 'perceptual' variables are more mixed.

However, there has also been growing recognition that individual variables explain only part of the gender differences in entrepreneurial performance and that the gender stratification of entrepreneurial activity also matters. In other words, it is not simply that women's enterprises perform less well than those of men but that they tend to be concentrated in sectors and activities that are generally less profitable. For instance, analysis of enterprise data from a number of sub-Saharan African countries by Hallward-Driemeier (2011) found that women were concentrated within services and traditionally lower value-added production sectors such as garments and food processing. Men are more likely to be in metals and other manufacturing activities. Female enterprises were also less likely to be registered than those of men. Using value added per worker as a measure of performance, she found a gender gap in labour productivity of 6%. However, once controls for entrepreneurs' education, size of enterprise, and line of business had been introduced, the gap in productivity shrank and virtually disappeared among formal enterprises. While Hallward-Driemeier concluded that it was women's small share of formal, registered enterprises that accounted for productivity differences rather than gender per se, we noted earlier that this does not dispense with a gender analysis. We still need to understand why women's share of formal enterprises was so small and why the impact of gender-related constraints on productivity appeared more significant at the informal, survivalist end of the continuum than at the formal, growth-oriented end.

Some insight into these questions is provided by two studies which used randomised control trials in Sri Lanka and Ghana to explore how male and female entrepreneurs respond to the provision of transfers of various kinds. De Mel, McKenzie, and Woodruff (2009) surveyed around 400 low-capital micro-entrepreneurs, both male and female, in Sri Lanka periodically between 2006–2008 to examine the impact of transfers of different sizes, half of which were provided as cash and half as equipment or working capital. The study found that monthly profits increased by around 9% of the grant amount in male-owned enterprises but did not increase at all in female-owned ones. Male owners invested between 60% and 100% of their cash transfers in their enterprises, depending on the size of transfer. Female entrepreneurs failed to invest any of the smaller grant in their enterprises and, while they did invest as much or more of the larger grant than men, they failed to realise any return.

The study explored and rejected various possible explanations for these gender differentials in returns, including gender differences in household wealth, number of wage earners (a proxy for liquidity), years of education, scores on the Digit-span recall test (a measure of short-term processing power), various measures of entrepreneurial ability (e.g. achievement motivation, trust, locus of control, passion for work, entrepreneurial self-efficacy), and risk aversion.

The most plausible explanation suggested by the study related to the marked gender segmentation of enterprise activities evident in the sample. The authors noted that sample enterprises could be divided between activities that were entirely or predominantly male (e.g. repairs), activities that were entirely or predominantly female (e.g. lace making), and some that were mixed (e.g. retail trade and bamboo). Only 2% of women worked in sectors that were less than 40% female, while only 7% of men worked in sectors with more than 55% female owners. Both levels of investment and returns decreased steadily as the percentage of female owners in the sector increased. For women receiving the larger transfer, post-transfer investment levels and profits both increased if they were in the mixed sectors but fell in female-dominated sectors such as coir and lace. For men, investment levels and returns increased to a greater extent in male-dominated, compared to mixed, industries.

It is very likely that the gender composition of different activities was a proxy for various gender-related norms and constraints of the kind we discussed earlier. The gender-stereotyping of activities was evident for instance in the fact that only 10% of their respondents considered repairing bicycles to be a socially acceptable activity for females while none considered lace making acceptable for males. There was also evidence of restrictions on women's physical mobility—74% of female owners operated out of their homes compared to 52% of male owners, while 48% of female owners reported that all their customers were within one kilometre of their business compared to 30% of male owners.

One of the limitations of the study was its focus on the survival end of the enterprise continuum. Hence it had little to say about the relevance of gender differences for enterprise returns at the accumulation end of the spectrum. A later experiment along the same lines carried out in Ghana did include different sized enterprises and offered some interesting insights into this question (Fafchamps et al. 2011). The Ghana study covered 793 microenterprises, selected on the criteria that none had paid employees. One group of entrepreneurs was given a cash transfer, a second group was given the equivalent in equipment, materials, and inventories of their choice, while the rest formed a control group. The study found that while cash grants did not increase profits for female-owned firms, in-kind grants did increase their profits, but only for the largest 40% of firms as measured by initial profits and capital stock. Those managing survival-oriented businesses saw no gains from access to additional capital. Returns for male-owned firms were obtained, regardless of size of the firm. Cash grants were generally associated with a smaller overall increase in profits.

The different effects of in-kind compared to cash transfers for women was attributed to the fact that it was easier for them to resist internal or external pressure to divert transfers when it came in the form of inventories or equipment rather than cash—although this difference was only relevant to women who had achieved a certain scale of activity. Women, particularly those with lower initial profits, spent most of their cash transfers on household expenditure or payments to non-household members. While males receiving cash grants also reported higher household expenditure, it was not significant. One factor that explained gender differences in returns on the transfers was thus the greater familial pressures on women than men to use these transfers on others.

The study also explored various explanations for the differences in enterprise outcomes between women at different points of the enterprise continuum. Differences in bargaining power within the household and external pressure to share the transfers did not prove significant. Nor were differences in industry or type of business activity. Instead, the main explanation appeared to lie in differences in initial scale of their enterprise in terms of profits, capital stock, and volume of sales. In fact, the largest 40% of women's businesses had larger profits than the average male-owned firms in the sample. They were also more educated, came from richer households, were more likely to keep accounts, to have taken out a formal loan, and been in business somewhat longer than women in the low profit group. They were also more likely to say that they had chosen the sector for its earning potential rather than because it had low capital requirements.

The findings of two studies suggest that one reason why gender disparities in earnings tend to be larger at the poorer, informal end of the enterprise spectrum is because poorer self-employed women cannot access the resources that better off women are able to in order to offset their gender disadvantage. Gender gaps in education, skills, contacts, and access to capital, including formal capital, are generally larger at the poorer end. In addition, as we noted in the previous section, poor women are more likely than those who are better-off to be restricted by their domestic obligations in their access to markets because they have less access to time-saving utilities and infrastructure. The gender segmentation of opportunities is therefore likely to be more marked at their end of the continuum.

The other point that comes out of a comparison of the two studies is the importance of context that was highlighted by our conceptual framework. As Fafchamps et al. (2014) note, the Ghanaian context is more favourable to women's entrepreneurial success than the Sri Lankan one. Women in Ghana have similar labour force participation rates to men as well as a long tradition of involvement in their own businesses. This contrasts sharply with Sri Lanka, where not only is there a wide gender gap in labour force participation rates but very small percentages of women have their own businesses. This regional pattern is broadly supported by an ILO survey (2018) of 13,000 enterprises in 70 countries. It found that Ghana reported some of the highest percentages of women who were owners or managers of enterprises. By contrast, South Asia had lower rates of FLFP and lower percentages of women-owned businesses.

This does not mean, of course, that women in contexts more favourable to female enterprise do not face constraints. The kinds of constraints they face are illustrated in a study of entrepreneurial activity in Ghana by Hampel-Milagrosa (2011). The author found very little gender difference in motivations for becoming an entrepreneur with both men and women stating the need for income, but men were more likely to be educated than women, to have formal businesses, to access formal sources of credit rather than relying on familial networks, and to express more positive attitudes about their business prospects. In addition, women were more likely to take responsibility for domestic tasks, to work fewer hours in their enterprise, and to report greater difficulty in balancing work and family responsibilities. These differences are likely to explain why overall net profits were higher for men than women, although this difference disappeared for formal enterprises. Education did not have an impact on the likelihood of men formalising their businesses, but women with higher education were more likely to register their business, a reflection perhaps of their greater self-confidence. It thus appeared that female education combined with access to formal services helped to offset some of the gender disadvantages experienced by women in the informal economy.

Additional qualitative data provided a more detailed account of some of the discrimination faced by women entrepreneurs. Their lower levels of education meant that they faced considerable problems in dealing with government officials, whether seeking to complete tax returns or register their businesses. In addition, several women spoke of the discrimination they faced as entrepreneurs from male customers and purchasing agents who refused to do business with them because of their gender.

The latter set of findings highlights the importance of qualitative research in teasing out some of the less easily observable barriers that reproduce gender inequalities in the market domain. This is noted by Hallward-Driemeier (2011) in her study of entrepreneurship in the African context. She points out that quantitative analysis appears to suggest that once enterprise characteristics are controlled for, gender differences in the obstacles faced by entrepreneurs would disappear. So, for businesses of similar size and in similar industries, men and women would report similar constraints. But, of course, they are not in similar sized firms or in similar industries.

Along with the various individual characteristics that explain why men and women occupy different positions in the enterprise continuum, focus group discussions revealed a number of challenges faced by women entrepreneurs that were 'different in kind (not just degree)' from those facing men. In particular, Hallward-Driemeier noted that the 'gifts' sought by suppliers, moneylenders, or officials from women traders often went beyond the financial to the sexual. Dolan (1997) has also noted that Kenyan women who acted as brokers in the marketing of French beans often had to use sexual services as part of the transaction: "that women should resort to exploiting their 'body capital' in this way, given their unfavourable access to capital and labour market opportunities, has been one of the less well-documented aspects of livelihood strategies in the region" (Whitehead and Kabeer 2001: 23).

Other examples of the gender-related obstacles that block women's progress up the business ladder, but that are less easy to capture through quantitative approaches, come from South Africa. Here the post-apartheid government passed the Black Economic Empowerment (BEE) Act which, among other things, seeks to increase the extent to which black women own and manage existing and new enterprises, and their access to economic activities, infrastructure, and skills training. Despite this evidence of official commitment, the consensus of businesswomen surveyed in a study, that included larger women's investment groups that had done well, was that "BEE is mainly a men's game, with women treated as minor partners, or add-ons". The study found that "corruption, old boys' networks, patronising procurement officials, difficult-to-come-by performance guarantees, a lack of working capital, and especially the lack of measurable targets" were frequently cited reasons why women lagged behind in preferential procurement opportunities. Out of 10 institutions surveyed by the study, only two included a gender breakdown on BEE procurement spending while statistics that were reported for women only ranged between just 2 to 5% (Naidoo, Hilton, and Melzer 2006: 6).

Finally, as we noted in the previous section, some research has suggested that women opt for self-employment because of its compatibility with their domestic responsibilities. There are also suggestions that it may be a default option, a reflection of limited alternatives. For instance, in relation to her Ghana study, Hampel-Milagrosa (2011) suggests that because of the dearth of formal job opportunities, many university-educated job seekers, particularly women, ended up setting up their own businesses. This would apply at the higher profit end of the enterprise continuum. At the other end of the entrepreneurial spectrum, the concentration of so many poor women in survivalist forms of self-employment, and their inability to grow their enterprises, has been attributed to a variety of missing and imperfect markets. As Emran, Morshed, and Stiglitz (2011) pointed out, where there are severe restrictions on women's mobility in the public domain, markets for women's wage labour are, for all intents and purposes, non-existent. Alternatively, gender-related constraints on women's ability to take up waged labour, along with greater costs of a job search, may increase transaction costs of their wage labour to such an extent that the market for female labour becomes irrelevant to certain households.

Where women's entrepreneurial activities are dictated by considerations other than the profitability of their enterprise, the chances of transition to the accumulation end of the spectrum are likely to be difficult, if not impossible (Emran, Morshed, and Stiglitz 2011). Not all of them will have the necessary entrepreneurial ability, their priorities may lie in ensuring their family's survival and welfare, they may find it difficult to hire and manage labour, and to exercise the requisite degree of mobility. The failure of microfinance to benefit very poor women has underscored the difficulties they face as entrepreneurs and possible discontinuities in the transition to the higher-value end of the enterprise spectrum.

The microfinance experience has thrown up two alternative responses to this finding. The first is that very poor women might benefit from different forms of support than the moderately poor who have made more of a success of their access to microcredit. The savings led self-help group approach adopted by PRADAN and other non-governmental organisations (NGOs) in India is one example of such an approach. It combines a stress on group savings as a means of strengthening financial management skills and as the first step on the ladder to more productive and diversified livelihoods. Another example is the Bangladesh Rural Advancement Committee's Targeting the Ultra Poor programmes in Bangladesh which combine the transfer of productive assets with intensive mentoring. This has been piloted, generally successfully, in different countries around the world.

An alternative response is that very poor women may be better off in reasonably paid wage labour. There is some scattered evidence to support this. As we noted earlier, very poor women, particularly household heads, tend to opt for wage work and, in Honduras, those in full-time waged work expressed greater satisfaction with their jobs than those in more flexible part-time work. A study by Dolan (2004) in Uganda found that while less than 10% of female household heads worked in wage labour compared to 40% of male heads, their employment put them in the middle-income tercile compared to those in self-employment who were in the lowest tercile. There is also evidence from Vietnam that many of the informal enterprises that closed over the period of the global economic crisis (2007–2008) did not do so for reasons of business failure but because of the increasing number of higher wage jobs (Cling, Razafindrakoto, and Roubaud 2011). We turn next to whether, and in what circumstances, wage labour might offer a preferred option for working women.

From exploitative to 'decent' work: gender and wage-labour continuum

Wage labour is not classified as 'vulnerable' work by the ILO, but it is a very heterogeneous category and can, like own-account activity, be conceptualised as a continuum encompassing 'bad' jobs at one end of the spectrum (e.g. poorly paid, highly exploitative, and often demeaning work) and 'good jobs' at the other, characterised by formal contracts, decent working conditions, regularity of pay, as well as social and legal protection. The transformative potential of wage labour will be closely associated with its location on this continuum.

Casual, daily agricultural wage labour generally represents the distress sale of labour. It is among the worst paid of occupations, the work is physically demanding, employment is prone to seasonal variation, and it is frequently associated with lack of social status (Winters et al. 2008). For instance, in sub-Saharan Africa,

> the fact that performing casual and manual wage work for neighbours in rural areas is often seen as a last resort and distress-driven job … reflects the stigma associated with this type of job in comparison with equally horrible jobs that are performed on workers' own land.
>
> *(Oya 2010: 27)*

Other forms of 'bad' jobs included paid domestic work, largely associated with women and characterised by personalised relations of servitude; work on construction sites, often associated with bonded labour in South Asia; and subcontracted home-based workers paid piece rate wages by intermediaries.

The workers concentrated at the 'bad' end of the waged work continuum tend to be located at the intersection of multiple inequalities. In the Indian context, men and women from the scheduled castes have the highest probability of working as casual agricultural wage labour; they are poorer and less likely to be educated than other sections of the poor, and, moreover, excluded on caste grounds from better paid forms of wage labour. In South Africa, black African women dominate in waged domestic work and, along with black men, in unskilled agricultural labour, the two poorest paid categories of employment. Overall black women earn less than black men (Casale and Posel 2005). In Brazil, Afro-descendant women have been overrepresented in paid domestic work consistently between 1960 and 2000 and continued to be so in 2013 (Kabeer and Santos 2017). Indigenous men and women have been consistently concentrated in agriculture, although Indigenous women are also found in paid domestic work. These are the two poorest paid occupations, with Indigenous women generally reporting the lowest earnings (Kabeer and Santos 2017).

Formal public sector employment epitomises the 'decent work' end of the wage labour continuum in many countries. As we saw earlier, it was also the type of work that held out greater potential to transform women's lives when compared to informal wage labour and various forms of self-employment. However, public sector employment has been declining steadily over the last 30 years, a result of economic liberalisation, privatisation of state enterprise and service provision, and labour market deregulation. There has been an increasing informalisation of jobs through processes of subcontracting, replacing formal labour with informal jobs, downgrading contractual obligations, and so on. This means not only that there is less formal employment available but that working for a formal enterprise does not necessarily guarantee formal employment conditions.

Das (2006) suggests that the absence of regular, salaried jobs may be one reason why education has not led to an increase in FLFP in the Indian context. The alternative, particularly in rural areas, is unpaid work on family farms and enterprises or poorly paid positions in petty vending, domestic service, or manual wage labour, none of them likely to appeal to educated women. Das concludes that "macro level gender inequality, as measured by wage discrimination and barriers to entry into preferred jobs are a disincentive to women entering the labour force" (Das 2006: 13). Similarly, in Egypt, the contraction of the public sector has led to a decline in FLFP since educated women are reluctant to put up with the poorly paid and lower quality employment found in the private sector.

What appears to be emerging not as necessarily 'good', but certainly 'better', forms of wage work for women in the face of shrinking public sector employment are private sector jobs at the larger-scale end of production. These do not belong at the 'decent work' end of the spectrum in the sense of being 'equal opportunity employers' of the kind described by Sholkamy (2012), but they represent an improvement on what is otherwise available.

One attempt to capture the continuum of wage labour can be found in Cramer, Oya, and Sender (2008) who classified rural wage employment in Mozambique into 'good' and 'bad' jobs. The criteria for 'good' jobs were monthly salary, regularity of income, along with the greater possibility of compensation for overtime, housing, meals, and, in some cases, union representation. These jobs were associated with larger scale, technologically dynamic and productive employers (large plantations, sometimes foreign-owned) featuring greater crop specialisation and with strong links to the global markets. 'Bad' jobs offered casual wage labour for less than 15 days a month, frequently paid less than the minimum wage, and regularly paid in kind. These were generally associated with smaller, resource-poor employers (small-scale farmers and traders), but the worst jobs were in domestic service which paid monthly wages but lower than those received in other work.

Women predominated in casual agricultural wage work and domestic service, making up between 60 and 68% of this workforce while they made up just 25 to 30% of the 'good' jobs. However, divorced and separated women, particularly those with some education, were able to access better jobs in female-intensive agribusinesses, such as tobacco. The authors were not able to establish whether it was the greater freedom of these women from patriarchal control at home that led to positive labour market outcomes or whether their access to better jobs allowed them to leave unsatisfactory marriages.

In their study of high value horticultural export supply chains in Senegal, focusing in particular on main crops such as green beans and tomatoes, Maertens and Swinnen (2012) support the association between different kinds of work and their empowerment potential. As we noted earlier, women farmers were largely excluded from contracts with agro-industrial firms. In the bean sector in Senegal, one out of 59 contracted bean farmers was a woman. Interviews with the French bean companies suggested that they were strongly biased toward selecting men as contracted suppliers for the reasons touched on earlier. In Senegal, an additional factor was women's lack of claims to water for irrigation and infrastructure, crucial for bean production in the region. It was therefore men who dealt with contracting firms and received the income derived from contract farming. Women participated as unwaged family labour, often diverting their efforts from family food production to provide the primary source of labour for contract farming but received no direct remuneration in exchange.

By contrast, there was less bias in favour of men in employment generated by modern supply chains. Maertens and Swinnen note that women made up 90% of agro-industrial employees in the bean sector in Senegal and 60% in the tomato sector. In other African countries, women make up 50 to 75% of employees but just 35% in Zambia. Women appeared to benefit more directly from such work because they were themselves the 'contracted party'. Wages earned in the bean sector made up around one-third of household income for those households involved in agro-industrial employment and 85% of this income was earned by women. Forty-five per cent of the income derived from the tomato export sector was earned by women. Additionally, they were far more likely to control the proceeds of their labour in the latter case.

In Latin America, Deere (2009) has pointed out that the cut-flower industry in Colombia, Ecuador, and Mexico offered examples of high-tech production processes that favoured female labour and offered year-round employment. Deere noted that most studies suggest that packing house jobs were among the best available to women and preferable to working in the field. The gender wage gap in these industries appeared to have gradually diminished and was certainly lower than elsewhere in these economies. Newman (2001) found that the gender gap in unpaid domestic labour was also lower in the households of women who worked in the cut-flower industry in Colombia.

Efforts to compare different kinds of private sector waged work outside the agricultural sector once again finds better jobs in larger enterprises. In Bangladesh, Kabeer and Mahmud (2004) compared different forms of paid work carried out by women within and outside the export garment sector. They found that women working in the large scale, mainly foreign-owned factories in the country's specifically demarcated export processing zones earned the highest monthly wages in the sample, and were more likely to have permanent status, to be given paid and maternity leave, childcare and transport facilities, and medical care. These were, however, women with higher levels of education and who came from wealthier households than the rest of the sample. Women working in domestically owned export factories had fewer benefits but were nevertheless better off than other categories of wage workers. Women in the export sector more generally were more likely to earn on a regular basis and to report increased income during the past year than other categories of wage workers.

In Vietnam, where export garment factories were owned both by the state and foreign capital, labour standards were generally much higher than those in Bangladesh (Kabeer and Van Anh 2006). They were also much higher in the state sector, both state-owned garment factories and other state employees, and in the private export garment sector than other forms of private waged employment. However, wages were higher in private waged work outside the garment sector and the hours of work were shorter. The closest approximation to 'decent work' in this sample was reported by state employees outside the garment industry.

Studies of various kinds of wage labour in the informal economy, as well as in the formal private sector, point to evidence of gender disparities in wages but, as with the enterprise continuum, wage disparities appear to be larger at the poorer end of wage distribution than at the higher (Ntuli 2007; Chi and Li 2008; Deshpande, Goel, and Khanna 2018). This 'sticky floor' phenomenon differs from the 'glass ceiling' (greater gender disparities in earnings at the higher end of the wage distribution) documented in studies of wage disparities in the Organisation for Economic Co-operation and Development context.

There have been several studies on gender wage disparities which explain the disparity in terms of gender differences in education, skills, work experience, levels of unionisation, as well as women's unpaid domestic responsibilities which restrict their employment options and reduce their bargaining power. In addition, we have noted how gender norms can be drawn on to assign women to lower paid tasks or to construct activities typically assigned to women as based on their 'innate' rather than 'acquired' skills and hence deserving of lower remuneration. But there has been less attention paid to the factors that might explain why gender wage disparities are larger at the lower end of the wage distribution. One obvious explanation is that much of the lower end of the wage distribution is in the informal economy where workers are generally not covered by minimum wages and labour legislation. Informal workers are also generally excluded from mainstream trade union organisations although there has been a rise in other forms of unions and associations in recent years which provide workers with some degree of collective bargaining power.

These features combine to make workers in the informal economy, or at the lower end of the wage distribution, far more vulnerable than those in formal employment, while giving employers considerable power in determining wages and working conditions. This is evident in the Mozambique study cited earlier. It found that employers of casual wage labour exercised a great deal of discretion in determining levels and forms of payment for different tasks and periods of time (even within the same farm, the piece rates for harvesting cashew nuts varied between 2000–10,000 MT). The same latitude could be exercised in determining the assignment of men and women to different activities and rates of remuneration to different activities. As we noted, women made up a disproportionate share of workers in 'bad' jobs; they were more likely than men to be hired on casual rather than permanent basis, to be more poorly remunerated, to be ascribed attributes that were considered suited to these poorer paid jobs (e.g. physically weaker, lacking in authority, patient, nimble-fingered), and more likely to be paid in kind, usually food or clothing. This latter practice made precise estimates of the monetary value of the wage difficult to calculate.

Restrictions of various kinds on female employment options have the effect of lowering their 'reservation wage' and their bargaining power. For instance, as the Mozambique study suggested, rural areas in which widespread poverty combines with poor infrastructure and fragmented markets create local labour surpluses. In such contexts, employers were often reluctant to hire women, even if they can be paid less, in order to avoid creating tensions in situations of high male unemployment (Cramer, Oya, and Sender 2008).

Elsewhere, employers have deployed their monopsony power in an array of tactics to manipulate the gender and ethnic composition of their workforce in order to divide the workforce and keep wages down (Oya 2010). For instance, Johnston (2007) notes how the horticultural farmers in South Africa employed migrant female workers from Lesotho because they were more willing than South African workers to work at 'acceptable' pay rates or as one farm manager put it, "they worked harder and were willing to work for less" (Johnston 2007: 508). These women came from very poor households, they were the primary breadwinners, many had children to support, and they had limited employment options either in Lesotho or elsewhere in South Africa.

Turning to the higher end of the wage distribution, one reason for lower gender wage disparities may be that gender differentials in education and skills are less stark among workers from better-off families. In addition, women who are better off are able to afford to hire others or access time-saving technologies which reduce the constraints of childcare and domestic chores. In addition, wages, benefits, and working conditions are regulated by law in the formal economy, there is more likely to be provision for maternity leave, hence fewer interruptions in women's work history, and there is less likely to be scope for overt forms of discrimination.

There may be other factors at play to explain lower gender wage gaps in the context of global value chains. As Cramer, Oya, and Sender (2008) point out, jobs in larger-scale multinational farms and firms are likely to pay higher wages (at least to their permanent staff), offer better working conditions, and keep gender discrimination to a minimum compared to local firms and the informal economy, not necessarily because they are 'nicer' but because they tend to be more productive, particularly when they are owned by foreign multinationals (Oya 2010). And, as foreign-owned companies and multinationals, they are also more likely to be on the radar of journalists, human rights activists, and NGOs who put them under constant pressure (Deere 2009; Oya 2010). As Maertens and Swinnen (2012) noted, daily wage rates in the tomato agro-industry in Senegal, which was controlled by one multinational company certified by the Ethical Trading Initiative, were 20–30% higher compared to the bean export industry where explicit standards were not used.

Conclusion

The point of departure for this chapter is the growing body of evidence that greater equality in women's labour force participation contributes not only to economic growth but also to more inclusive patterns of economic growth. This has in turn given rise to research and policy interest in the issue of women's 'economic empowerment' and how it is best achieved. While there have been various ways of defining the concept of economic empowerment, the premise that informs the analysis in this chapter is that, regardless of how it is defined, it is most likely to be strengthened by expanding and improving women's labour market opportunities. But this is not an easy objective to achieve.

First, as we noted, the larger macro-economic environment has not been particularly favourable for either men or women. There has been a steady contraction in the availability of forms of employment that offer the greatest promise of gender equity—formal, most often public sector, employment. Current patterns of deregulated, market-led growth have led the downsizing of the public sector, increasing levels of unemployment, and the expansion of the informal economy as increasing numbers of men and women take up part-time, irregular, casual, and temporary forms of work or simply fail to find work at all. The literature reviewed for this paper referred to demand deficits in the labour market as a factor in explaining the widespread absence of educated women from the labour market in South Asia, their withdrawal from the labour market in Egypt, their concentration in self-employment in Ghana, and their unsuccessful search for full-time jobs in Honduras.

This has led to growing arguments for the shift to employment-centred growth strategies which would generate a broad-based expansion of economic opportunities (UN Women 2015). Such strategies would also create a hospitable macro-economic environment for achieving the economic empowerment of women, generating demand for their labour, and increasing their bargaining power, without requiring them to compete with men for a shrinking pool of decent jobs.

However, an overall expansion in employment will not, on its own, overcome the various gender-related constraints that have curtailed women's capacity to take advantage of existing employment opportunities on equal terms with men. As this chapter has argued, women's lower levels of labour force participation relative to men and their concentration in the poorest segments of highly gender-segmented labour markets reflect the intersection of discriminatory customs and laws as well as the attitudes and behaviour of different institutional actors.

In other words, even if more jobs became available as a result of the shift to more employment-centred growth, gender inequalities in labour market outcomes are likely to persist. The economic empowerment of women thus requires a better understanding of how these constraints play out in different socioeconomic contexts and what can be done to transform them. These questions were explored in this paper through a more detailed analysis of the factors which determine women's workforce participation and what confines them to a more restricted set of opportunities than working men. They are picked up again in several GrOW-supported case studies in developing country contexts featured in part three of this volume.

We drew on the idea of 'continuums' in different categories of employment to help us address these questions. Our review of the literature suggests that gender inequalities in resources, capabilities, and returns appear to be far greater at the lower end of the enterprise and wage-earning continuums, where work is motivated by survival concerns, than at the higher end where considerations of choice and preference are more likely to come into play. In fact, the labour-intensive nature of distress-driven activities at the lower end of both continuums, their reliance on returns for their physical labour rather than on skills or assets, has led a number of authors to discuss them under the rubric of 'labour markets' using the term in a wider sense than commonly used in mainstream economics (Chen et al. 2005; Whitehead 2009). This helps to emphasise the economic continuities and discontinuities in the income generating possibilities facing the poor and the difficulties of drawing hard and fast boundaries between own-account and wage labour activities—the same woman who seeks wage labour in the morning may sell sex in the afternoon (Shah 2014).

The economic empowerment agenda from the point of view of these women is to provide pathways to better economic opportunities. Policy efforts to bring about their sustained transitions along the enterprise and wage labour continuums, as well their ability to diversify across continuums, would need to address the gender-specific constraints and deficits that block such transitions. Such policies would clearly need to be tailored to challenge transitions in different contexts, but the analysis in this paper has suggested certain forms of public action that could be combined to provide a more general foundation from which to address specific aspects of this challenge.

Education, training, and life-long learning would equip women with basic life skills that would help to build their self-confidence, their ability to make the most of the employment opportunities available to them, and also to take advantage of any new opportunities that may emerge. These efforts could also be used to tackle discriminatory attitudes among men and boys, which would be more effective if they start earlier rather than later in the life course. The promotion of childcare support and infrastructure provision would help to reduce the time demands of their unpaid domestic responsibilities, expanding their employment opportunity sets. Building their capacity to come together in groups and within organisations can help to overcome their social isolation, to negotiate better terms for their labour, and perhaps put pressure on male-dominated trade unions to take gender equality issues more seriously. Social protection could reduce the insecurity of their livelihood activities, allow them to cope with shocks and stresses, and provide the basis for planning for a better future. Finally, progressive legislation would help to counter rather than reinforce gender discrimination within governance structures and to catalyse the cultural change needed to challenge discrimination in everyday life.

Notes

1 Education and employment are the measures of economic resources most often available for macro-level analysis. Micro-level analysis has pointed to the relevance of a range of other resources that might have similar impacts, including finance, land, and housing.
2 This is the opposite of the effect suggested by the reserve army of labour thesis.

References

Anker, Richard, and Catherine Hein (1985). Why Third World urban employers usually prefer men. *International Labor Review* 124(1): 73–90.

Appendini, Kirsten (2010). Economic liberalization, changing livelihoods and gender dimensions in rural Mexico. In FAO, IFAD, and ILO, *Gender dimensions of agricultural and rural employment: Differentiated pathways out of poverty* (126–139). Rome: Food and Agricultural Organization of the United Nations, International Fund for Agricultural Development, and International Labour Office. www.fao.org/3/i1638e/i1638e.pdf.

Arrow, Kenneth (1973). The theory of discrimination. In Orley Ashenfelter and Aalbert Rees (Eds.), *Discrimination in Labor Markets* (3–33). Princeton, NJ: Princeton University Press.

Avirgan, Tony, L., Josh Bivens, and Sarah Gammage (Eds.) (2005). *Good Jobs, Bad Jobs, No Jobs: Labour Markets and Informal Work in Egypt, El Salvador, India, Russia and South Africa.* Washington, DC: Economic Policy Institute.

Barrientos, Armando (2002). Women, informal employment, and social protection in Latin America. IDPM Discussion Paper Series, Paper No. 66. Manchester: Institute for Development Policy and Management, University of Manchester. https://ageconsearch.umn.edu/record/30557/files/dp020066.pdf.

Becker, Gary S. (1971). *The Economics of Discrimination*, Second Edition. Chicago: University of Chicago Press.

Bergmann, Barbara (1974). Occupational segregation, wages and profits when employers discriminate by race or sex. *Eastern Economic Journal* 1(2): 103–110.

Bhalotra, Sonia, and Marcela Umaña-Aponte (2010). The dynamics of women's labor supply in developing countries. IZA Discussion Paper 4879. Bonn: Institute for the Study of Labor. http://ftp.iza.org/dp4879.pdf.

Brickell, Katherine (2011). The "stubborn stain" on development: Gendered meanings of housework (non)participation in Cambodia. *Journal of Development Studies* 47(9): 1353–1370.

Bridges, Sarah, David Lawson, and Sharifa Begum (2011). Labor market outcomes in Bangladesh: The role of poverty and gender norms. *European Journal of Development Research* 23(3): 459–487.

Budlender, Debbie (2008). The statistical evidence on care and non-care work across six countries. United Nations Research Institute for Social Development, Gender and Development (UNRISD) Programme Paper No. 4. Geneva: UNRISD. www.unrisd.org/80256B3C005BCCF9/(httpAuxPages)/F9FEC4EA774573E7C1257560003A96B2/$file/BudlenderREV.pdf.

Casale, Daniela, and Dorrit Posel (2005). Women and the economy: How far have we come? *Agenda* 64: 21–29.

Cerrutti, Marcela (2000). Economic reform, structural adjustment and female labor force participation in Buenos Aires, Argentina. *World Development* 28(5): 879–891.

Chen, Martha, Joann Vanek, Francie Lund, James Heintz, Renana Jhabvala, and Christine Bonner (2005). *Progress of the World's Women 2005: Women, Work and Poverty*. New York: UN Women. www.unwomen.org/en/digital-library/publications/2005/1/progress-of-the-world-s-women-2005-women-work-and-poverty.

Chhachhi, Amrita, and Renee Ilene Pittin (1996). Introduction. In A. Chhachhi and R. Pittin (Eds.), *Confronting State, Capital and Patriarchy. Women Organizing in the Process of Industrialization* (1–32). London: Palgrave Macmillan.

Chi, Wei, and Bo Li (2008). Glass ceiling or sticky floor? Examining the gender earnings differential across the earnings distribution in urban China, 1987–2004. *Journal of Comparative Economics* 36(2): 243–263.

Cling, Jean, Mireille Razafindrakoto, and Francois Roubaud (2011). *The Informal Economy in Vietnam*. Hanoi: International Labour Organization. https://www.ilo.org/wcmsp5/groups/public/---asia/---ro-bangkok/---ilo-hanoi/documents/publication/wcms_171370.pdf.

Cramer, Christopher, Carlos Oya, and John Sender (2008). Lifting the blinkers: A new view of power, diversity and poverty in Mozambican rural labour markets. *Journal of Modern African Studies* 46(3): 361–392.

Das, Maitreyi Bordia (2006). Do traditional axes of exclusion affect labour market outcomes in India? Social Development Papers No. 97, South Asia Series. Washington, DC: World Bank. http://documents.worldbank.org/curated/en/195941468034790110/pdf/369630sdp970web.pdf.

de Mel, Suresh, David McKenzie, and Christopher Woodruff (2009). Are women more credit constrained? Experimental evidence on gender and microenterprise returns. *American Economic Journal: Applied Economics* 1(3): 1–32.

Deere, Carmen Diana (2009). The feminization of agriculture? The impact of economic restructuring in rural Latin America. In Shahra Razavi (Ed.), *The Gendered Impacts of Liberalization: Towards "Embedded' Liberalism"?* (99–127). London: Routledge.

Deshpande, Ashwini, Deepti Goel, and Shantanu Khanna (2018). Bad karma or discrimination? Male–female wage gaps among salaried workers in India. *World Development* 102: 331–344.

Deutsch, Ruthanne (1998). Does childcare pay? Labor force participation and earnings effects of access to childcare in the favelas of Rio de Janeiro. Office of the Chief Economist, IADB. Working Paper 384. Washington, DC: Inter-American Development Bank. https://publications.iadb.org/publications/english/document/Does-Child-Care-Pay-Labor-Force-Participation-and-Earnings-Effects-of-Access-to-Child-Care-in-the-Favelas-of-Rio-de-Janeiro.pdf.

Dey Abbas, J. (1997). Gender asymmetries in intra-household resource allocation in sub-Saharan Africa: Some policy implications for land and labor productivity. In Lawrence Haddad, John Hoddinott, and Harold Alderman (Eds.), *Intra-household Resource Allocation in Developing Countries: Models, Methods and Policy* (249–262). Baltimore: Johns Hopkins University Press.

Doepke, Mathhias, and Michèle Tertilt (2011). Does female empowerment promote economic development? Policy Research Working Paper 5714. Washington, DC: World Bank. http://documents.worldbank.org/curated/en/108891468337155421/Does-female-empowerment-promote-economic-development.

Dolan, Catherine (1997). *Tesco is King: Gender and Labour Dynamics in Horticultural Exporting, Meru District.* PhD Dissertation, Birmingham University.

Dolan, Catherine (2001). The good wife's struggle over resources in the Kenyan horticultural sector. *The Journal of Development Studies* 37(3): 39–70.

Dolan, Catherine (2004). "I sell my labor now": Gender and livelihood diversification in Uganda. *Canadian Journal of Development Studies* 25(4): 644–661.

Eaton, Charles, and Andrew Shepherd (2001). Contract farming: Partnerships for growth. FAO Agricultural Services Bulletin 145. Rome: Food and Agriculture Organization of the United Nations. www.fao.org/3/y0937e/y0937e00.pdf.

Edgeworth, Francis Ysidro (1922). Equal pay to men and women for equal work. *Economic Journal* 32(128): 431–457.

Emran, M. Shahe, A.K.M. Mahbub Morshed, and Joseph E. Stiglitz (2011). Microfinance and missing markets. MPRA Working Paper 41451. Germany: University Library of Munich. https://mpra.ub.uni-muenchen.de/41451/.

Espino, Alma, and Paola Aznar (2006). Changes in economic policy regimes in Uruguay from a gender perspective 1930–2000. United Nations Research Institute for Social Development, Gender and Development (UNRISD) Background Paper. Geneva: UNRISD. http://www.unrisd.org/unrisd/website/document.nsf/(httpPublications)/EDD0BAA932320A4BC1256FEF0051D663?OpenDocument.

Fafchamps, Marcel, David McKenzie, Simon Quinn, and Christopher Woodruff (2011). When is capital enough to get female enterprises growing? Evidence from a randomized experiment in Ghana. Policy Research Working Paper 5706. Washington, DC: World Bank. http://documents.worldbank.org/curated/en/651731468253176197/When-is-capital-enough-to-get-female-enterprises-growing-evidence-from-a-randomized-experiment-in-Ghana.

Fafchamps, Marcel, David McKenzie, Simon Quinn, and Christopher Woodruff (2014). Microenterprise growth and the flypaper effect: Evidence from a randomized experiment in Ghana. *Journal of Development Economics* 106: 211–226.

Figart, Deborah M. (2005). Gender as more than a dummy variable: Feminist approaches to discrimination. *Review of Social Economy* 63(3): 509–536.

Folbre, Nancy (1994). *Who Pays for the Kids? Gender and the Structures of Constraint.* London: Routledge.

Fontana, Mariza, and Cristina Paciello (2010). Gender dimensions of rural and agricultural employment: Differentiated pathways out of poverty. A global perspective. In FAO, IFAD, and ILO, *Gender Dimensions of Agricultural and Rural Employment: Differentiated Pathways out of Poverty* (1–63). Rome: Food and Agricultural Organization of the United Nations, International Fund for Agricultural Development, and International Labour Office. www.fao.org/3/i1638e/i1638e.pdf.

Ghosh, Jayati (2009). Informalization and women's workforce participation: A consideration of recent trends in Asia. In Shahra Razavi (Ed.), *The Gendered Impacts of Liberalization: Towards "Embedded Liberalism"?* London: Routledge.

Hallward-Driemeier, Mary (2011). *Enterprising Women: Expanding Opportunities in Africa.* Washington, DC: World Bank. http://documents.worldbank.org/curated/en/802071468009940929/pdf/697710ESW0P111000Enterprising0Women.pdf.

Hampel-Milagrosa, Aimée (2011). *The Role of Regulation, Tradition and Gender in Doing Business: Case Study and Survey Report on a Two-Year Research Project in Ghana.* Bonn: German Development Institute. https://www.die-gdi.de/uploads/media/Studies_60.pdf.

Hossain, Mahabub, and Binayak Sen (1991). Determinants of poverty. In Hossein Zillur Rahman and Mahabub Hossain (Eds.), *Rethinking Rural Poverty: Bangladesh as a Case Study*. New Dehli: SAGE Publications.

ILO (2008). *Global Employment Trends for Women*. Geneva: International Labour Organization. https://www.ilo.org/global/about-the-ilo/newsroom/news/WCMS_091225/lang--en/index.htm.

ILO (2012). *Global Employment Trends for Women 2012*. Geneva: International Labour Organization. www.ilo.org/global/research/global-reports/global-employment-trends/WCMS_195447/lang--en/index.htm.

ILO (2016). *Women at Work: Trends 2016*. Geneva: International Labour Organization. https://www.ilo.org/wcmsp5/groups/public/---dgreports/---dcomm/---publ/documents/publication/wcms_457317.pdf.

ILO (2018). *World Employment Social Outlook: Trends for Women 2018*. Geneva: International Labour Organization. https://www.ilo.org/wcmsp5/groups/public/---dgreports/---dcomm/---publ/documents/publication/wcms_619577.pdf.

ILO (2019). *Women in Business and Management: The Business Case for Change*. Geneva: International Labour Organization. https://www.ilo.org/global/publications/books/WCMS_700953/lang--en/index.htm.

Joekes, Susan (1985). "Working for lipstick?" Male and female labour in the clothing industry in Morocco. In Haleh Afsher (Ed.), *Women, Work and Ideology in the Third World*. London: Tavistock Publications.

Johnston, Deborah (2007). Who needs immigrant farm workers? A South African case study. *Journal of Agrarian Studies* 7(4): 494–525.

Kabeer, Naila (2000). *The Power to Choose: Bangladeshi Women and Labour Market Decisions in London and Dhaka*. London: Verso.

Kabeer, Naila (2008). *Mainstreaming Gender and Social Protection in the Informal Economy*. London: Commonwealth Secretariat.

Kabeer, Naila (2010). Can the MDGs provide a pathway to social justice? The challenge of intersecting inequalities. Sussex and New York: Institute of Development Studies and UN Millennium Achievement Fund. www.mdgfund.org/sites/default/files/MDGs_and_Inequalities_Final_Report.pdf.

Kabeer, Naila, and Simeen Mahmud (2004). Globalisation, gender and poverty: Bangladeshi women workers in export and local markets. *Journal of International Development* 16(1): 93–109.

Kabeer, Naila, and Luisa Natali (2013). Gender equality and economic growth: Is there a win-win? IDS Working Paper 417. Brighton, UK: Institute of Development Studies. https://onlinelibrary.wiley.com/doi/abs/10.1111/j.2040-0209.2013.00417.x.

Kabeer, Naila, and Ricardo Santos (2017). Intersecting inequalities and the Sustainable Development Goals: Insights from Brazil. WIDER Working Paper 2017/167. Helsinki: UNU-WIDER. www.wider.unu.edu/sites/default/files/Publications/Working-paper/PDF/wp2017-167.pdf.

Kabeer, Naila, and Tran Thi Van Anh (2006). Globalization, gender and work in the context of economic transition: The case of Vietnam. GEM-IWG Working Paper Series 06–3. http://nailakabeer.net/wp-content/uploads/2006/09/06-3.pdf.

Kabeer, Naila, Ragui Assaad, Akosua Darkwah, Simeen Mahmud, Hania Sholkamy, Sakiba Tasneem, Dzodzi Tsikata, and Munshi Sulaiman (2013). Paid work, women's empowerment and inclusive growth: Transforming the structure of constraint. New York: UN Women. https://www.lse.ac.uk/gender/assets/documents/research/choice-constraints-and-the-gender-dynamics-of-lab/Paid-work-womens-empowerment-and-inclusive-growth.-New-York-UN-Women.pdf.

Klasen, Stephan (1999). Does gender inequality reduce growth and development? Evidence from cross-country regressions. Policy Research Report on Gender and Development, Working Paper Series No. 7. Washington, DC: World Bank. https://documents.worldbank.org/en/publication/documents-reports/documentdetail/612001468741378860/does-gender-inequality-reduce-growth-and-development-evidence-from-cross-country-regressions.

Klasen, Stephan (2002). Low schooling for girls, slower growth for all? Cross-country evidence on the effect of gender inequality in education on economic development. *World Bank Economic Review* 16 (3): 345–373. http://documents.worldbank.org/curated/en/382741468330879895/Low-schooling-for-girls-slower-growth-for-all-Cross-country-evidence-on-the-effect-of-gender-inequality-in-education-on-economic-development.

Lopez Boo, Florencia, Lucia Madrigal, and Carmen Pages (2010). Part-time work, gender and job satisfaction: Evidence from a developing country. *Journal of Development Studies* 46 (9): 1543–1571.

Maertens, Miet, and Johan F.M. Swinnen (2012). Gender and modern supply chains in developing countries. *Journal of Development Studies* 48(10): 1412–1430.

Maloney, William (2004). Informality revisited. *World Development* 32(7): 1159–1178.

Manning, Alan (2003). *Monopsony in Motion: Imperfect Competition in Labour Markets*. Princeton, NJ: Princeton University Press.

Minniti, Maria, and Wim Naudé (2010). What do we know about the patterns and determinants of female entrepreneurship across countries? *European Journal of Development Research* 22(3): 277–293. https://link.springer.com/article/10.1057/ejdr.2010.17.

Naidoo, Sharda, Anne Hilton, and Ilana Melzer (2006). Access to finance for women entrepreneurs in South Africa: Challenges and opportunities. Washington, DC: International Finance Corporation. www.ifc.org/wps/wcm/connect/dd73ba18-a3fd-4331-bca8-7ef9430a282c/Access%2Bto%2BFinance%2B-%2BWomen%2Bin%2BSouth%2BAfrica.pdf?MOD=AJPERES&CACHEID=ROOTWORKSPACE-dd73ba18-a3fd-4331-bca8-7ef9430a282c-jqetmCL.

Newman, Constance (2001). Gender, time use and change: Impacts of agricultural export employment in Ecuador. Policy Research Report on Gender and Development Working Paper Series 18. Washington, DC: World Bank. http://documents.worldbank.org/curated/en/944941468770087536/Gender-time-use-and-change-impacts-of-agricultural-export-employment-in-Ecuador.

Ntuli, Miracle (2007). Exploring gender wage discrimination in South Africa 1995–2004: A quantile regression analysis. IPC Working Paper Series No. 56. Ann Arbor: International Policy Centre, University of Michigan. http://citeseerx.ist.psu.edu/viewdoc/download?doi=10.1.1.603.9002&rep=rep1&type=pdf.

Oya, Carlos (2010). Rural inequality, wage employment and labor market formation in Africa: Historical and micro-level evidence. Working Paper 97, Policy Integration Department. Geneva: International Labour Organization. https://www.ilo.org/integration/resources/papers/WCMS_145084/lang--en/index.htm.

Parrado, Emilio, and René M. Zenteno (2001). Economic restructuring, financial crisis and women's work in Mexico. *Social Problems* 48(4): 456–477.

Phillips, Anne, and Barbara Taylor (1980). Sex and skills: Notes towards a feminist economics. *Feminist Review* 6: 79–88.

Polachek, Solomon William (1981). Occupational self-selection: A human capital approach to sex differences in the occupational structure. *The Review of Economics and Statistics* 63 (1): 60–69.

Posadas, Josefina, and Nistha Sinha (2010). Persistence of the added worker effect: Evidence using panel data from Indonesia. Washington, DC: World Bank. http://conference.iza.org/conference_files/worldb2010/posadas_j6007.pdf.

Quisumbing, Agnes (2003). Household decisions, gender and development: A synthesis of recent research. Washington, DC: International Food Policy Research Institute. www.ifpri.org/publication/household-decisions-gender-and-development-synthesis-recent-research.

Sathar, Zeba, and Sonalde Desai (1996). Work patterns in rural Pakistan: Intersections between gender, family and class. Population Council Research Division Working Paper 90. New York: Population Council, mimeo.

Sedlacek, Guilherme, Leah Gutierrez, and Amit Mohindra (1993). Women in the labour market. Education and Social Policy Department. Washington, DC: World Bank, mimeo.

Seguino, Stephanie (2007a). The great equalizer? Globalization effects on gender equality in Latin American and the Caribbean. In Anwar Shaikh (Ed.), *Globalization and the Myths of Free Trade: History, Theory and Evidence* (177–214). London: Routledge.

Seguino, Stephanie (2007b). *Plus ça change*: Evidence on global trends in gender norms and stereotypes. *Feminist Economics* 13(2): 1–28.

Sender, John (2003). Rural poverty and gender: Analytical frameworks and policy proposals. In Ha-Joon Chang (Ed.), *Rethinking Development Economics* (401–420). London: Anthem Press.

Shah, Svati P. (2014). *Street corner secrets: Sex, work, and migration in the city of Mumbai.* Durham: Duke University Press.

Sholkamy, Hania (2012). How private lives determine work options: Reflections on poor women's employment in Egypt. In Ayşe Buğra and Yalçin Özkan (Eds.), *Trajectories of Female Employment in the Mediterranean* (114–135). London: Palgrave Macmillan.

Treiman, Donald J., and Heidi I. Hartmann (Eds.) (1981). *Women, Work and Wages: Equal Pay for Jobs of Equal Value.* Washington, DC: National Academy Press.

UN Women (2015). Progress of the world's women 2015–2016: Transforming economies, realizing rights. New York: UN Women. www.unwomen.org/-/media/headquarters/attachments/sections/library/publications/2015/poww-2015-2016-en.pdf?la=en&vs=0.

Welter, Friederike, and Ingrid Andersson (2007). Challenges and opportunities. In Friederike Welter (Ed.), *Handbook on Women-Owned SMEs: Challenges and Opportunities in Policies and Programmes* (7–17). Malmö, Sweden: International Organisation for Knowledge Economy and Enterprise Development. www.iked.org/pdf/Handbook%20on%20Women-owned%20SMEs.pdf.

Whitehead, Ann (1979). Some preliminary notes on the continuing subordination of women. *IDS Bulletin* 10(3): 10–13. https://bulletin.ids.ac.uk/index.php/idsbo/article/view/2308.

Whitehead, Ann, and Naila Kabeer (2001). Living with uncertainty: Gender, livelihoods and pro-poor growth in sub-Saharan Africa. IDS Working Paper 134. Brighton: Institute of Development Studies. www.lse.ac.uk/gender/assets/documents/research/choice-constraints-and-the-gender-dynamics-of-lab/Living-with-uncertainty.pdf.

Whitehead, Ann (2009). The gendered impacts of liberalization policies on African agricultural economies and rural livelihoods. In Shahra Razavi (Ed.), *The Gendered Impacts of Liberalization: Towards "Embedded' Liberalism"?* (37–62). London: Routledge.

Winters, Paul, Ana Paula de la O, Esteban J. Quiñones, Thomas Hertz, Benjamin Davis, Alberto Zezza, Katia Covarrubias, and Kostas Stamoulis (2008). Rural wage employment in developing countries. Rome: Food and Agriculture Organization of the United Nations. www.fao.org/fileadmin/user_upload/riga/pdf/aj301e.pdf.

World Bank (2012). World development report 2012: Gender equality and development. Washington, DC: World Bank. https://openknowledge.worldbank.org/handle/10986/4391.

World Bank (2019a). Women, business and the law 2019: A decade of reform. Washington, DC: World Bank. http://hdl.handle.net/10986/31327.

World Bank (2019b). Women in half the world still denied land, property rights, despite laws. World Bank Press Release, March 25. www.worldbank.org/en/news/press-release/2019/03/25/women-in-half-the-world-still-denied-land-property-rights-despite-laws.

World Economic Forum (2018). The global gender gap report 2018. Geneva: World Economic Forum. www3.weforum.org/docs/WEF_GGGR_2018.pdf.

Zammit, Ann (2010). Value chains and decent work for women: What is to be done? ILO Policy Integration and Statistics Department, Programme Paper 88. Geneva: International Labour Organization.

PART II

Syntheses of GrOW-supported research on women's economic empowerment

2

STALLED PROGRESS

Why labour markets are failing women

James Heintz

Introduction

Paid employment has the potential to improve women's ability to make autonomous decisions that have substantive impacts on their lives (UN Women 2015). As a result, labour market dynamics have implications for women's agency, access to resources, and wellbeing. Labour market opportunities affect the timing of marriage and childbearing, educational attainment, women's access to independent sources of income, and networking possibilities outside of household and kinship relationships. Over time, changes in women's paid employment may change norms and gender roles that influence what women can do and what they can become in the course of their lives.

In this chapter, we adopt an expansive definition of labour markets. Labour markets refer to the collection of formal and informal institutions that govern the ways that people exchange their labour in order to realise an income. Most often this income takes the form of a financial payment, although, in some cases, people sell their labour in exchange for goods or services. A dominant view of labour markets involves an employee selling their labour to an employer in exchange for a wage. However, the self-employed also engage in labour markets. Although they do not receive a formal paycheque, they effectively sell their labour services in exchange for income. For the self-employed, labour markets frequently operate through other markets for the goods or services exchanged.

Labour markets are gendered institutions (Elson 1999). The rules and structures governing how men realise income from their labour differ from the rules and structures governing how women realise income from their labour. These gender differences in how labour markets function create economic inequalities between men and women. They also determine whether labour markets enhance, or undermine, women's empowerment.

This chapter draws on the diverse research papers and reports focused on a range of developing countries that have been generated by the Growth and Economic Opportunities for Women (GrOW) initiative. This body of work demonstrates that labour markets in developing countries are distinct from those of high-income countries, with more self-employment, high rates of informality, differences in gender roles, variations in household structure, and a range of sectoral compositions. Although the broad themes may be similar in both developed and developing economies, research on women and labour markets is necessarily context specific. Furthermore, the studies reviewed here show that it is critical to look beyond individual micro-level decisions and explore how household characteristics, institutional factors, and macro-level dynamics impact labour market outcomes. Women and men make individual choices, but within structures defined by norms, laws, households, the distribution of assets, policy, and the overall economic environment. A failure to recognise these various elements will result in an incomplete, and possibly erroneous, understanding of labour markets and women's empowerment. This chapter picks up many of the same threads around labour markets and inclusive growth raised in Chapter 1 of this volume, while narrowing in on the findings of GrOW-supported research studies.

Labour markets and women's economic empowerment

We begin with a consideration of a paradox that has emerged in recent decades. There have been improvements in a range of socioeconomic outcomes for women and advances in gender equality in many, although not all, parts of the world. These achievements include better educational outcomes for women, higher life expectancy, improved access to prenatal care and reproductive services, lower maternal mortality rates, larger shares of women being elected as political representatives, and stronger laws regarding intimate partner violence (IPV) (Peters et al. 2016). However, these indicators of gender equality do not always translate into improvements in the substantive choices women are able to make regarding their own lives (UN Women 2015). There is less evidence of general improvements in labour market outcomes for women. One of the reasons for the more stubborn persistence of labour market inequalities is that various institutional barriers, such as economic structures, social norms, the unequal burden of unpaid work, and legal biases, limit the choices available to women. Constrained choices feed into unequal outcomes. When gender inequalities with regard to paid employment do materialise, they are often uneven, and differences with regard to race, ethnicity, class, caste, and other social divisions are evident.

Before delving into the details behind this paradox, it would be useful to discuss the relationship between labour market outcomes and women's empowerment in general terms. One possibility is that the paradox is temporary, that improvements in labour market outcomes for women, reductions in gender inequality, and women's economic empowerment (WEE) will eventually be realised, as long as the world's economies continue to grow.

In this version of the story, economic growth and labour demand go hand-in-hand. As the production of goods and services expands and incomes rise, so does the demand for labour. This generates new opportunities for paid employment for men and women. In the past, men got the best of these jobs, but as economies continue to grow, women are pulled into the labour market. The availability of paid employment gives women new choices and causes them to reassess other decisions—the average age of marriage increases, fertility falls, and educational attainment rises. In the long-run, social norms and gender roles begin to change. Labour markets provide a pathway to women's empowerment and gender gaps will inevitably close. The disjuncture between improvements in some indicators of gender equality and labour market outcomes is not really a paradox. It is just a timing issue.[1]

This narrative of labour markets as the channel through which economic growth positively contributes to women's empowerment collapses when this channel breaks down. Faster rates of economic growth do not always yield increasing demand for labour, particularly when the growth rate of labour productivity, due to automation or technological change, outstrips the growth rate of output. Even when labour demand is expanding, women do not always have access to the paid employment opportunities created. Barriers to women's labour force participation limit women's ability to take advantage of new jobs when they become available. Furthermore, gender segregation of labour markets limits the kinds of jobs women can do without violating social norms, experiencing the disapproval of others, or placing themselves at risk. Women are typically either under or overrepresented in particular sectors (e.g. construction versus garment manufacturing).

Women are not always 'pulled' into the labour market by new opportunities. They often are pushed. When households experience shocks that squeeze income (e.g. an unemployment crisis or violent conflict), women may take up paid employment to try to make ends meet. There is a significant empowerment gap between paid work that is freely chosen and jobs that arise out of distress. This points to another place where the narrative about the positive relationship between paid employment and women's empowerment becomes derailed. Not all jobs are the same, and not all paid work is empowering. The type of employment matters (see, for example, Kabeer, Mahmud, and Tasneem 2011 or Chapter 1 of this volume). The effect paid work has on women's ability to make substantive choices in their own lives varies with the social context, the kind of employment, and the reasons why women do the work they do. Simply having a job does not inevitably lead to empowerment.

Drawing on the research studies carried out under the GrOW initiative, this chapter explores these complexities. It begins with a consideration of the barriers to women's labour force participation. It then explores, in turn, the gender segregation of labour markets; the dynamics of paid employment, household formation, and unpaid care work; and the impact of gender roles, norms, and violence. The aim is to highlight the connections between labour market outcomes and women's empowerment.

Barriers to women's labour force participation: an overview

There are several reasons why we would expect women's labour force participation rates to have risen in recent decades throughout the developing world. Women's educational attainment has, in general, improved significantly. These gains have led to a narrowing, and in some cases an elimination, of gender gaps in enrolment and attainment at the primary level and, less frequently, at secondary and tertiary levels. In general, fertility rates have fallen, and, in some countries, this decline has been dramatic. Per capita economic growth in the developing world has generally been higher on average since the 1990s than it was in previous decades. We would expect that better educated women, with fewer children and living in households with higher living standards, would have more opportunities for paid employment that would help push up labour force participation rates. These expectations are not always born out in the data.

Klasen (2019) drives this point home. This study focuses on labour market trends in developing countries over recent decades. Klasen shows, based on his analysis of modelled labour force participation rates generated by the International Labour Organization, that the only developing region with a clear upward trend in female labour force participation (FLFP) rates is Latin America and the Caribbean. Even in Latin America, the rate of increase slows down after 2005. In contrast, women's labour force participation rates have fallen in East Asia and South Asia. In the Middle East and North Africa regions, FLFP appears to be rising, but the growth is very slow, starting from one of the lowest levels of any region in the world.

One possible explanation for this trend is that, because of higher educational attainment, girls and young women are staying in school longer, and this brings down the FLFP rate. However, Klasen also looks at the trends for women in their prime working years (ages 25–54) and finds similar results.

The differences in levels and trends in FLFP are not always consistent with the 'feminisation U' hypothesis which argues that the relationship between FLFP and per capita income is U-shaped—that is, women's labour force participation is high in low-income countries, declines with increases in per capita income up to a point, and then begins to increase again. A changing economic structure provides the rationale for the feminisation U hypothesis (Goldin 1995; Klasen 2019). Women's labour force participation tends to be high in agricultural economies, which, with their extended family and household structures, allow women to combine market work with unpaid care work. During processes of industrialisation, average incomes rise, but women tend to withdraw from the labour force to specialise in unpaid work since industrial employment is harder to combine with caring labour. In later stages of industrialisation, the expansion of the service sector provides new job opportunities for women and, with rising educational attainment and falling fertility, women's labour participation begins to increase.

Variations in both the levels and trends of women's labour force participation rates, particularly among countries with similar per capita incomes, suggest that the feminisation U hypothesis is, at best, incomplete. Klasen suggests three factors that affect women's labour force participation which may help explain differences between countries and regions. These are:

1. differences in the relationship between household income and labour force participation;
2. social norms that underpin segregated labour markets and restrict women's employment opportunities in particular sectors and occupations; and
3. differences in the growth process that interact with structural barriers to women's labour force participation.

The relationship between household income and women's labour force participation varies. As household incomes increase, there is less need for women to engage in paid employment to generate the income families need to make ends meet. Given higher male earnings, gender norms that favour men's participation in paid work over women's, and differences in bargaining power, women may withdraw from the labour force and specialise in unpaid care work as incomes rise. There is some evidence that women's labour force participation is counter-cyclical—rising during times of economic stress and falling when household incomes recover (Bhalotra and Umana-Aponte 2010; Klasen 2019). However, this reaction is not universal, and, in some country contexts, women may withdraw from the labour force during crisis periods (Lee and Cho 2005). This suggests that women's labour force participation rates will respond differently to changes in household income, depending on the context.

When women's labour force participation increases because household resources are squeezed, women are "pushed" into employment due to economic distress, not because they are taking advantage of improved opportunities for paid employment. For instance, analysis of Indian survey data by Klasen and Pieters (2012) finds that, at lower levels of education, FLFP is driven by necessity rather than economic opportunity. In contrast, only relatively privileged women with high educational achievement seemed to be pulled into the labour market by attractive employment opportunities. Several of the GrOW studies find evidence of this kind of distress labour force participation on the part of women—for example in artisanal mining in Central and Eastern African countries (Buss et al. 2017; Rutherford and Buss 2019) and in the informal sector of South Africa (Makaluza and Burger 2018).[2]

Since labour markets are segregated, women do not have the same access to the better occupations or jobs in certain sectors as men. Moreover, labour market segregation appears to be remarkably stable over time (Borrowman and Klasen 2019). These persistent inequalities affect women's labour force participation by limiting their options for paid employment. Differences in economic structure and growth patterns across countries will therefore have distinct implications for women's labour force participation. An economic structure dominated by "male" sectors and occupations will provide fewer opportunities for women to engage in paid employment compared to alternative economic structures. If employment growth is concentrated in sectors dominated by men, FLFP may be relatively unresponsive to increases in the general employment level.

As a result, differences in men's and women's labour force participation rates are influenced by economic structure. Enchautegui (2017) uses fixed-effects panel analysis to estimate the relationship between the labour force participation rate gap and variables associated with the structure of the economy over the period from 1991 to 2014 for low- and middle-income countries (LMICs). The study finds that increases in the value-added of agriculture and manufacturing, as well as government consumption expenditures, relative to the value-added of the private service sector, are correlated with a lower gap between male and FLFP rates. Increases in the value of exports and net foreign direct investment flows are correlated with a larger labour force participation gap, while the value of imports is negatively correlated with the gap.

Social norms play a significant role in the ongoing gender segregation of labour markets. This is evident even in the face of major economic and social shocks. As documented in the chapter by Gunatilaka and Vithanagama in this volume, GrOW-supported research on female-headed households in Sri Lanka illustrates the power of persistent gender norms. A dramatic increase in female-headed households characterised the protracted conflict in Sri Lanka. With the rising share of female-headed households, we may expect that women would take on non-traditional gender roles, including greater participation in labour markets and in forms of employment not usually taken on by women. However, prevailing norms limited the ability of widowed or separated women to participate in labour markets in the absence of an adult male family member (Lakshman 2017). The conflict also raised the prevalence of gender-based violence (GBV), including in the workplace, which represented another barrier to labour force participation outside of the home (Kandanearachchi and Ratnayake 2017).

In addition to the factors emphasised in Klasen (2019), the gender division of labour between paid and unpaid work represents another factor limiting women's labour force participation. Specialisation in unpaid household work, including providing care services, curtails women's opportunities for paid employment. In part, this is an issue of time. Women's labour supply is divided between paid and unpaid activities. A larger responsibility for unpaid work diminishes the time available for paid work. But the nature of many types of unpaid work, specifically care work, place further limitations on labour market options. For instance, the primary caregiver for young children must be 'on call'—ready to step in if a child gets sick or needs extra time. Jobs that do not provide this flexibility may be impossible to combine with commitments to care for others.

Given the gender division of labour, we may expect falling fertility rates to be associated with more women participating in the labour force. But, here too, the issues are complex. In some situations, women enter paid employment specifically to help provide for their children. Fewer children may mean less pressure to participate in labour markets (Priebe 2011). In cases where older children also help with unpaid household work, fewer children in the household mean that adult women receive less assistance with care responsibilities and household tasks. There also are economies of scale in the household. The difference in the amount of unpaid labour required for households with three children compared to two children will be smaller than the difference in the amount of unpaid work required for households with one child compared to those with no children. Marginal changes in the number of children per household may not result in large time savings.

A number of interrelated factors explain differences in the levels of women's labour force participation and changes in participation rates over time. These include social norms, the structure of economies, the gender segregation of labour markets, household dynamics—including bargaining power between men and women, and the allocation of labour time to unpaid, non-market activities. The remainder of this chapter examines these issues in detail, drawing on the findings of the GrOW-supported research projects.

Labour market segregation

One of the primary sources of gender inequality in labour markets arises because of the segregation of employment, where women are underrepresented in some jobs and overrepresented in others. Segregation can occur along several fronts—occupation, sector, status in employment, and degree of informality. Borrowman and Klasen (2019) examined patterns and trends in occupational and sectoral segregation by gender in 69 developing countries over the period from 1980 to 2011. Over this period, the researchers found that occupational and sectoral segregation has grown in more countries over time than the number of countries where it has fallen. Moreover, income levels appear to have no impact on occupational or sectoral segregation. Increases in average incomes do not guarantee that women will have improved access to a more diverse array of paid jobs.

There are many explanations for observed patterns of labour market segregation. Social norms and conventions lead to gender typing of jobs and discriminatory behaviour. These norms and gender roles are slow to change. One reason for the durability of social norms that reinforce gender inequalities is that collective action on the part of men contributes to the persistence and reproduction of these norms. In this way, men protect their economic interests. Labour market segmentation may also arise from other forms of gender inequality. For instance, under-investment in women's and girls' education and gender-based differences in skills and training can lead to differences in the job opportunities available to women. The gender division of unpaid labour in the household also yields patterns of segregation in which women tend to work in the kinds of paid jobs that are more easily combined with unpaid work.

Neoclassical theories argue that women's preferences, with respect to types of work and degree of risk, help explain gender segregation. Women work in certain types of positions because they simply prefer those activities or because they have a greater aversion to risk than men and self-select into safe, predictable types of employment. One difficulty with this argument is that preferences are difficult to observe directly. Instead, the existence of preferences is assumed to be consistent with observed choices (Sen 1977). But if this is the case, the explanation collapses to a circular argument: women are assumed to have preferences for certain types of paid work simply because that is the type of work they do. Moreover, it is often difficult to separate preferences from norms. Women may articulate a preference for certain types of work because they want to conform to prevailing norms (see, for example, Heintz, Kabeer, and Mahmud 2017 or Chapter 5 in this volume). The assumption that women are, in all cases, inherently more risk averse than men has also been shown to be questionable (Nelson 2016).

An approach to labour market segregation that is consistent with many of the findings of the GrOW research is that women make labour market choices within a social structure defined by cultural norms, household relationships, the composition of economic activities, and the distribution of resources (such as household assets) and opportunities (such as education). The degree to which choices with respect to paid employment reflect their individual preferences will vary. One outcome of these structural realities is the persistence of labour market segregation.

GrOW research on school-to-work transitions in six African countries—Burkina Faso, Ethiopia, Ghana, Kenya, Tanzania, and Uganda—underscore the impact of labour market segregation (see Chapter 10 in this volume). Using the data from Demographic and Health Surveys (DHS) for each country, researchers compared education and employment outcomes over time. They found that, although there had been improvements in women's educational attainment, this was not always associated with better employment outcomes (IDRC 2017; Mariara et al. 2018). The mismatch between educational attainment and women's employment opportunities may also explain why better educational attainment does not always translate into higher labour force participation in many country contexts (Klasen 2019). Only in two of the countries among the six African countries studied—Ghana and Kenya—was there evidence that women moved out of traditional agricultural activities and diversified the types of paid work they did. In the case of Ghana and Kenya, the degree of diversification has been modest, particularly when contrasted with improvements in educational attainment. Segregated employment opportunities offer one explanation for these limited changes.

Labour market segregation occurs simultaneously with regard to occupation and sector. A number of GrOW research projects that look at women's work in the extractive sectors of selected African countries illustrate the interaction between sectoral and occupational segregation. Specifically, women tend to be underrepresented in extractive sectors and, when they are employed in those sectors, they are often confined to specific types of paid employment.

These studies of mining include research in Ghana, Côte d'Ivoire, the Democratic Republic of the Congo (DRC), Rwanda, and Uganda (Baah-Boateng, Baffour, and Akyeampong 2017; Buss et al. 2017; Konan and Atsin 2020; Rutherford and Buss

2019). Analysis of the Ghana Living Standards Survey revealed that representation of women in extractive industries is low—just 18% of total employment—and gender segregation by occupation is higher in extractive industries compared to other sectors (Baah-Boateng, Baffour, and Akyeampong 2017). In Ghana's mining sector, very few women participate in underground mining. Instead, women are generally concentrated in other forms of employment with lower earnings and weaker job security. A similar picture emerges from analysis of data from Côte d'Ivoire (Konan and Atsin 2020). As in the case of Ghana, women only constitute 18% of employment in mining, and jobs are segregated with women concentrated in marginal activities.

Norms and stereotypes help explain segregation in the mining sector. In both Ghana and Côte d'Ivoire, women are considered to be bad luck with regard to underground mining (Baah-Boateng, Baffour, and Akyeampong 2017; Konan and Atsin 2020). Women often do not have the training for certain mining activities. The qualitative research on artisanal mining in the DRC, Rwanda, and Uganda echoes these findings. There are norms and taboos that prevent women from participating in pit mining—women are also considered to be bad luck in these countries. In some cases, women working around the mine are assumed to engage in what is judged to be immoral behaviour, such as sex work, and they are subject to violence (Buss et al. 2017; Rutherford and Buss 2019). The types of mining activities that women participate in—stone crushing, washing, panning—tend to have low and more volatile earnings. Women's opportunities are constrained by their lower education on average, no or limited access to land, patriarchal family dynamics, and gendered norms. Women typically need the permission of their husbands to enter into subcontracting relationships, access credit, or to sell a piece of land (Buss et al. 2017). As a result of these norms, very few married women participate in mining.

With regard to labour market segregation, women are not only concentrated in specific sectors and occupations. They may also be disproportionately represented in informal jobs—unregulated forms of employment lacking basic social protections. As with the general analysis of segregation, gender-based constraints—including unpaid care and household work, norms, differences in women's access to and control over assets and finance, and unequal investments in capabilities—limit women's choices relative to men's and contribute to their greater representation in informal forms of employment (Heintz and Pickbourn 2012). Informal employment is heterogeneous. Gender segmentation occurs within informal employment itself, with regard to branch of activity, sector, and wage versus self-employment, and gender earnings gaps are often found in informal self-employment (Chen et al. 2005). This suggests that gender-based constraints continue to operate in informal labour markets, despite low barriers to entry and the absence of formal legal institutions.

Recent theoretical approaches to informal employment recognise the heterogeneity in informal activities and see informal employment divided into low- and high-end activities (Fields 1990; Perry et al. 2007). Individuals voluntarily choose the high-end segment as an alternative to formal employment, but barriers to entering these activities and limited numbers of formal job opportunities result in a fraction of the labour force having no choice but to work in low-end activities, where there are few barriers to entry.

Research on the nature of informal employment in South Africa finds that employment in informal enterprises primarily consists of these low-end activities (Makaluza and Burger 2018). Employment in the South African informal sector is characterised by harsh working conditions, low pay, and few prospects for upward mobility. There is also evidence of gender segregation. The study finds that approximately 40% of workers in low-end, survivalist activities in the informal sector are street vendors, an occupation dominated by women. In contrast, around 28% of the occupations in the higher-end, growth-oriented segment of the informal sector are related to the building industries, a male-dominated sector.

The prevalence of precarious and informal forms of employment with regard to women's paid work suggests that the concept of labour market segregation should be broadened beyond a consideration of occupation and sector to include the informality status of different kinds of paid work. Differences in status in employment (e.g. wage employment versus self-employment) should also be recognised since, in many countries, self-employment comprises the largest share of informal employment. Informal employment has a greater propensity toward precarity, with low and unstable earnings and few, if any, social and legal protections. Therefore, when women are disproportionately represented in informal activities, it contributes to gender inequalities associated with labour markets.

The gender-segregated nature of labour markets causes economic policies, including macroeconomic policies, to have different effects on women's and men's paid employment. Broad-based economic policies will have gender-specific effects when these policies interact with structural features of the economy, such as labour market segregation, intra-household inequalities and the distribution of unpaid work, to produce distinct outcomes for women and men (UN Women 2015). For instance, if the central bank raises interest rates as part of an inflation-targeting strategy, the policy choice will affect sectors differently, depending on how responsive sectoral output and investment is to interest rates. When women and men are unevenly employed in different productive sectors, we expect to see women's and men's employment respond differently to central bank policy.

Two GrOW research papers illustrate how gender segregation of labour markets produces different employment outcomes for men and women when governments pursue trade liberalisation policies. Braga (2018) examines trade liberalisation in Brazil, and Lepelle, Edwards, and Sundaram (2017) investigate the impact of a similar policy orientation in South Africa. The Brazilian research suggests that trade liberalisation has negative labour market effects for young low-skilled workers, with more significant negative effects for men than women (Braga 2018). The paper further links worsening labour market outcomes for men to lower fertility and delayed marriage among women. The paper uses decentralised regional data from Brazil to examine how trade shocks, measured in terms of changes in tariff exposure, affect regional outcomes. The economic structures of regions differ, resulting in a variation in trade exposure. This causes the effect of trade liberalisation to vary by region. Due to the sectoral segregation of employment by gender, changes to trade policy affect women's and men's employment differently.

A parallel story emerges in research from South Africa on trade liberalisation. Lepelle, Edwards, and Sundaram (2017) use a regional approach similar to the Brazilian analysis. They found that trade liberalisation had a negative effect on labour market outcomes for both men and women. However, the consequences for men's labour force participation are significantly larger than those for women. When the researchers restrict their attention to manufacturing, their analysis suggests that, in municipalities that had high exposure to trade, male employment grew while female employment declined. Again, labour market segregation explains these differences. In manufacturing, women are concentrated in labour-intensive activities that would be more responsive to a negative shock from trade liberalisation. Outside of manufacturing, men are concentrated in sectors with greater trade exposure than women. This could account for the stronger overall negative response of men's labour force participation to liberalisation compared to women's.

Household formation and unpaid care work

The gender division of labour between unpaid and paid work represents a structural constraint to women's labour force participation and affects their employment choices. Unpaid, non-market work includes activities such as household chores, carrying fuel and water, meal preparation, and caring for others.[3] In this section, we focus on unpaid care work—the provision of non-market services, usually within the household, such as childcare, care for the sick or disabled, and elder care. Typically, women perform the majority of unpaid care work. In many respects, the division of unpaid care work between women and men can be thought of as an extension of the gender segregation of economic activities in the market economy. However, there are important differences. Perhaps most significantly, women may enter and leave the labour market, rotating in and out of paid employment. However, women are rarely able to withdraw their unpaid caring labour without significant consequences.

Care for children represents an important component of unpaid labour. This means that changes in marital status and childbearing have a significant impact on women's labour force participation and employment outcomes. Several GrOW studies also uncovered evidence that women had difficulty continuing to participate in labour markets after they got married—a common finding across many types of employment, from garment factories in Bangladesh to artisanal mining in East African countries (Buss et al. 2017; Field, Nazneen, and Glennerster 2018).

A particularly important set of issues is the intersection of the choices regarding education, marriage, childbearing, and paid work that young women face, and the constraints that influence those choices. The direction of causality is complex, and these choices influence one another. The research on school-to-work transitions in

Burkina Faso, Ethiopia, Ghana, Kenya, Tanzania, and Uganda used nationally representative data to look at educational attainment and women's labour market outcomes, taking into account marriage, childbearing, and the presence of young children (IDRC 2017; Mariara et al. 2018). These studies found that early marriage had a particularly important impact on the gender gap in school attendance and educational attainment. According to a comparative synthesis of regression analysis, marriage is associated with lower education and literacy scores for both men and women, although the negative effect appears to be more pronounced for women. Similarly, having young children has a strong negative association with women's literacy and remaining in school through to the secondary level.

These findings are not restricted to these particular African countries. Research on early marriage in Bangladesh also found that delayed marriage was associated with increased years of schooling which would translate into better employment outcomes for women (Field et al. 2018). Qualitative research, based on in-depth interviews, on barriers to economic empowerment in Bangladesh provided additional insight into the relationship between marriage, childbearing, and paid employment (Field, Nazneen, and Glennerster 2018). In Bangladesh, many girls faced a rapid transition from childhood to adulthood because of early marriage. Once married, girls and young women face a different set of constraints and new household bargaining dynamics. Specifically, upon marriage, girls and young women would move to the households of their in-laws (they would move away from their families to households comprised of people not directly related to them). If they wanted to continue their education or participate in paid employment, they would need to negotiate this with their in-laws. Often, their in-laws would refuse. Traditional gender roles and cultural practices constrain women's economic participation, and these constraints are typically intensified by marriage.

In some cases, marriage or a return to traditional roles in the household served as an alternative to paid employment as an economic survival strategy for women. For instance, the GrOW research on Sri Lanka and the rise of female-headed households as a result of the conflict found that many female heads of households pursued one of two strategies when confronted with the challenge of being both breadwinner and caregiver: they typically either returned to their extended family or opted to remarry (Lakshman 2017).

The direction of causality does not simply run from marriage to labour market outcomes. Employment outcomes for men and women can affect marriage rates and patterns of household formation. Specifically, when men's employment outcomes deteriorate, marriage rates often decline (e.g. Brien 1997; Blau, Kahn, and Waldfogel 2000; Loughran 2002; Posel and Casale 2013). This suggests that policy changes that affect women's and men's employment differently may also have consequences for marriage and household formation. The study on trade liberalisation in Brazil found that higher exposures to trade were correlated with lower marriage rates (Braga 2018). One explanation for this relationship is that trade liberalism in Brazil appears to have had a larger negative effect on men's employment prospects than those of women.

Changes in marriage rates and household composition affect the distribution of the costs of children, with important consequences for women's economic welfare and labour market prospects. Falling marriage rates are often associated with a decline in fertility rates (e.g. Braga 2018). However, they are also associated with a larger share of children being born outside of marriage and more children being raised by single parents, most often single mothers. Depending on the policy environment (e.g. existence of family policies and enforcement of child support payments) and the fertility response of falling marriage rates, the costs of raising children, both in terms of unpaid labour and money, increase.

Household dynamics have a direct impact on the allocation of women's and men's labour. Therefore, households are, in many respects, labour market institutions. It is not just women's productive attributes, such as years of education, which determine their participation in labour markets and access to paid employment. The endowments of other household members and bargaining dynamics affect labour market outcomes. For instance, in India, married women's labour force participation declines with increases in their husbands' educational attainment (Klasen 2019). This suggests that household formation will affect women's employment outcomes, with consequences for WEE.

The effects of marriage, household formation, and childbearing on women's labour market outcomes raise questions about what policies could be adopted in order to expand the choices available to women in ways that would support economic empowerment. The research on early marriage in Bangladesh provides an instructive example. Bangladesh has a very high rate of child marriage, the second highest in the world (UNICEF 2014). According to the 2014 Bangladesh DHS (National Institute of Population Research and Training, Mitra and Associates, and ICF International 2016), 59% of Bangladeshis aged 20–24 were married before 18, the legal age of marriage (Field et al. 2018). One of the reasons for high rates of child marriage in Bangladesh is economic. Dowry costs rise with the women's age, providing an incentive for parents to marry their children early (Buchmann et al. 2017).

One of the GrOW projects conducted a randomised trial in Bangladesh to explore the effectiveness of different strategies to reduce child marriage and teenage childbearing (Buchmann et al. 2017). Selected communities were randomised into three treatment groups and one control group. Beginning in 2008, the girls in treatment groups received either a six-month empowerment programme, a financial incentive to delay marriage, or a combination of the empowerment programme and the financial incentive. The financial incentive was conditional on the girls remaining unmarried until age 18, rather than being conditional on girls remaining in school. Analysis of data collected on 15,739 girls four and a half years after the programme was over showed that girls eligible for the financial incentive for at least two years were less likely to be married under 18, less likely to have given birth under 20, and more likely to be in school at age 22. In contrast, the empowerment programme had no effect on child marriage or teenage childbearing, but it did have a modest positive impact on the likelihood that girls would remain in school.

Improving access to childcare services represents an important intervention that may expand women's choices with respect to paid employment. Evidence from high-income countries suggests that increasing the availability of daycare can improve economic outcomes for mothers. Research on these same issues for LMICs is less well-developed. One study pulled together evidence from 13 studies of developing economies on the effect of daycare provision on a range of socio-economic outcomes (Harper, Austin, and Nandi 2017). The research used a combination of narrative review and random-effects meta-analysis. The studies covered the following countries: Mexico, Colombia, Brazil, Argentina, China, Guatemala, Nepal, Ghana, and Ecuador.

Based on this synthesis of evidence, the researchers estimate that for each 30-percentage point increase in daycare utilisation, maternal employment would rise by six percentage points. This is a summary estimate. There was significant variation in the results reported in the studies reviewed. Important differences in the quality of daycare programmes, types of paid work available to women, household dynamics, and time constraints will lead daycare to have different impacts on mothers in low-income economies. Nevertheless, this study highlights the role of unpaid care work as a labour market constraint and the potential importance of access to childcare for mother's labour force participation.

Another GrOW project used a randomised control trial to look at how lowering the costs of childcare services, through a voucher system, would affect women's labour market choices and outcomes in Nairobi, Kenya (Clark et al. 2017, 2019). Some question whether access to childcare is less of an issue in sub-Saharan Africa, where women primarily work in the informal sector in forms of paid employment that allow them to more easily combine paid and unpaid work. To examine this question, this study used an experimental approach in which selected mothers, living in Korogocho—a slum area of Nairobi—received subsidised early childcare. Mothers who were not using one of the eligible daycare centres identified by the researchers were randomly assigned into control and treatment groups. The mothers who received the childcare subsidy were given 12 monthly vouchers, covering the months of January to December 2016, for all their children between the ages of one and three years.

The researchers found that uptake rates were significant. Over 80% of mothers who were given vouchers were sending their children to daycare a year into the project. With regard to paid employment, women who were given subsidised childcare were, on average, 17% more likely to be employed than those who did not receive the subsidy. Furthermore, working mothers who were given the childcare subsidy were able to work fewer hours without any reduction in their earnings.[4]

These examples illustrate how choices around marriage, childbearing, and employment are influenced by economic incentives, bargaining power, social norms, and changes in economic opportunities for men and women. Policies that seek to enhance WEE through labour markets and paid employment must pay attention to these social factors in addition to the characteristics of individual women.

Gender roles, norms, and violence

Gender roles refer to activities and behaviours adopted within a specific social context that are considered to be appropriate for a particular gender. Gender roles are defined by social norms, the informal rules and understandings that govern behaviour within a specific group. As already discussed, gender roles and norms affect the division of labour between paid and unpaid activities, women's labour force participation, and labour market segregation—including the degree of informality. Policies aimed at enhancing WEE must take these issues into account.

The importance of gender roles and unequal labour market outcomes affecting policy outcomes is reflected in research on skills and vocational training programmes in Punjab, Pakistan (Cheema et al. 2019). Using data collected from a survey of 10,946 households, the study examined the factors that would influence participation in skills development programmes, such as those supported by the Punjab Skills Development Fund (PSDF). The population surveyed has a high proportion of youth with few skills (including basic numeracy and literacy) and low educational attainment. Unemployment rates are particularly high and labour force participation rates are low among women. The survey asked households who, if anyone, they would nominate for a skills training programme. Over 92% of households nominated at least one household member for PSDF training. However, two-thirds of households nominated men for the training, regardless of educational attainment, because of the men's traditional role in paid employment and their higher earning potential. The study also found that responsibilities for household duties represented a constraint to accessing training. This suggests that government-sponsored training programmes may be gender biased if they do not take these issues into account.

Expanding on these themes, a different project on skills and vocational training in Punjab, Pakistan used a random control trial methodology to explore the constraints that prevented women from taking part in skills development initiatives in Punjab (Cheema et al. 2019). Individuals were assigned to one of three groups: a control group and two treatment groups, one with a basic voucher to provide an incentive to enrol in a training programme and a second with a "top-up" voucher of greater value. The study also tested the impact of bringing the training facility to a village in order to see whether distance represents a major constraint for women to access a facility.

The study found that it is extremely challenging for rural women to travel across village boundaries for vocational training and providing a stipend is often not sufficient to address these constraints. Providing in-village training significantly increases uptake among women in rural areas. One of the reasons for the significant increase in uptake when a training facility is in the village is the perception of safety. Women felt that it was unsafe to travel between villages, but they were able to move around their own villages in order to access training. The question of women's safety and GBV is discussed further below.

Gender roles representing informal social rules governing behaviour may become formalised and codified into social practices that may also be reflected in formal and customary laws. These practices represent barriers to WEE and labour force participation. The research on Sri Lanka emphasised the barriers that formal practices create for WEE. For instance, women in northern Sri Lanka cannot sell or manage land without their husband's permission (Lakshman 2017). This limits women's choices with respect to income-generating activities. In the case of Sri Lanka, these rules create significant problems, particularly with the rise in female-headed households due to the country's protracted conflict.

In many of the countries examined, the dividing line between individual preferences and social norms is fuzzy.[5] For instance, in Bangladesh, there are strong social norms for women to limit their market employment to activities that can be done within the home. Studies of women's employment choices show that they often express preferences for employment in the home rather than outside the home (Heintz, Kabeer, and Mahmud 2017). One of the reasons for these stated preferences is that conforming to social norms enhances women's status. For example, the study on artisanal mining in Central and East Africa shows that the desire to appear 'respectable' influences women's choices with regard to work in mining activities (Buss et al. 2017).

The importance of norms and traditional gender roles in determining labour market outcomes raises a critical question: can norms be changed? Several of the GrOW research studies suggest that the answer is yes, but it may be a long process and not all efforts to alter norms are equally successful. As described in the previous section, Bangladesh has a long-standing tradition of child and underage marriage. Research on this issue shows that financial incentives, conditional on remaining unmarried, actually make a difference by delaying marriage. However, simply offering an empowerment programme, without the financial incentive, has no effect.

The duration of interventions to change norms appears to matter. Research on the state-funded and state-run Mahila Samakhya (MS) empowerment programme in India illustrates how sustained engagement may shift gender norms (Mahendiran, Jha, and Ghatak 2017). MS was first introduced in 1989 in 10 districts in three states, Uttar Pradesh, Gujarat, and Karnataka. Since then, it expanded to more than 42,000 villages in 11 states by 2015–2016. There are four pillars associated with MS: political empowerment, social empowerment, economic empowerment, and personal empowerment. The study looked at the effectiveness of MS in the State of Bihar, the poorest state in India.

MS organises groups of women into *sangha*, or collectives (Menon 2017). As conceptualised within the programme, the *sangha* is a collective process through which women can reflect on, analyse, and resolve problems they face. A *sahayogini* is responsible for all the *sanghas* located in each cluster, usually consisting of ten villages. The *sahayoginis* work with the *sanghas* to develop women's knowledge and capacity for action.

The study used a quasi-experimental approach to assess the effect the MS programme has had on economic empowerment. Seven measures of empowerment were used—economic activity, political participation, intra-household decision-making, awareness about laws and entitlements, functional literacy, attitude toward violence against women, and self-efficacy. The paper estimates the long-term, medium-term, and short-term effects of MS to understand whether the effects vary with the duration of exposure to the programme. The researchers found that, in the short-run, MS had an impact on several measurements of empowerment, but no significant effect on intra-household decision-making and self-efficacy. This suggests that, in the short run, the programme did not have a notable effect on gender roles and norms. However, the assessment of the long-run effects of the programme do show evidence that these components of empowerment were affected, indicating that the programme has the potential to shift norms over a longer term.

Violence against women represents one way norms may be enforced. GBV restricts women's engagement with labour markets in a number of ways (Peters et al. 2016). Violence outside of the home may make it dangerous for women to engage in certain activities or work in particular locations. IPV within the home has a direct impact on household dynamics and women's ability to make independent decisions, including those regarding the allocation of their labour.

The research on Sri Lanka highlights how a culture of violence evolved during the years of conflict in that country. High levels of sexual and gender-based violence make it difficult for women to engage in economic activities outside of their home (Kandanearachchi and Ratnayake 2017; Lakshman 2017). Although Sri Lanka has put measures in place in an attempt to reduce violence against women, research revealed that women in the North still encounter problems due to the lack of enforcement of these laws (Kandanearachchi and Ratnayake 2017). The research on artisanal mining in African countries also found that violence against women, particularly around mining areas, constrained women's choices (Buss et al. 2017).

GBV also affects women's choices with respect to household formation and marriage. In societies in which violence against women outside the home is commonplace, marriage to a man provides women with some form of protection even if her husband himself is abusive (Kabeer 2018). The fear of sexual or GBV can restrict women's employment options, even when women have not experienced such violence directly. The research on Sri Lanka suggests that these dynamics are important in maintaining traditional gender roles. Given the prevalence of violence, marriage constitutes an agreement in which the husband provides for and protects his wife and children in exchange for the wife's unpaid household labour (Lakshman 2017). This bargain between husbands and wives reinforces gender roles and restricts women's ability to freely participate in labour markets.

The direction of causation does not only run from GBV to labour market outcomes. Women's participation in paid employment may also influence the likelihood that they experience some form of domestic abuse, but the issue is complex. Women's participation in paid employment could reduce the incidence of IPV and abuse when paid employment increases women's economic autonomy, improves their options outside of current partnerships, and gives them more bargaining power. These factors can lower the chances that women are subjected to abuse. However, this argument may not hold in traditional patriarchal societies in which divorce and separation is uncommon. Alternatively, improvements in women's economic position may threaten men's dominant gender roles. IPV and abuse may represent a form of backlash when masculinist identities come under threat.

Causality may also run domestic violence related to employment. Women who experience abuse may make different labour market decisions than women who do not. Furthermore, research into the relationship between women's employment and domestic abuse faces another challenge. Both employment and domestic abuse can be independently correlated with additional factors. If these factors are not considered (i.e. variables are missing), a relationship between women's employment and domestic violence may appear to exist, when in reality it is caused by a third factor. For instance, households experiencing economic stress may see an increase in women's labour force participation and a higher probability of domestic abuse. In this case, it is the economic stress, not women's employment, which is triggering the greater likelihood of IPV and abuse.

One study examined the relationship between women's employment and incidences of physical and psychological abuse directed at women within households (Khan and Klassen 2018). The researchers took care to address the possible problems of causality and missing variables, and created an economic model using quantitative data from 35 countries, drawn from DHS surveys. The study controls for issues of endogeneity that may result in biased estimates. They found a negative relationship between women's participation in paid employment and reported physical and psychological abuse—a result consistent with the argument that access to paid employment improves women's bargaining power and reduces domestic violence. It is important to note that regional variations were evident. Countries in Latin America and the Caribbean and East Africa appear to show a positive relationship between women's employment and incidences of abuse. This suggests that the relationship between women's employment and domestic abuse may be context specific and sensitive to factors such as the construction of masculinity and variations in gender roles.

Discussion and policy directions

The collection of GrOW research studies provides insights and detailed case studies that increase our understanding of gender inequalities in labour markets—why they exist and why they continue to persist. These studies help explain several counter-intuitive outcomes regarding gender inequality and women's paid employment. Why have labour market inequalities been stubbornly resistant to change despite a narrowing of other gender gaps, such as school enrolment rates and levels of educational attainment? When women's participation in paid employment increases, why do we not automatically see improvements in women's empowerment, defined as women's ability to make substantive choices about their own lives?

One core message that emerges from a consideration of the findings is that structural features of economies create barriers that entrench labour market inequalities between women and men. The most important of these structural features include segregated labour markets, social norms that reinforce gender roles, unequal distributions of assets and economic resources, women's disproportionate specialisation in unpaid work, and gender-biased laws and institutions.

If policymakers do not take these factors into account, efforts to improve labour market outcomes for women may not yield the desired results. Moreover, a focus on trying to improve a narrow set of indictors of gender equality, such as school enrolment gaps or labour force participation rates, may not translate into women having improved choices and opportunities relative to men (UN Women 2015). Not only does this mean that advances in true gender equality will likely prove elusive, but it also has implications for economic performance and wellbeing more generally. The inability of women to realise their full potential represents both a social injustice and a real economic cost.

Broad-based economic policies, such as macroeconomic and trade policies, interact with the gender structures of economies to produce employment outcomes that differ for women and men. The research projects that explored the impact of trade liberalisation on women's and men's employment in South Africa and Brazil demonstrated these dynamics (Braga 2018; Lepelle, Edwards, and Sundaram 2017). These kinds of research studies show how a gender impact analysis of all economic policies, not just those focused on women's employment or empowerment, can be performed. Policymakers could demand that similar gender impact analyses be routinised and incorporated into the development and design of a range of economic policies.

Women are often concentrated in informal, precarious, or marginal types of paid employment. In many developing countries, women's paid work is far more likely to be in self-employment than wage employment, and therefore it does not receive the social protections that standard labour laws provide. When crafting public policies, it is critically important to recognise these informal and marginal work arrangements. Specifically, informal employment represents an important source of income for women that has the potential to allow for savings, investments to improve livelihood opportunities, and more autonomous decision-making (Kabeer, Mahmud, and Tasneem 2011; Buss et al. 2017). Therefore, policies aimed at improving labour market outcomes for women must take into account the specific factors affecting workers in remunerative informal employment. These typically include access to markets, access to credit, appropriate infrastructure (e.g. water taps, sanitation facilities, and electrification), and asset and land ownership and control. The constraints limiting the opportunities of women in informal employment will vary by activity and sector.

Skills development and training programmes, if properly designed, have the potential to remove some constraints to women's labour market participation and choices with regard to paid employment. The project on vocational training and skills development in Pakistan provides useful policy insights (Cheema et al. 2019).

Skills development and training programmes should be designed to take account of the differences between men and women who participate. This is particularly important given that the men who participate will have different labour market experiences and positions within their families than the women who participate.

The skills emphasised in the training should also consider differences in the types of paid work women and men typically do. Research has indicated that vocational training may raise men's earnings but have little impact on women's, suggesting that there are gender biases in the content of the education received (Heintz and Pickbourn 2012). There is a tension here between the need to reduce gender segregation of labour markets while also providing women with the skills they need for the types of jobs they are likely to do. Skills development and training programmes should be coordinated with other initiatives to reduce gender inequalities in labour markets.

Formal institutions, such as the legal framework, frequently contain gender biases that constrain women's participation in paid employment. For instance, inheritance and family law may prohibit women from inheriting economic resources and give husbands power over their spouse's ability to participate in certain economic activities or make independent decisions (Peters et al. 2016). Research on female-headed households in war-torn Sri Lanka showed how customary law restricted women's livelihood choices and control over economic resources (Kandanear-achchi and Ratnayake 2017). In this case, the necessary policy interventions involve legal and institutional reforms to remove gender biases.

The policy challenge is more daunting when the rules that restrict women's choices and labour market activity arise, not from formal laws, but from informal social norms. One consistent message that emerges from the collection of GrOW research projects is that social norms matter, and matter greatly, for the types of work, paid and unpaid, that women do. Although norms are recognised as a constraint within which women make choices, the question of how to change these norms to advance gender equality is a difficult one. Several studies suggest that different gender roles and norms are possible. The research into programmes to reduce child marriage in Bangladesh found that well-designed financial incentives cause people to deviate from traditional behaviour and this may help shift norms (Buchmann et al. 2017). The cluster of studies of the MS programme in India indicate that this community-based empowerment programme had little impact on norms in the short-run, but long-term engagement appears to have an effect on altering gender roles.

Related to the question of norms, a number of studies found that GBV, or even the threat of such violence, has a significant impact on the choices available to women throughout their lives, but also with regard to the kinds of paid employment they are able to do or their ability to access training programmes. In many country contexts, this is a critically important contributor to gender inequalities in the labour market, one that requires attention when formulating policies to enhance women's positions in the economy.

The unequal distribution of unpaid labour and care work represents a significant barrier to labour force participation, limiting women's choices with regard to paid employment. Chapter 4 in this volume provides a comprehensive overview of these issues on care work. At a minimum, public policies seeking to improve women's paid employment must consider the demands of unpaid care if they are to have an impact on unequal labour market outcomes. However, to truly address this source of gender inequality, policymakers must explicitly consider adopting long-term strategies to reduce care burdens through public provisioning and gender egalitarian family policies.

A comprehensive approach to labour market policies must adopt a life-cycle perspective. Certain junctures in women's lives are particularly important in shaping future employment trajectories and the degree of economic vulnerability women face. One of these junctures is the school-to-work transition, which, for many young women, overlaps with transitions into marriage and childbearing. Studies on school-to-work transitions begin to shed light on the complex set of issues involved (IDRC 2017). However, more research in this area, particularly in the developing country context, is needed.

Overall, the projects that have contributed to the GrOW research initiative increase our understanding of the factors that underpin persistent gender inequalities in labour markets and employment outcomes. They provide guidance in designing new policies that could address the unevenness between women and men with regard to labour force participation, employment opportunities, and the quality of paid work. In the future, more work along these lines—with greater breadth, by increasing the countries, regions, and types of employment studied, and depth, by applying a rigorous gender analysis to examine unanswered questions—has the potential to transform thinking around employment policies in developing countries.

Notes

1 For a review of the literature concerning the relationship between economic growth and gender equality, see Chapter 1 in this volume.
2 Further exploration of women's labour force participation and gender norms in the mining sector can be found in Chapter 6 in this volume.
3 For a more complete, detailed and nuanced discussion of how to define care work, see Chapter 4 in this volume.
4 For information on the PhotoVoice methodology used to evaluate the impacts of this daycare intervention in Kenya, see Chapter 7 in this volume.
5 For an in-depth look at the relationship between gender, social norms, and women's economic empowerment, see Chapter 5 in this volume.

References

Baah-Boateng, William, Pricilla Twumasi Baffour, and Emmanuel Akyeampong (2017). Gender differences in the extractives sector: A case study of mining in Ghana. GrOW Working Paper, No. 1. www.interias.org.gh/sites/default/files/WP_1.pdf.

Bhalotra, Sonia, and Maria Umaña-Aponte (2010). The dynamics of women's labor supply in developing countries. IZA Discussion Paper Series, No. 4879. Bonn: Institute for the Study of Labor (IZA). http://ftp.iza.org/dp4879.pdf.

Blau, Francine D., Lawrence M. Kahn, and Jane Waldfogel (2000). Understanding young women's marriage decisions: The role of labor and marriage market conditions. *Industrial and Labor Relations Review* 53(4): 624–647.

Borrowman, Mary, and Stephan Klasen (2019). Drivers of gendered sectoral and occupational segregation in developing countries. *Feminist Economics* 26(2): 62–94.

Braga, Beno (2018). The effects of unilateral trade liberalization on marriage and fertility choices: Evidence from Brazil. 2nd IZA Workshop: Gender and Family Economics, April 20–21. http://conference.iza.org/conference_files/Gender_2018/braga_b25045.pdf.

Brien, Michael J. (1997). Racial differences in marriage and the role of marriage markets. *Journal of Human Resources* 32(4): 741–778.

Buchmann, Nina, Erica Field, Rachel Glennerster, Shahana Nazneen, Svetlana Pimkina, and Iman Sen (2017). Power vs money: Alternative approaches to reducing child marriage in Bangladesh, a randomized control trial. Research Paper. www.povertyactionlab.org/sites/default/files/research-paper/Power-vs-Money-Working-Paper.pdf.

Buss, Doris, Blair Rutherford, Jennifer Hinton, Jennifer Stewart, Joanne Lebert, Abby Sebina-Zziwa, Richard Kibombo, and Frederick Kisekka (2017). Gender and artisanal and small-scale mining in Central and East Africa: Barriers and benefits. GrOW Working Paper Series, GWP-2017–02. https://grow.research.mcgill.ca/publications/working-papers/gwp-2017-02.pdf.

Cheema, Ali, Asim I. Khwaja, Farooq Naseer, and Jacob Shapiro (2019). Glass walls: Experimental evidence on access constraints faced by women. Working Paper. https://khwaja.scholar.harvard.edu/files/asimkhwaja/files/glass_walls_draft_november_draft.pdf.

Chen, Martha A., Joanne Vanek, Francie Lund, James Heintz, with Ranana Jhabvala and Chris Bonner (2005). Progress of the world's women 2005: Women, work and poverty. New York: United Nations Development Fund for Women. www.unwomen.org/en/digital-library/publications/2005/1/progress-of-the-world-s-women-2005-women-work-and-poverty.

Clark, Shelley, Sonia Laszlo, Caroline Kabiru, and Stella Muthuri (2017). Can subsidized early child care promote women's employment? Evidence from a slum settlement in Africa. GrOW Working Paper Series. GWP-2017–05. http://grow.research.mcgill.ca/publications/working-papers/gwp-2017-05.pdf.

Elson, Diane (1999). Labor markets as gendered institutions: Equality, efficiency, and empowerment issues. *World Development* 27(3): 611–627.

Enchautegui, María (2017). Economic structure and gender inequalities in labor force participation. Working paper, mimeo.

Field, Erica, Rachel Glennerster, and Shahana Nazneen (2018). Economic empowerment of young women in Bangladesh: Barriers and strategies. The International Policy Centre for Inclusive Growth, Policy in Focus Vol. 15(1).

Field, Erica, Rachel Glennerster, Shahana Nazneen, Svetlana Pimkina, Iman Sen, and Nina Buchmann (2018). Age at marriage, women's education, and mother and child outcomes in Bangladesh. 3ie Impact Evaluation Report 68. New Delhi: International Initiative for Impact Evaluation (3ie). www.3ieimpact.org/sites/default/files/2019-01/IE%2068-Bangladesh-marriage.pdf.

Fields, Gary S. (1990). Labor market modelling and the urban informal sector: Theory and evidence. In David Turnham, Bernard Salomé, and Antoine Schwarz (Eds.), *The Informal Sector Revisited* (49–69). Paris: OECD.

Goldin, Claudia (1995). The U-shaped female labor force function in economic development and economic history. In T. P. Schultz (Ed.), *Investment in Women's Human Capital and Economic Development* (61–90). Chicago: University of Chicago Press.

Harper, Sam, Nichole Austin, and Arijit Nandi (2017). Daycare and women's health, social, and economic outcomes in low- and middle-income countries: Systematic review and evidence synthesis. GrOW Working Paper Series. GWP-2017–07. http://grow.research.mcgill.ca/publications/working-papers/gwp-2017-07.pdf.

Heintz, James, and Lynda Pickbourn (2012). The determinants of selection into non-agricultural self-employment. *Margin: The Journal of Applied Economic Research* 6(2): 181–209.

Heintz, James, Naila Kabeer, and Simeen Mahmud (2017). Cultural norms, economic incentives and women's labor market behavior: Empirical insights from Bangladesh. *Oxford Development Studies* 46(2): 266–289. doi:10.1080/13600818.2017.1382464.

IDRC (2017). From school to work in six African countries: How are women faring? Policy Brief. Ottawa: International Development Research Centre. https://idl-bnc-idrc.dspacedirect.org/bitstream/handle/10625/56368/IDL-56368.pdf?sequence=2&isAllowed=y.

Kabeer, Naila (2018). The fear of sexual harassment is robbing women of work around the world. *Ms. Magazine*, August 3. https://msmagazine.com/2018/03/08/fear-sexual-harassment-robbing-women-work-around-world/.

Kabeer, Naila, Simeen Mahmud, and Sakiba Tasneem (2011). Does paid work provide a pathway to women's empowerment? Empirical findings from Bangladesh. IDS Working Paper 375. Brighton: Institute of Development Studies. https://www.lse.ac.uk/gender/assets/documents/research/choice-constraints-and-the-gender-dynamics-of-lab/Does-paid-work-provide-a-pathway-to-womens-empowerment.pdf.

Kandanearachchi, Kethaki, and Rapti Ratnayake (2017). Post-war realities: Barriers to female economic empowerment. Report. Colombo: International Centre for Ethnic Studies. http://ices.lk/wp-content/uploads/2017/12/Post-War-Realities-For-Circulation.pdf.

Khan, Sarah, and Stephan Klasen (2018). Female employment and spousal abuse: A parallel cross-country analysis from developing economies. Courant Research Centre: Poverty, Equity and Growth Discussion Paper 249. Goettingen, Germany: Courant Research Centre. www2.vwl.wiso.uni-goettingen.de/courant-papers/CRC-PEG_DP_249final.pdf.

Klasen, Stephan (2019). What explains uneven female labor participation levels and trends in developing countries? *World Bank Research Observer* 34(2): 161–197. https://elibrary.worldbank.org/doi/abs/10.1093/wbro/lkz005.

Klasen, Stephan, and Janneke Pieters (2012). Push or pull? Drivers of female labor force participation during India's economic boom. IZA Discussion Paper No. 6395. Bonn: Institute for the Study of Labor (IZA). http://ftp.iza.org/dp6395.pdf.

Konan, Yao Silvère, and M. Atsin (2020). Does artisanal mining promote women's economic empowerment in Côte d'Ivoire? Paper accepted for presentation at the World Congress of the International Economic Association, Bali, July 3–7, 2020. Working paper, mimeo.

Lakshman, Iresha M. (2017). Impact of intimate relationships on livelihood activities of women affected by war in northern Sri Lanka. ICES Report. Colombo: International Centre for Ethnic Studies (ICES). http://ices.lk/wp-content/uploads/2017/12/Impact-of-Intimate-relationships-For-Circulation.pdf.

Lee, K. W., and K. Cho (2005). Female labor force participation during economic crises in Argentina and the Republic of Korea. *International Labor Review* 144(4): 423–450.

Lepelle, Refilwe, Lawrence Edwards, and Asha Sundaram (2017). Trade effects on gendered labor market outcomes in post-apartheid South Africa. Working paper, mimeo.

Loughran, David S. (2002). The effect of male wage inequality on female age at first marriage. *Review of Economics and Statistics* 84(2): 237–250.

Makaluza, Nwabisa, and Rulof Burger (2018). Job-seeker entry into the two-tiered informal sector in South Africa. In Frederick Fourie (Ed.), *The South African Informal Sector: Creating Jobs, Reducing Poverty*. Cape Town: HSRC Press.

Mahendiran, Shreekanth, Jyotsna Jha, and Neha Ghatak (2017). Understanding the impact of Mahila Samakhya on women's economic empowerment in Bihar. CBPS-GrOW Working Paper No. 1. Bengaluru: Centre for Budget and Policy Studies. Working paper, mimeo.

Mariara, Jane, Andy McKay, Andy Newell, and Cinzia Rienzo. (2018). Gender gaps in the path to adulthood for young females and males in six African countries from the 1990s to the 2010s. *IZA Journal of Development and Migration* 8:16. https://doi.org/10.1186/s40176-018-0124-8.

Menon, Niveditha (2017). *The methodology of Mahila Samakhya: Understanding the sangha as a space for empowerment.* Bangalore: Centre for Budget and Policy Studies. Unpublished Working Paper, mimeo.

Nelson, Julie (2016). Not-so-strong evidence for gender differences in risk taking. *Feminist Economics* 22(2): 114–142.

National Institute of Population Research and Training (NIPORT), Mitra and Associates, and ICF International (2016). *Bangladesh Demographic and Health Survey 2014.* Dhaka, Bangladesh and Rockville, MD: NIPORT, Mitra and Associates, and ICF International. https://dhsprogram.com/pubs/pdf/FR311/FR311.pdf.

Peters, H. Elizabeth, Nan Marie Astone, Ammar A. Malik, Fenohasina Maret, and Caroline Heller (2016). Women's economic empowerment: A review of evidence based on enablers and barriers. Washington, DC: Urban Institute. www.urban.org/sites/default/files/publication/84641/2016.09.28_womens_economic_empowerment_final.pdf.

Perry, Guillermo E., William F. Maloney, Omar S. Arias, Pablo Fajnzylber, Andrew D. Mason, and Jaime Saavedra-Chanduvi (2007). Informality: Exit and exclusion. Latin American and Caribbean Studies. Washington, DC: World Bank. https://openknowledge.worldbank.org/bitstream/handle/10986/6730/400080Informal101OFFICIAL0USE0ONLY1.pdf?sequence=1&isAllowed=y.

Posel, Dorrit, and Daniela Casale (2013). The relationship between sex ratios and marriage rates in South Africa. *Applied Economics* 45(5): 663–676.

Priebe, Jan (2011). Child costs and the causal effect of fertility on female labor supply: An investigation for Indonesia 1993–2008. CRC-PEG Discussion Paper No. 45, University of Göttingen. https://econpapers.repec.org/paper/gotgotcrc/045.htm.

Rutherford, Blair, and Doris Buss (2019). Gendered governance and socio-economic differentiation among women artisanal and small-scale miners in Central and East Africa. *Third World Thematics: A TWQ Journal* 4(1): 63–79.

Sen, Amartya (1977). Rational fools: A critique of the behavioral foundations of economic theory. *Philosophy and Public Affairs* 6(4): 317–344.

UNICEF (2014). Ending child marriage: Progress and prospects. New York: UNICEF. https://data.unicef.org/resources/ending-child-marriage-progress-and-prospects/.

UN Women (2015). Progress of the world's women 2015–2016: Transforming economies, realizing rights. New York: UN Women. www.unwomen.org/en/digital-library/publications/2015/4/progress-of-the-worlds-women-2015.

3

MACROECONOMICS AND GENDER

Recent research on economic growth and women's economic empowerment

Sophia Kan and Stephan Klasen

Introduction

Over the last two decades, women's economic empowerment (WEE) has become increasingly recognised as an important development outcome by governments and development stakeholders. WEE is not only a goal in and of itself, but a means for overall economic growth by expanding human capital and through spillover effects on families and children. Promoting WEE, however, is not straightforward. It requires thoughtful interventions that target gender inequality across a broad range of sectors, from education to employment to trade. To help address this challenge, this chapter provides a synthesis of the research commissioned by the Growth and Economic Opportunities for Women (GrOW) programme, focusing on an investigation of the linkages between macroeconomic growth and WEE. In total, 30 studies were included in the synthesis, including 11 cross-country analyses, seven on Africa, one on Europe, three on Latin America and the Caribbean, one on the Middle East and North Africa (MENA) region, six on South Asia, and one on Southeast Asia. The aim of this chapter is to expand the knowledge base and distil key messages on the linkages between macroeconomic changes and WEE.

The GrOW research portfolio aimed to target specific research gaps. For example, existing macro-level studies on the impact of gender gaps in employment on economic growth are few because of measurement challenges (although the small body of growing literature indicates that reducing the gaps is good for overall economic growth). Micro-level studies are also rather limited, but they show promising results that advancing WEE promotes economic growth. More studies are needed on key channels linking empowerment with economic growth, such as promoting higher productivity in agricultural work, increasing access to inputs and credits at the firm level, improving women's intra-household bargaining power, and enabling political empowerment.

Findings from the GrOW programme add valuable insight to the topic of WEE by contributing to research and empirical evidence on the topic. It includes studies that examine the impact of economic growth and structural change on WEE, and others that investigate the impact of gender inequality on economic growth. In addition to examining these linkages, the GrOW research portfolio includes ten studies on enabling factors—factors that help directly link growth to WEE. Studies focusing on these factors include three papers on education, three papers on transportation and public services infrastructure, one on childcare, one on financial inclusion, one on affirmative action policies, as well as one on asset accumulation.

This chapter begins by laying out the conceptual framework and key definitions. Then we provide an overview of the impact of gender inequality on growth in two parts: a review of the macro literature and a review of the micro literature. This is followed by a review of the literature on the impact of growth on gender inequality—we focus on employment, women's empowerment in households, trade, and the role of enabling factors. The conclusion lays out some of the key findings with a focus on policy lessons and actions that can promote WEE and economic growth.

Conceptual framework

Defining and measuring women's economic empowerment

The concept of women's empowerment—especially their economic empowerment—started to receive its own place in policy discussions only in recent decades. Kabeer (2012) explains that global commitments, such as the Beijing Platform for Action and the UN Millennium Development Goals, helped to strengthen and shape the topic by including policy goals and language to support women's empowerment, economic independence, and productive employment. This momentum eventually led to the recent inclusion of and focus on women's empowerment in the general development discourse.

Greater awareness of women's empowerment eventually led to the coining of the term "women's economic empowerment" by the World Bank in 2006, defined as "making markets work for women (at the policy level) and empowering women to compete in markets (at the agency level)" (World Bank 2006: 4). Another definition, which includes both women and men is

> the capacity of poor women and men to participate in, contribute to and benefit from growth processes on terms which recognise the value of their contributions, respect their dignity and make it possible for them to negotiate a fairer distribution of the benefits of growth. Economic empowerment means people thinking beyond immediate survival needs and thus able to recognise and exercise agency and choice.
>
> *(Eyben, Kabeer, and Cornwall 2008: 9–10)*

While the first definition emphasises shaping markets, the second includes a host of measures that reflect principles of equity and individual wellbeing. The concept of WEE has, and still does, reflect numerous perspectives and definitions. A recent literature survey of WEE, across 32 papers and research proposals from the GrOW programme, revealed more than 40 different measures of WEE (Laszlo and Grantham 2017). The most common measures were female labour force participation (FLFP), followed by education rates, autonomy and household decision-making power, gender inequality in social norms, and gender inequality in legal institutions. The range in definitions is, however, indicative of WEE's aim to encompass a comprehensive set of goals.

The academic literature on WEE in the field of economics, however, is typically limited to the analysis of labour markets and variables such as FLFP, hours worked, and earnings. This narrow focus on employment indicators, while clearly important, can be quite misleading. For example, on the one hand, an increase in FLFP means greater income and bargaining power for women. On the other hand, as shown by Gasparini and Marchionni (2015) and Klasen (2019), withdrawal from low-paid unattractive jobs can also be an improvement in wellbeing and empowerment, even if the loss of income might affect women's bargaining power within the home. This is one of the reasons for slow improvements in FLFP in developing countries over the past few decades (Klasen 2019). Alternatively, a decrease in FLFP could also be driven by a lack of suitable and well-paying job opportunities or relate to social stigmas for more educated women to work in certain sectors or occupations.[1] These examples demonstrate some of the complexities and limitations of using FLFP as a measure of WEE. As highlighted in the introduction to this volume, for a more accurate analysis of WEE it is critical to consider factors beyond FLFP, such as the quality of employment, including pay and working conditions, ease of access, etc.

How women's economic empowerment can promote growth

WEE pertains not only to the ability of women to determine the course of their lives but has direct implications for macroeconomic growth. WEE can promote economic growth through many channels, such as adding human capital to the economy, removing a gender-induced distortion in drawing on an economy's best talent, developing a comparative advantage in certain types of manufacturing and service sectors, and by promoting investments in child, household, and community welfare. To support these arguments with empirical evidence, we first measure the relationship between WEE and growth, which is challenging given the multi-faceted nature of WEE. In surveying GrOW projects, Laszlo and Grantham (2017) found that the measurement of WEE can be broken down into objective and subjective dimensions. Most of the existing literature focuses on outcomes (e.g. income) and there are fewer studies on processes (e.g. capabilities and agency). This may in part be due to data limitations and the challenges of measuring processes, whereas surveys can capture outcomes more easily and clearly.

Measurement is also complicated when going beyond individuals and households to assess macroeconomic effects. In a recent paper, Klasen (2018) explains that the effects of WEE on macroeconomic growth are difficult to measure due to several methodological challenges. These challenges include measuring whether micro-level effects can be generalized at the macro level; the difficulty in capturing positive spillovers that contribute to economic growth (e.g. decrease in child mortality); the difficulty in taking general equilibrium effects into account; and recognition that a sizable portion of women's work, especially care and housework, is not included in national accounts (gross domestic product (GDP) estimates).

The literature stemming from the GrOW programme reviewed below is a collection of studies that address both outcomes and processes of WEE and relate to macroeconomic growth. Despite the measurement challenges, the studies complement each other to paint a coherent picture of the linkages between WEE and economic growth. We also provide a framework for the discussion that attempts to address some of the measurement challenges associated with WEE.

Economic growth: how and under what conditions does it lead to WEE?

There are several channels through which economic growth can promote WEE. First, economic growth can stimulate labour demand which can draw women into the labour force. This will depend on the labour intensity of growth (i.e. how many new jobs are generated by growth) and whether the jobs are in sectors and occupations that women can easily access. Conversely, as discussed above, higher incomes resulting from growth may lead some women to leave undesirable jobs.

Second, economic growth can promote or accelerate structural change, with implications for WEE. The effect will depend on the direction of structural change (i.e. the nature of the growth process). For example, if growth is mostly based on expanding capital-intensive resource exploitation, it is likely to lead to fewer opportunities for WEE than growth that promotes female employment in export-oriented manufacturing or services.

Third, growth may relieve tight budget constraints at the micro and macro level. At the micro level, this could improve access to vital household infrastructure that might reduce women's unproductive and time-consuming activities (such as fetching water or wood). At the macro level, it can generate higher tax receipts that can be used to increase health and education spending, thereby lowering gender gaps in these areas.

Enabling factors

Enabling factors are policies at the macro and micro levels that link growth to WEE. At the macro level, trade policy can, depending on the policy and context, provide economic opportunities for women. Similarly, fiscal policy can provide resources to promote WEE by creating public employment opportunities for women in the health or education sectors, for example, or by relieving micro-level constraints to greater WEE, such as providing better, safe, and reliable transportation services or publicly funded childcare. For an overview on the linkages between childcare and WEE, see Chapter 4 in this volume.

Empirical findings: impact of gender inequality on growth

The GrOW portfolio included several literature reviews on the impact of gender inequality on economic growth, including three systematic reviews. We summarise these reviews below.

Theoretical mechanisms

A review by Klasen and Minasyan (2017a) presents four arguments for how gender gaps in education reduce economic performance. First, gender gaps in education can reduce female employment and thus reduce the size of the workforce and potential labour hours. Second, gender gaps in education can mute the positive externalities of education on growth, such as a decrease in fertility, reduction in child mortality levels, and intergenerational knowledge transfers via the mother. Decreasing fertility, for example, means the working-age population will grow faster than the dependent population. Third, a lower gender gap also increases the talent pool for employers, which should lead to better use of human capital with positive growth implications. Fourth, gender gaps in education can prevent countries from benefitting from some female-intensive competitive export-oriented manufacturing industries, industries that contributed to strong economic growth in East Asia. Therefore, reducing gender gaps in education is one way to foster gender-equitable change and economic growth.

Klasen and Minasyan (2017a) also identify four channels through which gender gaps in employment can hamper economic growth. The first is that it reduces the natural pool of female human capital and distorts the workforce. Second, gender gaps in employment reduce overall labour force participation. Third, these gaps hinder countries from taking advantage of female-intensive export-oriented manufacturing sectors. Last, gender gaps in employment can reduce women's take-home earnings and, in turn, decrease their bargaining power at home. This bargaining power can have several macroeconomic growth effects, including increased savings and greater expenditures on more productive investments such as the education and health of the children. Not surprisingly, many consequences and causes of gender gaps in education and employment are similar or overlap.

Compared to findings from this applied theoretical work, Santos-Silva and Klasen (2018) show that the 'growth theory' literature tends to focus on how gender gaps in education or employment affect fertility and the human capital of the next generation. Such effects play out over the long term and can lead to poverty traps for countries with large gender gaps, associated high fertility, and low human capital investments. These models also typically argue that exogenous technological change tends to erode incentives to maintain gender gaps in education or employment for two main reasons. First, new technologies will favour brain over brawn and thus erode the male advantage of physical strength. Second, technologies help increase the efficiency of care and housework and reduce the time spent (typically by women) on these activities.

While these mechanisms are plausible, other aspects of technological change may not be so benign. For example, the growing technology, science, and engineering sectors in many countries tend to be very male dominated, which could increase gender gaps in employment. Where initially there are gender gaps in education, skill-based technological change can also result in women losing out as demand for unskilled labour falls.

Last, in these models, there is usually a strong role for policy. Promoting female education or employment can help countries break out of their poverty traps and embark on a self-sustaining path of higher growth and greater gender equity.

Macro-level systematic review

Another component of the GrOW portfolio consists of systematic reviews of aggregate studies on the impact of gender inequality on economic growth (Klasen 2018; Minasyan et al. 2019). A fundamental problem in studying the relationship between macroeconomic growth and WEE is the complexity involved in capturing both measures as well as additional variables needed to demonstrate a causal effect. A study by Klasen (2018) outlines the specific challenges of measuring the effect of narrower gender gaps on macro-level growth effects. The first challenge is that changes in WEE can have many positive effects, such as improved health and education of children, but these are often difficult to measure. Second, to measure the effect of a change in gender equity, reactions by other actors must be considered (i.e. general equilibrium effects). For example, to measure the economic growth effect of an increase in FLFP, one cannot simply use basic accounting to calculate how much income additional female work would earn at prevailing wage rates. Instead, the effect of this change on male labour force participation, wage rates, or sectoral changes must also be considered.

Third, a sizable portion of women's work is often not captured in national accounts. Many types of domestic care such as raising children, caring for the elderly, and housework are not included in gross national income. Fourth, many studies estimate relationships between variables without necessarily considering the channels and mechanisms behind the relationship. These mechanisms, however, can provide insight and strengthen the estimations. Last, many studies cannot identify a causal effect to show which factor led to the other: did WEE improve economic growth or vice versa?

One area where there is a large, comparable, and robust literature that can be assessed in a systematic review and meta-analysis is the impact of gender inequality in education on economic growth. A study by Minasyan et al. (2019) looks at this topic. They conduct a systematic review of macro-level studies that includes all publicly available regression analyses using aggregate data that relate a gender-disaggregated education indicator or a gender gap measure to a measure of output or growth of output. The initial search of studies published in journals and of working papers yielded 1,421 potentially relevant studies. After screening for relevance and duplication, 264 studies remained. These were subjected to full-text screening by two independent screeners. After screening and the addition of five studies, based on expert recommendations, 54 studies were included in the systematic review. Since nearly all these studies include several different regressions, the number of regressions assessed is substantially larger.

Minasyan et al. (2019) find that most studies show that reducing gender gaps in education promotes economic growth. However, they note several issues that should be considered in the interpretation of the studies. Some of the studies use time series methods: although they support the overall conclusion, they are methodologically weak, and their findings should be treated with caution. Some studies also use male and female education as separate variables and find a negative impact of female education on growth. These should be treated with caution as they rely on a problematic model specification that is likely to lead to biased results. After disclosing these caveats, the authors then perform a meta-analysis of studies that uses the ratio of female-to-male education and find that reducing the gender gap in education has, on average, a sizable impact on promoting economic growth, which is not influenced by publication bias.

Regressions on the determinants show that the effect of the gender gap on growth is smaller if the model is estimated using fixed effects, when the share of female authors is larger, and when economic controls are included. The effect is significantly larger when the regression controls for average education includes social or institutional controls and uses enrolment rates instead of years of schooling. Whether it is published in a peer-reviewed journal or it also includes FLFP does not significantly change the effect. Based on these results, regression specifications that are arguably the most convincing—use fixed effects, years of schooling as the gap variable, and control for a large number of variables including average education—will carry a sizable and significant positive correlation coefficient, thus providing robust evidence that reducing the educational gender gap improves economic growth.

In addition to education, the analysis of gender gaps in employment is also an important area of study. Currently, the existing body of macro-level studies on the effect of gender gaps in employment on growth is still relatively small due to data challenges and endogeneity issues (Gaddis and Klasen 2014), as well as the measurement issues listed above. In Klasen's (2018) literature survey, key macro-level studies on this topic are identified. Below, the five most relevant and robust studies are summarised.

The first two studies (Cavalcanti and Tavares 2016; Cuberes and Teignier 2016) estimate the cost of gender discrimination in employment on economic growth. Cavalcanti and Tavares (2016) find that wage gaps increase discrimination and ultimately decrease FLFP and increase fertility. Specifically, a 50% increase in the gender wage gap decreases per capita income by 35% in the long run. The authors argue that their findings explain differences in economic growth between the US and countries such as India, Saudi Arabia, and Egypt. Cuberes and Teignier (2016) find that restrictions on female employment lead to an income loss of 27% in the MENA region, 19% in South Asia, and 10% in Europe.

The third study on gender gaps in employment and economic growth is a study by Klasen and Lamanna (2009) that analysed regional data over a 40-year period. It found that gender gaps in labour force participation negatively affect growth. For example, in the 1990s, employment gaps caused South Asia to lose some 0.2–0.4 percentage points annually in growth compared to East Asia. The results were particularly significant in the Middle East. Klasen and Minasyan (2017a) then apply this study to Europe and find that gender gaps in employment led to substantial losses, hampering annual per capita growth by 0.8 percentage points in Ireland in the 1980s and 1990s, Spain in the 1970s and 1980s, and Portugal in the 1970s.

Cumulatively, these countries lost about 17.3 percentage points in economic growth. This amounts to an 8.3 percentage points loss of output over a decade and 17.3 percentage points over two decades, compared to the top performers, which were Finland in the 1970s and 1980s and Sweden in the 1990s. For the United Kingdom, France, and Germany, the cumulative costs are more moderate but still amount to about 4 percentage points per decade.

A fifth study in India finds that gender gaps in employment and managerial positions have a negative effect on growth (Esteve-Volart 2004). Analysing 30 years of panel data across Indian states, the author finds that the gaps not only reduce income per capita but distort the allocation of talent.

In short, the studies that link gender gaps in employment to growth are limited, but they generally find a negative relationship—gender inequality hurts growth. However, there are many issues surrounding the measurement of macro-level effects, making it difficult to clearly estimate the direction and magnitude of the effect. Micro-level findings can perhaps help provide another level of evidence on the relationship between WEE and economic growth.

Micro-level findings

A small body of micro-level studies focuses on the linkages between WEE and economic growth. They have similar measurement challenges to the macro-level studies. They rely on accounting for positive externalities or spillover effects, making it difficult to ascertain the aggregate-level effects. However, the literature on micro-level findings is growing.

Klasen (2018) identified four research areas on this topic. The first relates to farm and agricultural work. Several papers find that gender inequality in terms of access to land, inputs, and agricultural technologies leads to reduced farm productivity (Udry 1996; Goldstein and Udry 2008; Croppenstedt, Goldstein, and Rosas 2013). For example, Goldstein and Udry (2008) find that inequality in land rights in Ghana leads women to shorten fallow periods (i.e. slash and burn agriculture), which can destroy the fertility and productivity of the soil. This inefficiency is estimated to cost 25% of output, which amounts to 1% of GDP. The second area of research is on the relationship between access to inputs, credit, and labour and firm efficiency. This is a nascent field of literature, and not yet resolved. Impact evaluations, however, seem to indicate that small-farm interventions may disproportionately benefit men over women (McKenzie and Woodruff 2014). The third research area largely pertains to other indirect factors that can strengthen WEE, such as women's greater intra-household bargaining power and political decision-making power. A host of robust studies show that greater intra-household bargaining power improves the health and education of children, which has a positive effect on economic growth. Finally, several studies (Chattopadhyay and Duflo 2004; Duflo 2012; Bhalotra and Clots-Figueras 2014) show that women's political empowerment can improve economic growth through the provision of public goods, better human capital, and reduced child mortality.

The GrOW portfolio also included a review of micro studies of interventions to promote WEE (Ibanez et al. 2018). It finds that interventions to promote WEE (e.g. improving financial access, promoting entrepreneurial activities, promoting employment, or supporting women farmers) have a modest impact on human development in low- and middle-income countries (LMICs). These interventions promote employment and increase income, subjective wellbeing, and income security. Some interventions also increase enrolment in training. Yet, there are no significant effects on savings, access to credit, or health. There are also no significant effects on female empowerment within households, domestic violence, or consumption. As these interventions focused on women, it is not clear whether the effects would have been similar for men.

To summarise, a large theoretical and empirical body of literature shows that reducing gender gaps and promoting WEE can boost economic growth.[2] There are robust findings on the impact of gender gaps in education on growth—the empirical findings on other dimensions of WEE on growth are fewer but generally support the positive linkage. The literature on the impact of policy and interventions is still quite specific and hard to generalise.

Empirical findings: impact of growth on gender inequality

To investigate the effect of macroeconomic growth on gender equality, GrOW researchers have focused on two main channels—employment and women's empowerment in the household. The studies on employment find that economic growth alone has no clear impact on female employment. Rather, employment depends strongly on the type of economic growth and the associated structural change. In some cases, economic growth can worsen occupational and sectoral gender segregation.

In terms of the second channel—women's empowerment in households—GrOW studies have found that economic growth increases women's empowerment and decision-making power, with strong positive externalities on other family members. However, as with employment, the relationship is nuanced and depends on the setting. For example, the impact of trade on gender inequality largely depends on the type and gender composition of manufacturing sectors and is therefore highly setting-specific. The trade studies included in this review, for instance, find a mixed effect in Brazil (Braga 2017) but a positive effect in Indonesia (Kis-Katos, Pieters, and Sparrow 2018).

In addition to the two channels, further research areas linking economic growth to WEE include studies on education, transportation and infrastructure, childcare, financial inclusion, and affirmative action policies.

Employment

Economic growth can have a very uneven impact on female employment (Klasen 2019). In some regions, most notably Latin America[3] and the Caribbean, economic growth has been accompanied with substantial increases in female employment in recent decades. However, in many Asian countries, including India and China, economic growth was accompanied by declining FLFP. This indicates that there are no universal trends linking growth and female employment, such as the feminisation U hypothesis (Gaddis and Klasen 2014). Instead, what matters is how women's employment decisions are made independently from the economic and social conditions of the households; the nature of social stigmas militating against (certain types of) employment for women, particularly those who are educated; and the growth of employment opportunities in sectors deemed appropriate for women.

Economic growth may also do little to increase the retention of women in the labour force. Using a nationally representative panel dataset for India, Sarkar, Sahoo, and Klasen (2019) show that women not only participate less in the labour force, but are dropping out at an alarming rate. To investigate the determinants of women's entry and exit from employment, they correct for selection bias due to initial employment and panel attrition. The results show that higher incomes of other members of the household lead to lower entry of and higher exit probabilities for women. This income effect persists even after controlling for the dynamics of the household's assets. Along with the effects of caste and religion, this shows the importance of cultural and economic factors in explaining India's decline in FLFP. They also explore other individual- and household-level determinants of women's employment transitions. Moreover, they find that a large public workfare programme significantly reduces women's exit from the labour force.

Closely related to these findings is evidence indicating that occupational and sectoral segregation persists with economic growth. A study by Borrowman and Klasen (2019) found that economic development (measured as GDP per capita) had no statistically significant effect on occupational or sectoral segregation. Their results confirm earlier findings by the World Bank (2012) that argued that economic development is insufficient for integrating labour markets along gender lines.

Borrowman and Klasen (2019) used panel data and country fixed effects to analyse 69 developing countries from 1980–2011, using the World Bank International Distribution Database. The final dataset included a sample of countries across sub-Saharan Africa (n=24), Latin America and the Caribbean (n=20), East Asia and the Pacific (n=10), Europe and Central Asia (n=5), and the MENA region (n=2).

Using several measures of segregation, they found that as economic development increased, occupational and sectoral segregation increased in more countries than it decreased. This is particularly the case for occupational segregation. Even when economic growth promotes female employment, women largely enter sectors and occupations that are already dominated by women. A nuanced view of the mechanism can be illustrated by a case study of Ghana's extractive sector (see below).

Given the existing gender segregation in employment, the impact of economic growth on FLFP will depend on which sectors expand and shrink because of growth or the pattern of structural change. For example, Gaddis and Klasen (2014) investigated the extent to which sectoral value-added growth led to greater FLFP. They find that rising shares of FLFP in the mining sector lead to lower female participation while rising shares of manufacturing and of some services are associated with greater female participation. In the following paragraphs, we review GrOW research that focuses specifically on this issue, evaluating the impact of structural change or sectoral developments on women's employment.

To begin, Enchautegui (2018) investigates the impact of the various components of GDP on FLFP of 94 LMICs over a 24-year period from 1991–2014. She finds that, compared to value-added growth in the service sector, the growth of the agricultural sector and of a broadly defined natural resources sector (water, gas, construction, mining, and electricity) is associated with reduced gender gaps in participation rates. She also finds that as the private sector contracts, gender inequality increases, which is rather surprising given that most private sector work is informal (where women are largely concentrated). Two possible explanations are posited: first, since the countries in the study are still developing, there are not enough white-collar positions available for educated women, and second, in many developing countries, as agriculture is still the main economic activity, the service sector is secondary and smaller. Using descriptive statistics, Enchautegui also shows that from 1991 to 2014, overall FLFP increased in total by 3.7 percentage points, while male labour force participation decreased by 2 percentage points. This helped close the gap from 28 to 22 percentage points. It is unclear whether some of the increase in FLFP is due to more men exiting the labour market. A variety of methodological and data issues with the study might also affect the results.[4]

The next set of studies are country- and sector-specific case studies. Baah-Boateng, Baffour, and Akyeampong (2017) conduct a case study on Ghana's mining sector and show how sectoral segregation can persist despite economic growth. They use the same segregation indices (Duncan Index of Dissimilarity, and the Karmel and MacLachlan Index) as Borrowman and Klasen (2019) and an Oaxaca-Blinder decomposition approach to identify the composition of earnings by gender. Analysing a sample of some 1000 men and women in the mining sector from the Ghana Living Standards Survey (2005–2006 and 2012–2013), Baah-Boateng, Baffour, and Akyeampong (2017) find that women are relegated to some of the worst occupations in the sector. For example, they often do the most menial and toxic work. In mining and petroleum, 60% of women and 42% of men have elementary job status. One rung up, in production, women compose 29% of workers while men account for 41% of workers. Women also earn, on average, 48 to 57% less than their male counterparts.

In the Ghanaian context, the authors cite rigid gender norms as the main determinant of gender and wage gaps, such as the belief that women are bad luck. Gender norms affect overall sectoral segregation in Ghana where women compose only about 19% of extractive sector workers. The shares of women in small-scale mining are much higher in Guinea (75%), Mali (50%), and Zimbabwe (50%). In short, despite an increase in economic growth and the growth of the mining sector, progress toward greater WEE must include addressing the barriers to occupational and sectoral equity, such as gender norms.

A second paper (Konan 2017) also explores the relationship between mining and gender. In the Ivory Coast, among those employed in mining, women earn less than men. This gender pay gap has been attributed to cultural norms and social barriers. The analysis was based on a 2016 survey that included 1,842 working men and women in 20 regions, between the ages of 15 and 60. The authors also created an empowerment index, and then used the index to employ propensity score matching to match miners and other workers to calculate the likelihood of being employed in small-scale mining. The authors used the Oaxaca-Blinder estimation method to investigate wage differentials and found that women earn 24% less than men. According to the decomposition, 52% of the salary difference between men and women was explained by gender.

The study also measured women's empowerment. Interestingly, being employed in small-scale mining was estimated to increase the probability of being empowered by 15%. While working in small-scale mining has a positive effect on empowerment, the effects are relatively small. This may be due to social and infrastructure barriers (e.g. distance, safe transportation, protection from theft, and physical violence). To reduce these barriers, the author recommends building schools for the workers' children near the mining facilities.

In summary, these studies show that economic growth can have varied effects on female employment. Factors such as cultural and social barriers and strong occupational and sectoral segregation mean that it is not just economic growth but the type of economic growth that will matter for improving WEE. For example, growth based on natural resources, such as mining, does little to promote female employment opportunities, but growth strategies based on export-oriented manufacturing can help promote women's employment, particularly those with medium levels of education. Similarly, growth in public or publicly financed service sectors, such as health, education, and public administration, can also improve women's employment opportunities.

Women's empowerment in households

Economic growth also has implications for women beyond employment; it can be empowering. In a large cross-country study, Braga et al. (2017) found that GDP growth improves female intra-household bargaining power. The study employs a sample of one million married women across 36 countries (a total of 99

Demographic and Health Surveys) from 2000–2014. There are two main outcome variables, indices developed by the authors. The first measures intra-household bargaining power based on whether women participated in decisions pertaining to major household purchases, visiting family and friends, and even their own healthcare. The second measure pertains to attitudes about domestic violence, which is based on five separate questions that measure a woman's willingness to justify the violence.

The authors found that a 4% annual growth rate in GDP per capita, over a five-year period, led to a 5% increase in the number of decisions in which a married woman participates. Education accounted for a 6.6% increase in decision-marking, and employment led to a 9% increase. Factors that decreased decision-making power were having children (although by a trivial 0.007 percentage points per child) and being Muslim (0.26 percentage points). The effects of economic growth on domestic violence were insignificant.

In a follow-up paper, Peters et al. (2018) used the same dataset to investigate the impact of economic growth on experiences with and attitudes toward domestic violence. Overall, their results suggest that attitudes toward violence do not respond directly to changes in national income. However, attitudes do change indirectly over time, following social and cultural changes that are associated with economic development. The experience of intimate partner violence (IPV), however, appears to be more resistant to change, either directly through changes in national income or indirectly through changes associated with economic growth. Moreover, because of the positive correlation between FLFP and IPV, economic growth may have a built-in backlash—as FLFP increases, men may be more likely to use violence to assert their power and control.

The question of whether women's employment leads to backlash and more violence was also investigated by Lenze and Klasen (2017) who analyse the effect of women's employment on domestic violence in Jordan. The authors find that without controlling for the endogeneity of domestic violence and employment, employment would have appeared to be positively associated with all forms of domestic violence. This endogeneity can be the result of reverse causality or the impact of some unmeasured third variable and it will bias the effect. After addressing this problem, they find that employment has no effect on IPV in general, although there is some evidence that it lowers sexual violence. The reduction in sexual violence is believed to be due to women's increased bargaining power at home.

Extending the above analysis to 35 countries, Khan and Klasen (2018) find that, without taking endogeneity into account, a woman's employment status increases violence by her spouse. After controlling for endogeneity, these results turn out to be the opposite, suggesting that women's employment status, especially formal employment, has a negative influence on domestic violence. Breaking down the estimation by regions shows that women's employment decreases domestic violence in all regions except Latin America and East Africa. Differentiating the results by employment type shows that women working in agricultural occupations experience more IPV.

Returning to the relationship between growth and intra-household bargaining power, van Biljon (2017) found that an increase in income (receiving pensions) increased female intra-household bargaining power and child health (measured as weight-for-height ratio). Analysing the state pension system in South Africa, van Biljon found that receiving pensions increased female bargaining relative to younger males and females in the household. For both men and women between the ages of 15 and 60, residing with a female pension recipient decreased the probability of being the primary decision-maker by 9 percentage points. This effect is smaller and less robust when the pension recipient is male, which leads to only a 2 percentage point decrease in the probability of younger household members being primary decision-makers.

When women are the recipients of old-age pensions, overall female bargaining power within the household increases. However, female bargaining power decreases when men receive pensions. Households with a female pension recipient are 5 percentage points more likely to have a female primary decision-maker. When considering the change within a household, a female receiving the old-age pension is associated with a 3–4 percentage point increase in the probability of a household having a female primary decision-maker. When a male household member receives a pension, the probability of having a female primary decision-maker decreases by 2 percentage points. It therefore seems that resources held by grandmothers enable women to be primary decision-makers in the household. This suggests that the increase in children's wellbeing is due to the greater bargaining power of women with pensions. In short, pensions given to women increase WEE and bargaining power, which leads to greater investment in the wellbeing of the children in the household.

The study by Konan (2017), described in the section on employment, gender, and mining, supports the above findings. Measuring differences in spending patterns between empowered and non-empowered women in the mining sector, Konan found that 90% of empowered women invested in education and health fees for their children.

In sum, there is some evidence that growth and women's rising incomes improve their empowerment in the home, but this pertains only to some indicators and seems far from guaranteed. The papers also confirm that greater female empowerment in the home leads to greater investments in child health and education.

Enabling factors

Trade

The relationship between trade and WEE is mixed. While both men and women benefit from cheaper goods, their employment opportunities are affected unevenly. For example, trade policies that favour female-intensive sectors can improve WEE. However, trade liberalisation often has a disproportionally negative economic and employment effect on men because there are more men in the tradable sector, where competition decreases employment. In contrast, women are often overrepresented in the service sector and are therefore less affected. Below, we provide a summary of diverse examples where women benefitted relatively by losing out less than men from trade reforms (Brazil), where women were hurt more than men (South Africa), where rising poverty associated with trade reforms led to higher female distress employment (India), and where women benefitted from trade reforms (Indonesia).

In Brazil, a study by Braga (2017) found that trade liberalisation had a surprisingly positive effect on women's empowerment as a result of higher male unemployment. Braga investigated the effect of the 1990–1995 changes in tariff rates across 411 micro-regions, municipalities in a state having similar economic characteristics, with varied levels of exposure to the tariff change. He then looked at the effect of the changes on low-skilled workers aged 20–35. Using a difference-in-differences estimation method, Braga found that trade liberalisation reduced work for pay for both women (1.6 percentage points) and men (2.8 percentage points). For women, the decrease in employment was then associated with a decline in the marriage rate, single-parenthood, and fertility rates. Because these women also became less likely to marry low-skilled men, it postponed marriage and childbearing. The effects were most pronounced for women without high school diplomas and for women in micro-regions that were most affected by trade.

A study by Gaddis and Pieters (2017) complements Braga's paper (2017) by also finding that employment rates often decline with trade liberalisation. Their study investigated changes in tariff rates from 1987–1998 on micro-regions in Brazil, analysing the impact on 1991–2000 data on labour force participation and employment rates of both men and women. The people studied were aged 25–55, working in paid, unpaid, formal, and informal work. Gaddis and Pieters found that Brazil's reduction in tariffs decreased labour force participation and employment for both men and women. The impact was two to three times greater for men, likely due to their larger representation in the tradable sector. This decreased the absolute gender employment gap, but not because women's participation increased. The people who were most affected were low-income men and women in the tradable sector. In addition, the authors found that men were able to relocate to the service sector more easily than women. For high-skilled workers, there was no significant association between trade liberalisation and labour force participation. The findings are in accord with Borrowman and Klasen (2019) who found that despite economic growth, segregation of men and women in the labour force persists.

Similar results were found by Lepelle, Edwards, and Liebbrandt (2018) in South Africa, where a decrease in tariffs had a negative effect on both female and male employment. The study investigated the differential effect of trade liberalisation on regional employment by gender from 1996–2011. They drew on employment data for 234 municipalities and exploited variations in pre-liberalisation industry composition of manufacturing to identify the effect of tariff reductions on employment in manufacturing and services. They found that trade reform reduced employment in manufacturing for both men and women, but its effect was significantly stronger for women.

The gender-specific effects found by Lepelle, Edwards, and Liebbrandt (2018) were driven by the industry-bias of tariff reforms against female-intensive industries, such as apparel, experiencing relatively strong reductions in tariffs. They also found no evidence that women benefitted from trade-induced technological change or the greater demand for skilled labour. In addition, they found that employment in the services sector fell in response to trade reform, although the effect is homogenous across gender. They argued that these results arise from reduced household income, a decline in derived demand for services, and reductions in infrastructure investment arising from the decline in manufacturing in these regions.

In a follow-up study, Lepelle, Edwards, and Leibbrandt (2018) look at the effects of trade reform on labour migration in South Africa. The extent to which labour markets are affected by trade liberalisation depends on the ease with which labour and factors of production reallocate across regions and sectors of the economy. This paper considers this key question by observing the effect of tariff reform on the spatial reallocation of labour across regions in South Africa from 1996–2011. The authors also examine how labour force impacts depend on migration frictions stemming from gender differences and disparities in the skill level of workers, among other factors. They find that tariff reductions on imports to South Africa induced a spatial reallocation of labour. They find no robust effect of tariff reform on the decision to migrate from a region but a strong influence on the destination region. Migrants select regions that have relatively low shares of manufacturing in total employment and that experienced relatively low reductions in exposure to tariffs. These results are robust regarding the inclusion of controls for infrastructure, income, aggregate employment, and firm entry.

The next study analyses trade's effect on female labour supply and its subsequent effect on poverty. Gupta and Pieters (2018) study India's trade liberalisation in the 1990s, which led to increased poverty in rural areas (Topalova 2007, 2010). Examining whether households resorted to sending women to work (which is stigmatised) to cope with the negative income effects of liberalisation, they found that tariff cuts did increase labour supply in the poorest 50% of districts. Among the very poorest quartile of districts, this increase is driven by men employed in public works. Since the public works programmes in the 1990s mostly targeted the lowest income quartile (Dutta, Murgai, and Howes 2010), this option was not available to households in less poor districts. Indeed, in the second-poorest quartile of districts, women increased their participation in unpaid agricultural work, and were less likely to primarily engage in domestic duties. Since most of the increase occurred among women who were less educated and belong to a lower social status, the authors concluded that this labour is used as an insurance against negative income shocks.

The final case study is set in Indonesia, where employment favours female-intensive sectors, which can have a positive effect on WEE. Kis-Katos, Pieters, and Sparrow (2018) found that a decrease in input tariffs increased FLFP. In Indonesia, trade liberalisation resulted in greater job opportunities as reductions in input tariffs made production in those sectors more competitive. A one standard deviation reduction from the mean in input tariffs led to a 5.8 percentage point increase in employment for women aged 20 and over. The increase also corresponded to an equivalent decrease in the share of women who considered their primary work as domestic work. The authors found that changes in output tariffs, however, did not influence FLFP, as was the case in Brazil.

In terms of sectoral segregation, the authors found that, surprisingly, female-intensive sectors benefitted from the input tariff liberalisation in low-skilled activities, which indicates a level of segregation. However, after the trade policy went into effect, women also moved into more male-dominated sectors. Kis-Katos, Pieters, and Sparrow (2018) also found some indirect support for technology-induced increases in demand for female workers. Furthermore, they discovered direct evidence that tariff reductions delayed the timing (but not the occurrence) of marriage among women aged 20–29 and men aged 30–39. This was not addressed in the paper but could have some strong positive social implications for childrearing and WEE. The case of Indonesia deviates from the cross-country study of sectoral segregation by Borrowman and Klasen (2019).

The above examples help illustrate the varied and uneven impact of trade on WEE. When lowering trade barriers increases the competitiveness of female-dominated sectors, it can be one path to strengthening WEE. But often, such policies lead to job losses and rising poverty, at least in the short to medium term. By understanding how country-level factors can shape the trade-WEE relationship, policymakers can be better equipped to anticipate appropriate steps in order to strengthen WEE in their respective countries.

Other enabling factors

As outlined above, there are several channels through which economic growth can either weaken or strengthen gender inequality. These channels can also be supported by several enabling factors, such as education, transportation and public services infrastructure, childcare, financial inclusion, and affirmative action policies. Each of these factors can strengthen and support the impact of growth on FLFP and WEE. We briefly summarise each of these factors in the following paragraphs.

As previously discussed, a large body of literature shows that reducing gender gaps in education has a positive effect on economic growth, with employment as a key intermediating variable. This functions via four well-documented mechanisms: an increase in the quantity of human capital available to society; a decrease in fertility rates; the ability to grow female-intensive export-oriented manufacturing industries; and through positive externalities that are passed onto the next generation (Seguino 2020; Klasen 2018).

The first mechanism lifts the artificial barrier placed on females, in which less qualified male equivalents are employed over more qualified female workers. The second mechanism alludes to the phenomenon of the demographic gift, where the dependent population shrinks relative to the working population, spurring economic growth. The third mechanism refers to growing industries that are largely dominated by women, such as in the case of Indonesia. The fourth mechanism refers to an increase in maternal education and how it can improve child nutrition and education.

Unfortunately, as discussed in Klasen (2019) and Klasen and Minasyan (2017a), closing the gender gap in education does not necessarily promote female employment in a commensurate way. In MENA and South Asia, massive improvements in female education have not been accompanied by increases in female employment for the reasons discussed above. Clearly, female education helps increase WEE, but it alone is not enough.

Education can improve WEE at the micro level, and vocational education can be particularly effective in bringing women into the labour force. In Nepal, the evaluation of the Adolescent Girls Employment Initiative, a large-scale vocational education programme that provided training to both men and women, found a disproportionately large effect for women (Chakravarty et al. 2018). The programme was targeted at people aged 16–24 and provided them with technical training in skills such as incense stick rolling, carpentry, tailoring, welding, and masonry. Depending on the skill, the courses lasted anywhere from four weeks to three months.

The evaluation of the programme found that the training had a strong positive effect on becoming and remaining employed. Training led to an increase of 28 percentage points (overall increase: 93%) in non-farm-related work, and a 71% increase in average monthly earnings. There was, however, no significant effect on farm-related work. The programme also increased overall employment hours by 62 hours per month. The impact on women was significantly larger: in 2012, while men experienced a 10% increase after the training programme, women's employment rate increased by 40%. The programme ran from 2009–2012, with around 4,500 female participants. This study shows that training programmes can bring immediate results in the short-run and be a useful intervention when targeting women.

Investments in transportation infrastructure can also strengthen the effect of economic growth on WEE. Zolnik, Malik, and Irvin-Erickson (2018) studied gender differences in the use of the Lahore Metro Bus System (LMBS) in Pakistan. The authors measured the strength of relationships between gender, trip purpose, and mode of transportation using odds ratios to measure effect size. They found that women are 78% less likely to work outside of their homes compared to males and 62% less likely to travel alone but are much more likely to use the LMBS daily. Women are also more likely than men to take the bus to and from their homes because they take the bus for purposes unrelated to their employment. They are also more likely to travel with other people (possibly for physical safety reasons). In short, transportation use differs strongly by gender, and safety may help increase the possibility for women to travel alone and use public transportation to commute to work.

In neighbouring India, Lei, Desai, and Vanneman (2017) found that improvements in transportation increase non-agricultural FLFP by facilitating access to work and providing more free time. Transportation also helps change gender attitudes. The authors analysed household data from the India Human Development Survey, collected in 2005 and 2012. Over 42,000 households, randomly sampled across 1,503 villages in 388 districts, were interviewed. For the panel analysis, 3,373 women and 5,605 men between the ages of 25–59 were included. The authors employed a cross-sectional analysis combined with panel analysis to identify first, the changes in non-agricultural labour force participation rates differentiated by gender, and second, the effects of roads and buses on FLFP (and accounting for gender norms, measured through *purdah*[5]).

An increase in bus services increased FLFP in non-farm work at the intensive margins, and an increase in paved roads and the frequency of bus services increased FLFP in non-farm work at the extensive margins. The authors then investigated how gender norms affect these results by controlling for the level of *purdah* practiced in the community. Results show that the positive effects are weaker in villages where *purdah* is considered common practice, "even when the women are provided easier access to non-farm jobs, they are unable to take advantage of the job opportunities due to restrictions on their physical mobility and norms preventing interactions with unrelated men" (Lei, Desai, and Vanneman 2017: 21). So, while expanding transportation infrastructure can bring women into the labour force, gender norms must also be considered.

Investments in public service infrastructure may also help women access greater employment opportunities. Research by von Fintel and Moses (2017) found that migration, for both black African men and women, is no longer primarily driven by marriage and familial considerations. Although female migration patterns tend to follow those of men, the increase in FLFP over the last two decades suggests intentional co-migration is no longer the dominant reason for female migration. Instead, black African women tend to move to regions where the earnings of (both black and white) men are high (not just of women). This implies that female migrants move based on information about earning potential which does not directly include them. One explanation is that women are drawn to better public services in areas with higher earnings. If women no longer move primarily for family reasons or relocate in response to labour market benefits that accrue specifically to them, better service provision may be a key motivator in their migration decision. This theory is supported by a positive association between the effective targeting of the Child Support Grant in a region and female migration flows to that region. Since public services matter for women's migration decisions, effective management of public resources may help improve WEE.

A report by Peters et al. (2016) also emphasises the importance of gender norms in facilitating meaningful changes for WEE. The report explains that infrastructure development such as electrification, public transportation, access to water, access to technology, and street lighting can help promote WEE, but they must be accompanied by safety measures for women. Infrastructure alone cannot help women if they are prone to harassment and violence when using the infrastructure. In short, while necessary, infrastructure is insufficient: norms must also change. Norms and attitudes can have a powerful role in preventing women from entering the labour market. As discussed earlier, despite optimal conditions for improvements in FLFP in India, such as income growth and gender equality in education, gender norms against female employment have kept women out of the labour force (Sarkar,

Sahoo, and Klassen 2017). For an in-depth review of the relationship between gender, social norms, and WEE, see Chapter 5 in this volume.

Peters et al. (2016) studied the role of childcare on FLFP and WEE. They conducted a literature review using these search terms: "women's labour force participation", "women's labour supply", "childcare", "time poverty", "gender certified firms", "workplace health", and "workplace violence", finding 400 reports since 1995. A large body of literature found that childcare has a positive relationship with FLFP, and either greater availability or a lower cost of childcare has a positive effect on FLFP. However, in terms of WEE, the authors argue that there is not enough evidence that childcare increases free time for women. For instance, it is unclear whether the hours freed from childcare are spent on other domestic work or even work outside the home. Also, the authors did not find evidence that childcare can help women move from the informal to the formal sector. On the other hand, access to childcare can have positive externalities conducive to economic growth. Childcare can, for example, improve children's developmental outcomes when they are placed in early childhood education programmes, and it can also generate jobs for childcare workers. However, the latter can be problematic as many of these jobs in developing countries tend to be informal and poorly paid.

Another enabling factor between growth and WEE is financial inclusion. A study by van Biljon, Pasha, and von Fintel (2018) found that formal financial inclusion increases a woman's intra-household bargaining power, which in turn increases the likelihood that she participates in the labour force. The authors evaluated a programme in South Africa, where women received a Child Support Grant cash transfer bank card. The grant is a proxy for financial inclusion, which is used as a measure of WEE. The authors control for reverse causality and endogeneity issues by instrumenting WEE with the cash transfer.

Findings from this study show that women who received a cash transfer gained more decision-making power within the household, which encouraged them to enter the job market. Those who became the primary household decision-maker increased their probability of employment by 92 percentage points. Women who already had autonomy before the treatment still experienced a 54 percentage point increase in the probability of working when they became primary decision-makers. Finally, women who were never the primary decision-makers in their households also experienced a 42 percentage point increase in the probability of working. Financial inclusion had a strong effect among women who did not have a bank account before the bank card rollout and a stronger impact on women who lived in male-dominated households. Findings support the standard non-cooperative theoretical model that posits that greater female autonomy increases female labour supply. Interestingly, the authors did not find a significant effect for men, which implies that gender norms drive the results—men may already possess a large degree of bargaining power.

Finally, affirmative action policies can also strengthen the linkages between growth and WEE. In South Africa, a study by Klasen and Minasyan (2017b) found that, when targeted appropriately, affirmative action policies can help bring women into the labour force, and also into top occupations, reducing occupational segregation. The authors estimate the effect of three different affirmative action policies on high-skilled black women in South Africa. They find that the Employment Equity Act of 1998 had a small, delayed impact; the Black Economic Empowerment Act of 2003 had a positive effect; and the Codes of Good Conduct of 2007 had a negative effect.

The Black Economic Empowerment Act of 2003 led to a 2.2% higher likelihood of women being employed in a top-level occupation. This was then set back by the Codes of Good Conduct of 2007, which led to a 3% decrease in the probability of women's employment in a top-level occupation. The authors suggest that the differences in effects are due to poor overall job growth and low compliance. However, when designed appropriately (such as the Black Economic Empowerment Act of 2003), affirmative action policies have the potential to help reduce gender gaps in employment by reducing occupational segregation.

In addition to these enabling factors, three studies found that some factors had no effect on WEE or even worked against WEE. The first study tested whether asset accumulation could strengthen the relationship between economic growth and WEE. A study by Desai and Barik (2017) investigated poor women in rural areas over 60 years using the Indian Human Development Survey, a nationally representative sample of households in 2011–2012. The authors found a strong relationship between extended household residence (inter-generational co-living) and land ownership. Older women were more likely to live with their children when the household owns land. For women, however, there was no relationship between land ownership and health expenditure (there is a positive relationship for older men in comparison to working-age men). For households with land, older men get more decision-making power, but there was no effect for women. In the long run, the importance of land (which has poor returns) is declining, and death of the patriarch leads to land fragmentation. This can be problematic as land was often used as informal payment by the parents for caretaking by the children. This study indicates that asset accumulation of land may not increase women's intra-household bargaining power or their general economic empowerment.

A second study by Patel et al. (2018) investigated the relationship between WEE and climate change. The authors created two indexes to measure WEE, the Women's Empowerment in Slums Index (WESI) and Empowerment in Slums Index (ESI). WESI uses 23 agency- and resource-related indicators that apply just to women, whereas the ESI is composed of 18 indicators that apply to both men and women. The construction of the index is based on the Alkire and Foster (2011) method. The study regresses WESI and ESI on 12 different environmental factors: nine are poverty-related environmental degradation factors and three are related to climate change events. The main empirical findings (pooled cross-section, controlling for cities) found that WESI was negatively associated with temporary housing (living less than two years in a household), poor street conditions, and being in an overcrowded house. The regressions, analysed at the country level (controlling for slums within the country), found that WEE was negatively associated with torrential rain, lack of drainage, and over-crowding in India; and flooding and lack of drainage systems in Pakistan. The study also found that women are systematically less empowered than their male counterparts. In short, climate change can work counter to the enabling forces supporting WEE.

A third study by Chopra and Zambelli (2017) found that balancing unpaid work with paid work is crucial for WEE since paid work can often have a negative effect on WEE. The authors conducted mixed-methods research on paid and unpaid work in four countries: India, Nepal, Rwanda, and Tanzania.[6] In each country, they interviewed participants from both NGO-led and public sector-led interventions that promote WEE. The study found that women's level of unpaid care strongly determined their physical mobility and the type, quantity, and quality of paid care they could engage in. Despite the increase in income, paid work often negatively affected women because it reduced the ability and quality of time they had with their children and families. Moreover, because of the low quality of available paid work, women's participation often led to lower empowerment and lower economic empowerment. Very few women were able to successfully manage both paid and unpaid work, and most women experienced "physical and emotional depletion" (Chopra and Zambelli 2017: 36). Their research demonstrated the importance of evaluating how women balance paid with unpaid work to assess whether FLFP is an appropriate indicator of WEE.

As illustrated above, many factors can help facilitate the linkages between macroeconomic growth and WEE, such as favouring female-dominated sectors, lowering the gender gap in education, investing in transportation and public services infrastructure, improving gender norms in favour of WEE, offering childcare, financial inclusion, and affirmative action policies. Many of these factors are also inter-related. For example, education has the power to shape not only wages but also gender norms and attitudes toward FLFP (Gasparini and Marchionni 2015).

The role of macroeconomic policy

The GrOW portfolio did not specifically analyse the role of macroeconomic policy, such as fiscal, monetary, or exchange rate policy, on WEE. A paper by Seguino (2020), however, provides useful discussion in this regard. It emphasises three points that are worth examining in future research. First, policies to stimulate aggregate demand can play an important role in providing a short-term boost to female employment opportunities. Second, a growth-oriented fiscal policy can promote many of the enabling factors for WEE discussed above. Conversely, austerity can reverse gains made by women by limiting employment opportunities, increasing care and other burdens, and by sometimes leading to distress employment. Last, monetary and exchange rate policy can be used to promote growth and aggregate demand and improve financial access for women.

Conclusion

Despite decades of research on WEE and its determinants, including much high-quality work in the GrOW programme, the linkages between growth and WEE are still not well understood. Many questions remain about the central role of employment in linking growth and WEE. Employment is a highly unspecific indicator, comprising good and bad jobs with different conditions. Evidence also exists that reducing employment gaps promotes growth, although more work is needed in this field. Growth has a highly variable impact on employment, related to strong occupational and sectoral segregation.

While policies to promote female-dominated sectors can promote WEE, trade liberalisation often does little to promote female employment opportunities. There is a growing literature on other enabling factors, but this is largely based on case studies and needs to be generalised. Building on the existing research—including GrOW-supported studies—clearly more work is needed to understand the complex linkages between economic growth and WEE.

In terms of policy, many of the studies discussed generate immediate implications. Maybe one overarching policy conclusion is that reliance on growth or increased trade alone will do little to promote WEE. Instead, more specific policies that take women's economic and social circumstances into account and focus on removing specific barriers to their empowerment are required. A second lesson from the research is that despite the overarching benefits of WEE for economic development, just relying on this 'win-win' argument is insufficient: gender equity should be a central goal in and of itself.

Notes

1 For an overview on how labour markets can shape WEE, see Chapter 2 in this volume.
2 For an in-depth review of the literature concerning the relationship between economic growth and gender equality, see Chapter 1 in this volume.
3 In Latin America, Gasparini and Marchionni (2015) investigated determinants of FLFP over a 20-year period. While FLFP increased, they found that the rate of increase slowed down after 2000. The reason for the deceleration is not well understood but possible reasons include sluggish overall employment growth (also for males); sectoral segregation that favours males; and improving household incomes and state transfers (particularly for poorer households) that might have enabled some women to leave low-paying or otherwise undesirable employment.
4 The study uses annual data which necessitates examining and adjusting for time series properties (e.g. autocorrelation, stationarity) which are only partly addressed. They do not include a lagged dependent variable but dynamic panel models are usually required for such analyses. One would then have to deal with biases of including a lagged dependent variable using generalized method of moments (GMM) methods. Lastly, they appear to focus on the age group 15+ where changes in education also greatly affect labour force participation rates which are not controlled for. This also explains the falling labour force participation of males.
5 The word *purdah* means seclusion and applies to the behaviour of women to seclude themselves in front of men, such as covering one's face or not being alone with a man in a public place.
6 Findings from this study on the bi-directional relationship of paid work and unpaid care are presented in Chapter 8 in this volume.

References

Alkire, Sabina, and James Foster (2011). Understandings and misunderstandings of multidimensional poverty measurement. *Journal of Economic Inequality* 9(2): 289–314.

Baah-Boateng, William, Pricilla Twumasi Baffour, and Emmanuel K.Akyeampong (2017). *Gender differences in the extractive sector: A case study of mining in Ghana*. Accra: University of Ghana International Institute for Advanced Studies, mimeo.

Bhalotra, Sonia, and Irma Clots-Figueras (2014). Health and the political agency of women. *American Economic Journal: Economic Policy* 6(2): 164–197.

Borrowman, Mary, and Stephan Klasen (2019). Drivers of gendered sectoral and occupational segregation in developing countries. *Feminist Economics* 26(2): 62–94.

Braga, Breno (2017). The effects of unilateral trade liberalization on marriage and fertility choices: Evidence from Brazil. GrOW Working Paper Series, GWP-2018–15. Montreal: Institute for the Study of International Development, McGill University. http://grow.research.mcgill.ca/publications/working-papers/gwp-2018-15.pdf.

Braga, Breno, Nan Marie Astone, H. Elizabeth Peters, and Tyler Woods (2017). National income changes and the empowerment of women within the household. Washington, DC: Urban Institute. https://paa.confex.com/paa/2017/mediafile/ExtendedAbstract/Paper14797/Braga_et_al_PAA2017.pdf.

Cavalcanti, Tiago, and José Tavares (2016). The output cost of gender discrimination: A model-based macroeconomics estimate. *Economic Journal* 126(590): 109–134.

Chakravarty, Shubha, Mattias Lundberg, Plamen Nikolov, and Juliane Zenker (2018). Vocational training programs and youth labor market outcomes: Evidence from Nepal. *Journal of Development Economics* 136: 71–110.

Chattopadhyay, Raghabendra, and Esther Duflo (2004). Women as policy makers: Evidence from a randomized policy experiment in India. *Econometrica* 72(5): 1409–1443. https://economics.mit.edu/files/792.

Chopra, Deepta, with Elena Zambelli (2017). No time to rest: Women's lived experiences of balancing paid work and unpaid care work. Global Synthesis Report for Women's Economic Empowerment Policy and Programming. Brighton: Institute of Development Studies. www.ids.ac.uk/publications/no-time-to-rest-womens-lived-experiences-of-balancing-paid-work-and-unpaid-care-work/.

Croppenstedt, André, Markus Goldstein, and Nina Rosas (2013). Gender and agriculture: Inefficiencies, segregation, and low productivity traps. *World Bank Research Observer* 28(1): 79–109. https://openknowledge.worldbank.org/bitstream/handle/10986/19493/wbro_28_1_79.pdf?sequence=1&isAllowed=y.

Cuberes, David, and Marc Teignier (2016). Aggregate effects of gender gaps in the labor market: A quantitative estimate. *Journal of Human Capital* 10(1): 1–32.

Desai, Solande, and Debasis Barik, D. (2017). Land live: Land ownership in rural India and intra household exchanges. India Human Development Survey, Working Paper No. 2017–1. New Delhi: National Council of Applied Economic Research.

Duflo, Esther (2012). Women empowerment and economic development. *Journal of Economic Literature* 50(4): 1051–1079. https://economics.mit.edu/files/7417.

Dutta, Puja, Rinku Murgai, and Stephen Howes (2010). Small but effective: India's targeted unconditional cash transfers. *Economic and Political Weekly* 45(52): 63–70.

Enchautegui, María E. (2018). Economic structure and gender inequalities in labor force participation. Washington, DC: Urban Institute and the University of Puerto Rico, mimeo.

Esteve-Volart, Berta (2004). Gender discrimination and growth: Theory and evidence from India. LSE STICERD research paper. London: London School of Economics and Political Science (LES). http://sticerd.lse.ac.uk/dps/de/dedps42.pdf.

Eyben, Rosalind, Naila Kabeer, and Andrea Cornwall (2008). Conceptualising empowerment and the implications for pro-poor growth: A paper for the DAC Poverty Network. Brighton: Institute of Development Studies. https://opendocs.ids.ac.uk/opendocs/bitstream/handle/20.500.12413/7203/Conceptualising%20Empowerment%20Cornwall%20et%20al.pdf?sequence=1&isAllowed=y.

Gaddis, Isis, and Stephan Klasen (2014). Economic development, structural change, and women's labor force participation. *Journal of Population Economics* 27(3): 639–681.

Gaddis, Isis, and Janneke Pieters (2017). The gendered labor market impacts of trade liberalization. *Journal of Human Resources* 52(2): 457–490.

Gasparini, Leonardo, and Mariana Marchionni (2015). Bridging gender gaps? The rise and deceleration of female labor force participation in Latin America. La Plata, Argentina: Centro de Estudios Distributivos, Laborales y Sociales (CEDLAS). http://labor-al.org/participacionfemenina/wp-content/uploads/2016/01/Bridging-gender-gaps_full-book.pdf.

Goldstein, Marcus, and Christopher Udry (2008). The profits of power: Land rights and agricultural investment in Ghana. *Journal of Political Economy* 116(6): 981–1022. https://openknowledge.worldbank.org/bitstream/handle/10986/5789/595561.pdf?sequence=2&isAllowed=y.

Gupta, Aarti, and Janneke Pieters (2018). Female labor as insurance: Trade liberalization and female labor force participation in India. Wageningen: Wageningen University, mimeo.

Ibanez, Marcela, Soham Sahoo, Pooja Balasubramanian, and Sarah Khan (2018). Women's economic empowerment at the community level has a positive impact on human development in low and middle income countries. *Campbell Systematic Reviews* 13(1): 1–50.

Kabeer, Naila (2012). *Women's economic empowerment and inclusive growth: Labour markets and enterprise development.* SIG Working Paper No. 2012/1. www.idrc.ca/sites/default/files/sp/Documents%20EN/NK-WEE-Concept-Paper.pdf.

Khan, Sarah, and Stephan Klasen. (2018). Female employment and spousal abuse: A parallel cross-country analysis of 35 developing economies. Poverty, Equity and Growth—Discussion Papers No. 249. Göttingen, Germany: Courant Research Centre.

Kis-Katos, Krisztina, Janneke Pieters, and Robert Sparrow (2018). Globalization and social change: Gender-specific effects of trade liberalization in Indonesia. *IMF Economic Review* 66(4): 763–793.

Klasen, Stephan (2018). The impact of gender inequality on economic performance in developing countries. *Annual Review of Resource Economics* 10: 279–298.

Klasen, Stephan (2019). What explains uneven female labor force participation levels and trends in developing countries? *World Bank Research Observer* 34: 161–197. https://elibrary.worldbank.org/doi/pdf/10.1093/wbro/lkz005.

Klasen, Stephan, and Francesca Lamanna (2009). The impact of gender inequality in education and employment on economic growth: New evidence for a panel of countries. *Feminist Economics* 15(3): 91–132.

Klasen, Stephan, and Anna Minasyan (2017a). Gender inequality and growth in Europe. *Intereconomics* 52(1): 17–23.

Klasen, Stephan, and Anna Minasyan (2017b). The impact of affirmative action on the gendered occupational segregation in South Africa. Poverty, Equity and Growth—Discussion Papers No. 236. Göttingen, Germany: Courant Research Centre. www2.vwl.wiso.uni-goettingen.de/courant-papers/CRC-PEG_DP_236new.pdf.

Konan, Y. S. (2017). Small scale mining, salaries disparities and women empowerment in Côte D'Ivoire. Abidjan: Centre Ivoirien de Recherches Économiques et Sociales, mimeo.

Laszlo, Sonia, and Kate Grantham (2017). Measurement of women's economic empowerment in GrOW projects: Inventory and user guide. GrOW Working Paper Series, GWP-2017–08.

Montreal: Institute for the Study of International Development, McGill University. http://grow.research.mcgill.ca/publications/working-papers/gwp-2017-08.pdf.

Lei, Lei, Sonalde Desai, and Reeve Vanneman (2017). Village transportation infrastructure and women's non-agricultural employment in India: The conditioning role of community gender context. India Human Development Survey, Working Paper No. 2017–12. New Delhi: National Council of Applied Economic Research. https://idl-bnc-idrc.dspacedirect.org/bitstream/handle/10625/59134/IDL-59134.pdf

Lenze, Jana, and Stephan Klasen (2017). Does women's labor force participation reduce domestic violence? Evidence from Jordan. *Feminist Economics* 23(1): 1–29.

Lepelle, Refilwe, Lawrence Edwards, and Murray Leibbrandt (2018). Trade effects on gendered labour market outcomes in post-Apartheid South Africa. Cape Town: University of Cape Town, mimeo.

McKenzie, David, and Christopher Woodruff (2014). What are we learning from business training and entrepreneurship evaluations around the developing world? *World Bank Research Observer* 29(1): 48–82. https://openknowledge.worldbank.org/bitstream/handle/10986/22564/wbro_29_1_48.pdf;sequence=1.

Minasyan, Anna, Juliane Zenker, Stephan Klasen, and S. Vollmer, (2019). Evidence on education gender gap and economic growth: A systematic review and meta-analysis. *World Development* 122:199–217.

Patel, Amit, Marcia D. Mundt, Hyunjung Lee, Hina Lotia, Muhammad Arshed Rafiq, and Ammar A. Malik (2018). Empowering women in South Asia's slums: The challenges of climate change and environmental degradation. GrOW Working Paper Series, GWP-2018–17. Montreal: Institute for the Study of International Development, McGill University. http://grow.research.mcgill.ca/publications/working-papers/gwp-2018-17.pdf.

Peters, H. Elizabeth, Nan Marie Astone, Ammar A. Malik, Fenohasina Maret, and Caroline Heller (2016). Women's economic empowerment: A review of evidence on enablers and barriers. GrOW Program Report No. 1. Ottawa: IDRC. https://idl-bnc-idrc.dspacedirect.org/bitstream/handle/10625/56943/IDL-56943.pdf?sequence=2&isAllowed=y.

Peters, H. Elizabeth, Breno Braga, Tyler Woods, Adaeze Okoli, and Nan Marie Aston (2018). Economic growth, intimate partner violence and attitudes towards wife-beating. Population Institute of America, 2019 Annual Meeting, Austin, TX, April 10–13. http://paa2019.populationassociation.org/uploads/193101.

Santos-Silva, Manuel, and Klasen, Stephan (2018). Gender inequality as a barrier to economic growth: A review of the theoretical literature. Courant Research Centre: Poverty, Equity and Growth—Discussion Papers No. 252. https://ideas.repec.org/p/got/gotcrc/252.html.

Sarkar, Sudipa, Soham Sahoo, and Stephan Klasen (2017). Employment transitions of women in India: A panel analysis. IZA Discussion Paper Series, No. 11086. Bonn: Institute for the Study of Labor (IZA). http://ftp.iza.org/dp11086.pdf.

Sarkar, Sudipa, Soham Sahoo, and Stephan Klasen (2019). Employment transitions of women in India: A panel analysis. *World Development* 115: 291–309.

Seguino, Stephanie (2020). Engendering macroeconomic theory and policy. *Feminist Economics* 26(2): 27–61.

Topalova, Petia (2007). Trade liberalization, poverty and inequality: Evidence from Indian districts. In Ann Harrison (Ed.), *Globalization and Poverty* (291–335). Chicago: University of Chicago Press. www.nber.org/chapters/c0110.pdf.

Topalova, Petia (2010). Factor immobility and regional impacts of trade liberalization: Evidence on poverty from India. *American Economic Journal: Applied Economics* 2(4): 1–41. https://pubs.aeaweb.org/doi/pdfplus/10.1257/app.2.4.1.

Udry, Christopher (1996). Gender, agricultural production, and the theory of the household. *Journal of Political Economy* 104(5): 1010–1046.

van Biljon, Chloé (2017). The effect of old age pensions on child deprivation: Revisiting the role of gender. Stellenbosch Working Papers Series No. 13/2017. Stellenbosch, South Africa: Department of Economics, Stellenbosch University. https://econpapers.repec.org/paper/szawpaper/wpapers289.htm.

van Biljon, Chloé, A. Pasha, and D. von Fintel (2018). Bargaining to work: The effect of female autonomy on female labour supply. Stellenbosch Working Paper Series No. 04/2018. Stellenbosch, South Africa: Department of Economics, Stellenbosch University. https://econpapers.repec.org/paper/szawpaper/wpapers297.htm.

von Fintel, Dieter, and Eldridge Moses (2017). Migration and gender in South Africa: Following bright lights and the fortunes of others? *Regional Science Policy & Practice* 9(4): 251–268.

World Bank (2006). Gender equality as smart economics: A World Bank Group gender action plan—fiscal years 2007–10. Washington, DC: World Bank. http://documents.worldbank.org/curated/en/295371468315572899/Gender-equality-as-smart-economics-a-World-Bank-Group-gender-action-plan-fiscal-years-2007-10.

World Bank (2012). World development report 2012: Gender equality and development. Washington, DC: World Bank. https://openknowledge.worldbank.org/handle/10986/4391.

Zolnik, Edmund J., Ammar Malik, and Yasemin Irvin-Erickson (2018). Who benefits from bus rapid transit? Evidence from the Metro Bus System (MBS) in Lahore. *Journal of Transport Geography* 71: 139–149.

4

DEVELOPING CARE

The care economy and economic development

Nancy Folbre

Introduction

Women's unpaid care for their families and communities shapes both gender inequality and the larger process of economic development. The recent proliferation of nationally representative time-use surveys in low-income countries clearly demonstrates the empirical magnitude of unpaid work, its impact on the length of women's workday, and the potential impact of policies to recognise, reduce, and redistribute unpaid care (Benería, Berik, and Floro 2015). Yet policy-relevant research on this topic remains, to date, far less extensive than research on trends in women's educational attainment, labour force participation, and political representation, despite the likelihood that the less visible 'care economy' is probably an important driver of these trends.

This chapter brings the analysis on unpaid care work that Kabeer points to in this volume (see Chapter 1) into focus and draws on the large portfolio of projects funded under the Growth and Economic Opportunities for Women (GrOW) initiative. The initiative brings unpaid care provision to the front and centre of research on gender and development and raises important questions about the definition of economic development itself. The results validate concerns regarding the impact of unpaid care demands and provide specific evidence of constraints on women's ability to earn market income. New estimates of the value of women's unpaid work provide additional evidence that strategic investments in physical and social infrastructure could improve household living standards.

This chapter puts these results in context and highlights their contributions. It begins with a broad overview of research on the care economy, with attention to key concepts such as the distinction between direct and indirect care and correct measurement of supervisory or 'on-call' responsibilities.[1] The next section summarises the most important new findings of the GrOW-supported research and includes a brief discussion of some complementary contemporaneous studies sponsored by other initiatives. The final section outlines some possible next steps for advancing the care policy agenda.

Background: current understandings on care and economic development

While 'care' has recently become a catch word in analysis of causes and consequences of the gender division of labour, the term is often used in a variety of ways. Most research on developing countries, including the reports under consideration here, focus on unpaid care work because it absorbs the bulk of women's labour time—their participation in formal employment remains relatively low. Still, it is important to locate unpaid care work in a broader context of a care economy that encompasses expenditures on children and other dependents, paid care work, and unpaid care of family, friends, and neighbours. A rough map of this conceptual territory helps demonstrate how specific research projects are expanding the larger frontier.

The System of National Accounts excludes domestic activities such as cooking, cleaning, and personal care of dependent family members. Yet these forms of unpaid care work contribute to the maintenance and development of human capabilities, generating important benefits for recipients and society as a whole. While investment in 'human capital' is often defined entirely in terms of future market income, investments in human capabilities point to a broader set of benefits that are difficult to measure and not necessarily captured in market transactions: they represent 'public goods'.

The value of time spent collecting wood or water or producing goods for household consumption (which should, in principle, include breast milk) falls under the purview of the System of National Accounts. As a result, it is not always included in definitions of unpaid care work. However, such work clearly contributes to family provisioning, and is often done while supervising children or others who cannot safely be left alone for long periods of time. It is sometimes included in measures of unpaid work, including some of the specific studies reviewed below (e.g. Chopra and Zambelli 2017; see also Chapter 8 in this volume).

The distinctions between direct and indirect care work, and between active and supervisory care, are economically significant. Indirect care work is less person-specific and can often be reduced through investments in physical infrastructure (such as centralised water and electricity) and consumer durables (such as improved stoves). In the course of development, market substitutes (such as food prepared by street vendors) often become available. In contrast, direct care work has person-specific characteristics, and continues to be quite important even with increased reliance on social infrastructure such as childcare, education, and health services.

Supervisory care can often be combined with domestic work, such as cooking and cleaning, but is typically difficult to combine with paid employment or other income-earning activities. While it is less intense than other forms of care, and may be enjoyable, it imposes significant time constraints. Young children and others unable to care for themselves cannot be left alone for long periods, even when they are sleeping. Paid child or eldercare services primarily relieve family members of supervisory responsibilities, with less impact on their direct care activities. For instance, when mothers drop children off at a childcare centre to engage in paid employment, they still devote significant time to feeding, clothing, bathing, and other activities at the beginning and end of the day.

What shapes the provision of care?

Economic development often leads to higher standards for household consumption, including demand for more complex meal, laundry, and cleaning services. However, the expansion of paid services, the increased availability of labour-saving devices, and greater access to electricity gradually reduce the time devoted to indirect care. Time devoted to the direct care of children and other dependents declines more slowly for a number of reasons. Changes in household structure often reduce the number of resident adults (such as daughters-in-law or grandparents) available to provide care. Publicly or privately provided childcare and education services are not always well-coordinated with hours of paid employment. Also, economic development often entails a shift toward more intensive parenting—with more time spent talking to, interacting with, and teaching children.

Elderly family members tend to require far less direct care than children, and they often contribute significantly to the care of grandchildren. However, their needs are highly variable and often unpredictable, sometimes demanding considerable attention. The care of sick or disabled family members can be especially time-consuming in communities with a high incidence of chronic illness such as HIV infection. The promise of care within families represents a form of insurance, providing benefits that are not necessarily revealed by direct expenditures of time and money.

Cross-sectional analysis of the time allocation of parents in the US shows that parental time devoted to childcare increases with education and family income, despite increases in the opportunity cost of parental time (Kimmel and Connelly 2007). Time devoted to housework, by contrast, goes down with education and family income. In affluent countries, direct care responsibilities impose far more significant constraints on maternal labour force participation than other forms of care work. Cross-sectional analysis of time-use data from 15 European countries (including several low-income countries such as Bulgaria) shows that the time that parents with co-resident children devote to childcare increases slightly with levels of per capita income (Folbre and Yoon 2008).

Growth in the percentage of families maintained by women alone in many countries shows that economic development can lead to a decline in male contributions to family income and care. Few internationally consistent surveys accurately measure parental co-residence, even in affluent countries with extensive statistical infrastructure (Strohschein 2017). Even fewer surveys attempt to measure contributions of fathers who are not living with their children (Greene and Biddlecom 2000). The US is one of the few countries that estimates parents' (mostly fathers') compliance with legal child support responsibilities—only about 50% pay any child support at all (Stykes, Manning, and Brown 2013).

In many developing countries, extreme poverty and forced migration often disrupt families. On the aggregate level, remittances from long-distance migrants are clearly significant, but the contribution they make to total household income is difficult to measure. In her comparative ethnographic research on the Gambia, the Philippines, and Costa Rica, Sylvia Chant points to a feminisation of responsibility and/or obligation, noting that the end result is often "an intensification of the difficulties faced by women in reconciling unpaid reproductive work with economic contributions to household livelihoods" (2014: 297).

How is the distribution of unpaid care time measured?

Efforts to measure the distribution of unpaid care time have a long history, often coloured by resistance from economists and statisticians (Waring 1988; Folbre 2009). Partly due to pressure from women's groups, data collection has gradually expanded. In 1985, the Third UN World Conference on Women in Nairobi passed a resolution calling for more attention to the nexus between unpaid work and gender inequality. The World Conference of 1995 amplified this point, noting that "[t]he care of children, the sick, and the elderly is a responsibility that falls disproportionately on women, owing to lack of equality and the unbalanced distribution of remunerated and unremunerated work between women and men".[2] Reducing the burden of unpaid work on women is considered an indicator in UN Sustainable Development Goal 5: Achieve gender equality and empower all women and girls.[3]

The data available to examine time devoted to unpaid care has increased significantly over the last 10 years, along with the proliferation of nationally representative time-use surveys. A recent review by Jacques Charmes (2019) consolidates descriptive results from 126 national-level surveys carried out in 75 countries. Unfortunately, many of these surveys do not disaggregate by gender, some sample only one person per household, and many fail to collect household-specific economic information. Lack of harmonisation limits their comparability. Many surveys use slightly different definitions of specific activities and aggregate them differently.

A number of other methodological problems remain unresolved. Surveys based on stylised questions such as, "How much time did you spend on unpaid work during the previous week?" yield much higher estimates than time diaries that ask respondents to describe their activities in specific time segments during the previous day. Stylised questions often evoke responses that describe overlapping activities, so that reports of activities during a day often add up to far more than 24 hours. They are also susceptible to social desirability bias—respondents may report what they believe interviewers would like to hear.

While time-diary results are generally considered more reliable, they often focus on activities, excluding supervisory or 'on-call' responsibilities, leading to significant under-estimates of the temporal constraints of care (Folbre et al. 2005). Because both active and supervisory childcare are often conducted in tandem with other activities, small differences in the wording of survey questions can lead to dramatic differences in responses, confounding cross-country comparisons (Folbre and Yoon 2007). These issues highlight the potential contribution of mixed method approaches that include qualitative research (one of the significant contributions of the GrOW research portfolio reviewed below and reflected through the case studies in this volume).

Despite their limitations, time-use data from a wide cross-section of countries provide strong evidence for three important generalisations regarding gender differences (Budlender 2010; UNRISD 2010; Charmes 2019):

1. women, especially mothers, devote significantly more time to care work than men do;
2. women, especially mothers, work longer hours overall than men do; and
3. when mothers enter paid employment they do not reduce their hours of unpaid work commensurately.

Inferences regarding the effect of economic development and fertility decline on women's formal labour force participation are less robust. The widespread assumption that women's formal labour force participation typically follows a 'u-shaped' pattern in the course of economic development—first declining, then increasing—is now viewed with considerable scepticism (Gaddis and Klasen 2014). Cultural tradition, sectoral composition, and public policy lead to significant variation in women's labour force participation trends, highlighting the need for more nuanced case-study approaches. Additional analysis of trends and barriers in women's labour force participation can be found in Chapter 2 in this volume.

How is care valued?

Growing recognition of the importance of unpaid care has not yet led to widespread valuation of its contributions to household consumption and living standards. Economists have been hesitant to assign a dollar value to such work, even where market substitutes or wage rates provide a benchmark estimate of its replacement cost. Concerns about the possible imprecision of such estimates often overshadow the reality that unpaid care is currently valued at zero—clearly a gross undervaluation.

Market-centric assumptions treat unpaid care as an activity that both women and men perform only when paid work is unavailable, rather than an essential complement to market income. Market-based measures of household income also ignore the potential impact of improvements in the productivity of unpaid work that could enhance household living standards, improve health and human capabilities, and afford more time for rest and recreation.

In countries with high levels of female employment, policies such as paid family leave, subsidised childcare services, and reduced penalties for part-time work can help both women and men balance competing demands. Such policies clearly offer social, demographic, and economic benefits (OECD 2011). In developing countries where women spend a large portion of their time tending to family needs, investments in basic infrastructure such as electricity, gas, and plumbing could significantly improve their overall productivity while increasing their ability to engage in paid employment. The payoff for public investments in such infrastructure is understated when the value of non-market work, including family care of young children, is not explicitly factored in (Agénor and Agénor 2014; Fontana and Elson 2014). Many of the case studies in the GrOW research portfolio reviewed here and featured in this volume make such payoffs visible at the local level.

What attention does care work get in public policies?

Poor measurement and undervaluation of unpaid care contribute to significant gender bias in public policies. Social spending shows up in government budgets; women's unpaid work does not. As a result, policymakers are tempted to offload social costs or resist their redistribution, just as they are tempted to ignore environmental costs that do not directly enter national accounting ledgers. Investments in publicly provided social services are often described as luxuries that poor countries cannot afford, even when they address basic needs that families struggle to meet on their own.

Empirical research shows that subsidised childcare has significant positive effects on mothers' employment in Europe—particularly among those with lower family income and less education (Del Boca 2015). Uneven provision of childcare and parental leave in the US helps explain the relatively slow growth of female labour force participation (FLFP) there in recent years (Blau and Kahn 2015). Investments in childcare provision can also promote local economic development from the demand side through employment of childcare workers (Warner 2006; Warner and Liu 2006). While less evidence is available from developing countries, the level of subsidised childcare has been shown to have a positive impact on women's hours of paid employment in Guatemala, Brazil, Mexico, and China (Hallman et al. 2005; Paes de Barros et al. 2011; Staab and Gerhard 2011; Calderón 2014; Song and Dong 2018). In this volume, Chapter 7 captures the perspective of mothers using subsidised childcare in an urban settlement in Kenya, and the positive impacts they identify for the safety of their children and their ability to access work.

Low-income countries typically face tight budget constraints and often face pressure from creditors to adopt austerity measures. Formal labour force participation rates are growing more slowly than expected and the informal sector, where workers generally lack both regulatory protection and social benefits, looms large. In most regions of the world, informal employment comprises more than half of non-agricultural employment, and in South Asia, sub-Saharan Africa, and Latin America and the Caribbean, the percentage of women income earners in informal employment exceeds that of men (Vanek et al. 2014).

Family care services represent, in some respects, an informal welfare state. A recent analysis of time-use data in the Republic of Korea shows that the value of family care provision for children and the elderly far exceeds state spending on these age groups (Yoon 2014). Likewise, studies of home-based care for HIV/AIDS in Botswana estimated the value of services per caregiver at about USD5,000 per year, a number that would substantially increase estimates of total spending on healthcare if it were included (Mmopelwa et al. 2013). Public spending on social services represents both a complement to and a substitute for family care. Cuts in public spending often increase burdens on women, redistributing care costs to those who can least afford to pay (Elson 2012).

Economists sometimes argue that it is inefficient to finance services that women are willing to provide at little or no cost to taxpayers (Rosen 1997). This argument ignores the opportunity cost of women's time and the potential to increase their productivity as well as the stress and strain unfairly imposed upon them. Public investments in physical and social infrastructure, including health and education, should be conceptualised as inputs into family care provision and the development of human capabilities. Public provision of childcare services, for instance, can reduce the constraints of supervisory care that otherwise keep mothers close to home, while also allowing them to devote more time to active, developmental care when they are at home.

Childcare services in urban areas can make it easier for mothers and fathers to take their children with them when migrating to areas with greater employment prospects. Current patterns of gender- and age-tilted migration often lead to prolonged geographical separation, undermining paternal engagement with children and leaving mothers, as well as children and the elderly, more vulnerable to desertion. In most developing countries, the slow growth of wage employment reduces market demand for childcare services. Predominantly male owners and managers often prefer to hire other men and efforts to require them to provide on-site childcare can backfire by making female workers more costly. Slow employment growth can intensify competition between women and men for jobs. Yet public policies that increase women's productivity in both unpaid care and paid work can improve living standards and boost economic development. Policy design should be informed by a better understanding of the care economy.

Emerging evidence from GrOW-supported research studies

A new wave of research sponsored by the GrOW programme illuminates the impact of unpaid care provision on economic development in general and women's economic empowerment (WEE) in particular. This research goes beyond using existing data sources to include innovative field research in specific communities, combining quantitative and qualitative methods, often including comparative, experimental, and quasi-experimental analysis of specific policy innovations.[4]

The findings address three central questions: How can the level, distribution, and value of unpaid care work be assessed? How do public policies and community-sponsored services—especially childcare provision—affect women's unpaid care work? What is the relationship between the social organisation of care provision and women's empowerment? The studies, including some of the case studies in this volume, offer some specific answers and provide models for more extensive future research.

Cross-national findings

GrOW-supported research led by the Institute of Development Studies (IDS) shows how gendered social norms constrain women's economic activities in a variety of policy environments (Chopra and Zambelli 2017; see also Chapter 8 in this volume for additional insights from this research initiative). It assesses eight programmes and policies with potential impacts on WEE in India, Nepal, Rwanda, and Tanzania, relying on a mixed-methods approach that includes semi-structured interviews and participatory exercises. The title of its synthesis report, "No Time to Rest," conveys its most important message: the effort to simultaneously provide care and contribute to family income in difficult economic circumstances disempowers women and threatens their physical and emotional wellbeing.

The empirical strategy stipulates consistent methodologies across 16 different sites, based on snowball samples of female respondents with at least one child under six and who were engaged in paid employment in the previous year. Several important descriptive results emerge from the pooled data: childcare tasks are more often shared by men than other household tasks, even though men seldom take sole responsibility for children. The burden of household work per woman is lower, on average, in extended households (though it is unclear how equally it is distributed among women).[5] Some tasks—notably animal care—are allocated in relatively gender-neutral ways.

This research highlights powerful gender norms. Almost all women who participated in the study (over 94%) expressed the opinion that they are better at household tasks than men are, while a smaller percentage (about 68%) expressed the opinion that women are better at direct care work. About 61% believe that men are better at paid work. The powerful and self-reinforcing effects of such perceptions help explain little observable difference in sharing of care tasks between women participating in WEE projects and other women.[6]

The gender division of labour is also evident—though less pronounced—among girls and boys; some tensions between unpaid work responsibilities and educational attainment are apparent for both.[7] Across the entire sample, men are significantly more likely than women to be engaged in formal or informal wage employment, and women's income earning activities are more likely to take the form of home-based work or informal self-employment. Women typically engage in a patchwork of part-time or seasonal activities, including economic empowerment programmes, which are seldom sufficient to offer income security. The high travel time, transaction costs, poor working conditions, and tenuous nature of these arrangements contribute to economic stress.

The time-use surveys employed in this study define direct care rather narrowly, making household work (or indirect care) loom much larger as a percentage of the workday. In practice, both household work and household-based employment are often combined with supervisory or on-call childcare. Survey results show that multi-tasking is extensive, taking place almost 15 hours per day on average. Such multi-tasking becomes more difficult when women are forced to leave their children at home to garner market income. The need to earn income often has adverse effects on family care. More than a third of all women in this study report that they are forced to leave some household tasks undone and sacrifice childcare time. They report physical and emotional exhaustion.

A recent quantitative study conducted by Oxfam amplifies the insights from the GrOW research and helps contextualise them. A cross-national survey collected data in five rural communities in Colombia, Ethiopia, the Philippines, Uganda, and Zimbabwe as part of the Women's Economic Empowerment and Care (WE-Care) initiative, funded by the Hewlett Foundation (Karimli et al. 2016). A baseline Household Care Survey launched in 2014 interviewed female and male respondents from 1,123 households, using stratified random sampling to select respondents in study districts in each of the five countries.

In 2015, Oxfam assisted local organisations in implementing various interventions that broadly tried to "recognise, reduce, and redistribute" unpaid care work. In November and December of 2015, a second and revised survey was carried out with an equal number of households, including some panel data.[8] The study zealously aimed to: (1) document levels of unpaid care work and its distribution across household members using time-use data and (2) identify factors contributing to a lower workload for women, controlling for family structure and household characteristics. The six factors considered were recognition of care work, women's decision-making abilities, use of time-saving equipment, access to public services, social norms, and participation in Oxfam's interventions.

The descriptive results confirm the general patterns described above. Both the 2014 and 2015 surveys found that women performed a large and disproportionate amount of care work relative to men (as did girls relative to boys); and that women devoted less time to leisure and personal care than men. Efforts to demonstrate causal linkages were less successful. The researchers found no significant correlation between households' socioeconomic characteristics (assets, education, and income) and time spent on care work. Nor did they find a consistent association between hours of care work and women's reported wellbeing.[9] The factors that were found to lower care loads and promote more equal distribution of care work were access to electricity, progressive social norms, and, in some contexts, participation in the WE-Care programmes, especially those likely to influence social norms. While results varied across different statistical model specifications, measures of women's decision-making ability had either an insignificant or a negative effect on care work hours. Access to public provision of water, health services, and childcare services was not associated with reduced hours of care, nor was time- or labour-saving equipment.

The study acknowledges several methodological limitations. The survey instruments offered very approximate measures of time use, and, in particular, omitted measures of supervisory care (ongoing survey efforts aim to remedy this problem).

Causal linkages are intrinsically complex. Levels of many explanatory variables may be the result—rather than the cause—of care work burdens. For example, time-saving equipment could be adopted *because* of an especially heavy care burden, in which case it would not have the effect of reducing work time.

The study breaks new ground in its attention to context-specific indicators and its application of quasi-experimental methods. However, it is intrinsically difficult to measure changes in the quality of care services provided. For instance, the study offers no way of assessing the possibility that public policies increase the productivity of care work, improving household living standards rather than reducing women's workdays—women might spend more time preparing better meals or interacting more directly with their children.

Country-specific insights

A number of country-specific case studies add texture and detail to this larger picture. The Counting Women's Work projects, funded by the International Development Research Centre (IDRC) and the Hewlett Foundation as part of the National Transfer Accounts agenda, use time-use data to measure total production, consumption, and transfers of unpaid time in a range of countries including Ghana, India, Mexico, South Africa, and Vietnam (Donehower 2013).

The India study helps explain why female employment in India has declined even as fertility rates have fallen: unpaid work makes significant contributions to household living standards. The data show a clear pattern of gender specialisation and inequality in time use, consistent with other analyses of the Indian Time Use Survey (Ladusingh 2017; Mukherjee 2017). This study adds depth to previous research by imputing the market value of women's non-market work and redefining the components of income and consumption over the life cycle to include non-market care work. Incorporating time spent on household production significantly increases estimates of transfers to children and reveals women's full contributions to household consumption. A more regionally focused study of low-income households in the Indian states of Rajasthan and Madhya Pradesh finds that the care of young children, in particular, constrains women's ability to earn income (Sengupta and Sacheva 2017). Research on Vietnam offers a refreshing contrast—somewhat less gender disparity in workplace and education outcomes (Huong, Thu, and Toan 2017).

The GrOW programme sponsored a parallel study of four sites in Nepal, including analysis of two WEE programmes: Oxfam's Enterprise Development Programme and the state-sponsored Karnali Employment Programme (Ghosh, Singh, and Chigateri 2017a). The findings from Nepal, which are part of the multi-country study led by IDS in partnership with the Institute of Social Studies Trust (ISST), testify to the physical and mental stress of unpaid care burdens and the constraints imposed on women's income-earning capabilities. They also show how very high rates of male outmigration may contribute to marital mistrust, leading, in turn, to sanctions against wives' mobility.

The extension of this study in Tanzania demonstrates the impact of gendered norms that hold women responsible for tasks that are particularly arduous and place them at risk of sexual violence.[10] It also emphasises the knock-on effects of inadequate public infrastructure. Women report that they engage in paid work because of inadequate family income, and interviews with all members of the community highlight a huge unmet demand for better-paying jobs (Zambelli et al. 2017).

Across all four countries included in the IDS-led research, the average number of hours that women devote to leisure and personal care is significantly low, particularly when compared to men. Here again, family size and composition mediate care burdens, as do secure rights to land and housing and the quality of paid jobs. Overall, women report feeling overworked, tired, and worried about their children.

Policies and programmes to support childcare and women's employment

Policy precedents set by now-affluent countries are not well suited to current trajectories of development in developing countries. The slow growth of formal employment and the large size of the informal sector are particularly problematic. A recent report sponsored by Women in Informal Employment Globalizing and Organizing (WIEGO) titled "Our children do not get the attention they deserve" asks how women working in the informal economy negotiate childcare (Alfers 2016). Its findings draw from interviews and focus groups with 159 female informal workers (90% with a child under six) in six WIEGO-associated member-based organisations across five different countries.

Like the GrOW-supported IDS research summarised above, this study emphasises feedback loops that reinforce low earnings and long total workdays: women need flexible jobs in order to provide family care, but these jobs tend to be insecure and poorly paid. Mothers constantly worry about possible trade-offs between additional income and quality childcare, and they face difficulties paying for organised childcare (particularly in South Africa, where private paid services predominate), synchronising schedules (centre-based hours seldom completely coincide with their working hours), and transporting children to and from centres.

Women make use of a wide range of childcare centres (public, non-profit, private/informal, and early education centres attached to schools) and their responses clearly indicate that the type and quality of care matter as much as the quantity. The preponderance of informal sector employment highlights the limitations of employer-provided childcare programmes. The WIEGO report (Alfers 2016) recommends establishing good quality, affordable public childcare centres that meet the needs of informal and formal sector workers, with convenient locations, opportunities for parental and community-based participation, and decent working conditions for the care workers that it employs.[11]

While this might seem like an unrealistic wish list, additional research by WIEGO singles out several promising public childcare models (Moussié 2016). In

India, with financial support from the state, the Self-Employed Women's Association (SEWA) established childcare cooperatives that enrol children under six at a nominal cost, providing both nutritious meals and educational activities. The municipality of Belo Horizonte, Brazil has set up a successful daycare centre in response to the demands of the local waste-pickers cooperative.

Several national childcare systems in Latin America also stand out. In Chile, for example, the government-supported Crece Contigo programme offers daycare centres for children between one and three years of age, and home-based services for those under one. In Mexico, the federal government subsidises up to 90% of the cost of daycare for children eligible through the Estancias programme. Among women benefitting from the programme, 18% more are now employed, working on average six additional hours each week. Estancias also provided training and employment in childcare for more than 40,000 women.[12] Separate research offers evidence that the Mexican programme has improved child outcomes, while increasing women's participation in paid employment (Calderón 2014; Pérez-Escamilla 2017).

Childcare provision need not be based on a single model; employer-led initiatives can both supplement and inspire public provision. A recent report published by the World Bank builds the business case for firm-level provision (Niethammer et al. 2017). In-depth case studies of ten companies operating in both developed and developing economies, and supplemental case studies of 14 other companies, demonstrate benefits such as improved recruitment and retention and greater employee productivity through reduced absences and greater work commitment. Possible employer-led supports range from the most resource-intensive (like workplace creches) to the least (information and referral services). Unfortunately, the characteristics of the relatively large and successful firms studied suggest that their employees are not very representative of the larger female workforce.

The distinction between public and employer-based provision of childcare is somewhat blurred by the growing importance of public-private partnerships and aid-supported social enterprise. For instance, Oxfam's Enterprise Development Programme, launched in 2011, is a livelihoods programme aiming to improve opportunities for small rural enterprises, focusing particularly on women. A recent GrOW-sponsored study of one specific initiative in the Surkhet District of Nepal prompted investments in time-saving technology such as seed-sorting machines, a biogas facility, and seed collection centres (to reduce the time spent in manually carrying seeds to the market) (Ghosh, Singh, and Chigateri 2017a). Many specific case studies provide additional evidence of the need for employers, non-governmental organisations, and government initiatives to address care constraints.

Nepal

The Karnali Employment Programme is a 35-day work guarantee aimed at low-income and female-headed households that mandates equal wages for men and women. GrOW research jointly carried out by IDS and ISST examines the ability of female participants to balance paid and unpaid care work. It analyses quantitative and qualitative data from a sample of 100 women engaged in paid work with at least one child under six years of age in two municipalities of Nepal, revealing the programme's significant limitations (Ghosh, Singh, and Chigateri 2017b). Women with children under one year of age are excluded, and those with older small children find it difficult to participate. A pilot innovation that incorporated creche facilities was unsuccessful because most of the small children refused to part with their mothers. Children, as well as adults, need time to adapt to new circumstances and the reassurance that comes from wider participation.

Women participants report that many work sites are more than a one-hour walk from their homes, despite a rule to the contrary. The manual labour required is often physically exhausting. Researchers recommend a number of changes: provision of onsite childcare facilities, along with safety gear and basic amenities such as drinking water and toilets, and sufficient monitoring to ensure strict adherence to the one-hour distance limit. The programme could better achieve such goals if it employed staff to focus on the care-responsiveness of working conditions, required a minimum percentage of female participation, and encouraged women to play a larger role in its decision-making bodies, such as Ward Citizens' Forums.

India

Another component of IDS and ISST research on paid and unpaid care work focuses on one of the most important components of India's social protection policy, the Mahatma Gandhi National Rural Employment Guarantee Act (MGNREGA) (Zaidi and Chigateri 2017). It offers a far less favourable assessment than previous research which focused primarily on the programme's positive impact on FLFP rates.[13]

The public works programme entitles rural households to 100 days of waged employment, with 33% reserved for women, equal wages for men and women, and the provision of creches at worksites. Such provisions are usually seen as a means of empowering women, but a survey of 100 women and in-depth interviews with a subsample of 16 in two districts of Rajasthan concludes that MGNREGA has had a detrimental impact on the physical and mental well-being of women participants (Zaidi and Chigateri 2017). The unskilled hard labour leads to reports of pain and fatigue. Childcare facilities at work sites are rare and of poor quality. Women who participate tend to earn lower wages because they are forced to come late or leave early to attend to care tasks. No allowances such as lighter work assignments are made for pregnant or breast-feeding women.

Despite these limitations, most women surveyed consider MGNREGA employment vital, especially as an alternative to private employment in the agricultural lean season. Inequalities in daily wages between men and women labourers in private agricultural work are widespread and MGNREGA's equal pay provision has improved paid work opportunities for women (Dasgupta and Sudershan 2011). Still, the programme could and should be more responsive to their care burdens.

Public investment in infrastructure could also reduce such burdens by improving rural access to water and fuel.

Kenya

GrOW-sponsored research in an informal settlement of Nairobi shows that childcare centres could improve women's income-earning opportunities, with broader implications for other areas of sub-Saharan Africa (Clark et al. 2018, 2019; see also Chapter 7 in this volume for methodological insights). This project—jointly carried out by McGill University and the African Population and Health Research Center—used a randomised study design to assess the impact of a daycare voucher programme on WEE in an informal settlement of Nairobi. Women aged 15–49 with children between one and three years of age were identified using census data and interviewed. Most were engaged in poorly paid work of low quality (vending, cleaning, washing clothes, or domestic work) and a substantial number were unemployed. Relatively few women were able to rely on kin networks for childcare, due to geographical separation (Clark et al. 2018). Fathers played a very limited role in caregiving, and sibling care was considered detrimental both in terms of the quality of care provided and the impact on the education of the older sibling.

Many mothers engaged in income-earning activities that precluded bringing their children along. As a result, about a third paid for daycare centre services, despite the high price, which averaged about 17% of the women's monthly wages. Many of them saw centre services as advantageous to their children's development, a perception validated by research findings that children attending daycare were less likely than others to suffer from cognitive delay. Though these findings do not establish a causal relationship, they support the study's conclusion that formal centre-based childcare plays a central role in allowing mothers to balance work and childcare obligations (Clark et al. 2018).

Women who received 12 monthly childcare vouchers for the period from January to December 2016 were 17% more likely to be employed than those in the study who were not (Clark et al. 2019). In addition to being more likely to be employed, mothers who worked for pay were able to earn the same amount of income despite working about five fewer hours per week. Affordable daycare could be the "key to unlocking women's earning power in Africa".[14]

Rwanda

GrOW-supported research conducted by IDS in partnership with the Bangladesh Rural Advancement Committee's Research and Evaluation Unit in Rwanda demonstrates that improvements in women's income and position in the household do not necessarily help them reduce the demands of unpaid care. ActionAid Rwanda (AAR)'s Food Security and Economic Empowerment project in Muko targets vulnerable smallholder farmers, including 1,200 women and 300 men. It aims to improve their food and economic security through increased agricultural profitability (Kennedy and Roelen 2017). Initiatives include farmer cooperatives, community seed banks, a maize processing plant and storerooms, and agricultural training sessions. The researchers recommend that AAR could: (1) build infrastructure directly or in concert with the state to reduce care loads; (2) expand the project's literacy development centres, where women leave their children while they work; and (3) include care-sensitive and gender-disaggregated indicators in monitoring and evaluation, and train staff to use them.

The research also finds that Rwanda's Vision 2020 Umurenge Programme, a national social protection scheme that aims to eradicate extreme poverty, appears to intensify rather than mitigate women's total work burdens. The programme combines public works, credit provisioning, and unconditional cash transfers for households not eligible for public works (Murphy-McGreevey, Roelen, and Nyamulinda 2017). Women greatly value the income provided, and describe increased expenditures on food, education, and health that improved their families' wellbeing. However, they also describe longer workdays that undermine their health and general wellbeing. As with the AAR project in Muko, research finds that gender norms limit the redistribution of care work, leaving women exhausted.

China

The Chinese government's distinctive development strategies have yielded relatively high rates of economic growth since 1978. Systems of collective and state-provided care provisioning that existed in the Mao era were dismantled, while rural-to-urban migration increased dramatically as employment shifted from agriculture to industry. Fertility rates declined rapidly, tilting the age structure of the population toward the elderly. Both educational attainment and health outcomes improved (Li et al. 2017). Data available from several national surveys make it possible to trace some impacts of these changes at the household level.

IDRC-supported analysis of this data, by the University of Winnipeg and Peking University, argues persuasively that measured growth in Chinese market output has imposed new stresses on the family care economy and has disadvantaged women. The migration of working-age women to urban areas has intensified demands on grandparents, especially grandmothers, to provide care for children left behind (Tran et al. 2017). According to the 2010 census, 61 million children—40% of all rural children—were left behind as a result of massive labour migration to be cared for either by grandparents or the remaining parent. The proportion of rural preschool-age children in grandparents' full custody rose sharply from 3% to 27% between 1991 and 2011. Both family income and child outcomes tend to be significantly lower in rural than in urban areas.[15]

Public service provision has proved inadequate. While enrolment in daycare programmes has increased somewhat in urban areas, these services remain unaffordable for low-income families. Private and informal sector employees seldom have access to maternity leave. The newly mandated "two-child policy" may exacerbate the resulting difficulties. Stresses are also apparent at the other end of the life cycle. Women are less likely to be employed in public-sector or urban firms that provide pensions. Their responsibility for care work reduces their lifetime employment and earnings and limits their occupational choices. Many of the elderly remain in rural areas, geographically separated from their adult children. Elderly women in particular face an increased risk of poverty and neglect.

Other findings from the same research highlight how specific policy changes have reinforced women's responsibility for unpaid care (Dong and Zhao 2017). The economic reforms of the post-Mao period dismantled the system of employer- or state-provided childcare, shifting responsibility back onto families and invoking Confucian cultural traditions. Reduced revenue flows to local governments led to steep declines in childcare and pre-school programmes. Growth in personal income, combined with fertility decline, eased these pressures for some families more than others. Newly instituted maternity leaves and maternity benefits were not offered to state employees on short-term contracts, informal workers, or private employees. As of 2012, only a third of urban women were estimated to be eligible for paid leaves, with an obvious negative impact on both their career opportunities and their ability to breastfeed infants. Families have limited ability to compensate for the lack of public care provision for children and the elderly. Research found that women constitute 68% of the elderly infirm who do not receive appropriate care.

Public policies have contributed to increased gender gaps in both employment and earnings. Care responsibilities hinder the ability of rural women, in particular, to access better-paid off-farm employment. Between 1990–2010, the gender employment gap rose from about 14% to about 20% while the earnings gap widened in both rural and urban areas despite an upward trend in the average wages of both men and women. This change occurred despite a significant improvement in female educational attainment over the period.

Time-use data indicate that women work longer hours than men (the total work of urban women exceeds that of their male counterparts by as much as 8.7 hours per week). Elderly women have become more economically vulnerable. The post-reform pension system is contributory, so pensions depend on labour market status: women typically have fewer years of employment and lower pre-retirement salaries than men. As a result, women over 60 receive only half the average pension that men do (Dong and Zhao 2017).

In sum, economic policy reforms in China have both increased care deficits for disadvantaged families and constricted women's economic opportunities. Explicit integration of care needs and gender equality into a new Chinese development agenda could increase public, private, and community-level care provision, improve workplace regulation, and promote more equitable sharing of care duties within families.

Women's wellbeing and empowerment

Economic development is not an end in itself but a means to empowerment and wellbeing. It is easier to endorse this general principle, however, than to agree on how it should be operationalised. The UN Development Programme first offered its Human Development Index as a policy compass superior to Gross Domestic Product in 1990 (Stanton 2007). Since then, many other indices have been proposed. Their very proliferation suggests the need for a dashboard approach, utilising different indices for different purposes.

Self-reported measures of subjective happiness have long been recognised as useful but limited by the impact of both cultural norms and personal adaptation to difficult circumstances (Nussbaum 2001). Individuals who experience extreme deprivation and exploitation, but perceive no possible alternative to their circumstances, may report themselves as relatively happy. At the other extreme, those in extremely comfortable economic circumstances who feel unfairly excluded from even greater levels of comfort may express serious dissatisfaction with their lives. More specific psychological constructs may be useful, especially when linked to specific sources of stress.

Measures of human capabilities offer an alternative to purely subjective measures, but it is easier to quantify individual attainments of education and health than to categorise the social environments in which such attainments may or may not deliver expanded choices (Cornwall and Rivas 2015). Measures that assess only women's participation in traditionally male activities should always be accompanied by measures that assess men's participation in and support for family care (Folbre 2006).

The GrOW research programme has emphasised the importance of women's empowerment from the outset (Khan 2016; de Haan 2017). The Nairobi study assesses women's empowerment as it relates to increased participation in the labour market, changes in the number of hours worked, and improvements in earning potential. Research in India, carried out by researchers from McGill University and the Chennai-based Institute for Financial Management and Research, links a range of indicators of empowerment to care work. Richardson et al. (2019) bring household decision-making into the picture and note that it may be more important than control over income in communities where relatively few women engage in paid employment. Richardson et al. (2017) persuasively show how long work hours—including unpaid work—contribute to mental distress in rural India. Increased bargaining power of women in the family contributes to their larger political and cultural empowerment, and vice versa. However empowerment is defined, women's commitment to unpaid care must be considered in terms of the choices available, resources provided, and responsibilities shared.

Implications for policy and future research

Much of the research reviewed here makes its own case for changes in public policy, which must be more attentive to the demands of unpaid care and the difficulty of modifying entrenched gender norms. New income-earning opportunities will have little empowering effect on women unless accompanied by explicit, large-scale, and long-lasting efforts to reduce their burdens through public care provision. This problem is rendered particularly urgent by the specific character of economic development in many developing countries—continued reliance on subsistence production in rural areas and the prominent role of the informal sector in urban employment.

Investment in social infrastructure represents an important means of promoting economic development as it improves the productivity of both paid and unpaid work. Conventional economic analysis focuses on the ways in which investments in human capital can increase future wages. Broader investments in human capabilities also offer a high rate of return in the form of improved physical and mental health, educational outcomes, and a shift toward a higher quality—accompanied by lower quantity—of unpaid work. Achievement of a better balance between paid and unpaid work is a precondition for women's increased participation in the public sphere (Ferrant, Pesando, and Nowacka 2014).

GrOW-sponsored research offers important conceptual and methodological innovations. It is hardly surprising that many of the analyses rely heavily on time-use data, since time is the only metric by which unpaid work can be easily measured. Unlike many national-level surveys, however, the more localised surveys described here and featured in a number of case studies in this volume, are explicitly contextualised by attention to family and community-level characteristics. As a result, they are better designed to assess the effects of local policy initiatives, especially when these are maintained for a significant period of time.

This research also vindicates mixed-method approaches. The qualitative results, analysed by field-based researchers who immersed themselves in local communities, call attention to the importance of social norms and subjective experiences. Even where findings are not conclusive, they point to the need to improve survey design to include more attention to supervisory responsibilities, household economies of scale, intra-family income flows, and community-level infrastructure. National statistical agencies should take heed: most conventional household and time-use surveys (including those conducted by affluent countries) fail to provide the information necessary to accurately assess actual living standards.

Attention to the value of unpaid care and intra-family transfers over the life cycle calls into question the very principles of the System of National Accounts. Increased participation in paid employment provides few genuine gains if it is invisibly subsidised and effectively financed by reductions in unpaid care or increases in overall levels of work. Unpaid care is a particularly important input into the development and maintenance of human capabilities, and it can also affect the fiscal sustainability of public pensions and healthcare for the elderly.

Precisely because the research reviewed here offers such new insights into the level and distribution of unpaid work, its limitations also deserve attention. A broader picture of the family economy would include more explicit consideration of demographic factors such as age at marriage, average family size, reproductive rights, separation and desertion, and the percentage of families maintained by women alone. Both the temporal constraints and the nutritional benefits of breastfeeding infants deserve attention. A better understanding of how economic resources are shared within families is also required. While both direct and indirect care of family members is unpaid, most women caregivers enjoy some financial assistance or support from men in their families—especially the fathers of their children. Specific patterns of income pooling and expenditure allocation remain unclear, though they clearly vary across countries and cultural contexts. As the National Transfer Accounts project points out, more attention to intra-family and intergenerational transfers over the life cycle puts public spending in a larger context.

Except for the research in China, most of the analysis of women's employment in the studies reviewed here emphasises the supply side of the labour market. This makes sense for public employment schemes, such as in the case studies in India and Nepal. Yet the very large role of the informal sector in most developing countries, as emphasised above, points to significant shortfalls on the demand side of the labour market. These shortfalls could increase the relative importance of technological change and increased labour productivity in the production of both goods and services for own consumption. Technological change could also increase the potential for more decentralised development strategies.

While it is important to consider women's position relative to men, empowerment is also shaped or limited by class, caste, race, and citizenship. An explicitly intersectional approach could address aspects of women's economic wellbeing that are not gender-specific, such as average wages, family income, and vulnerability to poverty. Closer attention to inequalities among women could help explain the difficulties of forging purely gender-based political coalitions. A broader conceptualisation of empowerment could help allay fears that women's gains come entirely at men's expense.

Bringing care to the front and centre of the development discourse belies the notion that economies are driven entirely by the pursuit of individual self-interest. Ideals of shared family responsibility can strengthen solidarity on the national and international level. The historical record reveals the potential for a virtuous circle in which economic, demographic, political, and cultural change combine to expand human rights and improve human capabilities. Women and men need to work together to set this circle into motion.

Notes

1 Further analysis on women's time use and supervisory responsibilities can be found in Chapter 8 in this volume.
2 See the United Nations World Conference Beijing Declaration and Plan of Action, p. 13, at www.un.org/en/events/pastevents/pdfs/Beijing_Declaration_and_Platform_for_Action.pdf.
3 United Nations, High Level Thematic Review of SDG #5, at https://sustainabledevelopment.un.org/content/documents/14383SDG5format-revOD.pdf.
4 Case studies in this volume, particularly those in Chapters 7 and 8, provide a deeper look into the diversity of research initiatives and methods employed in the GrOW programme related to the care economy.
5 Recent research using the Indian Time Use Survey for 1998–1999 suggests that the presence of a daughter or daughter-in-law reduces the time that older women devote to

care activities, and that these burdens are shared rather unequally by age (Mukherjee 2017).

6 WEE programmes are defined as "programmes aiming for women's economic empowerment, through either provision of jobs—mainly public works—or in cooperatives" (Chopra and Zambelli 2017: 50, n. 25).

7 Additional insights on the gendered aspects of educational attainment and unpaid work responsibilities in the home can be found in Chapter 10 in this volume.

8 Efforts to re-interview the initial respondents were thwarted by a high level of migration in certain sites. As a result, the fraction resurveyed varied widely across countries and panel analysis was conducted only for the Ethiopia and Zimbabwe samples.

9 They do not report estimates of correlation with total work hours.

10 For more insight on the role of gendered social norms beyond care responsibilities, see Chapter 5 in this volume.

11 Chapter 7 in this volume offers insights into the perspective of mothers who experienced using a subsidised childcare programme, and the kind of trade-offs that they take into account.

12 For a more detailed comparison of the Chilean and Mexican programmes, see Staab and Gerhard (2011).

13 See Dreze and Oldiges (2009), Khera and Nayak (2009), and Dasgupta and Sudershan (2011).

14 Blog post at www.idrc.ca/en/stories/could-affordable-daycare-be-key-unlocking-womens-earning-power-africa, IDRC, October 17.

15 Adverse effects of migration on children left behind in rural areas have also been observed in Vietnam (Nguyen 2016).

References

Agénor, Pierre-Richard, and Madina Agénor (2014). Infrastructure, women's time allocation, and economic development. *Journal of Economics* 113: 1–30.

Alfers, Laura (2016). Our children do not get the attention they deserve': A synthesis of research findings on women informal workers and child care from six membership-based organizations. Research Report. Cambridge, MA: WIEGO. www.wiego.org/sites/default/files/publications/files/Alfers-Child-Care-Initiative-Full-Report.pdf.

Benería, Lourdes, Günseli Berik, and Maria Floro (2015). *Gender, Development and Globalization*, 2nd edition. New York: Routledge.

Blau, Francine D., and Lawrence M.Kahn (2017). The gender wage gap: Extent, trends, and sources. *Journal of Economic Literature* 55(3): 789–865. https://www.aeaweb.org/articles?id=10.1257/jel.20160995.

Budlender, Debbie (Ed.) (2010). *Time Use Studies and Unpaid Care Work*. New York: Routledge.

Calderón, Gabriela (2014). The effects of child care provision in Mexico. Working Paper 2014–07, Banco de México. www.econstor.eu/bitstream/10419/100113/1/789443112.pdf.

Chant, Sylvia (2014). Exploring the 'feminisation of poverty' in relation to women's work and home-based enterprise in slums of the Global South. *International Journal of Gender and Entrepreneurship* 6(3): 296–316.

Charmes, Jacques (2019). The unpaid care work and the labour market: An analysis of time use data based on the latest world compilation of time-use surveys. Geneva: International Labour Organization. http://www.ilo.org/wcmsp5/groups/public/---dgreports/---gender/documents/publication/wcms_732791.pdf.

Chopra, Deepta, and Elena Zambelli (2017). No time to rest: Women's lived experiences of balancing paid work and unpaid care work. Global Synthesis Report for Women's

Economic Empowerment Policy and Programming. Brighton: Institute of Development Studies. https://www.ids.ac.uk/publications/no-time-to-rest-womens-lived-experiences-of-balancing-paid-work-and-unpaid-care-work/.

Clark, Shelley, Caroline Kabiru, Sonia Laszlo, and Stella Muthuri (2019). The impact of childcare on poor urban women's economic empowerment in Africa. *Demography* 56: 1247–1272.

Clark, Shelley, Midanna De Almada, Caroline W. Kabiru, Stella Muthuri, and Milka Wanjohi (2018). Balancing paid work and child care in a slum of Nairobi, Kenya: The case for centre-based child care. *Journal of Family Studies*, 1–20.

Cornwall, Andrea and Althea-Maria Rivas (2015). From 'gender equality' and 'women's empowerment' to global justice: Reclaiming a transformative agenda for gender and development. *Third World Quarterly* 36(2): 396–415.

Dasgupta, Sukti, and Ratna M.Sudershan (2011). Issues in labour market inequality and women's participation in India's National Rural Employment Guarantee Programme. ILO Working Paper No. 98. Geneva: International Labor Office. www.ilo.org/integration/resources/papers/WCMS_153042/lang--en/index.htm.

de Haan, Arjan (2017). The win-win case for women's empowerment and growth: A review of the literature. Concept Paper, GrOW Working Paper Series, GWP-2017–03. Montreal: Institute for the Study of International Development, McGill University. http://grow.research.mcgill.ca/publications/working-papers/gwp-2017-03.pdf.

Del Boca, Daniela (2015). The impact of child care costs and availability on mother's labor supply. ImPRovE Working Paper 15/04. Antwerp: Herman Deleeck Centre for Social Policy, University of Antwerp. https://ideas.repec.org/p/hdl/improv/1504.html.

Donehower, Gretchen (2013). Incorporating time and gender into NTA: National time transfer accounts methodology. Unpublished. www.ntaccounts.org/doc/repository/Incorporating%20Gender%20and%20Time%20Use%20into%20NTA,%20Version%203.docx.

Dong, Xiao-yuan, and Yaohui Zhao (2017). Care economy, gender and inclusive growth in post-reform China: How does unpaid care work affect women's economic opportunities and gender equality? Research Contribution Paper, GrOW Working Paper Series, GWP-2017–06. Montreal: Institute for the Study of International Development, McGill University. http://grow.research.mcgill.ca/publications/working-papers/gwp-2017-06.pdf.

Dreze, Jean, and Christian Oldiges (2009). Work in progress. *Frontline* 26: 4. www.frontline.in/static/html/fl2604/stories/20090227260410100.htm.

Elson, Diane (2012). Social reproduction in the global crisis. In Peter Utting, Shahra Razavi, and Rebecca Varghese Buchholz (Eds.), *The Global Crisis and Transformative Social Change* (63–80). London: Palgrave Macmillan.

Ferrant, Gaëlle, Luca Maria Pesando, and Keiko Nowacka (2014). Unpaid care work: The missing link in the analysis of gender gaps in labour outcomes. Paris: OECD Development Centre. www.oecd.org/dev/development-gender/Unpaid_care_work.pdf.

Folbre, Nancy. (2006). Measuring care: Gender, empowerment, and the care economy. *Journal of Human Development* 7(2): 183–199.

Folbre, Nancy (2009). *Greed, Lust, and Gender.* New York: Oxford University Press.

Folbre, Nancy, and Jayoung Yoon (2007). What is child care? Lessons from time use surveys of major English-speaking countries. *Review of Economics of the Household* 5(3): 223–248.

Folbre, Nancy, and Jayoung Yoon (2008). Economic development and time devoted to care. Background Paper for UNRISD Flagship Report on Combatting Poverty and Inequality. Geneva: United Nations Research Institute for Social Development. www.unrisd.org/unrisd/website/document.nsf/(httpPublications)/7783FF26A4DC0C83C12574E2002F53F3?OpenDocument.

Folbre, Nancy, Jayoung Yoon, Kade Finnoff, and Allison Sidle Fuligni (2005). By what measure? Family time devoted to children in the U.S. *Demography* 42(2): 373–390.

Fontana, Marzia, and Diane Elson (2014). Public policies on water provision and early childhood education and care (ECEC): Do they reduce and redistribute unpaid work? *Gender and Development* 22(3): 459–474.

Gaddis, Isis, and Stephan Klasen (2014). Economic development, structural change and women's labor force participation: A reexamination of the feminization U hypothesis. *Journal of Population Economics* 27(3): 639–681.

Ghosh, Anweshaa, Anjam Singh, and Shraddha Chigateri (2017a). A trapeze act: Balancing unpaid care work and paid care work by women in Nepal. National Report. Brighton: Institute of Development Studies. https://opendocs.ids.ac.uk/opendocs/handle/123456789/13338.

Ghosh, Anweshaa, Anjam Singh, and Shraddha Chigateri (2017b). Making Karnali employment programme more care-responsive. Programmatic Notes. Brighton: Institute of Development Studies. https://opendocs.ids.ac.uk/opendocs/handle/123456789/13147.

Greene, Margaret E., and Ann E. Biddlecom (2000). Absent and problematic men: Demographic accounts of male reproductive roles. *Population and Development Review* 26(1): 81–115.

Hallman, Kelly, Agnes Quisumbing, Marie Ruel, and Benedicte de la Briere (2005). Mother's work and childcare: Findings from the urban slums of Guatemala City. *Economic Development and Cultural Change* 53(4): 855–885.

Huong, Nguyen Thi Lan, Pham Minh Thu, and Pham Ngoc Toan (2017). Counting women's work in Vietnam. Counting Women's Work Country Report No. 3. https://www.countingwomenswork.org/news/2018/6/8/cww-country-report-vietnam.

IDRC (2017). Could affordable daycare be the key to unlocking women's earning power in Africa? Blog, October 17. https://www.idrc.ca/en/stories/could-affordable-daycare-be-key-unlocking-womens-earning-power-africa.

Karimli, Leyla, Emma Samman, Lucia Rost, and Thalia Kidder (2016). Factors and norms influencing unpaid care work: Household survey evidence from five rural communities in Colombia, Ethiopia, the Philippines, Uganda and Zimbabwe. Oxfam Women's Economic Empowerment and Care Report. Oxford: Oxfam UK. https://policy-practice.oxfam.org.uk/publications/factors-and-norms-influencing-unpaid-care-work-household-survey-evidence-from-f-620145.

Kennedy, Liam, and Keetie Roelen (2017). ActionAid's food security and economic empowerment programme in Muko Sector, Northern Rwanda: Guidelines for achieving the double boon. Programmatic Notes. Brighton: Institute of Development Studies. https://opendocs.ids.ac.uk/opendocs/handle/123456789/13231.

Khan, Themrise (2016). An evidential roadmap: Strengthening linkages between women's economic empowerment and growth. Background Paper for the UN High Level Panel on Women's Economic Empowerment. Ottawa: IDRC. https://idl-bnc-idrc.dspacedirect.org/bitstream/handle/10625/55633/IDL-55633.pdf?sequence=1&isAllowed=y.

Khera, Reetika, and Nandini Nayak (2009). Women workers and perceptions of the National Rural Employment Guarantee Act. *Economic and Political Weekly* 44(43): 49–57.

Kimmel, Jean, and Rachel Connelly (2007). Mother's time choices: Caregiving, leisure, home production, and paid work. *Journal of Human Resources* 42(3): 643–681.

Ladusingh, Laishram (2017). Counting women's work in India. Counting Women's Work Country Report No. 2. https://www.countingwomenswork.org/news/2018/6/8/cww-country-report-india.

Li, Hongbun, Prashant Loyalka, Scott Rozelle, and Binzhen Wu (2017). Human capital and China's future growth. *Journal of Economic Perspectives* 31(1): 25–48. https://pubs.aeaweb.org/doi/pdfplus/10.1257/jep.31.1.25.

Mmopelwa, Gagoitseope, Barbara Ntombi Ngwenya, Narain Sinha, and J.B.P. Sanders (2013). Caregiver characteristics and economic cost of home-based care: A case study of Maun and Gumare villages in North West District, Botswana. *Chronic Illness* 9(1): 3–15.

Moussié, Rachel (2016). Childcare from the perspective of women in the informal economy. Policy Brief for the UN Secretary General's High-Level Panel on Women's Economic Empowerment.

Mukherjee, Avanti (2017). *Three Essays on 'Doing Care', Gender Differences in the Work Day, and Women's Care Work in the Household.* PhD dissertation, University of Massachusetts Amherst. http://scholarworks.umass.edu/dissertations_2/1062/.

Murphy-McGreevey, Clare, Keetie Roelen, and Birasa Nyamulinda (2017). Making Rwanda's Vision 2020 Umurenge Programme Public Works care-responsive. Programmatic Notes. Brighton: Institute of Development Studies. https://opendocs.ids.ac.uk/opendocs/handle/123456789/13230.

Nguyen, CuoungViet (2016). Does parental migration really benefit left-behind children? Comparative evidence from Ethiopia, India, Peru and Vietnam. *Social Science and Medicine* 153: 230–239.

Niethammer, Carmen, Michelle Davis, Nathalie Hoffman, Amanda Devercelli, Benedicte Leroy De La Briere, Gharam Alkastani Dexter, Anna Kalashyan, Tazeen Hasan, and Rudaba Nasir. (2017). Tackling childcare: The business case for employer-supported childcare. World Bank Group Working Paper No. 121546. Washington, DC: International Finance Corporation, World Bank Group. http://documents.worldbank.org/curated/en/377711511422588789/pdf/121546-WP-Tackling-Childcare-Report-Final-October-2017-PUBLIC.pdf.

Nussbaum, Martha (2001). *Women and Human Development.* New York: Cambridge University Press.

OECD (2011). Doing better for families. Paris: Organization for Economic Co-operation and Development. www.oecd.org/social/family/doingbetterforfamilies.htm.

Paes de Barros, Ricardo, Pedro Olinto, Trine Lunde, and Mirela Carvalho (2011). The impact of access to free childcare on women's labor market outcomes: Evidence from a randomized trial in low-income neighborhoods of Rio de Janiero. Washington, DC: World Bank Group. http://citeseerx.ist.psu.edu/viewdoc/download?doi=10.1.1.258.5722&rep=rep1&type=pdf.

Pérez-Escamilla, R. (2017). Estancias infantiles y desarrollo infantil en México: Avances y retos [Childcare and child development in Mexico: Progress and challenges]. *Boletín Médico del Hospital Infantil de México* 74: 84–85.

Richardson, Robin, Arijit Nandi, Surinder Jaswal, and Sam Harper (2017). Are work demands associated with mental distress? Evidence from women in rural India. *Social Psychiatry and Psychiatric Epidemiology* 52(12): 1501–1511.

Richardson, Robin, Norbert Schmitz, Sam Harper, and Arijit Nandi (2019). Development of a tool to measure women's agency in India. *Journal of Human Development and Capabilities* 20(2): 26–53.

Rosen, Sherwin (1997). Public employment, taxes, and the welfare state in Sweden. In Richard B. Freeman, Robert Topel, and Birgitta Swedenbo (Eds.), *The Welfare State in Transition: Reforming the Swedish Model* (79–108). Chicago: University of Chicago Press.

Sengupta, Sudeshna, and Shubika Sachdeva (2017). From double burden of women to a "double boon": Balancing unpaid care work and paid work. IDS Policy Brief. Brighton: Institute of Development Studies. https://idl-bnc-idrc.dspacedirect.org/bitstream/handle/10625/56506/IDL-56506.pdf?sequence=2&isAllowed=y.

Song, Yueping, and Xiao-yuan Dong (2018). Childcare costs and migrant and local mothers' labor force participation in urban China. *Feminist Economics* 24(2): 122–146.

Staab, Silke, and Roberto Gerhard (2011). Putting two and two together? Early childhood education, mothers' employment and care service expansion in Chile and Mexico. *Development and Change* 42(4): 1079–1107.

Stanton, Elizabeth (2007). The Human Development Index: A history. Working Paper 127. Amherst, MA: Political Economy Research Institute, University of Massachusetts-Amherst. https://scholarworks.umass.edu/cgi/viewcontent.cgi?article=1101&context=peri_workingpapers.

Strohschein, Lisa (2017). Non-residential fatherhood in Canada. *Canadian Studies in Population* 44(1-2): 16–27.

Stykes, J. Bart, Wendy D. Manning, and Susan L. Brown (2013). Nonresident fathers and formal child support: Evidence from the CPS, the NSFG and the SIPP. *Demographic Research* 29(46): 1299–1330.

Tran, Olivia, Edgard Rodriguez, Arjan de Haan, Xiao-Yuan Dong, and Yaohui Zhao (2017). Caring across generations: Policy challenges for China. IDRC Policy Brief. Ottawa: IDRC. https://idl-bnc-idrc.dspacedirect.org/bitstream/handle/10625/56397/IDL56397.pdf?sequence=1.

UNRISD (2010). Combatting poverty and inequality: Structural change, social policy and politics. Geneva: United Nations Research Institute for Social Development. www.unrisd.org/unrisd/website/document.nsf/(httpPublications)/BBA20D83E347DBAFC125778200440AA7?OpenDocument.

Vanek, Joann, Martha Alter Chen, Françoise Carré, James Heintz, and Ralf Hussmanns (2014). Statistics on the informal economy: Definitions, regional estimates and challenges. WIEGO Working Paper (Statistics) No. 2. Cambridge, MA: Women in Informal Employment Globalizing and Organizing. www.wiego.org/sites/default/files/publications/files/Vanek-Statistics-WIEGO-WP2.pdf.

Waring, Marilyn (1988). *If Women Counted: A New Feminist Economics*. New York: Harper and Row.

Warner, Mildred E. (2006). Putting child care in the regional economy: Empirical and conceptual challenges and economic development prospects. *Community Development* 37(2): 7–22.

Warner, Mildred E., and Zhilin Liu (2006). The importance of child care in economic development: A comparative analysis of regional economic linkage. *Economic Development Quarterly* 20(1): 97–103.

Yoon, Jayoung (2014). Counting care work in social policy: Valuing unpaid child- and eldercare in Korea. *Feminist Economics* 20(2): 65–89.

Zaidi, Mubashira, and Shraddha Chigateri (2017). Making Mahatma Gandhi National Rural Employment Guarantee Act (MGNREGA) more care-responsive. Programmatic Notes. Brighton: Institute of Development Studies. https://opendocs.ids.ac.uk/opendocs/handle/123456789/13214.

Zambelli, Elena, Keetie Roelen, Naomi Hossain, Deepta Chopra, and Jeniphe Twebaze (2017). 'My mother does a lot of work': Women balancing paid and unpaid care work in Tanzania. National report. Brighton: Institute of Development Studies. https://opendocs.ids.ac.uk/opendocs/handle/123456789/13283.

5

GENDER, SOCIAL NORMS, AND WOMEN'S ECONOMIC EMPOWERMENT

Rachel Marcus

Introduction

Social norms are increasingly recognised as significant barriers to women's economic empowerment (WEE), even where progressive laws have been enacted (Hunt and Samman 2016; ILO 2018; Jayachandran 2019). Although the Growth and Economic Opportunities for Women (GrOW) programme did not specifically focus on norms, it generated a wide set of insights on social norm-related barriers to and enablers of WEE, with a particular focus on women's access to assets, employment, and entrepreneurship.[1] This chapter draws on the findings of more than 50 research outputs from GrOW-supported studies and on a rapid search and analysis of wider literature on social and gender norms and WEE.

While the GrOW studies, as a whole, provided considerable insights into positive policies that support WEE, few directly addressed questions of how to best reduce normative barriers. This is a question on which there are many recent experimental initiatives, as well as emerging insights about policies to support large-scale normative change (ALIGN forthcoming). Reflecting on this wider literature is outside the scope of this chapter. Instead we summarise emerging insights from the GrOW studies, situate them within the body of existing research on social and gender norms and WEE, and highlight knowledge gaps.

Most GrOW studies fell broadly within the discipline of economics and are based on analysis of large-scale datasets. These primarily provided indirect insights into social norms, focusing on indicators of gender equality and their relationship to economic phenomena rather than on the social relations that contribute to the observed patterns. The main exceptions were sets of studies led by Klasen (2018) and Peters et al. (2016) that relate trends in women's labour market participation to a range of factors, including social norms. GrOW also funded five mixed-methods studies, which directly illuminate the relationship between gender norms and

WEE.[2] These focused on women's economic opportunities in post-conflict northern Sri Lanka, artisanal mining in Central and East Africa, young women's transitions to work in East Africa, young women's work and marriage patterns in Bangladesh, and unpaid care work in South Asia and East Africa. This chapter draws substantially on these studies, four of which are also featured as case studies in this volume.

Definitions: social and gender norms

We understand social norms as "collective definitions of socially approved conduct, stating rules or ideals" (Pearse and Connell 2016: 31), and gender norms as "social norms that express how people of a particular gender, and often age, are expected to behave in a given social context" (ALIGN 2018). Gender norms both embody and contribute to reproducing gendered power relations, and thus to gender-based inequalities across many spheres of economic, social, and political life.

Norms can be held in place by expected sanctions for violating norms—such as gossip, social shunning, or violence—and by social approval for conforming to them (Mackie et al. 2015). Nonetheless, individuals may choose not to comply with them: for example, if they believe specific norms are wrong or that others in their 'reference group' (influential social group) do not comply with them; if they cannot afford to do so or can afford to risk sanctions for non-compliance; or their personal sense of agency is particularly strong (Marcus and Harper 2014). New norms can emerge when enough people do not support the old ones (Mackie et al. 2015; Vaitla et al. 2017).

Changes in norms can reflect the impacts of policies and programmes or structural forces of change, such as economic growth or decline, the spread of education, or greater access to information and communications technology (Marcus and Harper 2014). The GrOW studies highlight how processes of structural change have intersected with, and influenced, pre-existing norms to produce both new opportunities for and constraints to WEE and wellbeing more broadly.

Framework for understanding gender norms and women's economic empowerment

Gender norms, intertwined with stereotypes about men's and women's capabilities, affect access to resources, opportunities to develop human capital, livelihood opportunities, and time use. This chapter discusses two main sets of norms that affect WEE: norms specifically related to gender and economic activity—shown in darker grey in Figure 5.1—and broader norms that influence the behaviour of men, women, boys, and girls, shown in lighter grey.[3] These norms intersect to affect both access to work and women's experiences within formal and informal workplaces, and lead to patterns of work that disadvantage women, such as gendered work segregation and concentration of women in lower paid activities.

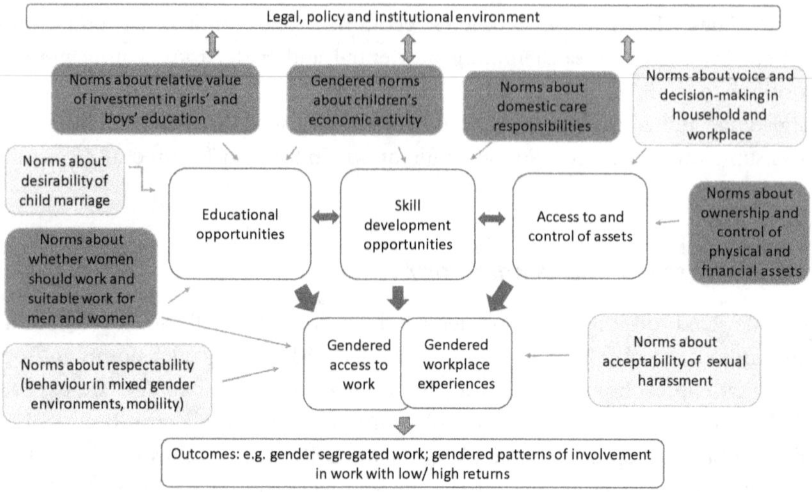

FIGURE 5.1 Relationship between gendered social norms and women's economic outcomes
Source: Author

Insights into the role of social and gender norms in facilitating or constraining women's economic activity

A macro-level view

Examining trends in gender gaps in various areas of social and economic life over the past two decades, Klasen (2018) shows that, although gender gaps in educational participation and outcomes have narrowed considerably, those in labour force participation and time use have declined much less. Globally women's labour force participation rates, at 48.5%, lag behind those of men by 26.5 percentage points (ILO 2018). Furthermore, there has been almost no progress in reducing occupational and sectoral segregation or unexplained gender pay gaps.[4]

Klasen suggests that the rapid closure of gender gaps in education reflects a combination of favourable circumstances related to economic growth, a supportive policy environment, and relatively malleable norms. By contrast, he argues that a combination of less favourable factors has contributed to weak progress in closing labour market gaps. These include structural changes in labour markets that have had varied effects on employment opportunities in different places (and have not universally opened up opportunities seen as suitable for women); a generally lower policy priority globally to reducing gender-based barriers to decent work than enhancing access to education; and a different set of norms related to paid and unpaid work, which may be more persistent as they relate to deeper-seated ideas about gender roles within and outside the home.

Normative opposition to women's labour force participation may explain why a set of factors that normally lead to increased labour force participation (rising levels of education, reductions in fertility in most regions, and economic growth and rising income) have only done so in some regions, such as Latin America (Klasen 2019).

As well as overall labour force participation rates, job segregation (clustering of women and men into certain occupations) has changed little over the last 40 to 50 years (Klasen 2018). As countries have become richer and as more women have entered the labour force, gendered job segregation has not notably reduced. Indeed, Klasen (2019) suggests that in contexts where the range of sectors considered appropriate for women to work in is relatively narrow, such as in South Asia and the Middle East, the supply of educated women has outstripped demand, leading to stagnating labour force participation rates. Even where it does not affect overall economic participation, gendered job segregation prevents people from fulfilling their potential, and often contributes to women being concentrated in less well remunerated occupations (Gallup and ILO 2017).

GrOW-supported research from six countries in sub-Saharan Africa (Burkina Faso, Ethiopia, Ghana, Kenya, Tanzania, and Uganda) confirms that, although levels of educational attendance and attainment have been rising faster among girls than boys, this has not translated systematically into greater labour force participation (Mariara et al. 2018). Growth in white-collar jobs has not kept pace with rising education levels, and there is a clear gender gap (male dominance) in these jobs in three of the six countries. Mariara and colleagues further found that women in white-collar jobs have higher literacy levels than men, perhaps indicating that they require higher skills or qualifications to obtain these jobs, or that discriminatory norms or stereotypes persist in recruitment. For more information on school-to-work transitions for young women in sub-Saharan Africa, see Chapter 10 in this volume.

However, in some countries and regions, GrOW studies show that women—particularly younger women—are moving into the labour force, such as in Indonesia following trade liberalisation (Kis-Katos, Pieters, and Sparrow 2018). As will be discussed in the following sections, there is also evidence both of gendered social norms interacting to constrain women's access to 'decent work', and of norms relaxing as people respond in different ways to economic opportunities and stresses in their particular context.

Norms about whether women should undertake paid work

Norms about the overall acceptability of women engaging in paid work are strongly related to three other connected sets of norms: the acceptability of work in specific sectors and activities; respectability and mobility; and norms concerning care responsibilities and domestic divisions of labour. I first present evidence of the broader norms and values, and then discuss each of these connected sets of norms in turn.

Data from a 2017 study conducted by Gallup and the ILO found that, globally, most men and women support women undertaking paid work, either as a sole responsibility or, more commonly, combined with taking care of the home and family. The one exception was North Africa, where more men (but not more women) preferred women to only take care of their families. This study found that family attitudes were a key influence—in households that do not consider it acceptable for women to work outside the home, 61% of women said that they preferred to stay at home. Men and women with university-level education and people in families without children were most supportive of women's paid work (Gallup and ILO 2017).

GrOW-supported studies from both East Africa and South Asia found considerable ambivalence toward women working for pay. Focus group participants in Uganda interviewed as part of a study on early labour market transitions reported strong male reservations about women working outside the home (Ahaibwe, Ssewanyana, and Kasirye 2018a). These reservations reflect fears that women may engage in sexual liaisons or may be sexually exploited by bosses, as well as the possibility that women earning their own money would be less subservient. They also express an underlying norm of married men's entitlement to their wives' time and labour:

> Men feel very insecure. It takes some years in marriage for a man to trust you to work. (Female focus group participant, Masaka)
>
> How do you donate your wife to another man to work for him? (Male focus group participant, Namayingo)
>
> Economically empowered women are big-headed, they often divorce. (Male focus group participant, Namayingo)
>
> *(all cited in Ahaibwe, Ssewanyana, and Kasirye 2018a: 22)*

Although conflict-related disruption can lead to women adopting new roles and norms changing to reflect common patterns of behaviour (Petesch 2013), GrOW-supported research on barriers to WEE in post-conflict northern Sri Lanka indicated little normative change.[5] A massive 82% of women in male-headed households said that household responsibilities were a barrier to wage work, and 42% reported family attitudes as a barrier (Gunatilaka and Vithanagama 2018; Jeyaseker and Ganeda 2018). A smaller proportion of female-headed households cited these factors as barriers to wage work (63% and 21%, respectively), perhaps because their need for income meant they were forced to violate norms. Around 10% of women reported community-level disapproval of women working as a barrier to wage work.

Field, Glennerster, and Nazneen's (2018) study in Bangladesh, also found considerable opposition to young women working, though this was nuanced by whether work could be undertaken at home or not. In about half the households studied, husbands and in-laws preferred young women not to work for pay at all or to undertake work they could do from home such as tailoring or tutoring. These findings are consistent with those of Heintz, Kabeer, and Mahmud (2017), who found that *purdah*[6] norms and the desire to avoid negative judgements from other community members, strongly influenced women's work preferences in Bangladesh. Indeed, Asadullah and Wahhaj (2016) estimated that *purdah* norms explained half of the male/female difference in labour force participation in Bangladesh.

While norms deterring women's paid work (both in general or in specific occupations, discussed in the next section) were strong, GrOW studies also found evidence of change. Research by Chopra and Zambelli (2017) on women's paid and unpaid work in India, Nepal, Rwanda, and Tanzania explored the tension between idealised gender norms and the economic pressures many households faced. The study concluded that:

> [M]en across the research sites valued their wives' engagement in paid work for the contribution that this made to the household budget. However, most men considered this engagement as a symptom of their household's poverty, rather than an idealized situation, and preferred that this work was either in their own fields or closer to home.
>
> *(Chopra and Zambelli 2017: 28).*

The authors also found—consistent with a long-standing qualitative and quantitative literature—that norms about women's engagement in any paid work, or about acceptable work for women and men, were of necessity looser in households living in extreme poverty.

The GrOW-supported baseline survey for the Punjab Economic Opportunities Programme in Pakistan explored households' willingness to send members for training. To the researchers' surprise, they found an openness to women taking part in training, so long as it took place in or near their villages. Similarly, half the unemployed women (31% of all women in their sample) reported that they were looking for work, as were 9% of women who were already working. Again, this indicates that norms prohibiting women from working may not be as strong as assumed, particularly if the work can be done close to home (i.e. not strongly violating norms about women's mobility) (Cheema et al. 2017).

Qualitative research in Kagera region, Tanzania, undertaken as part of GrOW-supported research by Kamanzi and colleagues on early labour market transitions, found that norms about paid work were changing rapidly among young women, reflecting generational change:

> Those days where our mothers were to ask for money from our fathers, even for simple things like underwear, are gone: we need our own money, and this means that we should work.
>
> Now like me who has gone to school, why did I go there? To stay at home and do what? … Do you need to go to school to remain at home? Why don't you stay there from the word go?
>
> *(Kamanzi et al. 2017: 15)*

However, parallel focus groups with young men also documented unease about women's work outside the home, particularly in terms of impact on family life.

Norms about suitable work for men and women

The gender typing of certain occupations in ways that reflect stereotypes about male and female capabilities and about suitable work for each gender continues to underpin gendered job segregation. For example, a GrOW-supported study undertaken in Pakistan found that 77% of women wanted to learn skills related to garment manufacturing and textiles, which can be done at home; 6% chose the next-most popular option, makeup and jewellery. Men's training aspirations were much less concentrated in one sector—agriculture, livestock-rearing, engineering, driving, and computer skills were each prioritised by 10–15% of male respondents (Cheema et al. 2017).

GrOW studies, and the wider literature, indicate that as new economic opportunities emerge, pre-existing norms and ideologies are often incorporated and mapped onto newly emerging work areas—sometimes morphing, sometimes relaxing, sometimes hardening (Ridgeway 2009; Munoz Boudet et al. 2012). For example, Field, Glennerster, and Nazneen (2018) found that tutoring, which has emerged as a new occupation for young women with secondary education, is seen as contributing to society, involves work with children (an extension of women's domestic roles), can be undertaken at home or in the village, and is generally considered prestigious work in rural Bangladesh. Consequently, young women undertaking tutoring generally do not meet family resistance. Indeed, Field, Glennerster, and Nazneen (2018) found tentative evidence that the returns from work of this kind available to secondary school graduates offset the higher marriage payments (dowries) frequently demanded for educated girls, who are perceived to be less docile wives.

By contrast, attitudes to garment work, another major growth sector for women's employment in Bangladesh over the past few decades, are much more ambivalent. Garment work involves a number of elements that violate idealised gender norms. These include working outside the home with boys and men, often living away from familial supervision, moving and speaking freely, and learning to negotiate and assert themselves. Some families tried to hide their daughters' work in the garment industry from potential in-laws for fear that an engagement would be annulled.

GrOW studies of the artisanal mining sector in Ghana (Baah-Boateng, Twumasi Baffour, and Akyeampong 2017) and in Central and East Africa (DRC, Rwanda, and Uganda) (Buss et al. 2017a) illustrate the processes by which gendered norms underpinning job segregation are enforced and their implications. Focus groups in Ghana highlighted men's perceptions that strength, endurance, and an ability to withstand tedious work in difficult and dangerous conditions were required in mining. Since these attributes are associated with idealised masculinity (Baah-Boateng, Twumasi Baffour, and Akyeampong 2017), they can deter women from entering certain kinds of work and can be mobilised to exclude women.

In both the Ghana and the Central and East Africa mining studies, norms deeming underground mining to be a male activity were related to beliefs about menstruating women bringing bad luck on miners, such as making gold harder to find or the ore harder to extract. This led to women's exclusion from pits and contributed to their concentration in less lucrative activities, such as crushing, washing, and sifting sand and rock after extraction, or in ancillary services such as food provision and sexual services (Baah-Boateng, Twumasi Baffour, and Akyeampong 2017; Buss et al. 2017a). In Uganda, where most tin miners worked in male-only 'gangs,' women were typically included only if they were related to a gang member who could vouch for them. As a result—and indicating women's agency in the face of constraining norms—some women formed their own gangs (Buss et al. 2017a).

Social norms theory highlights the use of social sanctions—including labelling, gossip, avoidance, intimidation, and violence—as ways of enforcing norms (Mackie et al. 2015; Cislaghi, Manji, and Heise 2018). The mining studies found that sexual harassment and intimidation were relatively common, particularly where women engaged in male-dominated activities such as machine operation or worked underground (Baah-Boateng, Twumasi Baffour, and Akyeampong 2017; Buss et al. 2017a). They also reported widespread gossip about women working outside the home, particularly in male-dominated sectors, framed in terms of women's violation of norms of respectable sexuality or the care they provide to their families.

For example, in Rwanda, Buss et al. (2017a) found moralistic stereotypes of women working in mining. These labelled young women working at the mines as liable to take drugs, become pregnant outside of marriage, and disobey their parents. Married women were portrayed as being in constant disputes with their husbands. Widows were presented as unable to 'control themselves'. These women were compared to those working in respectable (but usually less lucrative) occupations, such as agriculture. Similarly, Kodikara's (2018) study of livelihoods among female-headed households in north-east Sri Lanka found that widows or separated women who hired men to work for them, even for one-off casual jobs, were subject to considerable gossip, hinting that their economic relationship masked a sexual one. Driving an auto-rickshaw was also considered 'indecent' (Jeyaseker and Ganeda 2018).

In Uganda and Rwanda, women involved in mining were also subjected to negative gossip about their domestic skills. For example, women wolframite miners reported "community members saying that their houses are a mess, no one looks after their children, and their crops are not being properly looked after" (Buss et al. 2017a: 33). Lakshman's (2017) study of women's livelihoods in war-affected Sri Lanka likewise highlighted examples of women working in 'male spaces' being subject to gossip. When women perceived this to be personally shameful or detrimental to their children's—particularly their daughters'—reputations, they felt obliged to stop working.

As well as inviting gossip, engaging in non-traditional work can also challenge individuals' sense of how they are living up to community expectations. As a woman tin miner interviewed in Uganda explained:

> When I go to do the tin mining, I cannot provide that care to my own children and I think that is where I have deviated from one of the key makers of a real woman. A real woman is that one who digs and grows food crops and feeds the family but for me, I buy food using tin money which is also abnormal for a real traditional woman.
>
> *(Buss et al. 2017a: 32)*

Norms about respectability, decorum, and mobility

Norms about respectability and decorum exert substantial influence on whether women participate in work outside the home and contribute to workplace segregation. Respectability is closely related to chastity within heterosexual marriage in many of the social contexts in which GrOW studies were carried out. Safeguarding personal and family honour by behaving in gendered respectable ways is fundamental to social wellbeing and economic success.

The artisanal mining studies in Central and East Africa highlighted how norms of decorum, modesty, and the limits to appropriate contact between men and women feed into gendered job segregation. For example, a female focus group respondent in Uganda stated that in "the digging area, men dress badly! It is not good to see the body of a man who is not your husband!" (Buss et al. 2017a: 29). A male miner from Rwanda articulated something similar about norms for dressing appropriately and acceptable topics for discussion in mixed company, stating, "It is not good if someone else's wife finds you shirtless or only with a loincloth working in the shafts… And then us, the miners, we talk about everything while working! Sex-related nonsense." (Buss et al. 2017a: 29).

In South Asia, the imperative of safeguarding women's and girls' reputations often translated into norms constraining women's mobility and limiting their economic options. As a widow in northern Sri Lanka reported:

> A widowed woman has to go to Samurthi, DS office [social security] and everywhere all by herself, but all that people say is she is seeing a man. I am not exaggerating; this is what happens in the society. It's always a problem when there is no male travel companion with you.
>
> *(Lakshman 2017)*

As the study of women's economic opportunities in post-conflict northern Sri Lanka concluded:

> [C]onstrained by the narrow rules put in place by society, a majority of the women interviewed did not even consider such choices as feasible solutions to their problems. Driving a lorry or hiring a three-wheeler alone is not perceived as suitable solutions to the difficulties of walking under the blazing sun by a woman (once) married.
>
> *(Lakshman 2017: 19)*

Consistent with other studies from South Asia about the impact of male migration on gender norms, GrOW-supported research by Ghosh et al. (2017) found no clear loosening of norms about women's paid work in Nepal. In sites with high male out-migration, some women were now engaging in ploughing, traditionally a male-dominated activity. This reflected difficulties in securing male labour rather than shifts in gendered norms about appropriate work activities for men and women and was seen as a temporary measure until families could afford paid labour. Furthermore, the study found some evidence that restrictions on women's mobility and participation in paid work had tightened because of the norms associated with women's chastity and sexuality. Some of the women interviewed had husbands working in India who did not want them to work because they feared that they would meet other men through work and/or because of their own pride in being able to live up to prescribed norms of masculinity. They aspired to be breadwinners whose wives were not required to work outside the home.

In the Ugandan gold mine studied by Buss et al. (2017a), some women excavated mine shafts, others owned or rented processing machines, and a few were establishing themselves as 'big persons' in the mining zone. Similarly, at the tin mine, a few excavation teams were composed entirely of women, defying norms that preclude women from digging. Some of these women saw themselves as trailblazers, paving the way for others to occupy lucrative jobs traditionally held by men (Buss et al. 2017b).

While gender norms often contribute to job segregation, they are not unassailable constraints. Qualitative insights from GrOW studies indicate the possible start of a process of normative change, whereby a few determined women—often with familial support or support from an external organisation—have managed to break into relatively lucrative, male-dominated work sectors.

Some women interviewed by Jeyaseker and Ganweda (2018) were able to defy local gender norms to drive an auto rickshaw to do business further afield and access more lucrative opportunities. Others found some creative ways to work while still ostensibly abiding by norms that restricted their mobility. For example, some of the young women Field, Glennerster, and Nazneen (2018) interviewed in Bangladesh who were prevented from going to market by their husbands, in-laws, or their own internalisation of gender-based restrictions on mobility, attempted to overcome these restrictions by communicating with customers by mobile phone. While this was a partial solution, their isolation nevertheless impeded their businesses because they lacked knowledge of changing fashion and design, and thus of the changing needs and preferences of their customers.

Norms about care work, domestic work, and time use

Norms about whether, or in what circumstances, women should undertake paid work are deeply linked to norms about women's responsibility for unpaid household work: cooking; cleaning; care of children, the elderly, and sick people; and care of household assets. In this section, we discuss changes and continuity in gender norms about unpaid care responsibilities, the contexts or factors that support greater flexibility in gender divisions of labour, and the impacts of care responsibilities on women's economic opportunities.

Four GrOW-supported country studies—undertaken in India, Nepal, Rwanda, and Tanzania—exploring norms around women's paid and unpaid work found that most household work was normatively a female responsibility and that, in fact, women did more than twice the amount of unpaid care work than men. Girls were socialised into this work from an early age (Chopra and Zambelli 2017). However, there was some evidence of a divergence between people's private attitudes and actions, and what they perceived to be the cultural norm, particularly in Tanzania and Rwanda. For example, one male interviewee in Rwanda observed:

> [A]ccording to the culture, women have to handle the home activities. However, that is about the culture, but to me I feel well when everyone gets involved in the doing care work at home. This indicates that everyone has something to contribute to the family.
>
> *(Rohwerder et al. 2017: 22)*

Other men also said they felt it important to support their wives by completing some care tasks when they returned from work, although women in some focus groups indicated that this was rare (Rohwerder et al. 2017). Similarly, the Tanzania study found a disjuncture between the norms and values that men adhered to in public (for example, in a focus group discussion with other men) and their private attitudes. In focus group discussions, men agreed that "if you help your wife with [care] activities, she will think you're under her control," but in individual interviews they recounted undertaking a variety of unpaid care work activities (Zambelli et al. 2017: 28).

In some cases, men stepped-in to perform unpaid care work because their wives were away from home and they had no choice; in others, it was the recognition that "I can see that she is doing a lot for the family and I would not want her to be exhausted" (Zambelli et al. 2017: 29). Unusually, the Tanzania study found greater flexibility in the work children undertake as they get older. In most other contexts, norms about gender roles become more rigid during adolescence.

The study also found some sharing of household tasks in specific circumstances, such as during pregnancy, after childbirth, or when women were menstruating (in Nepal), as well as more task sharing among younger couples. Despite greater flexibility in the two African countries (Rwanda and Tanzania), men's involvement in all four countries was generally framed as 'helping' women, rather than viewing these tasks as a shared responsibility (Chopra and Zambelli 2017; Rohwerder et al. 2017). As the study concluded:

> [W]here women felt overburdened or unable to undertake tasks normatively framed as theirs, their first recourse was to daughters and older women, though in some interviews they expressed a desire for a more equal division of labour with their spouses.
>
> *(Chopra and Zambelli 2017: 39)*

While many women wished for more equal division of labour, they felt this was impossible in the context of poverty and need for men (and often women) to work long hours, or to migrate, to make ends meet (Chopra and Zambelli 2017; Ghosh et al. 2017). Social disapproval also dissuaded people from challenging norms about gender labour divisions. For example, a young woman in Nepal observed:

> If my husband helps me with my work by washing the dishes, even my mother-in-law teases him for doing so. Also, the other people look down upon me.... The people who want to help hesitate to do so due to the fear of being ridiculed by the village.
>
> *(Ghosh et al. 2017: 25)*

Kamanzi et al.'s (2017) study from a different part of Tanzania found similar patterns of norm change and tensions surrounding it. The young women interviewed generally expressed egalitarian views about childcare and gender divisions of labour. However, both young men and women reported that the older men held reservations:

> I think that there is no big problem with working mothers. Of course, older people like my father would not like to hear the story because they think women must be goalkeepers [sic] and therefore they should not work. (young woman)
>
> I do not care what they think. I just care what I think that it is a very good thing that a mother works. There are so many ways one can take care of children. (young woman)
>
> I know that some people think that such mothers are hopeless because they have left their families. For example, my father always complains about Mr X's wife because she goes to work and comes back in the evening. (young man)
>
> *(cited in Kamanzi et al. 2017: 15)*

Five studies in the GrOW portfolio explored the impact of gendered norms around care responsibilities for women on their economic opportunities; in all cases, they were significantly constraining. The study on young women's transition to the labour market in six African countries (Burkina Faso, Ethiopia, Ghana, Kenya, Tanzania, and Uganda) found that, in every country, the presence of young children in households reduced the likelihood of a young woman receiving a good education and thus obtaining a high quality job, irrespective of whether the children were her own or those of another female household member (McKay et al.

2018). This may reflect demands on young women and older girls to care for these children, although girls who have dropped out of school or live in places with few economic opportunities may also start families earlier (Mariara et al. 2018). Having children under six years of age—particularly if they are closely spaced—is negatively associated with women's non-farm employment (Ahaibwe, Ssewanyana, and Kasirye 2018b).

GrOW-supported research from the Centre for Budget and Policy Studies (CBPS 2018) found that the need to care for children was the single most commonly reported reason for women not working outside the home in Karnataka, India. However, this did not imply that women were not involved in economic activity—the need to work in a family business was the second most commonly given reason. Similarly, the study of artisanal mining in Central and East Africa found that 33% of women recorded family obligations as a major factor reducing their work hours, compared with 14% of men (Buss et al. 2017b). These reduced hours limit their earnings and their ability to network and build livelihood connections. The expectation that a woman's first duty is to her family and husband also tended to discourage married women from working in the mining sector—nearly 35% of women working in artisanal mining were divorced, separated, widowed, or never married, compared with only 23% of men. Norms about domestic responsibilities and mobility, as well as more limited access to transport, meant that women tended to sell minerals near the extraction zone where they received a lower price than men who were able to travel further afield.

This tension between paid work and care responsibilities is corroborated by GrOW research in northern Sri Lanka, where women—particularly those in female-headed households with little family support—mentioned that care work prevented or limited them from engaging in certain livelihood activities (Lakshman 2017). Safety concerns were paramount for single mothers with daughters. One respondent highlighted ambivalence toward women working outside the home, citing her sisters' reluctance to take care of her children (Lakshman 2017: 22). As a result, 56% of women respondents in Sri Lanka engaged only in livelihood activities that could be conducted from home (Jeyaseker and Ganeda 2018).

Norms around education, adolescent marriage, and childbearing

Overall, GrOW studies highlighted the negative impact of early marriage on women's economic outcomes and the malleability of norms around early marriage where economic or educational opportunities are expanding. For example, Kis-Katos, Pieters, and Sparrow (2018) found that trade liberalisation in Indonesia had increased women's labour force participation and contributed to a rising median age at marriage (early- to mid-20s).

The study of young women's transitions to the labour market in six African countries (Mariara et al. 2018) confirmed the importance of education for obtaining high quality work and highlighted the impact of discriminatory social norms on girls' educational and work outcomes. The overall positive policy environment for girls' education in many African countries (which has included fee waivers and incentives in some countries) has probably contributed to girls staying in school longer and a rising age of marriage or first birth among younger women (Mariara et al. 2018).

Research in Kenya undertaken for this study found a strong negative correlation between marrying or having a child before age 18 and the level of education attained (Kabubo-Mariara et al. 2016). The Uganda research team found that women who married or gave birth before 20 years of age were less likely to be in professional/technical and managerial positions and were more likely to work in subsistence agriculture (55% as compared to 40% of women who married later) (Ahaibwe, Ssewanyana, and Kasirye 2018a). The Uganda research team also found that having parents with secondary education greatly reduced young women's risk of early marriage, childbearing, and labour market entry (Ssewanyana, Ahaiwe, and Kasirye 2018).

Of the six countries, the research in Uganda best demonstrates the role of social norms in early marriage. Ahaibwe, Ssewanyana, and Kasirye (2018a: 16) found that traditional norms persisted about the relative value to households of a girl's education compared to obtaining bride price:

> It's better to marry off the girls early and get cows early so that they start reproducing rather than waiting for a girl to go through education with the hope of getting a job and provide for the family thereafter. By this time the cow would have reproduced and brought in more wealth and income. (male FGD participant, Yumbe)

More commonly, discriminatory norms intersected with limited educational availability. Having a primary school in one's village was associated with lower rates of marriage before age 18 (Ssewanyana, Ahaiwe, and Kasirye 2018). Focus groups indicated that where there was no secondary school nearby, families were willing for boys to travel by bicycle. Out of concerns about girls' safety, they felt that girls would have to board or rent a room near the school, both of which were prohibitively expensive. Furthermore, parents feared that girls living independently would get pregnant. Concerns for girls' safety also led parents to enrol them late, increasing the likelihood of dropping out before completing their schooling. Norms around girls returning to school after giving birth were generally negative. As focus group participants reported:

> Going back to school after giving birth is completely unheard of. Parents think it is a wastage of money, teachers think teenage mothers will spoil other pupils in school, and there is generally a lot of stigma around teenage mothers from fellow students and teachers.
>
> *(Ahaibwe, Ssewanyana, and Kasirye 2018a: 14)*

Ssewanyana, Ahaiwe, and Kasirye (2018) found that the prevalence of marriage among girls under 18 years of age influences others to also marry. This likely reflects peer pressure that normalises early marriage, supported by social norms. As one participant in Ahaibwe, Ssewanyana, and Kasirye's (2018a: 19) rural focus groups put it: "almost every girl gets married at around 15 or 16 years, so it's the order of the day." These focus groups also highlighted the lack of examples of young people who had been able to escape poverty after completing their education.

Once married, girls and women can face significant work restrictions, as outlined above. As a 17-year-old focus group participant said:

> My husband dictates the kind of work I can engage in, he even restricts me on the number of hours I can work.
>
> *(Ahaibwe, Ssewanyana, and Kasirye 2018a: 22)*

In a very different context, qualitative evidence from Bangladesh found stronger social support for women continuing education after marriage if they had already completed secondary school (i.e. they were attending tertiary-level education) than if they were still to complete high school (Field, Glennerster, and Nazneen 2018). This may reflect intersecting norms about schools being for children, and thus inappropriate places for married women, whereas, as adult education institutions, colleges may be attended by married or unmarried young people. It may also point to the importance of policies in this context that deter marriage before young people have completed secondary school.

Norms about sexual and gender-based violence

> It's common for men to make fun of us, whether we are married or not, when we go to work, we have to face those problems. We cannot say there are no issues. (participant in Sri Lanka)
>
> *(Subrahmaniam 2017: 23)*

Three GrOW studies reported that sexual and gender-based violence (GBV) deter women's economic activity. While they did not discuss norms about such violence directly, its prevalence and reactions to it indicate that it is widespread and unacceptable to women and some men.

Research in northern Sri Lanka found workplace sexual harassment to be common. Both women's own fear of violence and fear of violence against daughters left at home deterred them from working outside the home (Subrahmaniam 2017). Similarly, the artisanal mining studies found that night work was considered unsuitable for women in Uganda because of the risk of sexual violence, thus reinforcing job segregation (Buss et al. 2017a). In response, some women formed all-female digging teams to avoid sexual harassment or negative comments from men. In some mines, bosses were willing to act to counter harassment, including threatening to take the foremen of tunnels where it occurred to court. This shows that while a practice may be common, it is not necessarily accepted.

The GrOW-supported study by the Urban Institute on transport safety in Lahore, Pakistan, cites data showing that 82% of women bus riders have experienced sexual harassment at a bus stop and 90% have experienced it on buses (United Nations 2017 cited in Irvin-Erickson et al. 2020). As a result, 87% of men surveyed would recommend their female relatives use a women-only van for transportation. However, Irvin-Erickson et al.'s (2020) interviews indicated limited support for women-only transport. Instead they favoured educating men to 'behave'—to change norms and behaviour around sexual harassment. They also found that, although women were taking shorter journeys, they spent considerably more money per journey on transport, usually because they used more expensive services perceived to be safer than public transport, such as ridesharing or Uber. Irvin-Erickson et al. (2020) found that women were extremely reluctant to report harassment because of norms against reporting, they feared retribution, and they had little confidence that reporting would lead to change.

Three quantitative studies also explored another side of the relationship between economic empowerment and GBV—whether WEE is associated with increased intimate partner violence (IPV), as some studies have found (ICRW 2019). Using Demographic and Health Survey (DHS) data from 35 countries, Khan and Klasen (2018) found no robust evidence that women's employment is associated with IPV, except in Latin America and East Africa and among women working in agriculture. They speculated that women working in agriculture did not earn enough to offset the loss of control men experience when their wives are wage earners. Also examining DHS data, Peters et al. (2018) found that attitudes toward violence change indirectly over time as economic development leads to rising education levels, urbanisation, and media exposure, but that this is a slow process. They concluded that relying on economic development to weaken norms supporting violence is likely to be ineffective and that more focused policy attention is needed to change attitudes and practices.

Norms around ownership and control of assets

The most direct evidence from the GrOW portfolio of gender norms negatively affecting women's ownership of physical and financial assets came from research in Uganda:

> Men are hesitant to have joint investment with their wives; once a woman has money, she becomes uncontrollable and disobedient. (male focus group participant, Namayingo)
>
> Apart from working on the family farm, women are not allowed to engage in other economic activities or control assets. (male focus group participant, Yumbe)
>
> *(Ahaibwe, Ssewanyana, and Kasirye 2018a: 22)*

Discriminatory norms are influenced by and underpin legal and policy discrimination related to asset ownership. In Rwanda, for example, married women need their husbands as cosignatories on loan applications and agreements to sell land. This limited their opportunities to become mining subcontractors—men were not always willing to agree to sales or taking on loans because of the level of risk involved—and to engage in some of the more lucrative aspects of mining, such as becoming shaft or pit owners (Buss et al. 2017a).

Studies about the extent of women's involvement in decisions about household expenditures and the use of their earned income also provide some indirect insights into norms about financial asset use. For example, Mahendiran, Jha, and Ghatak (2017) found that more than 80% of women interviewed in Bihar, India, participated in decisions about household expenditures. However, a similar study in Karnataka showed that just over half of interviewees were involved in decision-making about the use of household income (CBPS 2018).

The wider gender norms and economic empowerment literature suggests that discriminatory norms about asset ownership are often stickier than norms about working outside the home (e.g. Munoz Boudet et al. 2012). This may be because the income benefits of work are evident and may require less ceding of control than independent land and property rights, which more deeply challenge patriarchal privilege and entitlement to resources (Baruah 2018). Peters et al.'s (2016) review of enablers and barriers to WEE highlights the positive impact of legal reforms that give women equal access to assets (e.g. through inheritance) or through land rights in their own names. However, this study also points out that, in some cases, egalitarian laws such as Namibia's land rights law have been subverted by local leaders who have discouraged younger women from applying for land rights.

What facilitates change in gender norms?

Supportive policy and institutional environment for women's economic empowerment

Gender norms and the legal, policy, and institutional environment are often discussed as separate "high level factors" influencing WEE (Hunt and Samman 2016; United Nations 2017). However, gender norms do not operate only at household, community, and workplace levels, but shape, and are shaped by, legal and policy frameworks. The GrOW portfolio of studies did not probe these relationships in detail; however, some insights emerged about their implications.

One group of studies examined the relationship between the extent of women's political representation, overall rights, and wellbeing, and found that in sub-Saharan Africa, where traditional (local or clan-based) political structures allow for female representation, women were significantly more educated than those in similar regions where only men occupy traditional political structures

(Anderson et al. 2018a). They were also more likely to have some ownership rights over their home and some land and have significantly higher household decision-making power. However, there was no relationship with labour force participation. Anderson et al. (2018b) also found a positive relationship between women's local political representation, better education and health outcomes, household decision-making, and reduced support for domestic violence. These studies point to the importance of norms that enable women's voice in decision-making as part of a broader enabling environment for WEE.

Norms around women's voice in economic governance also matter, as the studies of artisanal mining in Central and East Africa (Buss et al. 2017a) made clear. Governance arrangements varied significantly between the types of mines, with distinct implications. The formal company structures in Rwanda potentially provided more routes for women to challenge some forms of discrimination and barriers than less formal arrangements. However, they provided fewer accumulation opportunities for women than in "gold rush" sites in Uganda. Buss et al. (2017a) concluded that patriarchal norms infuse the relationships of governance and authority in different ways, limiting women's representation among locally powerful players, and affecting the royalties and other payments expected of them.

Economic empowerment programmes

Only five GrOW studies explored the impacts of economic empowerment programmes on gender norms. These cover a variety of approaches, including individual and collective empowerment; incentives for education, training and delaying marriage; and providing childcare to facilitate paid work. We now examine findings pertaining to each approach in turn.

Building individual and collective voice through broad-based empowerment

GrOW funded a set of studies on the Mahila Samakhya (MS) women's empowerment programme in India, which has been operational for over two decades. The core elements of MS included self-organisation into small groups (*sanghas*) for training, critical discussion and reflection, and linkage to government services. The studies of MS found that participants had greater self-confidence, were better able to voice their opinions, and had increased agency to make decisions and act on them individually and collectively (CBPS 2016). They found increases in women's level of education in districts with a MS programme, greater involvement of women in household decision-making, greater engagement in economic activities, and increased political participation (CBPS 2016, 2018; Mahendiran, Jha, and Ghatak 2017). Finally, these studies found somewhat reduced acceptance of IPV in various scenarios, including a woman getting a job or joining a collective without her husband's permission. Arguably, these aspects of empowerment are among the building blocks of norm change that also underpin WEE.

Incentives for education, training, and delaying marriage

Two studies directly examined the impact of incentives on norms about education, training, and the desirable age of marriage. Field et al. (2016) and Buchmann et al. (2018) explore the impact of both incentive payments and a community-based life skills and empowerment programme, called Kishoree Kontha, in delaying age of marriage and promoting girls' education in Bangladesh. The studies found that receiving an incentive (cooking oil worth a total of $16 per year) to remain unmarried until age 18 contributed to delaying marriage and childbearing and to girls remaining in school. Among girls who were eligible for the subsidy for at least two years, the likelihood of marriage under the age of 18 fell by 25%, and of marriage under 16 by 27%. These girls also completed 2.2 more months of schooling than their counterparts by age 22–25, and among girls who also attended the empowerment programme, this figure rose to 2.4 months of additional schooling. Furthermore, there was no evidence that the girls who received the incentive married shortly after turning 18; marriage rates among recipients and non-recipients only converged by age 22.

The authors suggest that these results may indicate a shift in norms about the desirable age of marriage, in part justified by the offer of an incentive. They may also indicate that parents are waiting to find the right match for their daughters or that girls negotiate to delay their marriages, both of which could reflect broader normative change. The extent to which incentives contribute to broader normative change around child marriage, both in this programme and others, remains controversial (e.g. White 2015; Chae and Ngo 2017; Kalamar, Lee-Rife, and Hinden 2016) and is a subject for broader empirical investigation.

By contrast, GrOW-supported research on the Punjab Economic Opportunity Program in Pakistan found that incentives to facilitate women's training were not enough to change deep-seated gender norms (Cheema et al. 2019). However, having training opportunities within the village increased women's participation in training by 35%. Providing safe transport to training opportunities outside the village also increased uptake by some 17–18%.[7] Overall, women themselves and their families found this form of engagement in paid work acceptable if women could work from their villages.

Providing childcare to facilitate paid work

The two studies of childcare provision—one from Kenya (Clark et al. 2017) and one from India (Richardson et al. 2018)—found that daycare was used where it was available, implying that norms about women looking after their own children are not binding. In the Kenya study, undertaken in a Nairobi slum, Clark et al. (2017) found that having access to an early childcare centre increased the likelihood of women being employed by 17%, rising to 20% among women who used these centres.[8] In rural Rajasthan, Richardson et al. (2018) found that 41% of mothers in hamlets with nongovernmental childcare centres used them to some extent.

However, these centres only reduced time spent on childcare by an average of 10.6 minutes per day and increased the probability of working year-round, rather than seasonally, by 2.2 percentage points. This relatively small increase in labour force participation may reflect limited employment opportunities in rural Rajasthan. These results are broadly consistent with the findings of Harper, Austin, and Nandi's (2017) systematic review, which found moderate positive impacts of childcare on women's labour force participation, mostly in Latin America. However, it did not examine impacts on norms about childcare or gendered divisions of labour.

The GrOW study on paid work and unpaid care, in India, Nepal, Rwanda, and Tanzania mentioned earlier, explored the impact of childcare provision on norms about the gendered division of labour. It found no difference in the sharing of care tasks between men and women, and among women who participated in economic empowerment programmes versus those who did not (Chopra and Zambelli 2017: 20).

Conclusions

Although few of the GrOW studies were designed to examine the implications of social and gender norms for WEE, they have generated many important insights. These studies indicate both persistence of and change in norms about women's economic activity and in wider norms that shape choices about that activity. Consistent with the wider literature, they suggest that increasing levels of education, widespread economic stress, and emerging economic opportunities in some contexts have contributed to 'relaxing' gender norms (Munoz Boudet et al. 2012), if not changing them. Elsewhere, however, norm-based constraints appear more binding and continue to limit women's economic options. The GrOW studies provide some evidence of emerging generational differences, with younger people adopting more flexible gender norms, particularly in East Africa.

Norms about women working

GrOW studies found that the strength of norms about work outside the home varies considerably by social and economic context. In many of the study contexts, norms idealising women's roles as homemakers are strong. However, as is recognised in the wider literature, low-income women are more likely to contravene prevailing gender norms to make ends meet, while economic opportunities for more highly educated women often lead to more flexibility among higher income groups. Studies of economic change (such as trade liberalisation) find an increasing entry of women into paid labour in some contexts, indicating that growing opportunities can lead to shifts in gender norms.

Norms about suitable work for women and men

Consistent with the wider literature, GrOW studies highlighted the role of gender norms in maintaining gendered work segregation. This was often enforced via gossip or intimidation, as well as outright prohibitions on women engaging in certain kinds of work (particularly in mining). These norms were closely tied to those governing propriety, women's mobility, contact between unrelated men and women, and responsibility for domestic care work. Women's unequal access to assets also contributed to work segregation; they were typically concentrated in self-employment activities that could be undertaken with limited capital.

Norms about mobility and respectability

Norms about whether women should work, and in which occupations, are also strongly tied to cultural values about decorum and respectability. The South Asian studies found a preference for women working from home; working in prestigious female-dominated activities, such as tutoring; or not engaging in paid work. In all cases, with family support, some determined women were able to defy these norms. Studies from Central and East Africa also found that norms of decorum, appropriate dress, and contact between men and women restricted women's involvement in underground mining.

Norms about unpaid care work

Norms assigning most of the unpaid household work to women emerged as a major constraint to their paid economic activity and affected their mobility. These norms were linked to idealised notions of womanhood and were partially enforced through fear of gossip and criticism from other community members. Norms about unpaid care were found to be stickier in South Asia than in sub-Saharan Africa, where some change in younger women's and men's attitudes and practices is evident. Prevailing norms support traditional gender divisions of labour, however.

Norms about asset ownership

The studies that probed asset ownership found that both informal norms and, in some cases, laws related to asset ownership undermined women's access to assets. Consistent with the wider literature showing that egalitarian inheritance and land rights laws have often been subverted locally, the mining studies found that legal frameworks tended to favour holders of mining rights over land holders, and that women's formal legal rights were often not understood or were ignored. GrOW studies also found discriminatory norms limiting women's access to property upon divorce. Norms about women's control of income varied depending on contexts.

Sexual and gender-based violence

Fear of sexual and GBV significantly constrained women's economic activity. The prevalence of such violence and harassment indicates that it may be a descriptive norm in some research contexts, although none of the studies probed the norms that uphold such behaviour. The two quantitative studies that used DHS data to examine whether women's increased labour force activity is associated with increased IPV found a clear relationship only in Latin America and East Africa, and for women working in agriculture. This suggests that the hypothesis that IPV is rising in backlash against gender norm change needs some qualification.

Norms about education, adolescent marriage, and childbearing

Studies of the relationship between education, child marriage, and labour market outcomes in East and West Africa highlight the central role of education in facilitating women's access to higher quality (better paid, more stable, formal sector) jobs. Child labour and adolescent marriage and childbearing are associated with lower levels of education and lower likelihood of quality work, and these are supported by societal norms in some contexts. There is some evidence of a trend toward later marriage (early- to mid-20s) where economic opportunities are expanding, or where educational incentive programmes are effective.

Economic empowerment programmes and norm change

The GrOW studies examined three main strategies: provision of childcare, provision of incentives, and broad-based empowerment approaches. For each strategy, there were a maximum of three studies, and insights about impacts on norms are thus suggestive rather than clearly established.

The childcare studies found that if good quality daycare is available, families are generally willing to use it, indicating that norms about family-based care are not binding. The studies of incentives indicate that in-kind incentives are helping girls stay in school and delay marriage in Bangladesh, which may lead to new norms about the appropriate age of marriage. Evidence from Pakistan suggests that incentives for vocational training were most widely taken up in activities and locations consistent with prevailing norms (they required little mobility and involved gender-segregated work). The studies of MS (a broad-based women's empowerment programme) also show some positive impacts on discriminatory gender norms in contexts of entrenched inequalities.

Gaps

Consideration of the relationship between social norms and WEE is a relatively young field, with many knowledge gaps. Assessment of the insights from GrOW and the wider literature suggests that future research could helpfully focus on filling several gaps.

First, no studies identified norms or beliefs that facilitate WEE, such as norms of respectful behaviour toward women as colleagues or customers. Buss et al. (2017a) found that women sometimes benefitted from stereotypes of women as more honest than men, although norms that limited women's economic opportunities were much more common. Further probing of supportive norms may help identify values and processes that could be strengthened to promote WEE. One possible entry point could be norms supporting women's involvement in non-traditional work areas.

Second, with some notable exceptions—such as Chopra and Zambelli (2018) and Irvin-Erickson et al. (2020)—norms of masculinity are rarely discussed in relation to WEE. This may reflect a primary focus on women and constraints on their economic activity or methodological issues such as lack of relevant data in the secondary data sets used. Further probing might reveal both relatively malleable and resistant norms and enable a stronger focus on more deeply entrenched norms in change campaigns.

Third, apart from geographical differences, the GrOW studies provide a relatively broad-brush overview of the ways that social and gender norms affect WEE. Many studies referred to women living in poverty or not far above poverty lines. More differentiated, intersectional analysis would be valuable, as norms are often stickier in some socio-cultural groups than others, and greater clarity would help develop more nuanced change strategies.

Fourth, many of the quantitative studies supported by GrOW indicated links between structural economic change (e.g. GDP growth and trade liberalisation) and social trends (e.g. trends in marriage and childbearing), without discussing their relationship with gender norms. Focused qualitative studies exploring norm change or lack of change associated with these trends would help understand the relative role of norms and other factors as supportive of, malleable in pursuit of, or putting the brakes on WEE.

Finally, a body of work on effective ways to support WEE is emerging, with growing attention to addressing norm-based barriers. A critical question is whether policies and approaches currently considered good practices in economic empowerment are effective in changing gender norms, since this means that effects are much more likely to be sustained over the long-term. Understanding this would require both qualitative and quantitative studies of specific policy changes, particularly those related to employment, where evidence lags behind self-employment and asset ownership.

Notes

1 The portfolio of studies also generated some insights on the role of economic empowerment programmes in shifting gender norms and the relationship between the policy and institutional environment, social/gender norms, and WEE.

2 Some other programmes had mixed-methods components with insights on gender norms (e.g. the research on transport safety in Lahore undertaken as part of the Urban Institute programme (Irvin-Erickson et al. 2020)).

3 Klein (2017) additionally distinguishes norms about the economy that disadvantage women, such as the devaluation of care work and of the informal sector where women are often overrepresented.

4 For a review of how gender overlaps with other socioeconomic inequalities in determining the position of men and women within the occupational hierarchies of the market, see Chapter 1 in this volume.

5 Chapter 9 in this volume explores the demographic, socioeconomic, institutional, and conflict-related factors that have influenced women's labour force participation in Sri Lanka's Northern Province.
6 The word *purdah* means seclusion and applies to the behaviour of women to seclude themselves in front of men, such as covering one's face or not being alone with a man in a public place.
7 This finding has some resonance with Lei, Desai, and Vanneman (2017) who found that the positive impact of transportation infrastructure on women's non-farm employment in India is stronger in communities with more egalitarian gender norms (measured by proportion of women practicing *purdah*). Where *purdah* is widely practiced, improved transport infrastructure has little effect as women are constrained by seclusion norms from taking up work outside the home.
8 For more information on the results of this study in Kenya, see Chapter 7 in this volume. For information about the relationship between women's unpaid care, paid work, and economic empowerment more broadly, see Chapters 4 and 8 in this volume.

References

Ahaibwe, Gemma, Sarah Ssewanyana, and Ibrahim Kasirye (2018a). Education, marriage, fertility and labour market experiences of young women in Uganda: Evidence from a qualitative assessment. Occasional Paper 46. Kampala: Economic Policy Research Centre. https://media.africaportal.org/documents/Education_marriage_fertility_and_labour_market_experiences.pdf.

Ahaibwe, Gemma, Sarah Ssewanyana, and Ibrahim Kasirye (2018b). Early labour market transitions of young women in Uganda. Occasional Paper 44. Kampala: Economic Policy Research Centre. https://eprcug.org/gemma-ahaibwe-publications/556-early-labour-market-transitions-of-young-women-in-uganda/download.

ALIGN (2018). Gender norms theory FAQS. ODI: ALIGN Project. www.alignplatform.org.

ALIGN (forthcoming). *Guide to Gender Norms and Women's Economic Empowerment.* London: ALIGN.

Anderson, Siwan, Sophia Du Plessis, Sahar Parsa, and James Robinson (2018a). Traditional female political representation in Sub-Saharan Africa. Montreal: GrOW. http://cournot.sun.ac.za/fppssa/docs/papers/fppssa-political-wp-april2018.pdf.

Anderson, Siwan, Sophia Du Plessis, Sahar Parsa, and James Robinson (2018b). Local female political representation in Sub-Saharan Africa. Montreal: GrOW. http://cournot.sun.ac.za/fppssa/docs/papers/fppssa-political-wp-april2018.pdf.

Asadullah, M. Niaz, and Zaki Wahhaj (2016). Missing from the market: *Purdah* norm and women's paid work participation in Bangladesh. IZA Discussion Paper Series, No. 10463. Bonn: Institute of Labor Economics (IZA). http://ftp.iza.org/dp10463.pdf.

Baah-Boateng, William, Priscilla Twumasi Baffour, and Emmanuel K. Akyeampong (2017). Gender differences in the extractive sector: A case study of mining in Ghana. Accra: University of Ghana International Institute for Advanced Studies, mimeo.

Baruah, Bipasha (2018). Women on wheels in New Delhi, India: Empowering women through an innovative training and employment program. GrOW Working Paper Series, GWP-2018-13. Montreal: Institute for the Study of International Development, McGill University. http://grow.research.mcgill.ca/publications/working-papers/gwp-2018-13.pdf.

Buchmann, Nina, Erica Field, Rachel Glennerster, Shahana Nazneen, Svetlana Pimkina, and Iman Sen (2018). Power vs money: Alternative approaches to reducing child marriage in Bangladesh, a randomized control trial. Cambridge: J-PAL. https://www.povertyactionlab.org/sites/default/files/research-paper/Power-vs-Money-Working-Paper.pdf.

Buss, Doris, Blair Rutherford, Jennifer Hinton, Jennifer Stewart, Joanne Lebert, Abby Sebina-Zziwa, Richard Kibombo, and Frederick Kisekka (2017a). Gender and artisanal and small-scale mining in Central and East Africa: Barriers and benefits. GrOW Working Paper Series, GWP-2017–02. Montreal: Institute for the Study of International Development, McGill University. https://grow.research.mcgill.ca/publications/working-papers/gwp-2017-02.pdf.

Buss, Doris, Blair Rutherford, Mary O'Neill, Alejandra Vargas, and Martha Melesse. (2017b). Empowering women in artisanal and small-scale mining in Central and East Africa. GrOW Policy Brief. Ottawa: IDRC. https://idl-bnc-idrc.dspacedirect.org/bitstream/handle/10625/56530/IDL-56530.pdf?sequence=2&isAllowed=y.

CBPS (2016). Why it is important to retain an independent Mahila Samakhya programme – A policy brief. Bengaluru: Centre for Budget and Policy Studies. https://cbps.in/wp-content/uploads/Final-MSPolicyBrief-28Jan2016.pdf.

CBPS (2018). Mahila Samakhya: A descriptive analysis of a baseline study in Haveri, Karnataka. CBPS-GrOW Working Paper No. 4. Bengaluru: Centre for Budget and Policy Studies. http://cbps.in/wp-content/uploads/CBPS-GrOW-Karnataka-Report_compressed-1.pdf.

Chae, Sophia, and Thoai D. Ngo (2017). The global state of evidence on interventions to prevent child marriage. GIRL Center Research Brief No. 1. New York: Population Council. www.popcouncil.org/uploads/pdfs/2017PGY_GIRLCenterResearchBrief_01.pdf.

Cheema, Ali, Asim I. Khwaja, Farooq Naseer, and Jacob Shapiro (2019). Glass walls: Experimental evidence on access constraints faced by women. Working Paper. https://khwaja.scholar.harvard.edu/files/asimkhwaja/files/glass_walls_draft_november_draft.pdf.

Cheema, Ali, Asim I. Khwaja, Muhammad Farooq Naseer, and Jacob Shapiro (2017). Designing active labor market policies in Southern Punjab: Evidence from household and community surveys. Working Paper. Punjab: Institute of Development and Economic Alternatives. https://ideaspak.org/wp-content/files_mf/1538545570PunjabEconomicOpportunitiesSkillsReport.pdf.

Chopra, Deepta, and Elena Zambelli (2017). No time to rest: Women's lived experiences of balancing paid work and unpaid care work. Global Synthesis Report. Brighton: Institute of Development Studies. https://www.ids.ac.uk/publications/no-time-to-rest-womens-lived-experiences-of-balancing-paid-work-and-unpaid-care-work/.

Cislaghi, Ben, Karima Manji, and Lori Heise (2018). Social norms and gender-related harmful practices: Theory in support of better practice. STRIVE Learning Report 2. London: London School of Hygiene & Tropical Medicine. http://strive.lshtm.ac.uk/system/files/attachments/STRIVE%20Norms%20Report%202.pdf.

Clark, Shelley, Sonia Laszlo, Caroline Kabiru, and Stella Muthuri (2017). Can subsidized early child care promote women's employment? Evidence from a slum settlement in Africa. GrOW Working Paper Series, GWP-2017–05. Montreal: Institute for the Study of International Development, McGill University. http://grow.research.mcgill.ca/pubs/gwp-05-2017.pdf.

Field, Erica, Rachel Glennerster, and Shahana Nazneen (2018). Economic empowerment of young women in Bangladesh: Barriers and strategies. The International Policy Centre for Inclusive Growth, Policy in Focus Vol. 15(1).

Field, Erica, Rachel Glennerster, Nina Buchmann, and Kyle Murphy (2016). Cost-benefit analysis of strategies to reduce child marriage in Bangladesh. Copenhagen: Copenhagen Consensus Center. www.copenhagenconsensus.com/sites/default/files/field_child_marriage.pdf.

Gallup, and ILO (2017). Towards a better future for women and work: Voices of women and men. ILO-Gallup Report. Geneva: International Labour Organization. www.ilo.org/wcmsp5/groups/public/---dgreports/---dcomm/---publ/documents/publication/wcms_546256.pdf.

Ghosh, Anweshaa, Anjam Singh, Shraddha Chigateri, Deepta Chopra, and Catherine Müller (2017). A trapeze act: Balancing unpaid care work by women in Nepal. IDS Working Paper 500. Brighton: Institute of Development Studies. https://opendocs.ids.ac.uk/opendocs/handle/123456789/13338.

Gunatilaka, Ramani and Ranmini Vithanagama (2018). Women's labour market outcomes and livelihood interventions in Sri Lanka's North after the war. Working Paper. Colombo: International Centre for Ethnic Studies. http://ices.lk/wp-content/uploads/2018/03/Women%E2%80%99s-Labour-Market-Outcomes-and-Livelihood-Interventions-in-Sri-Lanka%E2%80%99s-North-After-the-War.pdf.

Harper, Sam, Nichole Austin, and Arijit Nandi (2017). Daycare and women's health, social, and economic outcomes in low- and middle-income countries: Systematic review and evidence synthesis. GrOW Working Paper Series, GWP-2017–07. Montreal: Institute for the Study of International Development, McGill University. http://grow.research.mcgill.ca/publications/working-papers/gwp-2017-07.pdf.

Heintz, James, Naila Kabeer, and Simeen Mahmud (2017). Cultural norms, economic incentives and women's labour market behaviour: Empirical insights from Bangladesh. *Oxford Development Studies* 46(2): 266–289. https://www.tandfonline.com/doi/full/10.1080/13600818.2017.1382464

Hunt, Abigail, and Emma Samman (2016). Women's economic empowerment: Navigating enablers and constraints. Research Report. London: Overseas Development Institute. www.odi.org/sites/odi.org.uk/files/resource-documents/10683.pdf.

ICRW (2019). Women entrepreneurs need more than capital: What do women's businesses really need to grow and thrive? Washington, DC: International Centre for Research on Women. www.icrw.org/wp-content/uploads/2019/10/Women-Entrepreneurship-Beyond-Capital_final.pdf.

ILO (2018). World employment and social outlook: Trends for women 2018—Global snapshot. Geneva: International Labour Organization. http://www.ilo.org/wcmsp5/groups/public/---dgreports/---dcomm/---publ/documents/publication/wcms_619577.pdf.

Irvin-Erickson, Yasemin, Ammar Malik, Faisal Kamiran, and Mangai Natarajan (2020). Utility of ecological momentary assessments to collect data on fear of crime. *International Journal of Comparative and Applied Criminal Justice* 44(4): 307–319. https://www.tandfonline.com/doi/full/10.1080/01924036.2020.1719532.

Jayachandran, Seema (2019). Social norms as a barrier to women's employment in developing countries. Evanston, IL: Northwestern University. http://faculty.wcas.northwestern.edu/~sjv340/social_norms_flfp.pdf.

Jeyaseker, Vasuki and Ganeda, Savini (2018). Making ends meet: Women's livelihoods in post-war Sri Lanka. Colombo: International Centre for Ethnic Studies. http://ices.lk/wp-content/uploads/2018/03/Making-Ends-Meet-Women%E2%80%99s-Livelihoods-in-Post-War-Sri-Lanka.pdf.

Kabubo-Mariara, Jane, Anthony Wambugu, and Phyllis Machio (2016). Early labour market transitions of women in low-income African countries: A descriptive analysis of education outcomes, fertility decisions and labour market outcomes of youths in Kenya. Working paper. https://catalog.ihsn.org/index.php/citations/78428.

Kalamar, Amanda M., Susan Lee-Rife, and Michelle J. Hindin (2016). Interventions to prevent child marriage among young people in low- and middle-income countries: A systematic review of the published and gray literature. *Journal of Adolescent Health* 59(3): 16–21. https://jhu.pure.elsevier.com/en/publications/interventions-to-prevent-child-marriage-among-young-people-in-low.

Kamanzi, A., Andy McKay, Andy Newell, Cinzia Rienzo, and Wiktoria Tafesse (2017). Gender gaps in work outcomes after 19 years: Analysis based on the Kagera panel 1991–

2010. GrOW. https://editorialexpress.com/cgi-bin/conference/download.cgi?db_name=CSAE2018&paper_id=661.

Khan, Sarah, and Stephan Klasen (2018). Female employment and spousal abuse: A parallel cross-country analysis from developing economies. Courant Research Centre Poverty, Equity and Growth Discussion Paper 249. Göttingen: Courant Research Centre. www2.vwl.wiso.uni-goettingen.de/courant-papers/CRC-PEG_DP_249final.pdf.

Klasen, Stephan (2018). The impact of gender inequality on economic performance in developing countries. *Annual Review of Resource Economics* 10: 279–298. www.annualreviews.org/doi/pdf/10.1146/annurev-resource-100517-023429.

Klasen, Stephan (2019). What explains uneven female labor force participation levels and trends in developing countries? *World Bank Research Observer* 34: 161–197.

Klein, Elise (2017). Norms and women's economic empowerment. Background Paper for the UN Secretary-General's High-Level Panel on Women's Economic Empowerment. New York: United Nations. www2.unwomen.org/-/media/hlp%20wee/attachments/other-materials/briefing-papers/norms%20and%20womens%20economic%20empowerment.pdf?la=en&vs=1919.

Kis-Katos, Krisztina, Janneke Pieters, and Robert Sparrow (2018). Globalization and social change: Gender-specific effects of trade liberalization in Indonesia. *IMF Economic Review* 66(4): 763–793.

Kodikara, Chulani (2018). Doing this and that: Self-employment and economic survival of women heads of households in Mullaitivu. Colombo: International Centre for Ethnic Studies. http://ices.lk/wp-content/uploads/2018/03/Doing-This-and-That-Self-employment-and-Economic-Survival-of-Women-Heads-of-Households-in-Mullaitivu.pdf.

Lakshman, Iresha M. (2017). Impact of intimate relationships on livelihood activities of women affected by war in Northern Sri Lanka. Colombo: International Centre for Ethnic Studies. http://ices.lk/wp-content/uploads/2017/12/Impact-of-Intimate-relationships-For-Circulation.pdf.

Lei, Lei, Sonalde Desai, and Reeve Vanneman (2017). Village transportation infrastructure and women's non-agricultural employment in India: The conditioning role of community gender context. India Human Development Survey Working Paper No. 2017–2. New Delhi: National Council of Applied Economic Research. https://idl-bnc-idrc.dspacedirect.org/bitstream/handle/10625/59134/IDL-59134.pdf.

Mackie, Gerry, Francesca Moneti, Holly Shakya, and Elaine Denny. (2015). What are social norms? How are they measured? UNICEF: University of California, San Diego Center on Global Justice.

Mahendiran, Shreekanth, Jyotsna Jha, and Neha Ghatak (2017). Understanding the impact of Mahila Samakhya on women's economic empowerment in Bihar. CBPS-GrOW Working Paper No. 1. Bengaluru: Centre for Budget and Policy Studies, mimeo.

Marcus, Rachel and Caroline Harper. (2014). Gender justice and social norms – processes of change for adolescent girls. ODI Report. London: Overseas Development Institute. www.odi.org/sites/odi.org.uk/files/odi-assets/publications-opinion-files/8831.pdf.

Mariara, Jane, Andy McKay, Andy Newell, and Cinzia Rienzo (2018). Gender gaps in the path to adulthood for young females and males in six African countries from the 1990s to the 2010s. *IZA Journal of Development and Migration* 8(16):1–19. https://izajodm.springeropen.com/track/pdf/10.1186/s40176-018-0124-8.

McKay, Andy, Mary O'Neill, Alejandra Vargas, and Martha Melesse (2018). From school to work in six African countries: How are women faring? Montreal: GrOW. https://media.africaportal.org/documents/IDL-56368.pdf.

Munoz Boudet, Ana Maria, Patti Petesch, Carolyn Turk, and Angelica Thumala (2012). On norms and agency: Conversations about gender equality with women and men in 20 countries. Washington, DC: World Bank. http://documents.worldbank.org/curated/en/234151468324057689/pdf/NonAsciiFileName0.pdf.

Pearse, Rebecca, and Raewyn Connell (2016). Gender norms and the economy: Insights from social research. *Feminist Economics* 22(1): 30–53.

Peters, H. Elizabeth, Nan Marie Astone, Ammar A. Malik, Fenohasina Maret, and Caroline Heller (2016). Women's economic empowerment: A review of evidence on enablers and barriers. GrOW Program Report No. 1. Ottawa: IDRC. https://idl-bnc-idrc.dspacedirect.org/bitstream/handle/10625/56943/IDL-56943.pdf?sequence=2&isAllowed=y.

Peters, H. Elizabeth, Breno Braga, Tyler Woods, Adaeze Okoli, and Nan Marie Aston (2018). Economic growth, intimate partner violence and attitudes towards wife-beating. Population Institute of America, 2019 Annual Meeting, Austin, TX, April 10–13. http://paa2019.populationassociation.org/uploads/193101.

Petesch, Patti (2013). The clash of violent conflict, good jobs, and gender norms in four economies. Background Paper for the World Development Report 2013. Washington DC: World Bank. https://openknowledge.worldbank.org/bitstream/handle/10986/12130/WDR2013_bp_Clash_of_Violent_Conflict.pdf?sequence=1&isAllowed=y.

Richardson, Robin, Sam Harper, Norbert Schmitz, and Arijit Nandi (2018). The effect of affordable daycare on women's mental health: Evidence from a cluster randomized trial in rural India. *Social Science & Medicine* 217: 32–41.

Ridgeway, Cecelia (2009). Framed before we know it: How gender shapes social relations. *Gender & Society* 23(2): 145–160.

Rohwerder, Brigitte, Catherine Müller, Birasa Nyamulinda, Deepta Chopra, Elena Zambelli, and Naomi Hossain (2017). "You cannot live without money": Balancing women's unpaid care work and paid work in Rwanda. IDS Working Paper 498. Brighton: Institute of Development Studies. https://opendocs.ids.ac.uk/opendocs/bitstream/handle/20.500.12413/13337/Wp498_Online.pdf?sequence=657&isAllowed=y.

Ssewanyana, Sarah, Gemma Ahaiwe, and Ibrahim Kasirye (2018). Drivers for early labour market transitions of young women in Uganda: Evidence from the 2015 school to work transition survey. Occasional Paper 45. Kampala: Economic Policy Research Centre. https://media.africaportal.org/documents/Drivers_for_early_labour_market_transitions_of_young_women_in_Uganda_45_2.pdf.

Subrahmaniam, Jeevasuthan (2017). War and recovery: Psychosocial challenges in Northern Sri Lanka. Colombo: International Centre for Ethnic Studies. http://ices.lk/wp-content/uploads/2017/12/War-Recovery-Psychosocial-Chanlenges-For-Circulation.pdf.

United Nations (2017). Leave no one behind. A call to action for gender equality and women's economic empowerment, UN Secretary General's High Level Panel on Women's Economic Empowerment. New York: UN. www.unscn.org/uploads/web/news/UNSG-HLP-WEE-2nd-Report-.pdf.

Vaitla, Bapu, Alice Taylor, Julia Van Horn, and Beniamino Cislaghi (2017). *Social Norms and Girls' Well-Being: Linking Theory and Practice*. Washington, DC: Data 2.X.

White, Sarah C. (2015). Qualitative perspectives on the impact evaluation of girls' empowerment in Bangladesh. *Journal of Development Effectiveness* 7(2): 127–145.

Zambelli, Elena, Keetie Roelen, Naomi Hossain, Deepta Chopra, and Jenipher Twebaze Musoke (2017). "How can it be a problem if you need them both?" Women juggling paid and unpaid care work in Tanzania, IDS Working Paper 495. Brighton: Institute of Development Studies. https://jhu.pure.elsevier.com/en/publications/interventions-to-prevent-child-marriage-among-young-people-in-low.

PART III

Evidence from GrOW-supported case studies in developing country contexts

6

A MINE OF ONE'S OWN?

Gender norms and empowerment in artisanal and small-scale mining

Doris Buss, Blair Rutherford, Jennifer Stewart, Gisèle Eva Côté, Abby Sebina-Zziwa, Richard Kibombo, Jennifer Hinton, and Joanne Lebert

Introduction

This chapter explores the idea of change as it relates to gender norms and women's economic empowerment (WEE). Change is very much at the heart of the 2016 United Nations High-Level Panel Report on WEE. The final report of the Panel is a "Call to Action" with over a hundred pages of analysis and recommendations aimed at "breaking the constraints on women's economic empowerment" (United Nations 2016: 2). WEE is also about change; changing the power relations that shape and limit access to resources, self-conception, and realisation of full equality (Kabeer 2005, 2017; Cornwall and Rivas 2015).

Artisanal and small-scale mining (ASM) is an economic sector in which change, and calls for change, also figure. This form of mining, which generally uses limited mechanisation but with high labour inputs, is growing steadily, supporting an estimated 70 million people in sub-Saharan Africa alone (World Bank 2019: 13). Various efforts are focused on formalising the ASM sector—integrating it into the formal economy through legal regulation (licences, for example), taxation, financing, and the like—to improve its development potential (Hilson et al. 2017).

In 2018, an international meeting in Zambia was convened by the European Union, the Government of Zambia, the African Union, and several other governmental agencies to discuss ASM and its regulation. The resulting "Mosi-oa-Tunya Declaration" outlines an agenda for the formalisation of ASM, at "the heart" of which is empowered miners and quarry workers able "to chart their own vision of development". Women miners are also specifically referenced with calls to "create more avenues for women to participate in, benefit, and be empowered from mining and its value chains, including the removal of any underlying structural, cultural, social and economic barriers".[1]

Accounting for 30–50% (and in some cases up to 90%) of the ASM labour force (World Bank 2019: 9), women have nonetheless been largely excluded from the array of policy interventions aimed at formalising ASM. Some efforts to advance WEE through participation in mining activities (Hilson et al. 2018) are now being introduced to address this omission, at least in part. These two strands—the formalisation of ASM and the inclusion of women in (some) ASM initiatives—are unfolding, yet not always overlapping, but with calls for change at the heart of both.

In this chapter, we are interested in change in relation to gender norms and women's ASM livelihoods in two respects. The first is about the difference between a focus on chang*ing* versus change *in* gender norms. The High-Level Panel's depiction of gender norms as constraints (that need breaking) invokes a sense of norm fixity in which gender norms act like chains, holding back women's economic potential. The Panel's "Call for Action" is very much directed at change *in* gender norms (to unleash WEE). Our research, while certainly underscoring the importance of this first sense of change, considers gender norms as chang*ing* and changeable, and hence the social practices through which gender norms are constituted, navigated, and sometimes resisted. For the purposes of this chapter, our focus is specifically the gendered authority systems that shape women's ASM livelihoods.

Feminist scholars (Kabeer 2005, 2017; Cornwall and Rivas 2015) have urged an approach to empowerment understood as transformational; entailing change in power relations through which women's lives in the economic, political, and private spheres are navigated. Kabeer defines empowerment as including

> women's self-worth and social identity; their willingness and ability to question their subordinate status and identity; their capacity to exercise strategic control over their own lives and to renegotiate their relationships with others who matter to them; and their ability to participate on equal terms with men in reshaping the societies in which they live in ways that contribute to a more just and democratic distribution of power and possibilities.
>
> *(2008: 27, quoted 2017: 6)*

Cornwall and Rivas (2015: 407) observe that the relational dimension of gender and the transformation of power relations tend to be "closed from view in discourses of women's empowerment".

This chapter aims to place power relations and the authority relations that shape women's ASM livelihoods more centrally in the discussion about gender social norms and their impact on women's economic roles in this sector. We begin with a brief introduction to ASM and the current interest in its formalisation. From there, we draw selectively from our qualitative research from ASM sites in three countries to illustrate the importance, but also the complexity, of gender norms that operate in ASM. These norms, we argue, constrain and shape women's ASM livelihoods, but we suggest that the power of norms is better understood when viewed in terms of the social relations within which gender norms unfold. The third and last substantive section examines in more detail some of the authority relations at the study sites, demonstrating how these are profoundly gendered but also are shaped by other relations of inequality. We explore in this section how existing elites, mostly men, are well positioned to benefit from formalisation, even when it is justified as a route to empower miners. We argue through this chapter that analyses of relations of power and the ways in which existing power structures operate in relation to gender norms are essential if the objective of WEE is, in fact, changing power relations.

The research that informs this chapter was conducted across six ASM sites (two gold; the rest tin, tantalum, or tungsten): two in each of Democratic Republic of Congo (DRC), Rwanda, and Uganda. Research methods included participant observation at six sites which then informed a survey (878 people over the six sites plus a seventh site in eastern DRC), followed by focus group discussions (60 groups over six sites, involving over 400 participants), and finally life history interviews (28 in total) (see Buss et al. 2017). This paper draws mostly from the qualitative research results.

Formalisation and artisanal and small-scale mining in sub-Saharan Africa

'Artisanal and small-scale mining' is the term commonly used to refer to a form of mining that tends to use minimal technology, requiring large amounts of physically demanding, even dangerous labour, and routinely undertaken at the margins of formal legal sanction.[2] ASM has been historically ignored or disparaged by policymakers and some local communities, media, and researchers (see Huggins, Buss, and Rutherford 2017). Transnational policymakers, donor governments, and even ASM associations largely embrace the idea of ASM formalisation as the best route forward to address ASM's many perceived problems (exploitation, environmental damage, and armed conflict, to name a few),[3] and position it better for local development and poverty alleviation. While formalising ASM can include a number of interventions, such as training and capacity building, the dominant approach has focused on legalisation, such as requiring artisanal and small-scale mining licences and/or the formation of miners' associations as two common examples.

Just as ASM mainstreaming—to position the sector for economic development and as a hedge against its presumed risks—is unfolding, so too is a push for gender mainstreaming (see e.g. UN Women 2016: 24–25; Africa Union 2009; Perks and Orozco 2018). The justifications for and portrayal of women's ASM involvement in various policy contexts reinforce the 'either/or' narrative structure typically deployed to promote formalisation—women are either part of the untapped potential of ASM (hence ASM formalisation will strengthen WEE) or are a further reason for correcting the ills of ASM (in which 'women' figure primarily as victims or linked to child labour).

Our research unfolded against this backdrop, gathering qualitative and quantitative data on how women are involved in ASM livelihoods, the gendered norms and institutions that structure their livelihood options and trajectories, and the ways in which women navigate their ASM livelihoods. Gender norms, we discovered, were important—they shaped and constrained women's ASM livelihoods, but in uneven, sometimes contradictory ways (see Buss et al. 2017; Rutherford and Buss 2019). For the purposes of this chapter, our discussion is more narrowly focused on exploring a confounding result of the research; while gender norms are by definition variable, women's ASM livelihoods in the six sites seem to conform strongly with a gendered division of labour in which men predominate in digging roles, with women found largely in processing roles. This division would seem to suggest that gender norms, beyond some minor variance, are relatively stable over time and context. Yet, as we explore below, there *is* variability and change, but the appearance (or proclamations) of continuity is itself important. In the following discussion, we outline some of the gender norms shaping women's ASM livelihoods. We demonstrate that these findings also highlight the role of authority figures in shaping gendered normative orders, including the appearance of those orders as universal and timeless.

Gender norms and women's ASM livelihoods

The High-Level Panel identifies "adverse social norms" as posing one of four "systematic constraints" to WEE, with the other three being "discriminatory laws and lack of legal protection; the failure to recognize, reduce and redistribute unpaid household work and care; and a lack of access to financial, digital and property assets" (United Nations 2016: 2). Social norms are defined as the "rules of behavior that are considered acceptable in a group or society" (3). Pearse and Connell (2016: 35) define gender norms more specifically as the rules of behaviour specific to (and differentiated for) women and men, girls and boys. Social norms, including gender norms, are generally understood as having both a material and an ideational dimension; they are convictions or beliefs, and unfold and operate, sometimes with the force of violence, in specific settings (Bell and Cox 2015; Pearse and Connell 2016). Their effects are necessarily uneven, not always or even principally 'constraining' action. Women and men, girls and boys, navigate, resist, contest, and conform to norms in ways that also change their meanings and effects (Butler 1993).

Over the course of our research, we found a gendered division of labour that seemed to be replicated in those mine sites where women were permitted to do some mining work.[4] Broadly, digging roles in mine sites and shafts are done by men, with women found in processing roles and/or doing ancillary businesses (e.g. cooking and selling food, goods, and sexual services) (see Buss et al. 2017). This division of labour was often accompanied by social norms (sometimes described as 'customs' or 'rules') prohibiting women in certain mining roles. Various reasons were given by women and men in our study for this division, many of which seem to confirm that gender norms act to constrain women's economic opportunities in mining. As one example, men in a cassiterite site in South Kivu, eastern DRC, said in focus groups and interviews that women are too weak to hold the heavy tools to be diggers or that women would be exposed to 'illnesses' and unable to stay at night to do mining work. Women explained these prohibitions in slightly different terms. In addition to taboos against women entering shafts, they said, male miners viewed women as 'doors of misfortune', suggesting they would bring bad luck if they went into the mine shafts.

These justifications echo similar rationales offered in other sites we studied in which norms against women performing certain mining roles, often going into mine shafts, were explained in terms of women's physical weakness, putative lack of courage, pollution or bringing bad luck, or the sexual impropriety of women being in the shaft (Heemskerk 2003; Buss and Rutherford 2017; Buss et al. 2017; Danielsen and Hinton 2020). These explanations point to the multiplicity of gender norms—about women's proper place (in the home; caring for their families), sexual conduct, and capability—that intermingled (Pearse and Connell 2016: 46) to produce a seemingly coherent gendered social order. But gender norms also act in contradictory ways and not always simply as constraints. For example, some women miners in our research were not required to pay taxes in the same way as some men (Buss et al. 2017: 180), and women in ASM sites are commonly described as more honest or better money managers than men: "We men like beer. ... Women are economists" (quoted in Danielsen and Hinton 2020: 25). These conceptions of women's differences sometimes meant that women were seen as more desirable in certain mining roles that offered better chances for remuneration, such as gold buyers (see e.g. Hayes and Perks 2012: 535; Bashwira et al. 2014: 112). But, as Danielsen and Hinton note in their research on gender and ASM in Africa's Great Lakes Region "perceptions that view women favourably tend to have less significant effects in organizing behaviour and actions of mining stakeholders" (2020: 25).

The overall result from our research was that the types of mining roles women performed, and the way these roles were organised in the six study sites, reinforced a view of women's mining work as supplementary to the main mining activity. Women's mining roles mirrored their household responsibilities (carrying water, providing food, supporting others) and were accorded less value than mining roles done by men, including by women themselves. Mining work was balanced with women's other household demands limiting their time in the mine (see Buss et al. 2019: 1105–1107, for further discussion), all impacting women's access to mining skills, knowledge, and better remunerated work.

Hence, gender norms in the sites appear to be organised in ways that uphold a gender hierarchy in which women are systematically disadvantaged. If gender norms are chang*ing* and changeable, the seeming durability of these norms and the ways they affected women's livelihoods across different countries and multiple sites seems contradictory. Pearse and Connell (2016: 46) suggest some reasons why gender norms can also be durable. Research on gender norms, they explain, underscores these as not simply

> attitudes in individuals' heads, but also as embedded in organizational structures and practices, discursive systems, commercial transactions, and collective

> identities. This is a complex social terrain, and the multiplicity of gender norms is one of the most important points to recognize.

The authors further note (2016: 40) that "the persistence of gender norms must be understood relationally, as part of a larger social process".

In the course of research in the cassiterite mine site in South Kivu, researchers made a surprising finding echoing Pearse and Connell's observations about the importance of examining gender norms within larger social processes and structures. This site, like many others, reflected the gendered division of labour discussed above, with women and men describing a customary rule against women doing digging work in the mine and mine shafts. But in focus groups and interviews with women working in the mines, we heard a different explanation for the prohibitions on women in shafts and as diggers. Three women said they once were diggers at the site, but not any longer. One woman explained:

> There are no exceptions for the moment; no woman goes down into the shaft because our custom does not allow it. But before, the women did it, because the mining company had just abandoned this concession [c. 1983] and the chiefs did not count much on the artisanal exploitation.

According to these women, once the chief (the customary leader) realised the value of the minerals, he began to say that women should not mine.

The women's explanation of the operation of gendered norms is notable on several levels. First, it suggests that even when a custom or practice seems to have widespread conformity, this apparent consensus can, itself, be an enactment of power; an assertion that obscures other practices and histories. What appears to be a widely held practice, further, may be navigated and resisted in many ways, including by offering a different version of a social 'reality' to visiting researchers. Finally, these women's account points to the importance of decision-making and authority relations—in this case the customary chief—as sites where gender norms may be embedded and given further force (see also Rutherford and Chemane-Chilemba 2020: 139). The role of the chief, at least in this account, suggests that other (gendered) social practices may also have an impact on WEE. To the extent that gender norms may act as constraints on women, so too do other social dynamics, such as the authority structures that operate in the mine sites (and the particular social groups they may privilege that may themselves be defined by ethnic, linguistic, familial, and, importantly, patriarchal characteristics).

The importance of other social practices in relation to gender norms becomes particularly acute in the ASM context because of the efforts to formalise the sector. As noted above, formalisation efforts in sub-Saharan Africa have tended to concentrate on legalisation—formal legal regulations that specify the conditions in which miners can secure mining title, often through requirements that miners form themselves into associations or cooperatives. The extant research on formalisation in different sub-Saharan African countries, more detailed than we can explore here, finds that formalisation has tended to benefit and reinforce elite dominance, including efforts to encourage miners' associations or cooperatives (e.g. de Haan and Geenen 2016). For example, Fisher (2007), in an early study of formalisation in Tanzania, found that formalisation efforts unfolded in ways that presume homogenous ASM populations without recognising the complex array of institutions and relationships as well as the differences (gender, age, education, disability) operating within ASM sites, all of which importantly affect the ways individuals can be included or excluded in these formalisation interventions. Fisher concludes that "the process of formalisation conceals social and power relations that make people's access to these resources highly unequal" (2007: 747).

While our research of women's ASM livelihoods was not designed as a study of formalisation, our research results suggest that the gendered authority relations in the mine areas also reflected elite, masculine dominance. In the following discussion, we highlight a few examples. These are gendered authorities and they play a role in ordering and maintaining the apparent coherence of order in the sites. As we explore below, they also serve to highlight questions about what empowerment means in the context of ASM.

Gendered authority, ASM formalisation, and the prospects for empowerment

At our study sites, authority structures were occupied largely by men and/or are given meaning and assigned traits that define them as masculine, even patriarchal. The range of authorities, and their governance functions, in these sites were varied, including local state structures engaged in policing and tax collection, mine-specific management structures (such as mining committees, miners' associations, or cooperatives), land owners, shaft owners, mine work teams, and family units. For this chapter, we focus only on licence holders, mine-site management structures (i.e. committees), and miners' cooperatives/associations because these are the key structures implicated in formalisation schemes. Hence, these structures, and the individuals (usually elite men) who occupy them, are often in the strongest position to access licences and lead the miners' associations prioritised in some formalisation initiatives. In this section, we explore how authority and decision-making structures at the study sites remain out of reach for most of the women, and some of the men.

Licence holders

Across all sites, state structures (local mining ministry offices) and, if present, customary authorities (chiefs, for example) were male dominated. For example, different local and state authorities governing the tin mining area in DRC were all male dominated. When asked in focus group discussions about the role of women in their organisations, the officials replied, "There are no women in these services!" But, they added, sometimes women are hired on a day-to-day basis when there is a large amount of ore production or when they are needed to do an "inventory of all the diggers". Researchers found women were usually employed in the office, and they were expected to stay in the office, in the background, and undertake only duties to support their male colleagues. Focus group participants said women could not do the work of SAESSCAM[5] and mining agents because some agents are subject to insult or injury. In the offices of the *chefferie* (chiefdom administrative level), women are hired as cleaners, clerks, and secretaries. All the women hired in these roles were from the family of the *mwami's* (traditional leader's) wife, hinting at other authority relations at work.

Almost all licences at the six sites were held by men or by male-dominated corporate bodies. For example, the four *Administrateurs de Foyer Minier* (Directors of the Mine, AFM), the de jure or de facto licence holder in the gold mining communities in Ituri, DRC, were men. In the Uganda gold mine, a group of five men obtained a location licence to mine (see further below; Sebina-Zziwa and Kibombo 2020). In Rwanda, meanwhile the expensive artisanal mining licences are held by either cooperatives or corporations, as required by the law in operation at the time of our study (2015–2018; see Nsanzimana, Nkundibiza, and Mwambarangwe 2020). A 2017 study of the gendered composition of Rwanda's mining cooperatives, conducted by the Canadian non-governmental organisation IMPACT (formerly called Partnership Africa Canada), found that men were the vast majority of the shareholders and only three cooperatives had been managed by women between 2013–2016 (see Buss et al. 2019: 1107–1108).

Mine site management structures

Many of the sites had some kind of a committee that was seen to manage the overall organisation of the site. The roles and authority of these various management bodies varied widely, with some largely defunct at the time of the study, such as the system of 'hill leaders' in the Uganda tin mine, and others more active in asserting overall control. While different in scope and effect, all were male dominated. In the DRC gold site, as one example, the AFM as licence holder, appointed a *Président Directeur Général* (PDG, the equivalent of a chief executive officer), who looks after the day-to-day management of the mine. The PDG was normally a male relative of the AFM (son, brother, etc.), and the administrative positions under the PDG (the *chef de camp, directeur technique,* etc.) were all men with the exception of the *mère cheffe* (mother chief), a position usually held by the camp commander's wife. Many diggers said that they had a paternalistic relationship with the AFM like sons to a father. In return, the diggers paid a premium for the 'father's protection' in terms of giving the AFM a percentage of their gold. The management structure at this site was male dominated but also patriarchal in norms and idioms.

In Rwanda, the licence holders managed the mine sites but subcontracted the management of labourers. Both management and sub-contractors tended to be male, though at the cassiterite site two of the four sub-contractors were women, both of whom were known to the mine owner. In the wolframite site, in comparison, only two of 17 sub-contractors were women. Sub-contractors at the two sites required access to capital (to develop new tunnels, buy equipment, pay for health insurance, and so on), the ability to take the financial risk of making an investment that might not generate sufficient returns, and knowledge of mining and ore seams. All posed specifically gendered challenges for women taking on sub-contracting roles (see Nsanzimana, Nkundibiza, and Mwambarangwe 2020).

Hence, while each of the mining areas studied had different site-level authority structures in place that made decisions about security, movement of people, or quotidian aspects of organising the site, they were all largely dominated by men, or, in some rare cases, the female family members of senior men. These structures were also masculine and patriarchal. For some women, the patriarch in the form of the licence holder or senior male mine manager was one level of male authority they negotiated, alongside the permissions of their husbands or other male family members.

These gendered exclusions become both more acute and normalised in the trend to encourage miners' associations or cooperatives that are themselves formed within the uneven, highly gendered social topography of mining. Even while exacerbating existing, gendered inequalities, the preference for associations and the seemingly communitarian structure of 'cooperatives', ironically gives them a 'grass-roots' patina that is representative of the 'people' who mine. The literature on cooperatives in other sectors in the region should make one wary of assuming such egalitarian tendencies (Huggins 2017; Chapter 6). Indeed, across the research sites, there were different examples of cooperatives forming (and sometimes disbanding), each with marked gendered organisation and elite dominance. The gold mine site in Uganda offers one such example as discussed below.

Miners' associations/cooperatives

The Uganda gold research site was under an exploration licence, during the research period (2015–2018), but there was an agreement that the five male licence holders would establish a miners' association to organise the artisanal miners (see Sebina-Zziwa and Kibombo 2020). The association comprised the five men who provided most of the capital to pay for the licence and a further group of about 40 founding members (mostly men), including some local landowners. The association tried to organise the various miners working at the site, levying a fee, and making changes to improve some mining health and safety issues. In practice, all decisions within the association were made by the five founding directors.

The experience of this association, with control centred within a core group of men, drawn from what de Haan and Geenen (2016: 827) would classify as traditional elites (e.g. landlords, political authorities) and new elites (e.g. mine shaft owners/investors), illustrates how gendered exclusions in local authority structures are likely to be replicated and deepened through formalisation efforts that are inattentive to social inequalities. As women are underrepresented among 'traditional' elites—customary authorities, landowners, political leaders—they are unable to access membership through these routes. Female family members of 'traditional' elites would be an exception but without significantly challenging dominant gender norms and institutions. Equally, women's circumscribed mining roles mean they are underrepresented as shaft owners and other mining-related business owners. Hence, they are generally, with some exceptions, also underrepresented as 'new' elites. Mining associations/cooperatives form, such as at the Uganda gold site, reflect, and entrench the gendered exclusions that are already in place, meaning that women, and likely other groups as well depending on the particular social contexts of the mine site, are excluded from membership and decision-making.

Conclusion: a mine of one's own?

Feminist scholars have argued that women's empowerment, if it is to have the transformational effect desired, must be "fundamentally about changing power relations" (Cornwall and Rivas 2015: 405). The discourse of empowerment, and its linkage with gender norms, can sometimes distract from this transformational conception of empowerment, to something more likely to celebrate women's access to economies or, in our case, mining roles. Kabeer (2017: 9) cautions against such an approach noting that "access to markets does not necessarily address the terms on which poor women and men enter different market arenas or their ability to negotiate a fairer deal for themselves." Focusing on access without addressing the 'durable inequalities' that structure access, she notes, can end up reproducing those inequalities, while "rewarding the powerful and penalizing the weak" (Kabeer 2017: 9; see Chapter 1 in this volume on the relationship between economic growth, labour force participation, and gender equality).

The research from our study reveals the powerful operation of gender norms that shape women's ASM livelihoods. We have suggested that attending to gender norms requires close consideration of the social practices and authority structures that can concentrate gender norms and (seemingly) congeal normative orders. Our focus here has been on authority relations in mine sites to explore how formalisation efforts, even while motivated or justified by efforts to empower miners, can end up consolidating the power of mining elites. As most of these elites are men, and often embedded within patriarchal social relations, the effects of formalisation, perversely, may be to further exclude women (and some categories of men) from accessing licences or becoming decision-makers in miners' associations.

This result, we suggest, begs the question about the kinds of transformations that are hoped for or intended by empowerment initiatives, including those for WEE. In our research, gender norms were powerfully invoked by women and men at the study sites to limit women's access to digging roles, and sometimes work with equipment and/or in mine shafts. It can be tempting to offer a 'solution' to this finding by promoting changes in gender norms so that, for example, women are allowed, even encouraged, to be diggers or work in mine shafts. Is the goal for WEE in ASM for women to become diggers, mine owners, or something altogether different? Our research suggests that empowerment narratives and initiatives, like those that characterise contemporary formalisation interventions, can unfold in ways that obscure the consolidation, rather than the rupturing of power relations that WEE advocates may have intended. Empowerment initiatives in ASM might need to begin by considering how women and men miners, and not just mine/licence owners, have voice in the range of decisions made about mining and mining labour.

Notes

1 See Appendix 1 of the Report of the International Conference on Artisanal and Small-scale Mining, Quarrying and Development. 11–13 September 2018, Livingstone, Zambia (found at http://www.developmentminerals.org/index.php/en/resource/studies-handbooks?view=download&id=39).

2 The term 'ASM' is not without complication. It encompasses distinct types and scales of mining with very different implications for legal regulation and economic development, and some scholars have noted that 'artisanal' may not accurately reflect the challenging contexts of this sector (Lahiri-Dutt 2018: 3). We use ASM because it is in wide circulation particularly in relation to the current momentum around formalisation.

3 The construction of ASM's presumed problems is a complex process that should also be seen in terms of the resulting constructions of large-scale mining, both topics beyond our remit here. See Huggins, Buss, and Rutherford 2017 as well as Hilson and McQuilken 2014 for further discussion.

4 Depending on region and mineral, women can sometimes be 'banned' from mine sites altogether, though these bans, like the bans on women in digging roles discussed later in this chapter, can be variable (see Rutherford and Chemane-Chilemba 2020).

5 '*Service d'Assistance et d'Encadrement de l'Exploitation Minière Artisanale et à Petite Échelle*', a specialised mining service for artisanal mining. The body changed names after data collection and, as of 2019, is known as SAEMAPE (*Service d'accompagnement et d'encadrement de l'exploitation minière artisanale et à petite échelle*).

Acknowledgements

We are extremely grateful to Aline Providence Nkundibiza, Patricie Mwambarangwe, Bernard Nsanzimana, Bibiche Liliane Salumu Laumu Omeyaka, Véronique Minyego, Matthieu Mamiki Kebongobongo, Zacharie Bulakali, Janvier Kilosho Buraye, Joy Zawedde, Rosette Kyarisiima, Jonathan Ngobi, and Thomas Kanooti who conducted much of the research in Rwanda, DRC, and Uganda. We would also like to thank Sriyanchita Srinivasan for her close reading of and assistance with preparing this manuscript.

References

African Union (2009). Africa mining vision. Addis Ababa: African Union. https://au.int/en/ti/amv/about.

Bashwira, Marie-Rose, Jeroen Cuvelier, Dorothea Hilhorst, and Gemma Van der Haar (2014). 'Not only a man's world': Women's involvement in artisanal mining in eastern DRC. *Resources Policy* 40: 109–116.

Bell, David, and Mary Cox (2015). Social norms: Do we love norms too much? *Journal of Family Theory & Review* 7: 28–46.

Buss, Doris, and Blair Rutherford (2017). 'Dangerous desires': Illegality, sexuality, and the global governance of artisanal mining. In Diane Otto (Ed.), *Queering International Law: Possibilities, Alliances, Complicities, Risk* (35–52). London: Routledge.

Buss, Doris, Blair Rutherford, Jennifer Hinton, Jennifer Stewart, Joanne Lebert, Gisèle Eva Côté, Abby Sebina-Zziwa, Richard Kibombo, and Frederick Kisekka (2017). Gender and artisanal and small-scale mining in central and East Africa: Barriers and benefits. GrOW Working Paper Series, GWP-2017–02. Montreal: Institute for the Study of International Development, McGill University. http://grow.research.mcgill.ca/publications/working-papers/gwp-2017-02.pdf.

Buss, Doris, Blair Rutherford, Jennifer Stewart, Gisèle Eva Côté, Abby Sebina-Zziwa, Richard Kibombo, Jennifer Hinton, and Joanne Lebert (2019). Gender and artisanal and small-scale mining: Implications for formalization. *Extractive Industries and Society* 6(4): 1101–1112.

Butler, Judith (1993). *Bodies that Matter: On the Discursive Limits of Sex*. New York: Routledge.

Cornwall, Andrea, and Althea-Maria Rivas (2015). From 'gender equality' and 'women's empowerment' to global justice: Reclaiming a transformative agenda for gender and development. *Third World Quarterly* 36(2): 396–415.

Danielsen, Katrine, and Jennifer Hinton (2020). A social relations of gender analysis of artisanal and small-scale mining in Africa's Great Lakes Region. *Canadian Journal of African Studies* 54(1): 17–36.

de Haan, Jorden, and Sara Geenen (2016). Mining cooperatives in Eastern DRC: The interplay between historical power relations and formal institutions. *Extractive Industries and Society* 3(3): 823–831.

Fisher, Eleanor (2007). Occupying the margins: Labour integration and social exclusion in artisanal mining in Tanzania. *Development and Change* 38(4): 735–760.

Hayes, Karen, and Rachel Perks (2012). Women in the artisanal and small-scale mining sector of the Democratic Republic of the Congo. In Päivi Lujala and Siri Aas Rustad (Eds.), *High-Value Natural Resources and Peacebuilding* (529–544). London: Earthscan.

Heemskerk, Marieke (2003). Self-employment and poverty alleviation: Women's work in artisanal gold mines. *Human Organization* 62(1): 62–73.

Hilson, Gavin, Abigail Hilson, Roy Maconachie, James McQuilken and Halima Goumandakoye (2017). Artisanal and small-scale mining (ASM) in sub-Saharan Africa: Re-conceptualizing formalization and 'illegal' activity. *Geoforum* 83: 80–90.

Hilson, Gavin, Abigail Hilson, Agatha Siwale, and Roy Maconachie (2018). Female faces in informal 'spaces': Women and artisanal and small-scale mining in sub-Saharan Africa. *Africa Journal of Management* 4(3): 306–346.

Hilson, Gavin, and James McQuilken (2014). Four decades of support for artisanal and small-scale mining in sub-Saharan Africa: A critical review. *Extractive Industries and Society* 1(1): 104–118.

Huggins, Chris (2017). *Agricultural Reforms in Rwanda: Authoritarianism, Markets and Zones of Governance*. London: Zed Books.

Huggins, Chris, Doris Buss, and Blair Rutherford (2017). A 'cartography of concern': Place-making practices and gender in the artisanal mining sector in Africa. *Geoforum* 83: 142–152.

Kabeer, Naila (2005). Gender equality and women's empowerment: A critical analysis of the third millennium development goal. *Gender & Development* 13(1): 13–24. http://nailakabeer.net/wp-content/uploads/2005/09/13552070512331332273.pdf.

Kabeer, Naila (2008). Paid work, women's empowerment and gender justice: Critical pathways of social change. Institute of Development Studies, RPC Pathways of Women's

Empowerment, Working Paper No. 3. http://eprints.lse.ac.uk/53077/1/Kabeer_Paid-work_Published.pdf.

Kabeer, Naila (2017). Women's economic empowerment and inclusive growth: labour markets and enterprise development. GrOW Working Paper Series, GWP-2017–01. Montreal: Institute for the Study of International Development, McGill University. http://grow.research.mcgill.ca/publications/working-papers/gwp-2017-01.pdf.

Lahiri-Dutt, Kuntala (2018). Extractive peasants: Reframing informal artisanal and small-scale mining debates. *Third World Quarterly* 39(8): 1561–1582.

Nsanzimana, Bernard, Aline Providence Nkundibiza, and Patricia Mwambarangwe (2020). Promoting gender equality in the Rwandan ASM: Efforts and obstacles. *Canadian Journal of African Studies* 54(1): 119–138.

Pearse, Rebecca, and Raewyn Connell (2016). Gender norms and the economy: Insights from social research. *Feminist Economics* 22(1): 30–53.

Perks, Rachel, and Diana C. B. Orozco (2018). Closing the gender gap in extractives: What has been done and what have we learned? *Livewire: A knowledge note series for the Energy & Extractives Global Practice* 87: 1–7. Washington, DC: World Bank Group. https://openknowledge.worldbank.org/bitstream/handle/10986/30389/129731-BRI-PUBLIC-VC-LW87-OKR.pdf?sequence=1&isAllowed=y.

Rutherford, Blair, and Doris Buss (2019). Gendered governance and socio-economic differentiation among women artisanal and small-scale miners in Central and East Africa. *Third World Thematics* 4(1): 63–79.

Rutherford, Blair, and Laila Chemane-Chilemba (2020). The governance of artisanal and small-scale mining in Manica District, Mozambique: Implications for women's livelihoods. *Canadian Journal of African Studies* 54(1): 139–156.

Sebina-Zziwa, Abby, and Richard Kibombo (2020). Licensing of artisanal mining on private land in Uganda: Social and economic implications on spouses and women entrepreneurs. *Canadian Journal of African Studies* 54(1): 101–117.

United Nations (2016). Leave no one behind: A call to action for gender equality and women's economic empowerment. UN Secretary-General's High-Level Panel on Women's Economic Empowerment. www.empowerwomen.org/-/media/files/un%20women/empowerwomen/resources/hlp%20briefs/unhlp%20full%20report.pdf?la=en&vs=2916.

UN Women (2016). Building on good practices: Report on the regional sharefair on gender equality in the extractive industries. Nairobi: UN Women. https://africa.unwomen.org/en/digital-library/publications/2016/01/report-on-the-regional-sharefair-on-gender-equality-in-the-extractive-industries.

World Bank (2019). State of the artisanal and small-scale mining sector. Washington, DC: World Bank. https://delvedatabase.org/uploads/resources/Delve-2019-State-of-the-Artisanal-and-Small-Scale-Mining-Sector.pdf.

7

PICTURING CHANGE THROUGH PHOTOVOICE

Participatory evaluation of a daycare intervention in an urban informal context

Milka Nyariro, S.M. Hani Sadati, Claudia Mitchell, Stella Muthuri, and Milka Njeri

Introduction

In many societies throughout sub-Saharan Africa, childcare is largely the responsibility of mothers and other female family members. The time and resources that are required for childcare can act as limitations to the options that the female members of the family have in terms of economic activities. Many women in low-income contexts are limited to participating in informal work that takes place in the home because it is 'child-compatible'. In urban areas, however, factors such as wage labour, the monetised economy, and the cost of living compel women to take on other employment options in order to be economically independent or contribute to their household income. Thus, balancing work and childcare remains a dilemma for many women. In countries across Africa, including Kenya, tensions between work and childcare have contributed to a downward trend in fertility rates (Bongaarts 2008).[1]

Poorer segments of Kenya's population, which are also less likely to be educated and have fewer employment options, continue to have higher than average fertility rates when compared to the rest of the country. In Korogocho, one of Nairobi's largest slum settlements, the total fertility rate in 2009 was 3.7 children born per woman, while in Nairobi that figure was estimated at 2.8 children per woman (Emina et al. 2011). With more children and fewer opportunities for employment, mothers in low-income contexts like Korogocho struggle to balance childcare and employment responsibilities. Grappling with such economic and social constraints can translate negatively on the health and wellbeing of mothers and their children.

A complex interaction of economic, social, political, and environmental challenges predisposes children living in low-income contexts to higher health risks and infant mortality rates. Within the family, factors such as low educational levels of parents, especially of the mother, and economic constraints increase the chances of infant mortality. At the community level, workplace and environmental hazards such as open sewage and garbage dump sites are factors that can expose children to diseases or injury (Kimani-Murage et al. 2014). A participatory study with children aged eight to 13 years living in eight informal settlements in Nairobi further confirms that, from the perspectives of the children themselves, life is very dangerous, both in relation to environmental issues as well as social issues related to gender-based violence (Mitchell et al. 2016). What this study also confirmed is the benefit of the use of visual methodologies in getting at the perspectives of those most affected. In a country like Kenya, where there is an absence of adequate social policies and legal protections for vulnerable populations, Muthuri, Oyolola, and Cheikh (2017) advocate for interventions that provide an economic cushion, particularly to single mothers and those living in urban low-income contexts. For example, the establishment of reliable and affordable or subsidised daycare services may help women to balance childcare and employment responsibilities.

Chapter 4 in this volume notes the research in the GrOW programme benefitted from using innovative field research in specific communities to provide an analysis of potential solutions and policy innovations. This chapter provides greater insight into one of the methodological processes, and the findings it generated by examining the use of PhotoVoice for a participatory evaluation conducted as part of a larger randomised study, which provided vouchers for subsidised daycare to selected mothers living in the Korogocho slum in Nairobi. We consider the ways in which PhotoVoice can be used as a tool for participatory evaluation. To explore this idea, we organise the chapter into four sections. First, we briefly describe PhotoVoice as a participatory visual methodology that is useful to conduct research with marginalised populations (Nyariro 2018). We then continue to look at the use of PhotoVoice as a tool for programme evaluation, focusing on other studies that have used PhotoVoice in this way. In the third section, we describe the use of PhotoVoice in this study and some of the key findings that emerged. In the final section, we elaborate on key findings to discuss lessons learned about the use of PhotoVoice as a method of participatory evaluation in social research.

PhotoVoice as a useful tool for conducting research with marginalised groups

PhotoVoice is a community-based participatory and visual research methodology in which a collaborative partnership is formed between researchers and communities (Mitchell 2011). The practice of PhotoVoice involves the provision of cameras to community members, who are asked to take photos representing their own experiences with, and perspectives on, a particular issue in their community. In a sense, the photographs taken can act as a visual voice for participants, helping to express their needs and to tell stories that may not otherwise be captured by more traditional, researcher-driven methods. The actual term 'PhotoVoice' was first coined by American researcher Caroline Wang in the 1990s through her work with women and policymakers on health issues in rural China (Wang 1999). It is now a well-established approach for doing qualitative research and for conducting participatory research with socially marginalised groups in particular (Mitchell 2008; Mitchell and Sommer 2017).

Owing to its focus on capturing the experiences of marginalised groups, especially the experiences of women and girls, PhotoVoice is deeply rooted in feminist research methodologies. It is commonly implemented in feminist research on women's bodies and women's health. As such, it is highly appropriate to use this method when researching poor women's experiences of balancing work and childcare, as we do in this study. Feminist researchers use PhotoVoice to amplify women's voices, to identify and address their needs, and to encourage self-representation and reflexivity.

PhotoVoice is a useful tool to see 'through the eyes' of individuals who have historically been marginalised by society and by traditional research processes (Wang 1999). This method gives participants the opportunity to:

1. document and record their experiences and the conditions in which they live;
2. critically reflect on these experiences and conditions; and
3. develop strategies to reach policymakers.

A particular strength of PhotoVoice lies in the fact that it is not just researchers analysing the photographs produced during the research process, rather the participants themselves analyse, interpret, and narrate their own stories and experiences behind the photographs. In some cases, PhotoVoice participants may be given the opportunity to participate in community events like photo exhibitions, where they can display and discuss their work with local audiences (Mitchell 2011; Nyariro 2018).

PhotoVoice as a tool for programme evaluation

The concept of participatory evaluation was first introduced in the 1970s to address the knowledge and power gaps that existed between international development project staff and local beneficiaries (Moschetti 2003). Like traditional evaluation approaches, the goal of participatory evaluation is to measure the impact of an intervention in order to understand and improve its outcomes. Understanding programme impacts as they play out in local contexts is complex and will depend on whose eyes are observing the impacts. Long-standing assumptions about researcher objectivity and neutrality in the positivist research paradigm have historically worked to exclude local beneficiaries and stakeholders from the evaluation process, marginalising their perspectives and opinions.

By adopting the principles of collaboration that underlie participatory research, participatory evaluation goes beyond traditional impact evaluation processes in which outsiders, often foreign researchers, hold exclusive decision-making power. Instead, the voices and viewpoints of local beneficiaries and stakeholders are deliberately prioritised. In this way, participatory evaluation is participant-led or participant-driven and facilitates the process of self-reflection on the part of the various research partners. By adopting the principles of collaborative and community-driven research, participatory evaluation, when properly implemented, is an inherently inclusive process that has at its core the active involvement of local beneficiaries and stakeholders.

Mitchell, De Lange, and Moletsane (2017) explore the use of participatory evaluation to examine changes resulting from community-level interventions. They refer to the work of Davies and Dart (2005), Serrat (2009), and Lemaire and Lunch (2012), among others, who have conducted programme evaluations using participatory visual methods, such as participatory video, and what is referred to as the 'most significant change' approach. For these methods, community members are asked to produce videos or images using artwork, cameras, or cell phones to capture what they see as being key changes in the community resulting from an intervention (see also Mitchell and De Lange 2011). Researchers who use these methods argue that programme impact is only truly observable through the eyes of community stakeholders who are directly involved and impacted by a project (Mitchell, De Lange, and Moletsane 2017). Researchers such as Cousins and Earl (1992) make the case for participatory evaluation on the basis that it is inclusive, ethical, and empowering for participants, and because it has the potential to improve project sustainability well into the future. They argue that participatory evaluation is not merely about gathering information on social issues, it is also about taking action to address those issues.

PhotoVoice is another example of a participatory visual methodology that can be used to evaluate community-level development interventions. Research by Mitchell, De Lange, and Moletsane (2017) highlights several studies where PhotoVoice has been used as a method to carry out participatory evaluation. In one study that took place at Nelson Mandela University in South Africa, a group of young women involved in a project to address campus-based violence used cameras to study problems contributing to women's lack of safety at the school (De Lange, Moletsane, and Mitchell 2015). They identified issues such as poorly lit campus walking paths and the presence of undocumented male visitors in dormitories late at night. Following the implementation of a campus safety intervention, the women took another set of photos to capture which, if any, of these types of problems had been addressed. These before and after photos were included in an exhibition titled, *Seeing How It Works*, organised so that other students and campus authorities could understand the changes taking place from their perspective (see Garcia et al. 2020).

In another study, also in South Africa, teacher educators, who were responsible for implementing an HIV and AIDS awareness curriculum, used photographic images to document the impact of their teaching on the campus and wider community (Mitchell, De Lange, and Moletsane 2011). A key feature of this project was that it highlighted the significance of exhibiting the images publicly to promote understanding and discussion. In this case, the photos produced by the teachers became part of a travelling exhibition titled *Seeing, Believing, and Acting for Change in HIV and AIDS: Integrating HIV/AIDS in Higher Education Curricula*. The exhibition allowed audiences across South Africa to learn about the impact of the curriculum, initiating a broader conversation about the national HIV/AIDS epidemic.

Other studies adopting PhotoVoice as a method of participatory evaluation have been conducted throughout Africa, including projects evaluating the experiences of children living in informal slum settlements in Kenya (Mitchell et al. 2016), homeless girls living on the streets in Rwanda (Umurungi et al. 2008), and girls living in poverty in Mozambique (Sajan Virgi and Mitchell 2011).

Our study

The PhotoVoice participatory evaluation discussed in this chapter was nested within a larger randomised intervention study that sought to create better economic opportunities for women in Nairobi slums by providing access to subsidised daycare. Selected mothers in Korogocho were provided vouchers for free childcare at one of 48 registered daycare centres in the community included in the project. A detailed description of this intervention and its findings are presented elsewhere (see Clark et al. 2019; Clark et al. 2017, and additional information is provided in Chapter 4 of this volume).

The decision to conduct a PhotoVoice exercise as part of this larger study had a dual purpose. First, it allowed the research team to explore, from early in the study, the issue of childcare from the perspectives of the mothers themselves. As will be discussed below, the specific nature of the intervention was determined in part by the findings of the PhotoVoice exercise. Second, it evaluated the impact of the interventions from the mothers' perspectives. Through the PhotoVoice process, researchers were drawn to the relatively holistic, participant-led nature of PhotoVoice, with its built-in processes for generating community engagement and reflection.

Methodology: using PhotoVoice to evaluate programme impact

The PhotoVoice exercise was conducted in two phases. The first phase involved 47 mothers between 15 and 49 years old, with at least one child between the ages of one and four, in Korogocho. These mothers were asked to identify the challenges that they experienced living in the slum area and balancing work and childcare responsibilities. The research team provided them with cameras and asked them to take photos responding to the following questions: (1) how does childcare affect your work? and (2) what are some of the challenges and potential solutions to these issues?

In total, approximately 115 photos were taken by the mothers during this phase. The mothers were then asked to use these photos to create thematic poster-narratives (see Figure 7.1), which are visual boards featuring selected photos and captions to identify their significance (Mitchell 2011). In total, 16 poster-narratives were created by the 47 participants. The mothers were then interviewed in focus groups about the meaning behind their photos and poster-narratives. Drawing on an analysis of the photos, poster-narratives, and interview transcripts, the research team identified thematic areas that best

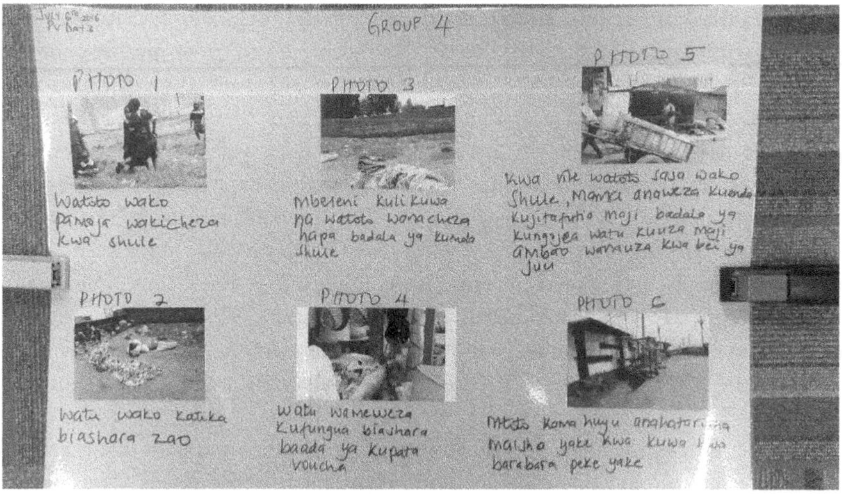

FIGURE 7.1 Sample of a poster-narrative
Source: Authors

captured the mothers' perspectives on balancing work and childcare, discussed in greater detail below. Findings from this first phase of the PhotoVoice exercise, along with survey data collected by researchers from the mothers and daycare operators, helped to frame and determine the implementation of the intervention.

Phase two of the PhotoVoice exercise engaged a sample of 31 mothers who participated in the intervention in order to understand the changes they experienced resulting from access to subsidised daycare. In this phase, the mothers were provided with cameras and trained on how to use them. Working in small groups, they were asked to take photos capturing their responses to the question: how has your life, or the lives of your family members, changed as a result of participating in the voucher programme? This component of the study set out to understand what was working, or not, with regard to the intervention, and how the project could be improved. Again, in groups, the mothers worked together to create poster-narratives of their photos.

Findings: 'through the eyes of mothers'

Findings from the PhotoVoice participatory evaluation suggest that, as a result of the intervention, mothers saw numerous improvements in their general wellbeing and that of their families. The following discussion outlines the changes that the mothers captured through their poster-narratives and during the follow-up interviews. The figures presented are a sample of the photos taken by the women, as well as the captions they wrote to accompany them.

The first finding to emerge from the PhotoVoice evaluation is that fewer children accompanied their mothers to their places of employment. Mothers remarked that since the start of the daycare intervention they no longer had to take their children with them to work (see Figure 7.2). According to some mothers, this had positive ripple effects on child nutrition. Before the introduction of the daycare programme, children who accompanied their mothers to work regularly missed meals because feeding them on the job was often not possible. For children who did not accompany their mothers to work, they may not have eaten at all because their mother was not home to feed them or due to a lack of food in their household. Evidence from Victora et al. (2008) and Grantham-McGregor et al. (2007) has shown that lack of proper nutrition for children has adverse health implications that can negatively affect brain growth and development. While it was beyond the scope of our study to definitively show improved nutrition, the comments of the mothers do suggest they felt that the changed situation was beneficial for their children.

The second finding that emerges from the PhotoVoice evaluation is that there was a reduced number of children playing unattended in the streets. The mothers indicate that following the implementation of the voucher programme, a reduced number of children could be found playing unattended or loitering in the streets because they were now attending daycare. In this way, daycare attendance reduced children's exposure to injuries and accidents, like those involving vehicles and

FIGURE 7.2 Quote from a participant for this photo: "This mother no longer goes early to the market with her child"

Source: Authors

motorcycles in the community. Before the intervention, mothers highlighted that there were several cases of children who were unattended being locked up in the house by their parents or left to loiter in the streets as the mothers worked or went to look for work. All the above were risky because of the high rates of insecurity, spontaneous fires, and child abduction and rape cases in the neighbourhood. As such, provision of daycare was found to improve the safety and security of the women's children while they attended work.

Closely related to the previous point, the PhotoVoice evaluation suggests that access to daycare reduced children's exposure to hazardous environments. In the first phase of the PhotoVoice exercise, women took photos of children playing in and around garbage, open sewage, and unsafe drainage systems. During the second phase of PhotoVoice, the mothers' photos captured the fact that children were no longer playing in these dangerous environments, and they attributed this to the introduction of the intervention (see Figures 7.3 and 7.4). With reduced exposure to hazardous environments, the mothers reported a decrease in incidences of child injury and illness. This subsequently resulted in household savings on medical expenses—money that could instead be used to buy food or invest in small businesses, for example (see Figure 7.5).

FIGURE 7.3 Quote from a participant for this photo: "There are no children playing in the drainage like before"
Source: Authors

FIGURE 7.4 Quote from a participant for this photo: "There are no children playing in the sewage following the voucher programme"
Source: Authors

The PhotoVoice evaluation also points to an increase in work and employment opportunities for the mothers following the introduction of the voucher intervention. The mothers acknowledged that access to reliable and affordable daycare services had given them more time to find and participate in paid employment or to work with their husbands as part of family businesses. This resulted in increased household income. Before the programme, mothers indicated that they often carried their children to look for work, which was not acceptable to potential employers and hence reduced their chances of finding work. In addition, having their children accompany them to their work negatively affected the quality of their work because of the divided attention, which further reduced their chances of being considered for subsequent jobs by the employers.

The improved wellbeing of family members was also identified as an outcome of the intervention. Access to affordable and reliable daycare not only contributed to the economic wellbeing of the mothers and their families but also to their physical and emotional wellness. For example, assurance that their children were safe and well taken care of in daycare centres gave the women the peace of mind to go about their work, to participate in social and leisure activities, as well as to have some rest (see Figure 7.6). Other family members also benefitted. For example, access to subsidised daycare eliminated the obligation of older siblings to step in as

FIGURE 7.5 Quote from a participant for this photo: "We have now managed to start businesses and expand them"
Source: Authors

secondary caregivers when their mothers were at work (see Figure 7.7). They were subsequently able to devote their time to other activities such as attending school and finishing their homework. Some even had time to play with friends and simply be children, experiencing real childhood time.

Finally, the PhotoVoice evaluation identified numerous intervention gaps and the need for follow up. The women who participated in the research project pointed to remaining gaps in community services, making it clear that there were still areas for potential improvement and expansion of the daycare programme. For example, they acknowledged that many mothers in the community still did not have access to childcare, meaning their children were still being exposed to danger and hardship daily.

These findings were presented as part of the previously mentioned travelling exhibition, *Picturing Change*. When included as part of an international stakeholders' conference in Nairobi, the exhibition offered what might be described as 'visual verification' of the mothers' experiences and complemented the more technical and academic presentations taking place at the conference. When it was exhibited several months later during a research dissemination event at the Korogocho community centre, it gave community members an opportunity to learn, through an accessible medium, about the findings of the study from the perspective of the mothers who participated. Several of the mothers involved in the

FIGURE 7.6 Quote from a participant on this photo: "This mother is going home to rest after work because her children are in daycare"
Source: Authors

PhotoVoice evaluation were present during these events to discuss the meaning behind their photos with attendees.

Interestingly, each of these public events had the potential to provide further opportunities for data collection and contribute to the findings of the participatory evaluation. As Mitchell (2015) highlights in an analysis of the value of PhotoVoice exhibitions, audience responses can offer an additional layer of data by including different perspectives and usually taking place at a later point in the project cycle. In this study, discussions with the community members during the research dissemination event and PhotoVoice exhibit in Korogocho indicated that cases of poor child health and malnutrition had increased since the voucher programme ended. Community leaders who attended this event also reported that cases of children playing unattended in the streets, exposed to environmental hazards, had likewise increased. These changes were attributed to the fact that most mothers in the intervention could not afford to pay the daycare fee for their children in the post-intervention period. The need for concerted efforts by local government, organisations, and community members to provide reliable and affordable daycare services for mothers was recommended as one strategy to sustain the positive changes resulting from the intervention, including benefits to maternal employment, household wellbeing, and child health and safety.

FIGURE 7.7 Quote from a participant on this photo: "This older child is left to care for his sibling instead of going to school"
Source: Authors

Discussion

While the PhotoVoice exercise was only one of the methods used to measure the overall effectiveness of the voucher programme, it was without doubt the most collaborative and participatory method. The exercise provided an opportunity for mothers to reflect on the changes they had experienced, and it gave community members an opportunity to participate in the evaluation process by attending the exhibition and sharing their perspectives. Research indicates that traditional evaluation data collected by external evaluators are not always shared with communities. It may also be difficult for community members to understand the significance of the data (Guba and Lincoln 1981; Kramer et al. 2013). The visual nature of the data in this case made it very accessible.

We consider PhotoVoice, as used in this study, to be a uniquely collaborative, participatory, and transparent approach to programme evaluation. We argue that PhotoVoice challenges the assumed primacy of traditional researcher-led approaches by prioritising the views of local beneficiaries and stakeholders. The mothers who participated in this PhotoVoice exercise, especially in the second phase, were extensively engaged in thinking about the changes to their lives, their households, and their communities that resulted from the intervention. This was not a small task as it required time and dedication to go out and find the right scene, to take

FIGURE 7.8 A participant mother explains an exhibited photo to conference attendees
Source: Authors

the picture from the best angle, and to make any number of other artistic considerations. Participating in the workshop, choosing which pictures best represented the programme's impact, and captioning those photos was also thoughtful and time-consuming work. We saw their willingness and dedication to this exercise as evidence that they were engaged and able to think critically about the impacts of the voucher programme. This type of locally engaged participation is too often missing from conventional evaluation approaches.

Making this exercise public through community exhibitions was also key to allowing the mothers who participated in the PhotoVoice exercise to discuss their photos and the impact of the intervention with attendees. At the same time, the mothers had a chance to see their work being appreciated by the community. The exhibition also created space for community members themselves to gain awareness of the changes that had taken place and to add their own perspectives and experiences to the conversation. These events created space to engage in what Mitchell, De Lange, and Moletsane (2017: 176) refer to as "tracking change" from multiple perspectives and at numerous points during the project cycle.

Conclusion

In this chapter, we make the argument that PhotoVoice can be used as a participatory method for documenting changes resulting from community-level development interventions. In keeping with the broader goals of the study, we drew on the participation of mothers to understand the challenges of balancing work and childcare responsibilities with an extension of the value of participatory research methods in playing a role in the evaluation process. There are implications for further research that stems from our experience here, particularly in relation to the role of participatory visual methodologies for programme evaluation and the value of community engagement and reflection in social research. Other researchers such as Theron (2012) have used visual exercises in an evaluative way, asking teachers participating in a project on HIV, AIDS, and resilience to depict their views on programme impact. Researchers adopting participatory visual methods to examine 'most significant change' have likewise found that the process of media making can be central to the overall effectiveness of their projects since it calls for community engagement and reflection. Given the many challenges to conducting community-level development projects and ensuring their sustainability, participatory evaluation through visual and creative exercises offers 'good value', both socially and economically, for funders, researchers, and participants alike.

Note

1 For additional insight into the dynamics of the care economy and women's economic empowerment, please see Chapter 4 in this volume.

Acknowledgements

We thank all the women who participated in the initial conversations to identify the issues that affect them and other women in the community, which led to an effectively designed daycare intervention. In addition, we thank the mothers for participating in the intervention project while monitoring what works and identifying what remains to be done, which culminated in the participatory evaluation aspect of the project. We also thank the Korogocho community members, non-governmental and community-based organisations working in Korogocho, and community representatives for making time to participate and share their experience with the project.

This project was made possible by funding from Canada's International Development Research Centre (IDRC), the Foreign, Commonwealth and Development Office (FCDO), and the William and Flora Hewlett Foundation, and a valuable research partnership between McGill University, the African Population and Health Research Center (APHRC), and Participatory Cultures Lab (PCL).

References

Bongaarts, John (2008). Fertility transitions in developing countries: Progress or stagnation? *Studies in Family Planning* 39(2): 105–110.

Clark, Shelley, Sonia Laszlo, Caroline Kabiru, and Stella Muthuri (2017). Can subsidized early child care promote women's employment? Evidence from a slum settlement in Africa. GrOW Working Paper Series, GWP-2017–05. Montreal: Institute for the Study of International Development, McGill University. http://grow.research.mcgill.ca/publications/working-papers/gwp-2017-05.pdf.

Clark, Shelley, Caroline W. Kabiru, Sonia Laszlo, and Stella Muthuri (2019). The impact of childcare on poor urban women's economic empowerment in Africa. *Demography* 56: 1247–1272.

Cousins, J. Bradley, and Lorna M. Earl (1992). The case for participatory evaluation. *Educational Evaluation and Policy Analysis* 14(4): 397–418.

Davies, Rick, and Jess Dart (2005). The 'Most Significant Change' (MSC) technique. A guide to its use. www.researchgate.net/publication/275409002_The_'Most_Significant_Change'_MSC_Technique_A_Guide_to_Its_Use.

De Lange, Naydene, Relebohile Moletsane, and Claudia Mitchell (2015). Seeing how it works: A visual essay about critical and transformative research in education. *Perspectives in Education* 33(4): 151–176.

Emina, Jacques, Donatien Beguy, Eliya M. Zulu, Alex C. Ezeh, Kanyiva Muindi, Patricia Elung'ata, John K. Otsola, and Yazoumé Yé (2011). Monitoring of health and demographic outcomes in poor urban settlements: Evidence from the Nairobi Urban Health and Demographic Surveillance System. *Journal of Urban Health* 88(2): 200–218. https://link.springer.com/content/pdf/10.1007/s11524-011-9594-1.pdf.

Garcia, Chloe K., Mindy R. Carter, Milka Nyariro, Maria Ezcurra, Lori Beavis, and Claudia Mitchell (2020). 'There is a crack in everything/that's how the light gets in': Reflections in selected arts interventions used to bring awareness to sexual violence at McGill University. In Diane Crocker, Joanne Minaker, and Amanda Nelund (Eds.), *Violence Interrupted: Confronting Sexual Violence on University Campuses*. Montreal: Queens-McGill Press.

Grantham-McGregor, Sally, Yin Bun Cheung, Santiago Cueto, Paul Glewwe, Linda Richter, Barbara Strupp, and the International Child Development Steering Group (2007). Developmental potential in the first 5 years for children in developing countries. *The Lancet* 369(9555): 60–70. www.thelancet.com/journals/lancet/article/PIIS0140-6736(07)60032-4/fulltext.

Guba, Egan G., and Yvonna S. Lincoln (1981). *Effective Evaluation: Improving the Usefulness of Evaluation Results Through Responsive and Naturalistic Approaches*. San Francisco: Jossey-Bass.

Kimani-Murage, Elizabeth W., J.C. Fotso, Thaddaeus Egondi, Benta Abuya, Patricia Elungata, Abdhalah K. Ziraba, Caroline W. Kabiru, and Nyovani Madise (2014). Trends in childhood mortality in Kenya: The urban advantage has seemingly been wiped out. *Health & Place* 29: 95–103. www.ncbi.nlm.nih.gov/pmc/articles/PMC4158907/.

Kramer, Leila, Pamela Schwartz, Allen Cheadle, and Susan Rauzon (2013). Using PhotoVoice as a participatory evaluation tool in Kaiser Permanente's community health initiative. *Health Promotion Practice* 14(5): 686–694.

Lemaire, Isabelle, and Chris Lunch (2012). Using participatory video in monitoring and evaluation. In Elisabeth-Jane Milne, Claudia Mitchell, and Naydene De Lange (Eds.), *The Handbook of Participatory Video* (303–317). Lanham, MD: AltaMira Press.

Mitchell, Claudia (2008). Getting the picture and changing the picture: Visual methodologies and educational research in South Africa. *South African Journal of Educational Research* 28(3): 365–383. www.ajol.info/index.php/saje/article/view/25163.

Mitchell, Claudia (2011). *Doing Visual Research*. London: SAGE Publications.

Mitchell, Claudia (2015). Looking at showing: On the politics and pedagogy of exhibiting in community-based research and work with policy makers. *Educational Research for Social Change* 4(2): 48–60. http://ersc.nmmu.ac.za/articles/Vol_4_No_2_Mitchell_pp_48-60_October_2015.pdf.

Mitchell, Claudia, and Naydene De Lange (2011). Community-based video and social action in rural South Africa. In Eric Margolis, and Luc Pauwels (Eds.), *The SAGE Handbook of Visual Research Methods* (171–185). London: SAGE Publications.

Mitchell, Claudia, Naydene De Lange, and Relebohile Moletsane (2011). Before the cameras roll: Drawing storyboards to address gendered poverty. In Linda Theron, Claudia Mitchell, Ann Smith, and Jean Stuart (Eds.), *Picturing Research: Drawing as Visual Methodology* (219–232). Rotterdam: Sense.

Mitchell, Claudia, Fatuma Chege, Lucy Maina, and Margot Rothman (2016). Beyond engagement in working with children in eight Nairobi slums to address safety, security, and housing: Digital tools for policy and community dialogue. *Global Public Health: An International Journal for Research, Policy and Practice* 11(5-6): 651–665.

Mitchell, Claudia, and Marni Sommer (2017). *Participatory Visual Research in Global Health.* London: Routledge.

Mitchell, Claudia, Naydene De Lange, and Relebohile Moletsane (2017). *Participatory Visual Methodologies: Social Change, Community and Policy.* London: SAGE Publications.

Moschetti, Wendy Peters (2003). An exploratory study of participatory evaluation and Hope VI community supportive services. Institute of Urban and Regional Development. Working Paper 2003–07. Berkeley, CA: University of California, Berkeley. www.econstor.eu/obitstream/10419/23610/1/WP-2003-07.pdf.

Muthuri, Stella K., Maharouf Oyolola, and Faye Cheikh (2017). Trends and correlates of single motherhood in Kenya: Results from the Demographic and Health Survey. *Health Care for Women International* 38(1): 38–54.

Nyariro, Milka (2018). Re-conceptualizing school continuation and re-entry policy for young mothers living in an urban slum context in Nairobi, Kenya: A participatory approach. *Studies in Social Justice* 12(2): 310–328.

Sajan Virgi, Zainul, and Claudia Mitchell (2011). Picturing policy in addressing water and sanitation: The voices of girls living in abject intergenerational hardship in Mozambique. *International Education* 40(2): 40–57.

Serrat, Olivier (2009). The most significant change technique: Knowledge solutions. Manila: Asian Development Bank. https://www.adb.org/sites/default/files/publication/27613/most-significant-change.pdf.

Theron, Linda C. (2012). Does visual participatory research have resilience-promoting value? Teacher experiences of generating and interpreting drawings. *South African Journal of Education* 32(4): 381–392. www.scielo.org.za/scielo.php?script=sci_arttext&pid=S0256-01002012000400005.

Umurungi, Jean-Paul, Claudia Mitchell, Myriam Gervais, Eliane Ubalijoro, and Violet Kabarenzi (2008). PhotoVoice as a methodological tool for working with girls on the street in Rwanda to address HIV & AIDS and gender violence. *Journal of Psychology in Africa* 18(3): 413–420.

Victora, Cesar G., Linda Adair, Caroline Fall, Pedro C. Hallal, Reynaldo Martorell, Linda Richter, and Harshpal Singh Sachdev (2008). Maternal and child undernutrition: Consequences for adult health and human capital. *The Lancet* 371(9609): 340–357.

Wang, Caroline (1999). PhotoVoice: A participatory action research strategy applied to women's health. *Journal of Women's Health* 8(2): 185–192.

8

PAID WORK AND UNPAID CARE WORK IN INDIA, NEPAL, TANZANIA, AND RWANDA

A bi-directional relationship

Deepta Chopra

Introduction

This chapter draws from primary research with women living in low-income families in four countries—India, Nepal, Rwanda, and Tanzania—as they strive to balance their various work responsibilities and make a living for themselves and their families. Specifically, this chapter focuses on the relationship between women's paid work and unpaid care work to shed light on how these activities feed into women's economic empowerment (WEE).

The data for this chapter is drawn from the research project 'Balancing unpaid care work and paid work: Successes, challenges and lessons for women's economic empowerment', funded through the Growth and Economic Opportunities for Women (GrOW) programme. The research was conducted from 2015–2017 and used an innovative, mixed-methods approach for data collection across 16 sites in the four study countries, including a survey of 800 women; 126 qualitative case studies of women's lived experiences based on interviews with women, men, and children; and a series of participatory exercises with women, men, and adolescents in the study communities. This chapter presents a summary of the research findings on the links between women's paid work and unpaid care work across the four countries,[1] and their relationship to WEE. Additional insights from the research are also available in Chapter 4 of this volume.

The research defines unpaid care work as encompassing different types of tasks, all uncompensated, including childcare and care for older individuals (e.g. the elderly, the ill), housework, ancillary tasks such as water and fuel collection, and care for animals. The world over, women perform the majority of all unpaid care work in their homes and communities, regardless of the share of household income that they earn (Elson 1995; Razavi 2007; Budlender 2008; Eyben and Fontana 2011; see also Chapter 4 in this volume). This unpaid care work occupies large amounts of women's time and constrains their participation in broader economic, political, civil, and social spheres. As Razavi (2007: 22) has argued, the constraints imposed by women's disproportionate burden of unpaid care work increases their risk of "economic disempowerment". However, there is little documented understanding of the dynamics by which this risk plays out for women as they endeavour to juggle their multiple responsibilities of daily life. This chapter aims to fill this gap in understanding and documenting women's lived experiences of balancing paid work and unpaid care work in India, Nepal, Tanzania, and Rwanda, as well as its impact on their economic empowerment.

The assumption that women will achieve economic empowerment through participation in the labour market has been problematised elsewhere in this volume, including in Chapter 1, and I pick up this thread again here. While WEE has been discussed and understood by some international development agencies as the mere inclusion of women in the labour market (World Bank 2006; OECD-DAC 2011), ongoing critiques of this approach have focused on the dual (i.e. paid work and unpaid care) responsibilities that women and girls shoulder, and the constraints imposed by labour markets and gendered social norms that push women into informal, low paid, and insecure work (Razavi 2007; Antonopoulos 2008; see also Chapters 1, 2, and 5 in this volume).

This chapter sets out to explore how and whether women's paid work in these situations is conducive to their empowerment. In doing so, I adopt the idea of 'empowerment' as a process rather than an outcome (Kabeer 2008; Schuler, Islam, and Rottach 2010; Kabeer, Mahmud, and Tasneem 2011; Chopra and Müller 2016). Empowerment is understood as a process through which there is a change in power relations—involving a holistic notion of power *over*, power *to*, power *with*, and power *within*—and a privileging of the relational dynamics of women's lives embedded within their families and communities, rather than an exclusive focus on an individual's incorporation into the labour market.

Finally, this chapter aims to shed light on the consequences of women's engagement in multiple domains of work on their emotional and physical wellbeing. In doing so, it puts forth the argument that there is a critical, yet under-recognised bi-directional relationship between paid work and unpaid care work that underpins WEE.

The chapter is structured as follows. It begins by presenting the relational dynamics of how care is organised across the 16 research sites and the conditions affecting the intensity and drudgery of care work for women living in low-income households. Next, the types of paid work that women undertake—specifically their working conditions and the choices and trade-offs they make in order to engage in paid work—are examined. Then the efforts that women exert and the strategies they employ to balance their paid work with unpaid care work are highlighted—including strategies of extreme multi-tasking and time-stretching. In addition, the consequences of this double burden on women themselves, their children, and their families, in terms of their physical and mental depletion, are discussed. I conclude by unpacking the complex dynamics of the relationship between paid work and unpaid care work that underpin WEE.

Unpaid care work: dynamics and patterns

Gendered divisions of labour

The most important aspect of the social organisation of care across the 16 research sites was that women always undertook the bulk of the responsibility for providing unpaid care work in their households, including childcare, household work, ancillary tasks, and animal care. Interestingly, we found that while men helped more than we had initially assumed, their participation was sporadic and often performed in response to the absence of any female in the household. Figure 8.1 below shows the large extent of the feminisation of care responsibilities in the study communities.

Figures 8.2 through 8.5 show the distribution of the different care tasks by country, and the pattern of women's disproportionate responsibility for unpaid care work holds true for most. Women were largely responsible for childcare in their households, although, in nearly a third (28%) of the families surveyed, men were also involved, which could reflect the flexibility of social norms around this activity. Household work was, however, performed largely by women. In India, as much as 89% of women took on household work without help. While the sharing of household work between men and women was most common in Nepal, this was still skewed mostly in favour of female respondents bearing this responsibility. As one woman from Depalgaon in Nepal said, "Everything has to be taken by the women—housework is personal to her". Two-thirds of all women (including female respondents and other female family members) surveyed across all 16 research sites were responsible for the collection of fuel and water for their families.

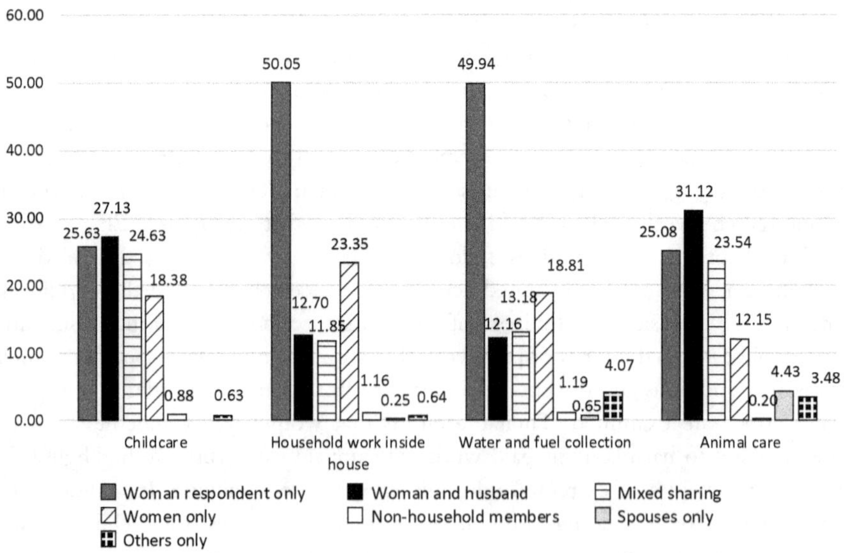

FIGURE 8.1 Social organisation of all unpaid care work across countries (%)
Source: IDS GrOW data, author's depiction

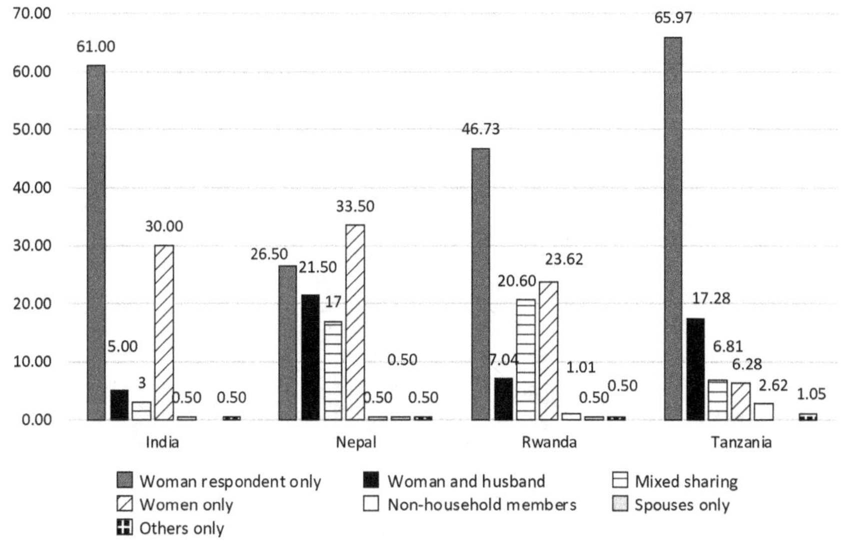

FIGURE 8.2 Social organisation of household work by country (%)
Source: IDS GrOW data, author's depiction

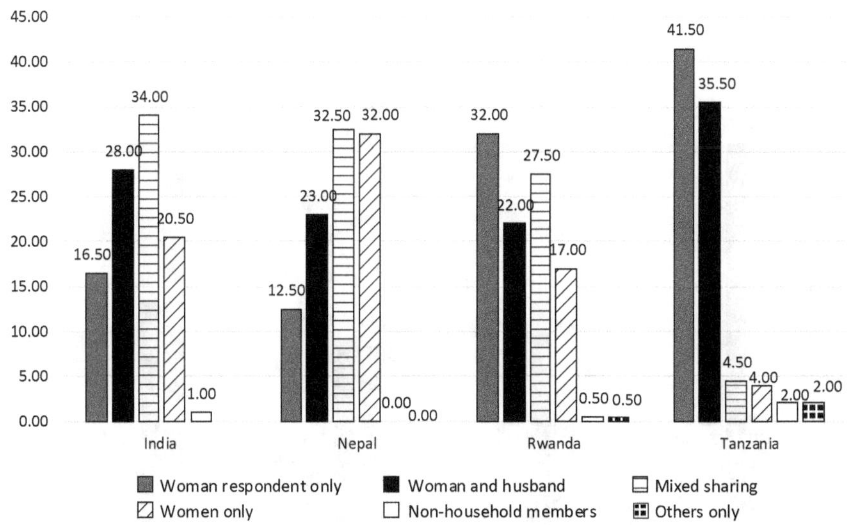

FIGURE 8.3 Social organisation of childcare by country (%)
Source: IDS GrOW data, author's depiction

Animal care was the most equitably distributed of all the care tasks, with men's sole responsibility in animal care being greater than any of their other care responsibilities. As Chopra and Zambelli (2017) have reflected, this perhaps reflects

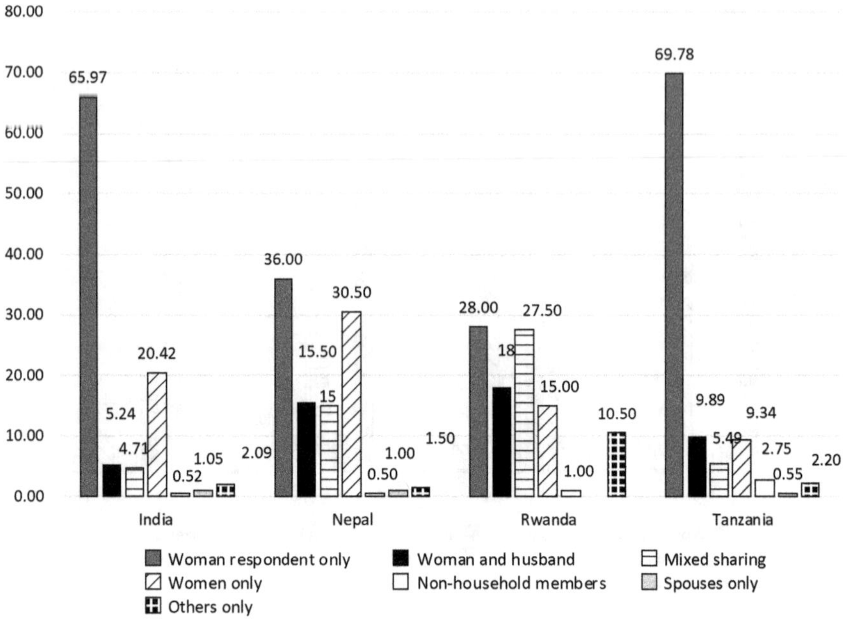

FIGURE 8.4 Social organisation of ancillary tasks (collecting water, fuel, and wood) by country (%)

Source: IDS GrOW data, author's depiction

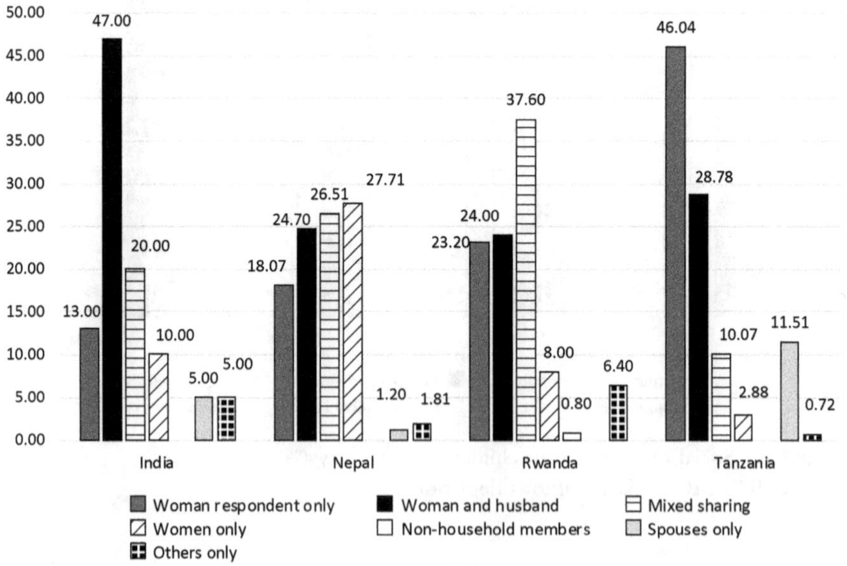

FIGURE 8.5 Social organisation of animal care by country (%)

Source: IDS GrOW data, author's depiction

the importance of the care of livestock as an income-generating task and hence considered part of men's domain of responsibility as the breadwinner.

Study results suggest that some care activities were squarely within women's domain of work, and for these activities there were deeply entrenched gender norms and expectations at play. For example, in Nepal, only married women were allowed to carry baskets on their back—these baskets being used for collection of firewood and fodder for animals.[2] Participants from Nepal and India commented on the strict gendered division of labour around this task:

> [S]owing and carrying woven baskets should not/cannot be done by men (*dokos*).
>
> *(Boy in Depalgaon, Nepal)*

> Only women bring water, and the men in the family do not go [to bring water]. And [boys] go only if they wish … [my] daughter-in-law and my daughters now take care of everything.
>
> *(Indumati Khair, Udaipur, India)*

Household structures were found to impact the social organisation of care. In extended households, the amount of unpaid care work was greater but also shared across a larger number of female family members. We also found that across the study countries, support from neighbours and community members was minimal. This was mainly because the low incomes and subsequent financial pressures experienced by most households in the study communities left little or no resources to help others. In some cases, if children were left home alone while their parents worked, neighbours would stop by periodically to see if they were alright.

The study documented a high incidence of intergenerational transfer of care to children. Over 22% of women reported that their older children undertook care work more than two to three times per week. There was also a gendered division of labour between girls and boys—with girls taking on more responsibilities within the house, such as childcare and housework like cooking and cleaning, while boys were more involved in shopping and caring for animals. However, this distribution of tasks was less rigid among children compared to adults (as similarly reported by Fontana and Natali 2008: 11). While the gendered division of labour between men and women was found to be flexible during lifecycle changes such as pregnancy and post-natal care, it always reverted to previous patterns once the child was born. A male respondent from Mehelkuna in Nepal expressed this well when he claimed to "do it all when the women cannot", adding that, "generally women have more responsibilities in domestic tasks".

Interestingly, in Rwanda, the involvement of boys was most prevalent in the collection of water and fuel (Chopra and Zambelli 2017: 20), which was not the case in other countries. This trend was accompanied by a recognition of the ill-effects on boys of performing ancillary tasks:

> My son gets tired too since he combines school and unpaid work at home. It is so tiresome, and he does not get enough time to play with friends due to some duties assigned to him by me and at some point this affects his performance at school.
>
> *(Denise Nishimwe, Rwanda (cited in Chopra and Zambelli 2017: 20))*

In other countries too, standard gender divisions of labour were found to be flexible amongst children. In India, we documented instances of boys helping mothers to cook and clean. In Nepal, we found that boys who did not have elder sisters at home contributed more to care-related tasks than those who did. As a mother of two boys explained:

> Both my sons help me. They know that their parents cannot work. I carry the manure and they do it too. They go to school in the afternoon. After returning from school one of the sons help to carry and the other makes food. And I rest near the stove. Whenever I can, I make the food but when I am unwell they make it.
>
> *(Kamla Giri, Jumla, Nepal)*

Despite the rare cases where gendered divisions of labour were ignored for specific purposes, what was most significant is the effect that the largely feminised responsibility of care had on women and girls. In fact, care tasks were considered as the main barrier for women to rest and were often very physically demanding to perform.

The drudgery of unpaid care work

The lack of childcare facilities and basic infrastructure, such as water and electricity, amplified the drudgery of women's unpaid care work. Across the four countries, women reported being exhausted and experiencing physical ailments and injuries because of the long distances travelled to collect or buy water and firewood, and the arduousness of the task. As a female respondent in Lushoto, Tanzania noted:

> Fetching water affects my health because I fetch a lot of water and I get the water far from my home so I get too tired walking while carrying a bucket of water, and also I get chest problems because of carrying a lot of buckets and climbing mountains with [heavy] loads.
>
> *(Cited in Zambelli et al. 2017b: 4)*

Women in Nepal recurrently complained about lack of water and especially electricity, which impacted their ability to grind wheat into flour that they could then use for cooking.

> If we had electricity, I would have finished my household work after returning from work. If we had gas we could have cooked faster unlike now.
>
> *(Hema Raut, Jumla, Nepal)*

> … the water taps are very far, if there were taps in various parts of the village it would be easier. The mills too are far from the houses. The mills in Jumla run on electricity but we hardly get electricity here. It would be nice to have mills in various locations in the village.
>
> *(Key Informant, Jumla, Nepal)*

In Tanzania as well, the lack of water facilities affected women's time use as they had to "suffer from long distance walks in search for water to water the vegetables" (Mama Harriet, Korogwe District, Tanzania). Women in Tanzania also spent large amounts of time travelling to access healthcare facilities due to lack of roads, and one woman expressed her concerns as follows:

> [T]he government should extend clean water services to our homes and even electricity. We would also like some hospital in our area so that we access medical services from our neighbourhood. Our nearest government hospital is far and that distance is too much for the sick person in case of an emergency.
>
> *(Baba Robin, Lushoto, Tanzania)*

The lack of water and electricity made childcare-related tasks, like feeding and bathing children, even more difficult. The lack of childcare facilitates across all 16 research sites gave women few alternatives and was particularly felt by women with children under the age of three.

The intensity of unpaid care work activities was also affected by seasonality in terms of weather conditions, as well as community and educational events such as festivals, children's school exams, etc. During the hot, dry season, women spent longer times collecting water in Tanzania and India; while in the rainy season, it was hard to wash and dry clothes or find dry wood to make fires for cooking (Zambelli et al. 2017a).

We can conclude from the above discussion that unpaid care work was largely feminised across the research sites, with men's participation characterised as sporadic at best. The lack of public services and infrastructure (including childcare, gas, electricity, water, and roads) emerged as the most important factor contributing to the drudgery of care work for women. This in turn limited women's ability to rest and take care of themselves, as comes through clearly in this quote from an 18-year old woman living in urban India:

> One has to lift [water] and get it. It is very far, you take it on your head and bring it, one's head too hurts. Once you are back with water, one does all the

> work like cleaning and cooking, all the work, to bathe and clean the kids, take shower oneself, clean clothes. All the work and then there is no rest at all.
>
> *(Manjari Rajkumar (cited in Chopra and Zambelli 2017: 22))*

However, this was not the only factor impacting women's rest and wellbeing. As Figure 8.6 shows, women's paid work also contributed significantly to their being unable to rest, second only to care work.

Paid work: dynamics and choices

This section captures the characteristics and conditions of paid work performed by women at the research sites.

Paid work activities

Across the four study countries, women spent an average of six hours per day on paid work. Notably, at any given point in time, nearly half of women respondents were simultaneously engaged in two or more paid work activities.

> I am a trader, I also do farming.... I trade, go to small saving schemes and sometimes if the season is good, I sell some of my harvests like cassava and sweet potatoes.
>
> *(Mama Jolly, Korogwe, Tanzania)*

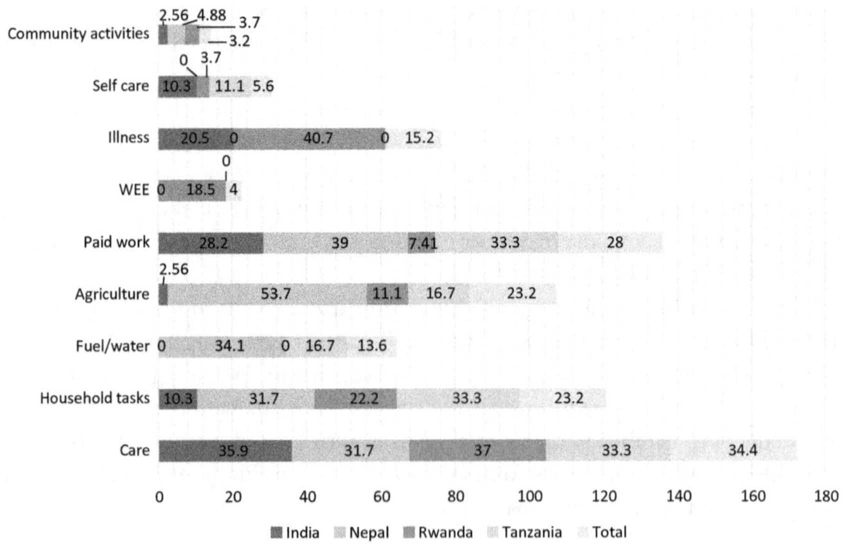

FIGURE 8.6 Tasks that prevented women from resting
Source: IDS GrOW data, author's depiction

> Mostly it is my husband and I. We own a small piece of land in the valley where we cultivate beans, maize, and yams. But we also do day labour jobs if someone wants their farm cleared.
>
> *(Mama Janice, Korogwe, Tanzania)*

These quotes highlight two important findings. First, most of the jobs that women were undertaking were very low-paid, which necessitated women doing multiple jobs in order to eke out mere survival for their families. Second, the economic conditions faced by the women and their families were dire enough for them to accept, and indeed value, any type of paid work opportunity available to them, irrespective of the conditions and time commitment involved. The following quotes highlight the difficulties faced by men and women alike in performing paid work activities:

> We do agricultural work otherwise something or the other.... If we find time then we go on other's fields to work, if we don't get time, we do it on our own fields. Yes, I have to do daily wage work [in MGNREGA] depending on my time availability. If I am not left with time I don't go.
>
> *(Raamu Daabi, speaking for himself and his wife Maya Daabi, Udaipur, India)*

> It is definitely difficult, we have to constantly work hard, and we get just 2 or 3 rupees per kilogram; we face many difficulties while selling, farming seems like an easy task but it is a painful work at last, we have to do the digging, then grow it, if that doesn't work we have to take the water, it might spoil, it is difficult.
>
> *(Sarita Kunwar, Mehentada, Nepal)*

There were significant differences in the employment patterns of men and women across the four study countries, as seen in Figures 8.7 and 8.8, with 40% of men engaged in daily wage labour and 11.6% working in factories or offices as employees (compared to just 1% of women engaged in these activities). In contrast, nearly 25% of women were engaged in home-based work, and almost 50% were either engaged in informal wage work or were self-employed. Self-employment constituted the main type of paid work for women respondents, but there were wide variations across the four study countries—from their engagement in informal waged employment being the highest in Nepal and the lowest in Tanzania to participation in public works programmes being the highest in Rwanda (Chopra and Zambelli 2017: 24).

Conditions of paid work

Across the four countries, paid work for both women and men was predominately of low pay and precarious, and, for women in particular, conducted mostly in informal and agrarian settings. Low earnings often went hand-in-hand with

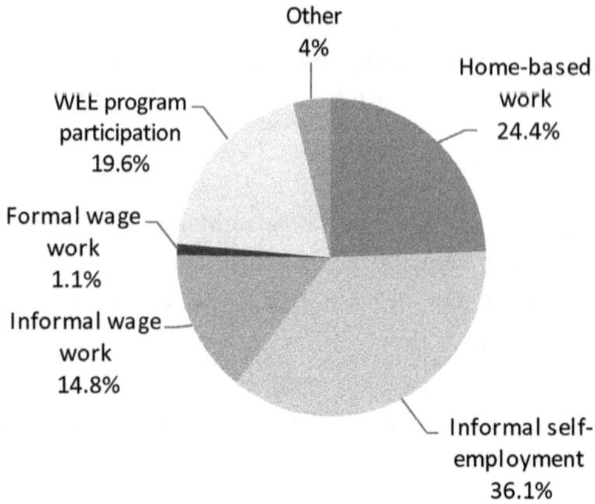

FIGURE 8.7 Types of paid work that women are engaged in (%)
Source: IDS GrOW data, author's depiction

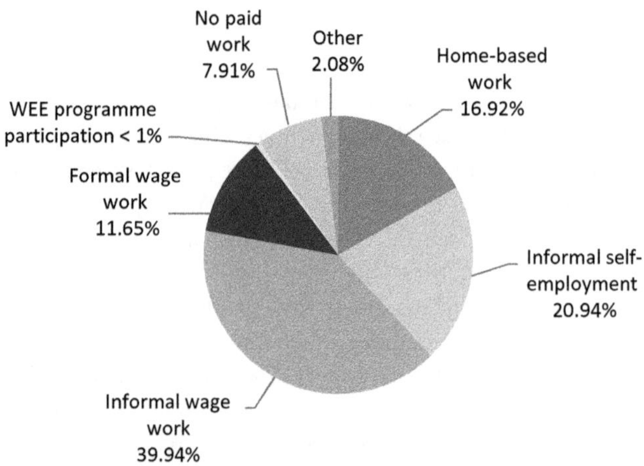

FIGURE 8.8 Types of paid work that men are engaged in (%)
Source: IDS GrOW data, author's depiction

delayed and refused payments. Self-employment and home-based work (which constituted 60% of women respondents' paid work activities) was also characterised by arduous labour with low returns, which left women feeling exhausted and depleted.

> Works like … carrying heavy loads to the market. Even if there is a place that we think is wrong, we do not have the option of quitting that work … she

> brings firewood from the forest and sells the same in the market. What can we do? That is also a problem.
>
> *(Jeevan Rokaya, husband of Pramila Rokaya, Jumla, Nepal)*

Lack of public services, such as roads for connectivity to markets and worksites, put additional time constraints and pressure on women's paid work activities. For 36.9% of women, paid work activities took place at their houses, but for the rest it involved travel to work sites. Women largely travelled on foot to their workplaces due to a lack of public transportation.

Women reported adverse effects to their health because of the strenuous nature of their paid work activities—this included back headaches, back and hand injuries, respiratory difficulties, and, in one case in Nepal, a serious condition called uterine prolapse.

> We sometimes carry the stones, sometimes the mud, sometimes we throw the mud. Sometimes our hands would get injured, sometimes our legs would. It is exhausting for the body. I did not even have energy to walk because of the tiredness.
>
> *(Radhika BK, Jumla, Nepal (cited in Ghosh et al. 2017: 5))*

> Yes, I face problems. I have to sit the whole day to roll *agarbattis* [incense sticks] due to which my hands hurt a lot and so does my back.
>
> *(Roshni Mimroth, Ujjain, India)*

Women were also keenly aware of the poor working conditions that their children—who shadowed them at work due to lack of alternative childcare—were exposed to. In fact, while this is underreported, we saw several instances of children being engaged in paid work alongside their mothers.

> They [sons aged 10 and 8, and daughters aged 12 and 4] are unable to study but what do we do? It is necessary to work also.... When they help in agarbatti making, we get more money... Three persons can make more than one person can.... When they have exams, they don't make *agarbattis*.... They make them for 1.5–2 hours [per day] and then study after that.
>
> *(Roshni Mimroth, Ujjain, India)*

> He plays on the roadside with mud and sand used at the [construction] site.... I do feel scared [for the child's safety], but there is no choice as I have to work. There is constant moving traffic on the road, and I need to cross the road at times to bring the construction material so I leave him on the roadside. When he was an infant, I used to leave him in the hammock.
>
> *(Malavika Gaur, Indore, India)*

A crucial element that affected women and constrained their ability to both seek out and perform paid work opportunities was the lack of childcare services. Women across the 16 sites spoke about their preferences for paid work that was home-based to accommodate their childcare and housework responsibilities.

> I make her [four-year-old daughter] sleep and then make the *agarbattis*. She is quite young and doesn't understand anything, she starts eating the raw material used for making the *agarbattis*.
>
> *(Roshni Mimroth, Ujjain, India)*

> If possible, it would be easy if the workplace was close to my house, if not that, then, improved roads would make things a little easier.
>
> *(Urmila Dhakal, Mehelkuna, Nepal)*

Women also reported being late for work or missing their shift all together because they were busy with childcare or other household tasks. While at work, women described being distracted due to worrying about their children or exhausted from performing unpaid care work and therefore less productive. Despite facing reprimand from their employers, many women were left with no choice but to bring their children to work due to a lack of options:

> There is no place to keep the kids at the workplace.... They [other women workers] have to bring older kids to take care of their younger kid, as they need to travel on foot for nearly two kilometres to work.
>
> *(Indumati Khair, Udaipur, India)*

As a result of the constraints they faced at every turn, some women reduced the amount of time spent on paid work to accommodate their unpaid care workloads, subsequently reducing their income. Others dropped out of the workforce temporarily or permanently when they became pregnant or while their children were still young. This demonstrates the common trade-off women are faced with between women's paid work and unpaid care responsibilities, which is discussed further the next section.[3]

Balancing care work and paid work: strategies and outcomes

The research documented a 'bi-directional relationship' between paid work and unpaid care work: not only did women's care work impact their paid work opportunities and engagement, but, conversely, paid work impacted the extent, timing, and nature of women's unpaid care activities. The following quote illustrates this relationship:

> I'm unable to clean the house—instead of [cleaning] I quickly cook the food and run to the farm, ordering my daughter to do a few tasks at home.

> Sometimes I [arrive] late to bring water. There are times when I can't clean my house or wash my [three] children's clothes. Either I am able to finish all the chores and unable to start the work at [the] farm, or if I finish the farm work, my house becomes messy.
>
> *(Rukmini Bk, Mehentada, Nepal)*

Women in all four study countries found that childcare and household tasks were the most difficult to combine with paid work, as shown in Figure 8.9. Nearly one-third of all women in the study reported that they left their household tasks undone in order to engage in paid work, while another third reported going to work without lining up childcare if necessary (Chopra and Zambelli 2017: 29). Activities such as unpaid agriculture activities (e.g. tending of their own farm) and collecting fuel and water were also difficult to undertake alongside paid work, but less so according to the research.

Strategies for balancing care work and paid work

To balance their dual workloads women employed several types of strategies. Some women reported getting up extremely early or staying up late, just to get everything done—a concept that our team titled "time stretching" (Chopra and Zambelli 2017: 31).

> Sometimes I have to go collect grass, I have to broom and clean the house, I have to cook food, I have to wake up at 4am, and … a few days ago I went to

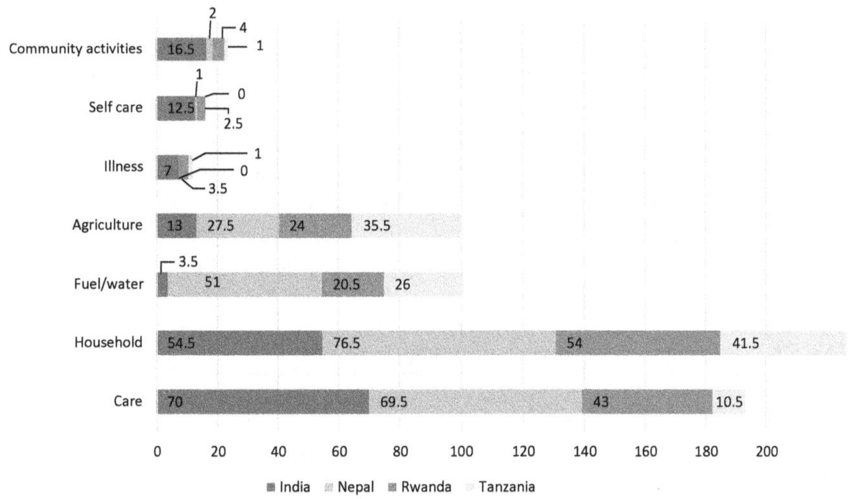

FIGURE 8.9 Activities that are problematic to combine with work
Source: IDS GrOW data, author's depiction

> collect grass taking my child with me because there was no one to look after her at home. And I do that while going to collect the firewood as well. I can only leave her if there is someone to take care of [her]. I cannot just go to work leaving my child home.
>
> *(Menuka Dhital, Depalgaon, Nepal (cited in Chopra et al. 2020: 28))*

Other women became adept at multitasking in order to accomplish both their paid work and unpaid care responsibilities, sometimes simultaneously. Not only did women multi-task during their waking hours, they also regularly had their sleep interrupted by the need to perform care-related tasks. On average, women respondents from the four study countries were found to be multi-tasking around 11 hours each day. Table 8.1 shows the average number of hours per day that women spent multitasking in each country.

Other strategies that women used to combine paid work and childcare, which were previously discussed, included the intergenerational transfer of care responsibilities to daughters, leaving children with relatives or home alone, and taking children to work with them. The fact that childcare responsibilities do not decrease, irrespective of the type and amount of paid work that women undertake, explains why women respondents expressed a preference for wanting to work closer to home or at home and in jobs that allow them the flexibility to look after their children at the same time (Chopra and Zambelli 2017: 36). This preference was especially strong for women with younger children. In the absence of any other options, "… if the child is very small, then we carry the child in our hands and then go to work" (woman in Udaipur, India).

Impacts of combining paid work with unpaid care

Regardless of which strategies they employed, women respondents struggled to balance their responsibilities for paid work and unpaid care, leaving them no time to rest or recuperate. As a result, women frequently reported feeling physically exhausted, drained, and anxious, unable to balance everything on their plate:

> The entire week I have to work, how do I explain my tension to you? Should I wake up at four o'clock or five o'clock? Should I do this work or that? My brain just doesn't function!
>
> *(Sangeetha Sohan Damra, Dungarpur, India)*

TABLE 8.1 Number of hours women spent multitasking

	India	*Nepal*	*Rwanda*	*Tanzania*	*Overall*
When awake	11.74	10.72	8.15	13.63	11.06
Interrupted while sleeping	2.43	3.69	3.33	4.47	3.48
In total (whether awake or asleep)	14.17	14.41	11.48	18.10	14.54

Source: IDS GrOW data, author's depiction

> [B]ecause there are times when I delay in the plantations and that means I am going to prepare lunch late, and washing my children's uniforms will also be late, but I can try to do whatever I had to do. In other words, everything becomes disorganized and I end up getting tired and exhausted although I fail to finish them all.
>
> *(Mama Juliet, Korogwe, Tanzania)*

> It's complicated because you have to do both at the same time and with the school-going children. You have to work here and there but it's difficult and you may end up declining in the business.
>
> *(Mama Joy, home-based worker in Korogwe, Tanzania)*

Children also reported mixed feelings about their mother's paid work having seen them regularly overworked and sleep deprived:

> [My mother] does a lot of work.... I know that working is good but she over works so I would like her to get some rest after her work. But again, she needs to do the digging so that we have food. So, I don't know [if her paid work is good or not].
>
> *(Justine's five-year-old daughter, Lushoto, Tanzania (cited in Zambelli et al. 2017a: 25))*

Across all four countries, it was found that women did not get enough sleep to feel rested the following day. In some cases, it seemed that women got a healthy amount of sleep each night in terms of total hours, but upon closer look it became clear that much of this sleep was interrupted and intermittent. The likelihood of women sleeping for several hours without waking up to perform paid or unpaid work was low, particularly in Rwanda and Tanzania (as shown in Figure 8.10). Further, women who have young children are always 'on call' to perform childcare work—signifying, as Chopra and Zambelli have labelled, "the absence of complete rest" (2017: 31).

Women's overlapping paid work and unpaid care responsibilities also ate into the time they had to spend on personal care, hygiene, and leisure. Over time, women became physically, emotionally, and mentally depleted. Many reported injuries including back pain and headaches, and illnesses including vision problems and even lung disease. In addition, women felt near-constant anxiety from worrying about their ability to support their families economically, or, conversely, feeling guilty and worried about their families while at work. It was an impossible situation for these women.

Women also reported concerns about transferring their unpaid care work to their daughters, yet feeling helpless about the situation since they needed to continue with their paid work to earn income for survival. As one woman painfully explained:

> I have lots of work but very little time. I get torn between work and baby's care is not managed well.... Yes, they [daughters] have been forced to grow

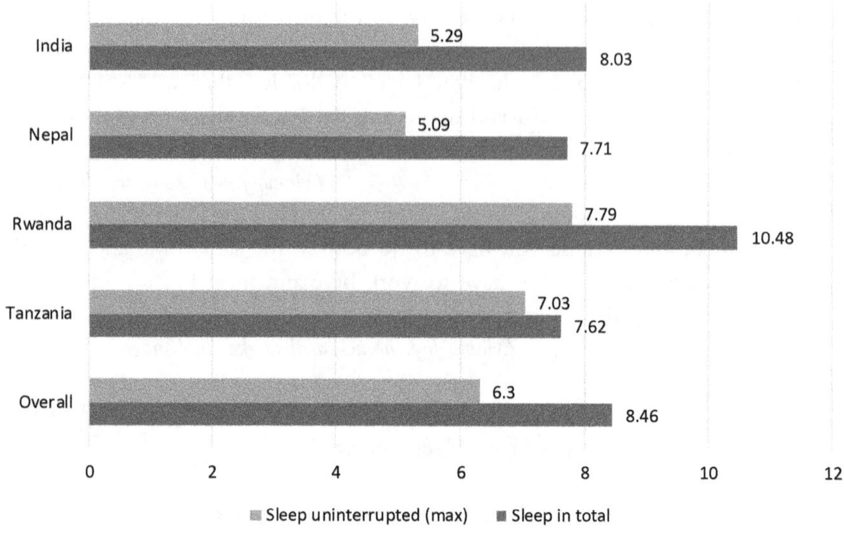

FIGURE 8.10 Women's hours of sleep per night
Source: IDS GrOW data, author's depiction

> up. I yell at them. At this age, they are supposed to be put in our laps, fed by us, but they clean themselves up, change their clothes, and go on their own because I am busy. Hence, if you consider the age of my daughter, she should be carried and taken to her bus, that is the service I should provide them, but I beat them up instead. I am burdened by the work; I get angry and end up beating them.
>
> *(Malati BK, Mehentada, Nepal)*

Children in turn felt the negative effects of women's double burden—both in terms of taking on the role of care provider (which impacted their education and time use), and in terms of experiencing lower quality and quantity of care themselves. Children who shadowed their mothers at paid work were often exposed to hazardous environments, and some were removed from school. Children also reported feeling lonely, sad, or angry at being left alone at home. One boy expressed feeling angry when he had to cook *roti* [bread], while another said he is unable to study when his mother goes away (Zaidi et al. 2017: 18).

Conclusion: women's economic empowerment or depletion?

It is clear from the research reflected in this chapter, and elsewhere in this volume, that simply engaging in paid work is not the easy answer to achieving WEE. Without a commensurate change in unpaid care work responsibilities, women's engagement in paid work only adds another dimension to their overall burden of work. This is not to say that women do not want to engage in paid work—quite the opposite—our research found that women are keen to engage in paid work, mainly to earn income for their cash-strapped families. However, as this chapter has shown, their choices are extremely constrained—both in terms of having to undertake poorly paid, informal sector work that hardly gives them a liveable income, as well as undertaking unpaid care work activities that are gruelling and undervalued.

In summary, four critical aspects of women's paid work and unpaid care work determine their experience, and whether they move toward empowerment or slide into further physical and mental depletion.

The first aspect is the drudgery of unpaid care work. This can be exacerbated by the presence of more young children and infants, as well as the lack of childcare support from family members. Women who were either sole adult earners and carers, or had limited familial support, felt their double burden more acutely and struggled the most. The absence of public services like childcare, and basic infrastructure including water, electricity, gas, and roads, further accentuated the drudgery that women experienced in fulfilling their care responsibilities. As summarised by Zambelli et al. (2017: 20): "Poor water and electricity infrastructure, distant health facilities, and bad roads all have a knock-on effect on the time that women spend doing a number of care tasks, which subtracts from the time they can invest in cash-earning activities". Access to these public services and supports is therefore critical for promoting WEE.

Second, the arduous nature of women's paid work can adversely impact women's time and energy. The lower-paying their work, the more hours women must work in order to make a living—often compelling them to combine multiple jobs and work for very long hours under adverse conditions. This only added to their physical and emotional depletion. The absence of childcare facilities especially heightened women's depletion, as they were forced to either leave their children alone at home or bring them to work. In either case, children were exposed to hazardous environments and neglect. Older girl children, to whom the responsibility for childcare was sometimes transferred, experienced negative outcomes such as loss of education and leisure time. Here, access to decent work opportunities, combined with reliable and quality public services and infrastructure, can greatly improve women's income and working conditions, and in turn promote their empowerment.

The third aspect is related to a household's poverty level. Economic insecurity and poverty were seen to push women (and men) more rapidly into precarious jobs with difficult working conditions. We saw that women from poorer households were undertaking paid work in order to provide much-needed income for their families, often regardless of the pay or working conditions. Therefore, this could not be seen as a "choice or a sign of women's positive inclusion in the labour market" (Chopra and Zambelli 2017: 40), but rather as a stopgap coping mechanism to ensure their families survival. Where women's paid work activities involved long hours of arduous work under poor conditions just to make ends meet, this cannot be considered empowering. Here again, access to decent work opportunities is critical to promoting WEE.

The final aspect that affected women's outcomes was related to community or institutional support. Better support from their community—both for undertaking paid work (such as rotational responsibilities for agriculture and livestock), and for taking care of children—was found to enable a more healthy and positive balance between women's paid work and unpaid care work. In addition, as discussed above, institutional support in the form of accessible and reliable public services would be critical in reducing the drudgery of both paid work and unpaid care work.

Ultimately, the study results show that women's empowerment is underpinned by a complex dynamic between women's paid work and unpaid care work. There is a bi-directional relationship at play: unpaid care work affects women's opportunities and engagement in paid work, and thus the income that women can earn; paid work in turn affects the quantity, quality, and outcomes of women's unpaid care work. The more that women have access to decent work opportunities, public services and basic infrastructure, and familial and community support, the more women's engagement in paid work will lead to empowering outcomes. These empowering outcomes, which have been termed as the 'double boon' (Chopra and Zambelli 2017), involve women having a fairer share of unpaid care work responsibilities and access to decent paid work, such that the labour market becomes a source of empowerment, rather than drudgery and depletion for women and their families.

In summary, the "drudgery and depletion of women's bodies and minds is neither a necessary nor an inevitable consequence of their participation in the labour force" (Chopra and Zambelli 2017: 41). Instead, well-funded public services combined with decent paid work is critical to ensuring a reduction in drudgery of both paid work and unpaid care work, and in cementing women's ability to achieve economic empowerment.

Notes

1 Country specific details are available in four working papers, namely: Zaidi et al. (2017) for India; Rohwerder et al. (2017) for Rwanda; Ghosh et al. (2017) for Nepal; and Zambelli et al. (2017a) for Tanzania.
2 For more on the discussion on the role of social norms and WEE, see Chapter 5 in this volume.
3 Other chapters in this volume explore the trade-off between paid work and unpaid care work, including Chapters 4 and 7.

Acknowledgements

The author is thankful to IDRC, the UK's Foreign, Commonwealth and Development Office (FCDO), and the Hewlett Foundation for their project grant to IDS under their GrOW programme, which this chapter draws all its data from. Meenakshi Krishnan (PhD scholar, IDS) provided the research assistance for writing this chapter, for which I am very grateful. Amrita Saha (Research Fellow, IDS) contributed the figures used in the chapter; many thanks to her for also checking all the quantitative data used in this chapter.

References

Antonopoulos, Rania (2008). The unpaid care work-paid work connection. The Levy Economics Institute Working Paper No. 541. Annandale-on-Hudson, NY: The Levy Institute. www.levyinstitute.org/pubs/wp_541.pdf.

Budlender, Debbie (2008). The statistical evidence on care and non-care work across six countries. United Nations Research Institute for Social Development, Gender and Development (UNRISD) Programme Paper No. 4. Geneva: UNRISD. www.unrisd.org/80256B3C005BCCF9/(httpAuxPages)/F9FEC4EA774573E7C1257560003A96B2/$file/BudlenderREV.pdf.

Chopra, Deepta, and Catherine Müller (2016). Introduction: Connecting perspectives on women's empowerment. *IDS Bulletin* 47(1A): 1–10. https://opendocs.ids.ac.uk/opendocs/bitstream/handle/20.500.12413/9700/IDSB_47_1A_10.190881968-2016.113.pdf?sequence=5.

Chopra, Deepta, and Elena Zambelli (2017). No time to rest: Women's lived experiences of balancing paid work and unpaid care work. Global Synthesis Report. Brighton: Institute of Development Studies. https://www.ids.ac.uk/publications/no-time-to-rest-womens-lived-experiences-of-balancing-paid-work-and-unpaid-care-work/.

Chopra, Deepta, Amrita Saha, Sohela Nazneen, and Meenakshi Krishnan (2020). Are women not 'working'? Interactions between childcare and women's economic engagement. IDS Working Paper 533. Brighton: Institute for Development Studies. https://www.ids.ac.uk/publications/are-women-not-working-interactions-between-childcare-and-womens-economic-engagement/.

Elson, Diane (1995). *Male Bias in the Development Process*, second edition. Manchester, UK: Manchester University Press.

Eyben, Rosalind, and Marzia Fontana (2011). Caring for wellbeing. The Bellagio Initiative. Brighton: Institute of Development Studies. https://opendocs.ids.ac.uk/opendocs/bitstream/handle/20.500.12413/3674/Bellagio-Eyben%20and%20Fontana.pdf?sequence=1.

Fontana, Marzia, and Luisa Natali (2008). Gendered patterns of time use in Tanzania: Public investment in infrastructure can help. Paper prepared for the IFPRI Project on Evaluating the Long-Term Impact of Gender-focused Policy Interventions. Brighton: University of Sussex. https://pdfs.semanticscholar.org/ed54/c1b13365dfdebee86142bc041af62ed3151a.pdf?_ga=2.84080479.719353871.1591816984-1151907925.1591816984.

Ghosh, Anweshaa, Anjam Singh, Shraddha Chigateri, Deepta Chopra, and Catherine Müller (2017). A trapeze act: Balancing unpaid care work and paid work by women in Nepal. IDS Working Paper 500. Brighton: Institute of Development Studies. https://opendocs.ids.ac.uk/opendocs/bitstream/handle/20.500.12413/13338/Wp500_Online.pdf.

Kabeer, Naila (2008). Paid work, women's empowerment and gender justice: Critical pathways of social change. Institute of Development Studies, Pathways of Women's Empowerment, Working Paper No. 3. http://eprints.lse.ac.uk/53077/1/Kabeer_Paid-work_Published.pdf.

Kabeer, Naila, Simeen Mahmud, and Sakiba Tasneem (2011). Does paid work provide a pathway to women's empowerment? Empirical findings from Bangladesh. IDS Working Paper 375. Brighton: Institute of Development Studies. https://www.lse.ac.uk/gender/assets/documents/research/choice-constraints-and-the-gender-dynamics-of-lab/Does-paid-work-provide-a-pathway-to-womens-empowerment.pdf.

OECD-DAC (2011). Women's economic empowerment. Issues paper. OECD-DAC Network on Gender Equality (GENDERNET). Paris: OECD Publishing. www.oecd.org/dac/gender-development/47561694.pdf.

Razavi, Shahra (2007). The political and social economy of care in a development context: Conceptual issues, research questions and policy options. United Nations Research Institute for Social Development, Gender and Development (UNRISD) Programme Paper No. 3. Geneva: UNRISD. www.unrisd.org/80256B3C005BCCF9/(httpAuxPages)/2DBE6A93350A7783C12573240036D5A0/$file/Razavi-paper.pdf.

Rohwerder, Brigitte, Catherine Müller, Birasa Nyamulinda, Deepta Chopra, Elena Zambelli, and Naomi Hossain (2017). 'You cannot live without money': Balancing women's unpaid care work and paid work in Rwanda. IDS Working Paper 498. Brighton: Institute of Development Studies. https://opendocs.ids.ac.uk/opendocs/bitstream/handle/20.500.12413/13337/Wp498_Online.pdf.

Schuler, Sidney Ruth, Farzana Islam, and Elisabeth Rottach (2010). Women's empowerment revisited: A case study from Bangladesh. *Development in Practice* 20(7): 840–854. www.ncbi.nlm.nih.gov/pmc/articles/PMC2941240/.

World Bank (2006). Gender equality as smart economics: A World Bank Group gender action plan (Fiscal years 2007–10). Washington, DC: World Bank. http://documents.worldbank.org/curated/en/295371468315572899/Gender-equality-as-smart-economics-a-World-Bank-Group-gender-action-plan-fiscal-years-2007-10.

Zaidi, Mubashira, Shraddha Chigateri, Deepta Chopra, and Keetie Roelen (2017). 'My work never ends': Women's experiences of balancing unpaid care work and paid work through WEE programming in India. IDS Working Paper 494. Brighton: Institute of Development Studies. https://opendocs.ids.ac.uk/opendocs/bitstream/handle/20.500.12413/13203/Wp494_Online.pdf.

Zambelli, Elena, Keetie Roelen, Naomi Hossain, Deepta Chopra, and Jenifer Twebaze Musoke (2017a). 'How can it be a problem if you need them both?' Women juggling paid and unpaid care work in Tanzania. IDS Working Paper 495. Brighton: Institute of Development Studies. https://opendocs.ids.ac.uk/opendocs/bitstream/handle/20.500.12413/13204/Wp495 Online.pdf?sequence=760.

Zambelli, Elena, Keetie Roelen, Naomi Hossain, Deepta Chopra, and Jenifer Twebaze Musoke (2017b). 'My mother does a lot of work': Women balancing paid and unpaid care work in Tanzania. National Report. Brighton: Institute for Development Studies. https://opendocs.ids.ac.uk/opendocs/handle/20.500.12413/13283.

9

WOMEN'S LABOUR FORCE PARTICIPATION IN SRI LANKA'S NORTH

Ramani Gunatilaka and Ranmini Vithanagama

Introduction

Sri Lanka's female labour force participation rate, at 37% of the population over 15 years of age in 2017, is one of the lowest in the region (Department of Census and Statistics [DCS] 2019). Yet women's workforce participation in Sri Lanka's Northern Province is even lower (28% in 2017) and a greater cause for concern. The region suffered significant damage during the decades-long military conflict which ended in 2009, making economic recovery and the creation of decent work opportunities an ongoing challenge. Most northern districts remain among the poorest in the country despite some recent improvements in poverty rates (DCS 2018). While analyses of female labour force participation at the national level have identified underlying factors such as unpaid care and household work, skills deficits, and gender discrimination (Gunatilaka 2013, 2016; Gunewardena 2015; Solotaroff, Joseph, and Kuriakose 2018; Samarakoon and Mayadunne 2018; Seneviratne 2019a, 2019b), few comparative studies exist for women in Sri Lanka's Northern Province.

Workforce participation for women in the north was low during and even before the conflict began in 1983. By 1985, 18% of women aged ten years and above were in the workforce, compared to 32% across the country (DCS 1987). Only in the Eastern Province were participation rates lower, at 15% (DCS 1987). By 2017, only the participation rates of women 15 years and older were reported but, even according to these data, women's participation rates in all but one of Northern Province's five districts (Vavuniya) were below the national average, including two districts (Kilinochchi and Mannar) that reported some of the lowest rates in the entire country, at 22.8% and 23.8%, respectively (DCS 2019). Women's representation in the workforce in the north has remained low but improved from just a fifth (20%) in 1985 to a quarter (25%) in 2016 (DCS 1987,

2019). In contrast, women's representation in the national economy has been higher, rising from 29% to 37% over the same period (DCS 1987, 2019).

This chapter explores the various demographic, socioeconomic, institutional, and conflict-related factors that have influenced the labour force participation of women in the Northern Province and quantifies the contribution of these factors to the probability of labour force participation. The analysis uses primary data collected from approximately 3,000 women-headed households and 1,000 male-headed households from all five districts in the province. The next section sets out the background and regional context of the study, which is followed by a review of the literature on the implications of armed conflict for women's labour force participation. A description of the research methodology, data, and analysis of the study results follows. The concluding section summarises the findings and discusses policy implications.

Background and study context

Sri Lanka's ethnic conflict was rooted in unequal access to good jobs and higher education that prevailed in the late 1960s and early 1970s. During this period, an individual's ethnicity and language conditioned their chances of obtaining a university degree or quality employment. While a restrictive trade regime, nationalisation of industries, and anti-private sector policies made employment in the public service the only option for most educated young people, a language-based standardisation policy and district quota system to govern university admissions reduced the proportion of Tamils entering university—and subsequently, the public sector. These policies heightened ethnic tensions and encouraged Tamil youth to revolt against the state (de Silva 1999; Abeyratne 2004). Many of these language-based standardisation policies were dismantled by the late 1970s. The economy was liberalised in 1977 to encourage foreign direct investment and private sector-led export and job growth (Athukorala and Jayasuriya 1994). Yet by that time, the country's Tamil-majority areas in the north and east were already engulfed in a violent military conflict, spurred on by sub-continental geopolitical forces and financed by the Tamil diaspora (de Silva 1999).

Northern Province also suffered the worst damage during the war (Chandran 2016; Tilakaratne and Siriwardena 2013). The region was the Liberation Tigers of Tamil Eelam's (LTTE) headquarters and the focus of government offensives to defeat it. The war further prevented the region from benefitting from the country's economic liberalisation policies during the late 1970s, which catalysed growth in the southern part of the country. Yet following the defeat of the LTTE by government forces in 2009, Sri Lanka's government invested heavily in post-war reconstruction and the development of infrastructure. While this investment created the necessary conditions for economic growth, it was not sufficient to generate the required number of decent jobs. In fact, across the entire country, only a quarter of the number of jobs created between 2006 and 2014 were in the formal sector (Majid and Gunatilaka 2017), and, as of 2017, close to half of all jobs in the non-agricultural sector were informal (DCS

2019). Yet while the proportion of non-agricultural informal sector jobs was 42% and 38%, respectively, in the economically advanced districts of the Western Province, only in Northern Province's Vavuniya district was the share at 49% slightly above the national average of 48% (DCS 2019). In the other four northern districts, employment in the non-farm informal sector ranged from 53% in Mannar to 62% in Mullaitivu, among the highest country wide (DCS 2019).

The region's adverse geography constrained economic growth and development in Northern Province long before the war broke out. Much of the land mass is in the 'dry zone,' while Jaffna peninsula and the province's western seaboard is in the 'arid zone' despite being irrigated by underground aquifers. Lagoons and islands impede intra-provincial connectivity. The provincial capital, Jaffna, is nearly 400 kilometres from Sri Lanka's capital, Colombo, and seven and a half hours drive by road (see map in Figure 9.1). Nearly half of the province's population of one million inhabitants lives on the Jaffna peninsula while the rest is scattered across its four southern districts, making Mullaitivu, Kilinochchi, Vavuniya, and Mannar among the least densely populated of all of Sri Lanka's districts (DCS 2015a).

The province's economy remains largely undiversified and dependent on agriculture and services. While Northern Province was the least industrialised in 1996 when provincial GDP data was first estimated, it remains the province with the smallest manufacturing sector and the largest services sector. Its share of the total number of non-farm commercial establishments is small and may have been smaller before the war. While Jaffna District accounted for 3% of non-farm commercial establishments nation-wide in 2013–2014, the other northern districts accounted for less than 1% each (DCS 2015b). The region continues to contribute the least to the national economic output: its share of 2.4% in 1996 had increased only marginally to 4.5% in 2017; whereas Western Province, where the country's capital city of Colombo is located, accounts for about 37% of GDP (Central Bank of Sri Lanka 2008, 2019). While Northern Province accounted for only 6% of five million Sri Lankans working in 1985–1986, this share had slipped to 4.5% by 2012 due to outmigration southwards, particularly of skilled individuals (DCS 2015a). In 2017, agriculture accounted for 28.3% of total employment while the services industry accounted for nearly 50% (DCS 2019). Foreign remittances from relatives in the Tamil diaspora continue to sustain many northern households.

The implications of armed conflict for women's labour force participation

War can change women's labour market prospects in several different ways. War intensifies women's burden of unpaid work, especially their work in providing care. Caregiving constrains mobility, while damage to infrastructure renders household activities much more laborious and time consuming (Rehn and Sirleaf 2002). Dislocation and displacement also destroy assets necessary for income generation. Health status as a dimension of human capital is often impaired due to poor nutrition and psychological trauma (Blattman 2010). The formation of skills

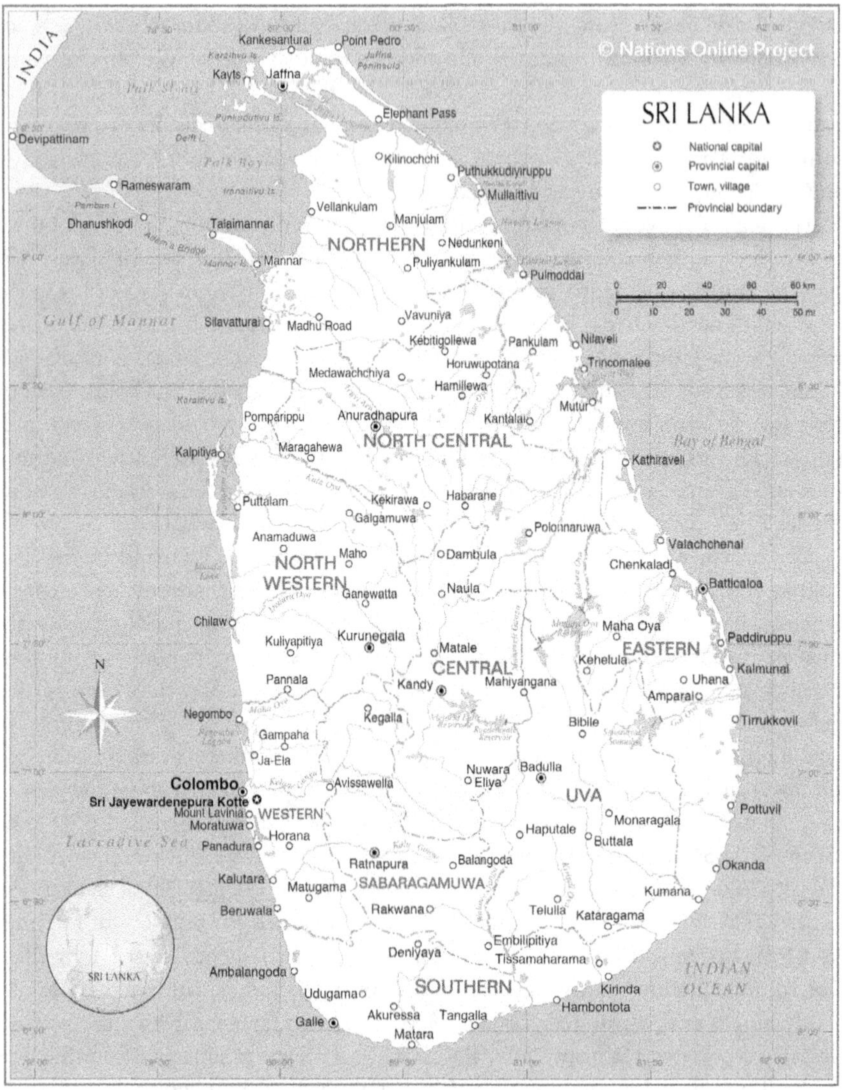

FIGURE 9.1 Sri Lanka's administrative districts
Source: www.nationsonline.org/oneworld/map/sri_lanka_map.htm

and human capital through schooling is disrupted, and equipment, arable land, productive trees, and livestock are destroyed. Social capital and social networks are decimated (El Jack 2003). Traditional gender inequalities in access to resources, information, basic services, and income are compounded by displacement (Birkeland 2009). Even where women benefit from displacement—in the form of training and development programmes in health, education, and income-generating activities—these programmes do not necessarily help create more equitable gender relationships (El Jack 2003).

Nevertheless, war and violence can also increase women's workforce participation by propelling them into jobs that are often precarious and involve self-employment and unpaid family work (Iyer and Santos 2012). As primary breadwinners, women can become entrepreneurs in the informal sector and exploit opportunities created by the conflict such as selling supplies to the rebels or providing food to the displaced (Hudock, Sherman, and Williamson 2016). Since armed conflict makes it dangerous for people to engage in traditional income-generating activities like agriculture in the open, such opportunities for informal livelihood activities can enable survival in labour markets stressed by conflict (Kumar 2001; Petesche 2011). Post-conflict, women's informal employment can increase as it requires little heavy investment, whereas the formal sector, which needs larger investments, may resuscitate only after political stability is restored (Kumar 2001; Bouta and Frerks 2002) A study of the impact of the 1996–2001 civil conflict in Nepal showed that women's likelihood of employment was strongly and positively related to the conflict, while an economic shock such as the loss of job for a man at home had no impact (Menon and van der Meulen Rodgers 2015).

The gendered socioeconomic impacts of Sri Lanka's conflict have received some attention in the literature. Ruwanpura and Humphries (2004) looked at the female headship of households in the conflict-affected Eastern Province. They argued that while the conflict may have increased the number of women-headed households, they were poor even before the war began. They were also heavily dependent on support networks of relatives and community, and financial support from male relatives outside the immediate family was much less important than the women's own efforts and the contributions of their children. Amirthalingam and Lakshman (2009) investigated how women leveraged assets that they held, mainly jewellery, to survive the economic consequences of displacement brought about by both the war and the 2004 tsunami.

In another study of gendered differences in the holding of assets after the war ended in Eastern Province, Kulatunga (2017) found considerable differences between female-headed and male-headed households. Kulatunga attributed these differences to ethnic differences, differences in the age of the household head, and the gender of children, as well as to differences in access to public resources, labour markets, and spatial factors. While economic backwardness and gender-based marginalisation were important in explaining gender-based differences in patterns of income generation, some of the differences could be attributed to cultural, religious, and social factors (Kulatunga 2014).

The war may have also compounded institutional disadvantages that women face in accessing productive resources. The inheritance schedules of Sri Lanka's Land Development Ordinance stipulate that if the person allotted the land dies without making a will, only the eldest son could inherit the land (Alailima 2000). These provisions may have resulted in women from such households losing access to land with the loss of their husbands and sons during the war. Meanwhile, the customary law of *Thesawalamai* that applies to those born in Sri Lanka's Northern Province recognises women's ownership of land but not their command over it. Such restrictions also may have had a bearing on women's labour market outcomes in Northern Province. Yet Sarvananthan, Suresh, and Alagarajah (2017) argue that gender-based discrimination by state institutions or the presence of the military in the north have been less hostile to women's non-traditional employment than the covert ethno-feminist and sub-nationalist agendas of those who have criticised the recruitment of Tamil women into Sri Lanka's armed forces.

Research data, methodology, and analysis

Data

The analysis in this chapter is based on data collected through a household survey conducted in the poorer divisions of the five districts of Northern Province during the latter half of 2015. The survey covered 3,021 women heading their households and 1,004 women in male-headed households. The sample of women-headed households was randomly selected from the registries of women-headed households available from the Divisional Secretariats in the five districts. Of these women, only those who did not have a spouse living with them were included. The closest male-headed household to every third such female-headed household in the sample was selected to make up the sample of women in male-headed households.

The respondents in the sample of female heads were selected for interview only if they were between 20 and 65 years of age and were primarily responsible for managing household affairs. Of them, 68% were widows, 23% had separated, 5% were single, and just 1% were married. The women in male-headed households were selected as the primary respondents if they were of the same age cohort and if they were married to the male head and responsible for managing the household. Female heads of households tended to be older: 60% were between 40–60 years of age and 17% were less than 40 years of age. In contrast, nearly half the women from male-headed households were less than 40. As Figure 9.2 shows, women heading their households are propelled into the labour market earlier, and more of them seem to continue to work even into their sixties.

An overwhelming 92% of the sub-samples of women-headed and male-headed households were ethnic Sri Lankan Tamils. The long war and ethnic cleansing by the LTTE of Muslims and Sinhalese, who had long been residents in the north, displaced most to other provinces. Nearly half the sample was from Jaffna district in keeping with its share of the total population in Northern Province according to the Population Census of 2012.

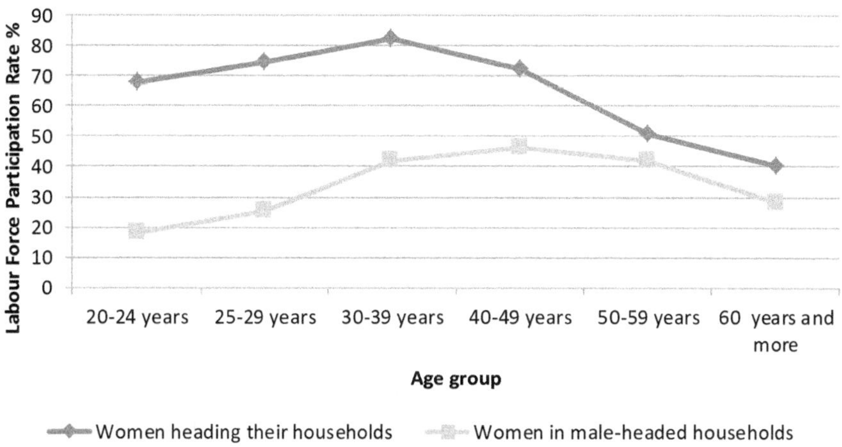

FIGURE 9.2 Labour force participation rates by age cohort
Source: Survey conducted for GrOW Study on Identifying Post-War Economic Growth and Employment Opportunities for Women in Sri Lanka's Northern Province, 2015

Methodology

Factors associated with the probability of participation

The probability of women's participation in the workforce was estimated separately for the sub-samples of women-headed and male-headed households, using the following model:

$$P_i = F(\alpha + \beta X_i)$$

In the above equation, the binary dependent outcome p took the value one if respondent i was a participant, and zero if not. The parameters α and β of the logit function $F(z) = e^z / (1 + e^z)$ were estimated by maximum likelihood. The vector X consists of several groups of factors hypothesised as conditioning women's workforce participation and were derived from an adaptation of the UK's Department for International Development's [DFID] (1999) Sustainable Livelihoods Framework. It should be noted that the model does not address the issue of causality to distinguish whether participation is a cause or a consequence of various individual and other characteristics.

We define the dependent variable first. Since none of the women in the sample were seeking employment, those in the workforce were essentially those who were employed. The employed were in turn defined as those engaged in any income-generating activity during the previous month, a somewhat broader definition than the standard International Labour Organization definition of employment, which uses the previous week as the reference period.

The analysis focuses on the relationships between the probability of workforce participation and six groups of characteristics: the expected wage; individual demographic characteristics; household characteristics; human, physical, and social capital attributes; spatial characteristics including connectivity; experiences with war-related shocks; and features of the institutional environment. Since wages are observed only for the employed, the Heckman procedure (Heckman 1979; Blau and Kahn 2007; Heim 2007; Klasen and Pieters 2012) using Maximum Likelihood Estimation (MLE) was used to impute wages for those who were not employed (Gunatilaka and Vithanagama 2018). Individual demographic characteristics included the individual's age and its square. Household characteristics based on its demographic composition, economic situation including household per capita expenditure and income from transfers, and attributes of male working members were covered. The human capital attributes of the respondent such as her health status and educational attainment were incorporated as well as variables denoting the household's ownership of physical assets such as house and land, financial assets, and productive assets such as crop trees and livestock. The social capital variables denoted membership in organisations and indicators of the strength of bonds with networks of relatives and friends. Spatial characteristics and connectivity were represented by characteristics of the structure of the local economy, access to vehicles, the time taken to go to the nearest administrative centre and market, and the administrative district of residence. The influence of war-related experiences such as displacement, loss of employment, damage to property, and disruption of schooling were covered. Yet family members dying or disappearing due to the war were not included, as the sample used for analysis was made up of women who headed their households and who may have headed their households because they had lost key family members for these reasons. Characteristics that captured the institutional environment and participation in livelihood development programmes were also covered in the specification.

Contribution of factors to the probability of labour force participation

The contribution of factors to the difference in labour force participation among the two groups was investigated by using the non-linear decomposition technique developed by Fairlie (see Fairlie 1999 and Fairlie and Robb 2007). The technique implements the Oaxaca-Blinder decomposition for categorical outcome variables by computing the differences in the probability of labour force participation between the two groups of women and quantifying the contribution of the group differences in the explanatory variables to the outcome differential.

The contribution of each group of characteristics to the probability of participation among women heads and women in male-headed households was investigated by implementing the Shapley value decomposition. The method is based on Shapley's (1953) solution to the problem of calculating the real power of any given voter in a coalition voting game with transferable utility, when all orders of coalition formation are equally probable. While Shorrocks (2012) showed that the Shapley value decomposition can be applied to any function, the method has been used in the economics literature to decompose income inequality (Sastre and Trannoy 2001; Gunatilaka and Chotikapanich 2009; Devicienti 2010), inequality in health outcomes (Deutsche, Pi Alperin, and Silber 2018), and poverty (Kolenikov and Shorrocks 2005; D'Ambrosio, Deutsch, and Silber 2009). Following D'Ambrosio, Deutsch, and Silber (2009), we use the technique of decomposing the Likelihood Ratio Index (LRI) into the marginal contributions of each category of explanatory variables. The sum of the marginal contributions is equal to the LRI which is also a measure of goodness of fit of the regressions, like the R^2 used in linear regressions.

Overview of analysis

The means and standard deviations of the characteristics hypothesised as correlating with the probability of participation for the two sub-samples of women are set out in Table 9.1. The table also presents the results of the differences in means and their statistical significance in the last column.

The share of women heading their households participating in the workforce was 20 percentage points higher than for women in male-headed households and the difference was statistically significant at the 1% critical level. The differences in mean characteristics between the two groups of women were also statistically significant for the most part, and the gap favoured women in male-headed households along many key dimensions such the log of expected wage, human capital, attributes related to almost all types of assets including the extent of land held, ownership of house with deed, and all three characteristics of social capital.

Proportionately more women heads also had experienced economic shocks related to the war and the differences in means are statistically significant. A larger share of women heading their households also received cash or direct transfers. Proportionately more of them also took longer to go to the nearest market. However, the differences in the means of characteristics of the two groups relating to location and perceptions about the helpfulness of institutions are not significant.

Results

Covariates of the probability of labour force participation

Table 9.2 compares the results of estimating the probability of labour force participation of women heads of household who were not living with a spouse with the results for married women living with their husbands in male-headed households. Standard errors of the estimates are set out alongside.[1]

Among the war-related experiences, only the experience of being displaced and having to live with friends and relatives and the disruption of the education of a household member are associated with a lower likelihood that women heads participate in the labour force. The marginal effect of the expected wage on the probability of labour force participation is positive, large, and significant at the 10% critical level only for women heading their households. This contrasts with the

TABLE 9.1 Means of characteristics of women heading their households and of women in male-headed households

	Sample means and proportions		*Standard deviation*		
	Women heading households	*Women in male-headed households*	*Women heading households*	*Women in male-headed households*	*Difference in means and whether statistically significant*
Participates in the labour force	0.5909	0.3904	0.4918	0.4881	0.2005***
Log of expected wage	8.9521	9.1301	0.3254	0.4077	-0.1780***
Demographic and household variables					
Age	50.3409	41.7241	10.1999	11.4682	8.6168***
Age squared	2638.2152	1872.2898	986.9737	997.6207	765.9254***
Share of children less than 5 years	0.0132	0.0722	0.0733	0.1297	-0.0590***
Share of children between 5 and 15 years	0.1142	0.1644	0.2102	0.1912	-0.0502***
Share of other adult females	0.6669	0.4726	0.3593	0.1727	0.1943***
Share of elderly household members (>70 years)	0.0279	0.0245	0.1022	0.0795	0.0034
Share of members who are ill	0.0196	0.0189	0.0936	0.075	0.0007
Share of employed males in the household	0.1283	0.3979	0.2175	0.1829	-0.2696***
Respondent's father a white-collar worker	0.1106	0.1036	0.3136	0.3049	0.0070
Housing infrastructure score	9.1337	9.3765	1.8073	1.5442	-0.2428***
Household receives transfer income	0.8716	0.6793	0.3346	0.467	0.1923***
Assets					
In poor health	0.3532	0.1783	0.478	0.3829	0.1749***
Primary education or less	0.3436	0.1345	0.475	0.3413	0.2091***

GCE O' Levels	0.234	0.3735	0.4235	0.484	-0.1395***
GCE A' Levels and more	0.0497	0.1384	0.2173	0.3455	-0.0887***
Extent of land held by household	4.5204	6.3343	10.4861	14.3951	-1.8139***
Household owns house with deed	0.4912	0.5319	0.5	0.4992	-0.0407**
Log of net financial assets held jointly	1.2549	1.4945	3.6125	3.9033	-0.2396*
Log of respondent's net financial assets	4.0897	3.9832	5.8399	5.9983	0.1065
Household has livestock	0.477	0.511	0.4996	0.5001	-0.0340*
Household has crop trees	0.7534	0.7958	0.4311	0.4033	-0.0424***
Strength of relationships with relatives '	3.048	3.3167	0.8585	0.7507	-0.2687***
Strength of relationships with friends '	3.09	3.3108	0.7533	0.7304	-0.2208***
Access to material support from relatives	3.5389	3.7859	1.0636	0.999	-0.2470**
Access to emotional support from friends	3.809	4.0269	0.9439	0.8101	-0.2179***
Respondent is a member of at least one community organisation	0.2827	0.2709	0.4504	0.4447	0.01180
Spatial variables and connectivity					
Log of per capita share of industrial and construction establishments in DS division	4.6224	4.6218	0.3591	0.3606	0.0006
Log of per capita share of trading establishments in DS division	3.966	3.9634	0.3278	0.3312	0.0026

(Continued)

Table 9.1 (Cont.)

	Sample means and proportions		*Standard deviation*		
	Women heading households	*Women in male-headed households*	*Women heading households*	*Women in male-headed households*	*Difference in means and whether statistically significant*
Log of per capita share of service establishments in DS division	4.0289	4.0253	0.3792	0.3790	0.0036
Household owns mechanised transport	0.1430	0.4273	0.3730	0.5484	-0.2843***
Minutes taken to go to the nearest market	23.8255	22.1165	19.8118	18.5939	1.7090**
Minutes taken to go to the Divisional Secretariat	44.9265	43.9541	31.0871	55.4348	0.9724
Jaffna	0.5713	0.5767	0.495	0.4943	-0.0054
Kilinochchi	0.0993	0.0996	0.2991	0.2996	-0.0003
Mullaitivu	0.0993	0.0996	0.2991	0.2996	-0.0003
Mannar	0.0993	0.0996	0.2991	0.2996	-0.0003
Vavuniya	0.1308	0.1245	0.3372	0.3303	0.0063
War experiences					
Displaced and stayed in camp	0.5839	0.5209	0.4930	0.4998	0.0630***
Displaced and stayed with relatives or friends	0.5396	0.5488	0.4985	0.4979	-0.0092
Damage to property	0.5789	0.5149	0.4938	0.5000	0.0640***
Loss of employment	0.4803	0.4472	0.4997	0.4975	0.0331*
Loss of assets	0.6696	0.6275	0.4704	0.4837	0.0421**
Education disrupted	0.3688	0.3357	0.4825	0.4725	0.0331*

Other damages due to war	0.0139	0.0110	0.1171	0.1041	0.0029
Institutions					
Perception of helpfulness of Divisional Secretariat	4.1401	4.1720	0.7160	0.6547	-0.0319
Perception of helpfulness of *Grama Niladhari*	4.2406	4.2652	0.7621	0.7088	-0.0246
Interventions					
Cash only	0.0692	0.0528	0.2538	0.2237	0.0164*
Direct interventions only	0.3724	0.3884	0.4835	0.4876	-0.0160
Cash and direct interventions only	0.1831	0.1863	0.3868	0.3895	-0.0032
Number of observations	3021	1004			

Source: Estimated with data from the survey conducted for the GrOW Study on Identifying Post-War Economic Growth and Employment Opportunities for Women in Sri Lanka's Northern Province, 2015. Data related to number of establishments and population in the divisions from Department of Census and Statistics (2015b, 2015c).

Notes: ***, **, and * denote statistical significance at the 1%, 5%, and 10% levels, respectively.

TABLE 9.2 Factors associated with the probability of women heading their households and women in male-headed households participating in the labour force: marginal effects of logistic regression

	Women-headed households		*Women in male-headed households*	
	Marginal effect	Standard error	Marginal effect	Standard error
Log of expected wage	0.0879*	(0.043)	0.0208	(0.057)
War experiences				
Displaced and stayed in camp	-0.0065	(0.018)	-0.0469	(0.033)
Displaced and stayed with relatives or friends	-0.0379*	(0.018)	-0.0144	(0.039)
Damage to property	-0.0337	(0.025)	0.0420	(0.031)
Loss of employment	0.0227	(0.027)	-0.0523	(0.047)
Loss of assets	0.0337	(0.025)	0.0685	(0.054)
Education disrupted	-0.0428*	(0.021)	0.0147	(0.050)
Other damages due to war	0.0778	(0.051)	-0.0177	(0.098)
Demographic and household variables				
Age	0.0057	(0.006)	0.0462***	(0.010)
Age squared	-0.0002*	(0.000)	-0.0006***	(0.000)
Share of children less than five years	-0.3371*	(0.145)	-0.0551	(0.149)
Share of children between five and 15 years	0.0819	(0.076)	0.0738	(0.073)
Share of other adult females	-0.0147	(0.024)	-0.0235	(0.068)
Share of elderly household members (>70 years)	-0.0800	(0.066)	-0.4362	(0.226)
Share of members who are ill	-0.0363	(0.090)	0.2737*	(0.136)
Share of employed males in the household	-0.5137***	(0.072)	-0.4482***	(0.111)
At least one male member in a white-collar job	0.0192	(0.044)		
Respondent's father a white-collar worker	-0.0107	(0.041)	-0.0570	(0.045)
Housing infrastructure score	-0.0135**	(0.004)	-0.0111	(0.011)
Household receives transfer income	-0.1315***	(0.033)	-0.0197	(0.041)
Husband's characteristics				
Husband's years of education			-0.0033	(0.008)
Employed in a white-collar job			0.0916	(0.050)
Employed in the manufacturing sector			0.0039	(0.029)
Employed in the services sector			0.0351	(0.054)

(Continued)

Table 9.2 (Cont.)

	Women-headed households		*Women in male-headed households*	
Assets				
In poor health	-0.1697***	(0.020)	-0.0665**	(0.025)
Secondary education	-0.0469*	(0.024)	0.0478	(0.067)
GCE O Levels	-0.0739	(0.039)	0.0172	(0.065)
GCE A Levels and more	0.0399	(0.046)	0.1301	(0.094)
Extent of land held by household	0.0039***	(0.001)	0.0020*	(0.001)
Household owns house with deed	0.0178	(0.021)	0.0559	(0.030)
Log of net financial assets held jointly	-0.0007	(0.002)	0.0020	(0.003)
Log of respondent's net financial assets	-0.0001	(0.001)	0.0019	(0.003)
Household has livestock	0.0618	(0.040)	0.1752**	(0.066)
Household has crop trees	-0.0432***	(0.013)	0.0555	(0.033)
Strength of relationships with relatives	-0.0543***	(0.013)	-0.0293	(0.021)
Strength of relationships with friends	0.0418**	(0.015)	0.0551*	(0.027)
Respondent is a member of at least one community organisation	0.1082***	(0.023)	0.1017*	(0.049)
Spatial variables and connectivity				
Log of per capita share of industrial and construction establishments in DS division	-0.5446	(0.307)	-1.2480***	(0.353)
Log of per capita share of trading establishments in DS division	0.3204*	(0.125)	0.5042**	(0.177)
Log of per capita share of service establishments in DS division	-0.1909	(0.124)	0.1697*	(0.077)
Household owns mechanised transport	-0.0413*	(0.017)	0.0051	(0.036)
Minutes taken to go to the nearest market	0.0012	(0.001)	0.0011*	(0.001)
Minutes taken to go to the Divisional Secretariat	-0.0002	(0.001)	0.0003	(0.000)
Kilinochchi	0.2943***	(0.083)	0.2740	(0.151)
Mullaitivu	0.3762***	(0.063)	0.0564	(0.136)
Mannar	0.6650***	(0.173)	1.1928***	(0.267)
Vavuniya	0.1025	(0.070)	-0.0397	(0.033)
Institutions				
Perception of helpfulness of Divisional Secretariat	-0.0317	(0.022)	-0.0279	(0.027)
Perception of helpfulness of *Grama Niladhari*	0.0190	(0.013)	0.0367	(0.030)

(Continued)

Table 9.2 (Cont.)

	Women-headed households		*Women in male-headed households*	
Interventions				
Cash only	-0.0306	(0.047)	0.0948	(0.111)
Direct interventions only	0.0134	(0.035)	-0.0672	(0.047)
Cash and direct interventions only	0.0117	(0.036)	0.1290	(0.073)
Likelihood ratio index (LRI)	0.201		0.160	
Number of observations	2969		920	
Labour force participation rate	0.590		0.378	

Source: Estimated with data from the survey conducted for the GrOW Study on Identifying Post-War Economic Growth and Employment Opportunities for Women in Sri Lanka's Northern Province, 2015. Data related to number of establishments from Department of Census and Statistics (2015c)

Notes: A constant term was included in the model. Reference categories for groups of dummy variables are as follows: single; number of children 16 years and older living in household; primary, secondary and O levels (husband's education); primary or no schooling (principal female respondent's education); agricultural sector; Jaffna District, neither cash nor direct interventions. The likelihood ratio index (indicating goodness-of-fit) is defined as LRI = 1 - (1n L/1nL), where ln L is the maximal value of the log-likelihood and ln L is the log-likelihood obtained when only a constant term is introduced. ***, **, and * denote statistical significance at the 1%, 5% and 10% levels, respectively. Both models have been clustered at Divisional Secretariat's Division level for robust standard errors and include constants.

absence of a statistically significant relationship between the expected wage and workforce participation in earlier studies on Sri Lanka and India (Gunatilaka 2013; Klasen and Pieters 2015).

An increase in the share of employed males in the household has a profound negative impact, 45 percentage points for women in male-headed households and 51 percentage points for women heads. Having children less than five years of age appears to hold women heads back from participation. Yet an increase in the share of sickly members in the household appears to propel women in male-headed households into paid work. The probability of participation increases with age for both groups of women, but only significantly for women in male-headed households. The wealthier the household, the less likely that a woman heading her household participates in the labour force, suggesting that economic distress likely drives women heads from poor households to take up paid work. The income effect of receiving transfer income appears to significantly obviate the necessity of the woman heading her household going out to work. Poor health has a larger negative impact on workforce participation of women heads. The relationship between education and labour force participation for women heading their households suggests a U-curve, such as Klasen and Pieters (2015) suggested for India.

A household's ownership of land has a slightly larger and positive effect on the participation of women heading their households than on the participation of women in male-headed households, and the results are statistically significant. These findings recall Emran and Shilpi's (2017) findings that restrictions on the sale of land distributed by the government increased women's labour force participation in local labour markets in Sri Lanka. On the other hand, the marginal effects on various forms of productive capital other than landholding, suggest that women in male-headed households may be better able to leverage these assets for the purposes of their employment.

Almost all the variables denoting access to social capital are statistically significant predictors of the participation of both groups of women, and the magnitudes of the marginal effects are similar. A strong bond with relatives makes it significantly less likely that a woman heading her household is engaging in paid work. The social capital denoted by this variable could influence workforce participation both directly and indirectly. Material help from relatives flowing from a strong relationship could obviate the need for the respondent to work. However, strong kinship ties could also subject women to more binding social norms which discourage labour force participation. On the other hand, the strength of the respondent's relationship with friends has a slightly smaller but positive and significant effect, and its effect for women in male-headed households is slightly larger. Compared to both these forms of social capital, membership in organisations is positively and significantly associated with an increase in the probability of participation. These results, however, need to be interpreted with some caution as the independent variables could be endogenous.

The marginal effects of the local market variables suggest that a local market with a relatively high density of trading and service sector establishments offer women more opportunities for engaging in livelihood activities. Neither of the institutional variables is a significant predictor of women's labour force participation. Participation in livelihood interventions is not significantly associated with the workforce participation of either group of women.

Decomposition of the difference in the probability of participation

Table 9.3 presents the results of the Fairlie decomposition to identify the factors underlying the difference in workforce participation of our two groups of respondents. The coefficients were estimated by drawing 1,000 random samples with replacement from the larger group of women heads to match the number of women in male-headed households. The sequence of variables was also randomised.

Group differences in the distribution of characteristics explain 29% of the difference in participation when the coefficients of male-headed households are used for the decomposition. It explains 34% of the negative difference if the coefficients of female-headed households are used. The biggest driver of differences in workforce participation between the two groups is employment outcomes of male household members, as would be expected. Differences in demographic

TABLE 9.3 Fairlie decomposition of the difference in the probability of participation

Pr (women heads of households)	*0.590434*			*(N=2969)*		
Pr (women in male-headed households)	*0.378261*			*(N=920)*		
Difference	*0.212174*					
	At coefficients of women in male-headed households			*At coefficients of female-headed households*		
	Coefficients	*Standard errors*	*Contribution to total explained %*	*Coefficients*	*Standard errors*	*Contribution to total explained %*
Expected wage	-0.0122**	0.004	-19.77	0.0124**	0.004	-17.44
War-related experiences	-0.0003	0.001	-0.49	0.0004	0.001	-0.54
Demographic characteristics	-0.0423***	0.009	-68.45	0.0365***	0.008	-51.35
Household characteristics	0.0004	0.009	0.64	-0.0001	0.009	0.14
Employment characteristics of male members	0.1415***	0.011	229.18	-0.1431***	0.012	201.10
Wealth status of household	0.0029**	0.001	4.69	-0.0032**	0.001	4.52
Receipt of transfers	-0.0153***	0.004	-24.72	0.0160***	0.004	-22.56
Respondent's health	-0.0278***	0.003	-44.96	0.0245***	0.003	-34.45
Respondent's education	0.0061	0.005	9.81	-0.0043	0.005	6.06
Physical and financial capital, livestock and crop trees	-0.0072***	0.002	-11.69	0.0083***	0.002	-11.66
Respondent's social capital	0.0043*	0.002	6.97	-0.0044*	0.003	6.16

Local market conditions and connectivity	0.0109	0.008	17.71	-0.0119	0.008	16.70
District characteristics	0.0009	0.006	1.48	-0.0025	0.006	3.54
Institutional environment	0.0003	0.001	0.48	-0.0003	0.001	0.38
Participation in livelihood interventions	-0.0005	0.001	-0.88	0.0004	0.001	-0.59
Total gap explained	0.0618		100.00	-0.0711		100.00
Unexplained	0.9382			0.9289		

Source: Estimated with data from the survey conducted for the GrOW Study on Identifying Post-War Economic Growth and Employment Opportunities for Women in Sri Lanka's Northern Province, 2015. Estimates generated by implementing Jann's (2006) fairlie.ado. See Fairlie (1999) for details of the methodology.

***, **, and * denote statistical significance at the 1%, 5%, and 10% levels, respectively.

characteristics, age and age squared, are the next largest contributors, but they do so by helping to reduce the difference. Differences in the health characteristics of the two groups and differences in their receipt of cash or direct transfers also help reduce the gap.

However, from a policy perspective, with the exception of health status, the characteristics that emerged as the most important drivers of participation gaps between the two groups are difficult to address. What remains are the characteristics related to assets. Yet in order to formulate and target appropriate strategies in relation to these attributes, we need to see their contributions to the probability that women heads, and women in male-headed households, participate. In the next section, we use the Shapley value decomposition to do exactly that.

Shapley value decomposition of the probability of participation

In the Shapley value decomposition, the marginal effects of the independent characteristics on the probability of labour force participation are eliminated one by one and weighted according to the stage of exclusion. The weights are assigned in such a way that all exclusion trajectories have equal weights. The results of the decomposition are set out in Table 9.4. The composition of the groups of factors, where different from the order in Table 9.2, is explained in the notes to the table. The second and third columns show the Shapley values derived from the decomposition. The fourth and fifth columns show the results of their application to decompose the log likelihood ratio into contributing groups of factors.

The table shows distinct differences in the contributions of groups of factors to the probability of participation of the two groups of women that can provide information to both prioritise and target policy interventions. As far as women heads of households are concerned, demographic and household-related characteristics, including the productive characteristics of male members together, account for more than half the probability that this group of women will participate in the workforce. In fact, employment characteristics of male members contribute most to the likelihood of participation, accounting for 17% of the likelihood ratio whereas for women in male-headed households, access to physical and financial capital appear to matter almost as much. The productive characteristics of male members account for 13% of the LRI of this group. Age-related factors contribute almost as much for women heads while health conditions account for 14%. The latter is more amenable for policy intervention than either demographic or household characteristics.

Conclusion

This chapter looked at the factors associated with women's labour force participation in Sri Lanka's north after the war. The analysis used primary data from a survey comparing women heads of household with women in male-headed households. It disaggregated the gap in participation between the two groups into contributing factors

TABLE 9.4 Shapley value decomposition of the probability of labour force participation: marginal contributions of characteristics

	Shapley value		*Marginal contribution to probability of participation %*	
	Women heads	*Women in male-headed households*	*Women heads*	*Women in male-headed households*
Expected wage	0.0082	0.0056	4.09	3.53
War-related experiences	0.0089	0.0052	2.81	3.27
Demographic characteristics	0.0713	0.0006	17.27	12.12
Household characteristics	0.0648	0.0006	12.94	5.88
Employment characteristics of male members	0.0438	0.0026	17.73	13.22
Wealth status of household	0.0042	0.0193	1.53	0.37
Receipt of transfers	0.0020	0.0093	2.28	0.38
Respondent's health	0.0398	0.0210	14.26	1.64
Respondent's education	0.0063	0.0068	2.23	4.27
Physical and financial capital, live-stock and crop trees	0.0150	0.0265	5.32	16.66
Respondent's social capital	0.0201	0.0167	7.82	10.54
Local market conditions and connectivity	0.0133	0.0180	6.51	11.36
District characteristics	0.0053	0.0152	2.59	9.57
Institutional environment	0.0122	0.0114	2.62	7.19
LRI or Total Explained	0.2005	0.1589	100.00	100.00
Residual	0.7995	0.8411		

Source: Estimated with data from the survey conducted for the GrOW Study on Identifying Post-War Economic Growth and Employment Opportunities for Women in Sri Lanka's Northern Province, 2015.

Institutional factors: Respondent's perception of how helpful the Divisional Secretariat is, how helpful the *Grama Niladhari* Office (village administration) is, and whether any member of the household participated in livelihood development programmes involving cash only, direct interventions only, or both.

using the Fairlie decomposition, and then decomposed the probability of participation of each group into contributing factors using the Shapley value decomposition. Given the nature of the data and the analytical methods that could be applied, we have not been able to establish causality or correct for endogeneity of variables. Nevertheless, the analysis has identified some key covariates of women's labour force participation in Sri Lanka's north which can help inform policy.

Economic distress drives women heads of household to find paid work. Receiving cash or direct transfers and living with men who are employed appear to ease some of the financial pressure on women, while poor health and the responsibility to care for young children are financial stressors. The need to engage in paid work is far less compelling for women in male-headed households and their labour supply is much more elastic in relation to age. These women also appear more capable of leveraging assets such as crops and farm animals for their employment compared to women heads of household.

The share of employed males in the household is the biggest contributor to the probability of labour force participation as well as to the explained difference between the probabilities of participation rates of the two groups of women. This not only reflects prevailing social norms but is also likely to be symptomatic of significant gender differences in the labour market prospects of men and women.[2]

Nevertheless, the contribution of human capital and other assets to the probability of participation suggests space for policy interventions. A macroeconomic and investment climate in line with the comparative and competitive advantages of the region can help make the economic environment more conducive to women entering the workforce in northern Sri Lanka. Enhancing skills through information technology-based education services can help develop women's human capital by improving critical shortfalls in teaching quality and materials. Interventions that facilitate the building of assets, including social capital, may condition positive labour market engagement. Yet most importantly, appropriate policies and designing a strategy to address the physical (e.g. non-communicable diseases such as diabetes, arthritis, and high blood pressure) and psychological (e.g. isolation, trauma, and depression) health issues that women heading their households grapple with are urgently needed. Mobile health clinics can help address problems of physical health. Community-based initiatives such as community gardens, art and craft circles, yoga, qi gong, and tai chi can help address physical as well as psychological health issues and help build trust and social networks.

Notes

1 The robustness of the results to the addition or omission of different variables was tested following Barslund et al.'s (2007) procedure. See Gunatilaka and Vithanagama (2018) for details.

2 For further discussion on the impact of gender equality and social norms on women's labour force participation, see Chapters 1 and 5, respectively, in this volume.

Acknowledgements

This research was made possible by the generous financial support of the Growth and Economic Opportunities for Women (GrOW) Programme sponsored by Canada's International Development Research Centre (IDRC), the UK's Foreign, Commonwealth and Development Office (FCDO), and the William and Flora Hewlett Foundation. The insightful comments of Nisha Arunatilake and two anonymous referees are gratefully acknowledged. Usual disclaimers apply.

References

Abeyratne, Sirimal (2004). Economic roots of political conflict: The case of Sri Lanka. *World Economy* 27(8): 1295–1314.

Alailima, Patricia J. (2000). The human development perspective. In Weligamage D. Lakshman and Clement Alan Tisdell (Eds.), *Sri Lanka's Development since Independence: Socio-economic Perspectives and Analyses* (41–60). New York: Nova Science Publishers, Inc.

Amirthalingam, Kopalapillai, and Rajith W.D. Lakshman (2009). Displaced livelihoods in Sri Lanka: An economic analysis. *Journal of Refugee Studies* 22(4): 502–524.

Athukorala, Premachandra, and Sisira Jayasuriya (1994). Macroeconomic policies, crises, and growth in Sri Lanka, 1969–90. Washington, DC: World Bank. http://documents.worldbank.org/curated/en/121561468777266972/Macroeconomic-policies-crises-and-growth-in-Sri-Lanka-1969-1990.

Barslund, Mikkel, John Rand, Finn Tarp, and Jacinto Chiconela (2007). Understanding victimization: The case of Mozambique. *World Development* 35(7): 1237–1258.

Birkeland, Nina (2009). Internal displacement: global trends in conflict-induced displacement. *International Review of the Red Cross* 91(875): 491–508.

Blattman, Christopher (2010). Post-conflict recovery in Africa. In Ernest Aryeetey, Shantayanan Devarajan, Ravi Kanbur, and Louis Kasekende (Eds.), *Oxford Companion to the Economics of Africa*. Oxford: Oxford University Press.

Blau, Francine, and Lawrence Kahn (2007). The gender pay gap: Have women gone as far as they can? *Academy of Management Perspectives* 21(1): 7–23.

Bouta, Tsjeard, and Georg Frerks (2002). Women's roles in conflict prevention, conflict resolution and post-conflict reconstruction. The Hague: Netherlands Institute of International Relations Clingendael. https://reliefweb.int/sites/reliefweb.int/files/resources/D946B37BBFD5E431C1256D56002EB960-NetherlandsWomenRole.pdf.

Central Bank of Sri Lanka (2008). *Annual Report 2007, Central Bank of Sri Lanka.* Colombo: CBSL, mimeo.

Central Bank of Sri Lanka (2019). *Annual Report 2018, Central Bank of Sri Lanka.* Colombo: CBSL. www.cbsl.gov.lk/en/publications/economic-and-financial-reports/annual-reports/annual-report-2018.

Chandran, Nyshka (2016). Battle scars: Sri Lanka's North counts the cost of a 26-year war. CNBC News, April 27. https://www.cnbc.com/2016/04/27/sri-lanks-northern-province-poorer-undeveloped-after-26-year-civil-war-with-tamil-tigers.html.

D'Ambrosio, Conchita, Joseph Deutsch, and Jacques Silber (2009). Multidimensional approaches to poverty measurement: An empirical analysis of poverty in Belgium, France, Germany, Italy and Spain, based on the European panel. *Applied Economics* 43(8): 951–961.

Department for International Development (1999). Sustainable livelihoods guidance sheets. London: DFID. www.livelihoodscentre.org/documents/114097690/114438878/Sustainable+livelihoods+guidance+sheets.pdf/594e5ea6-99a9-2a4e-f288-cbb4ae4bea8b?t=1569512091877.

Department of Census and Statistics (1987). Labour force and socio economic survey – 1985/86. Colombo: Government of Sri Lanka, mimeo.

Department of Census and Statistics (2015a). Census of population and housing – 2012. Colombo: Government of Sri Lanka. www.statistics.gov.lk/PopHouSat/CPH2011/Pages/Activities/Reports/CPH_2012_5Per_Rpt.pdf.

Department of Census and Statistics (2015b). Non-agricultural economic activities in Sri Lanka – Economic census 2013/2014. Colombo: Department of Census and Statistics, mimeo.

Department of Census and Statistics (2015c). Non-agricultural economic activities in Sri Lanka – Economic census of 2013/2014. Colombo: Department of Census and Statistics, mimeo.

Department of Census and Statistics (2018). Household income and expenditure survey – 2016. Final results (January to December 2016). Colombo: Department of Census and Statistics. http://www.statistics.gov.lk/IncomeAndExpenditure/StaticalInformation/HouseholdIncomeandExpenditureSurvey2016FinalReport.

Department of Census and Statistics (2019). Sri Lanka labour force survey. Annual report – 2017. Colombo: Department of Census and Statistics. http://www.statistics.gov.lk/LabourForce/StaticalInformation/AnnualReports/2017.

De Silva, K.M. (1999). *Reaping the Whirlwind: Ethnic Conflict Ethnic Politics in Sri Lanka*. New Delhi: Penguin Books India.

Deutsche, Joseph, María Noel Pi Alperin, and Jacques Silber (2018). Using the Shapley decomposition to disentangle the impact of circumstances and efforts on health inequality. *Social Indicators Research* 138(2): 523–543.

Devicienti, Francesco (2010). Shapley-value decompositions of changes in wage distributions: A note. *Journal of Economic Inequality* 8(1): 35–45.

El Jack, Amani (2003). Gender and armed conflict: Overview report. Brighton: BRIDGE. www.bridge.ids.ac.uk/reports/CEP-Conflict-Report.pdf.

Emran, Shahe, and Forhad Shilpi (2017). Land market restrictions, women's labour force participation and wages in a rural economy. *Oxford Bulletin of Economic and Statistics* 79(5): 747–768.

Fairlie, Robert (1999). The absence of the African-American owned business: An analysis of the dynamics of self-employment. *Journal of Labor Economics* 17(1): 80–108.

Fairlie, Robert, and Alicia Robb (2007). Families, human capital, and small business: Evidence from the Characteristics of Business Owners Survey. *Industrial and Labor Relations Review* 60(2): 225–245.

Gunatilaka, Ramani, and Duangkamon Chotikapanich (2009). Accounting for Sri Lanka's expenditure inequality 1980–2002: Regression-based decomposition approaches. *Review of Income and Wealth* 55(4): 882–906.

Gunatilaka, Ramani (2013). Women's participation in Sri Lanka's labour force: Trends, drivers and constraints. Colombo: International Labour Organization. https://www.ilo.org/colombo/whatwedo/publications/WCMS_215445/lang--en/index.htm.

Gunatilaka, Ramani (2016). Women's activity outcomes, preferences and time use in Western Sri Lanka. In *Factors Affecting Women's Labour Force Participation in Sri Lanka*, 43–113. Colombo: ILO Country Office for Sri Lanka and the Maldives. https://www.ilo.org/wcmsp5/groups/public/---asia/---ro-bangkok/---ilo-colombo/documents/publication/wcms_551675.pdf.

Gunatilaka, Ramani, and Ranmini Vithanagama (2018). Women's labour force participation in Sri Lanka's north. GrOW Working Paper Series, GWP-2018–18. Montreal: Institution for the Study of International Development, McGill University. http://grow.research.mcgill.ca/publications/working-papers/gwp-2018-18.pdf.

Gunewardena, Dileni (2015). Why aren't Sri Lankan women translating their educational gains into workforce advantages? The 2015 ECHIDNA Global Scholars Working Paper. Washington, DC: Centre for Universal Education at Brookings. www.ungei.org/Why_arent_sri_lanken_women_translating_edu_gains_into_work_gunewardena_2___.pdf.

Heckman, James J. (1979). Sample selection bias as a specification error. *Econometrica* 47(1): 153–161.

Heim, Bradley (2007). The incredible shrinking elasticities: Married female labour supply, 1978–2002. *The Journal of Human Resources* 42(4): 881–918.

Hudock, Ann, Karen Sherman, and Sarah Williamson (2016). In Roslyn Warren, Alexandra Z. Safir, and Tricia Correia (Eds.), *Women's Economic Participation in Conflict Affected and Fragile Settings*. Occasional Paper Series. Washington, DC: Georgetown Institute for

Women, Peace and Security. https://giwps.georgetown.edu/wp-content/uploads/2017/08/Occasional-Paper-Series-Womens-Economic-Participation.pdf.

Iyer, Lakshmi, and Indhira Santos (2012). Creating jobs in South Asia's conflict zones. Policy Research Working Paper No. 6104. Washington, DC: World Bank. https://openknowledge.worldbank.org/handle/10986/9315.

Jann, Ben (2006). *Fairlie: Stata Module to Generate Nonlinear Decomposition of Binary Outcome Differentials*. Boston: Department of Economics, Boston College.

Klasen, Stephan, and Janneke Pieters (2012). Push or pull? Drivers of female labor force participation during India's economic boom. IZA Discussion Paper No. 6395. Bonn: Institute of Labor Economics (IZA). https://ideas.repec.org/p/iza/izadps/dp6395.html.

Klasen, Stephan, and Janneke Pieters (2015). What explains the stagnation of female labor force participation in Urban India? *The World Bank Economic Review* 29(3): 449–478. https://openknowledge.worldbank.org/handle/10986/27684.

Kolenikov, Stanislav, and Anthony Shorrocks (2005). A decomposition analysis of regional poverty in Russia. *Review of Development Economics* 9(1): 25–46.

Kulatunga, Sasini T.K. (2014). Income generation in conflict-affected communities: With special reference to female-headed households in the Eastern Province of Sri Lanka. Paper presented at the International Conference on Revisiting Social Responsibility in Contexts of Crisis Challenges and Possibilities in Sri Lanka, University of Colombo, Colombo, Sri Lanka, November 17, mimeo.

Kulatunga, Sasini T.K. (2017). Unpacking household asset inequality between male and female headed households in the post war economy of eastern Sri Lanka: A decomposition analysis. Paper presented at the 5th International Economics Research Conference of the Sri Lanka Forum of University Economists. Conference Proceedings, Volume I, 1–10. University of Kelaniya, Sri Lanka. www.slfue.org/images/SLFUE_downloads/2016/SLERC_2016_Proceedings_Full_Paper_Series.pdf.

Kumar, Krishna (2001). *Women and Civil War: Impact, Organizations, and Action*. Boulder, CO: Lynne Rienner Publishers.

Majid, Nomaan, and Ramani Gunatilaka (2017). The welfare dimensions of employment change in Sri Lanka and sustainable growth. In *Fostering Workforce Skills through Education: Employment Diagnostic for Sri Lanka* (49–59). Manila and Geneva: Asian Development Bank and International Labour Organization. www.adb.org/sites/default/files/publication/382296/sri-lanka-employment-diagnostic.pdf.

Menon, Nidhiya, and Yana van der Meulen Rodgers (2015). War and women's work evidence from the conflict in Nepal. *Journal of Conflict Resolution* 59(1): 51–73.

Petesche, Patti (2011). Women's empowerment arising from violent conflict and recovery: Life stories from four middle-income countries. Washington, DC: USAID. www.usip.org/sites/default/files/Gender/Petesch_Women_and_Conflict.pdf.

Rehn, Elizabeth, and Ellen Johnson Sirleaf (2002). Women, war, peace: Progress of the world's women 2002. New York: United Nations Development Fund for Women. https://www.unwomen.org/en/digital-library/publications/2002/1/women-war-peace-the-independent-experts-assessment-on-the-impact-of-armed-conflict-on-women-and-women-s-role-in-peace-building-progress-of-the-world-s-women-2002-vol-1.

Ruwanpura, Kachana N., and Jane Humphries (2004). Mundane heroines: Conflict, ethnicity, gender and female headship in eastern Sri Lanka. *Feminist Economics* 10(2): 173–205.

Samarakoon, S.J.M.N.G., and Geetha Mayadunne. 2018. An exploratory study on low labour force participation of women in Sri Lanka. *Sri Lanka Journal of Social Sciences* 41(2): 137–151. https://sljss.sljol.info/articles/abstract/10.4038/sljss.v41i2.7701/.

Sarvananthan, Muttukrishna, Jeyapraba Suresh, and Anushani Alagarajah (2017). Feminism, nationalism, and labour in post-civil war Northern Province of Sri Lanka. *Development in Practice* 27(1): 122 128.

Sastre, Mercedes, and Alain Trannoy (2001). Shapley inequality decomposition by factor components: Some methodological issues. *Journal of Economics* 77(1): 51–89.

Seneviratne, Prathi (2019a). Married women's labor supply and economic development: Evidence from Sri Lankan household data. *Review of Development Economics* 23(2): 975–999.

Seneviratne, Prathi (2019b). Explaining Changes in Sri Lanka's wage distribution, 1992–2014: A quantile regression analysis. *Oxford Development Studies* 47(2): 238–256.

Shapley, Lloyd (1953). A value for n-person games. In H.W. Kuhn and A.W. Tucker (Eds.), *Contributions to the Theory of Games*, Volume 2 (307–317). Princeton, NJ: Princeton University Press.

Shorrocks, Anthony F. (2012). Decomposition procedures for distributional analysis: A unified framework based on the Shapley value. *Journal of Economic Inequality* 11(1): 99–126.

Solotaroff, Jennifer L., George Joseph, and Anne T. Kuriakose (2018). Getting to work: Unlocking women's potential in Sri Lanka's labor force. Washington, DC: World Bank. http://documents1.worldbank.org/curated/en/281511510294264126/pdf/121117-PUB-PUBLIC-Getting-to-Work-Unlocking-Womens-Potential-in-Sri-Lankas-Labor-Force-Overview-Ebook.pdf.

Tilakaratne, Kokmadua Mudalige, and Wanasekara Aarchchilage Siriwardena (2013). Former foes restore war-torn Sri Lankan infrastructure and livelihood together. ADB Knowledge Showcases. Manila: Asian Development Bank. https://think-asia.org/bitstream/handle/11540/437/restore-war-torn-sri-lankan-infrastructure.pdf?sequence=1.

10

THE SCHOOL-TO-WORK TRANSITION FOR YOUNG FEMALES IN SUB-SAHARAN AFRICA

Comparative qualitative evidence from six countries

Jane Kabubo-Mariara, Adalbertus Kamanzi, and Andy McKay

Introduction

The transition from school to work is a very important stage in the life of a young person. Of particular interest here is the type of early work opportunities young people can obtain after completing their education. An individual's first full-time job is potentially very important as this early work experience is likely to shape their subsequent opportunities. For young people in low- and lower-middle-income countries, the challenge of successfully transitioning from school to work is often much greater as many key 'family formation' events (e.g. marriage, pregnancy, childbirth) can occur simultaneously, especially in countries where early marriage or childbirth is common. The decisions to complete school, start a family, and begin work, for example, can all be interconnected.

The school-to-work transition for young people in the developing world has been widely studied in recent years. Helpful reviews are presented by Nilsson (2019) and Alam and de Diego (2019). A large amount of data was also collected by the ILO and MasterCard Foundation School-to-Work Transition Surveys (STWTS) (under the Work4Youth project), conducted in 34 countries between 2012–2016 (ILO and MasterCard Foundation 2016). Many studies have utilised this data, including important overview studies by Matsumoto and Elder (2010) and Manacorda et al. (2017), as well as cross-country studies on specific aspects of this transition such as rural development (Elder et al. 2015), gender differentials (Elder and Kring 2016), and educational qualifications (Sparreboom and Staneva 2014). To add to this, there are country-specific STWTS data and reports available for almost all countries on the ILO's website.[1]

The school-to-work transition is particularly challenging for young women. During this transition, schooling, work, and choices related to family formation (e.g. marriage, childbirth) can all interact to shape young women's experiences and opportunities in unique and complex ways. For example, young women are likely to marry earlier than young men and to be disproportionately responsible for childcare, both of which can limit their work opportunities and educational attainment.[2] These issues are even more predominant for women and girls from poorer backgrounds. This gender dynamic is not widely considered in existing studies on school-to-work transitions.

This chapter presents the results of a study which looked at the school-to-work transition of young women in six countries in sub-Saharan Africa—Burkina Faso, Ethiopia, Ghana, Kenya, Tanzania, and Uganda—taking full account of issues related to family formation. A fundamental challenge in addressing these issues is the potentially complex interaction between factors such as educational attainment, entering the workforce, marriage, pregnancy, and childcare. For example, a young person's decision about how long to stay in school may depend on what work prospects they expect it will provide or a young woman may drop out of school when she becomes pregnant. The extent of interdependency between these factors ('endogeneity' in economics language) means it can be very difficult to understand the reasons and motivations underlying the observed outcomes using only quantitative data. The research therefore included a qualitative component—which is the focus of this chapter—to help understand the relationship between these early life events for young people and to provide deeper explanation, nuance, and context to interpret study findings than quantitative data alone could provide.

In this chapter, we present some of the main insights and trends related to school-to-work transitions that emerged from the qualitative research across the six study countries. The first section provides the study context and background information on the countries of focus. The next section describes the qualitative approach adopted for the research, followed by a presentation of study findings related to education, family formation, and work outcomes, respectively, while emphasising the extent of interdependency between them. Finally, the conclusion summarises key lessons and policy insights emerging from the analysis.

Country context: basic evidence on gender differences in education, family formation, and work outcomes

Data for this research was collected in 15 communities across six countries in sub-Saharan Africa. Table 10.1 presents basic measures of key outcomes in the school-to-work transition for all six countries, including indicators for educational attainment, early marriage, early childbirth, and access to skilled or professional work. These indicators have been provided for young people aged 15 to 29 using Demographic and Health Survey (DHS) data. They are reported for the latest available year for each country, disaggregated by gender, and calculated using population weights to make them representative. This data source has the advantage of allowing the construction of comparable measures across countries and over time within countries.

TABLE 10.1 Background statistics on the six study countries

	Any post-primary education		*Married below 18 years*		*First child before 18 years*		*In skilled or professional work*	
	female	*male*	*female*	*male*	*female*	*male*	*female*	*male*
Burkina Faso 2010	16.2%	26.4%	44.3%	2.2%	23.8%	0.5%	6.8%	13.4%
Ethiopia 2016	22.4%	29.1%	38.0%	4.7%	21.6%	1.1%	6.1%	11.1%
Ghana 2014	70.6%	78.7%	17.8%	1.7%	15.0%	0.4%	15.7%	24.8%
Kenya 2014	47.5%	51.9%	21.3%	2.3%	20.5%	1.5%	3.9%	15.4%
Tanzania 2015–2016	31.4%	35.1%	27.9%	2.7%	20.1%	0.9%	6.3%	17.3%
Uganda 2016	39.4%	43.7%	29.3%	4.8%	24.4%	2.4%	17.0%	33.9%

Source: USAID DHS data (https://dhsprogram.com/), Authors' depiction

The first two columns in Table 10.1 report the percentage of young women and men in the 15 to 29 age range who have attained an education above the primary level. The numbers for both females and males are highest in Ghana and Kenya and lowest in Burkina Faso and Ethiopia. In both years and in all countries, more males than females have some post-primary education. What is striking from these figures, for all countries other than Ghana, is that only a minority of the population has attained this level of education.

The subsequent columns in Table 10.1 report the extent to which young women and men were married or had their first child before the age of 18. Again, there are significant differences across countries with Burkina Faso having a much higher incidence of early marriage and early childbirth than the other countries. What is most striking here is the very large gender difference—very few men were married or had children under the age of 18 compared to women. This implies that women who were married or gave birth before the age of 18 predominantly did so with older men.

There is a limit to the information available on work in the DHS data, but the final column of Table 10.1 reports the proportion of young men and women in skilled or professional work. The numbers are low in general and lowest in Burkina Faso and Ethiopia. A higher level of education is important for enabling young people to access skilled or professional employment, and early marriage and childbirth will make it much more difficult; the data show these correlations.

What is clear from the indicators reported in Table 10.1 is that there are significant gender differences. Young women are less educated than young men, much more likely to marry and give birth before age 18, and less likely to obtain skilled and professional work. Significant numbers of young women marry or give birth before the age of 18 in the six countries, and, in all countries, large numbers fail to reach secondary education levels.

The data reported do not present changes over time, but the same indicators are available for earlier years. When compared against data for the 1990s, the numbers of men and women attaining post-primary education, though currently low, have increased significantly over the past 15 or 20 years. The extent of early marriage and childbirth has also decreased substantially in all countries during this period. All of this indicates positive progress over time. However, the number of men and women that report working in skilled and professional jobs has increased only marginally over this period in most countries. These data also represent national-level trends, and closer analysis reveals significantly better outcomes in urban versus rural areas and in wealthier versus poorer households.

With this background in mind, we can now turn to documenting and understanding individual perspectives on schooling, work, and choices related to family formation, and how they interact in the school-to-work transition.

Research approach and methodology

The research aimed to provide a comparative qualitative analysis across the six study countries, with fieldwork and analysis in each country led by one or more local experts and active participation from several other researchers on the country team. The sites chosen for the work included: one rural and one urban community in Burkina Faso, one rural *kebele*[3] in Ethiopia, one rural and one urban community in Ghana, two rural and one urban communities in Kenya, two rural and two urban communities in Tanzania, and two rural and one urban communities in Uganda. In communities where data was collected, livelihoods ranged from traditional activities like agriculture and fishing to business activities and different forms of wage employment. The communities were comprised of various ethnic groups with mixed Christian and Muslim populations. In every community, there was educational infrastructure that provided schooling for both females and males.

Data for the study was collected using several tools including a community profile, focus group discussions, life stories, and individual interviews. The community profiles aimed to develop an understanding of the local context and of community-level factors contributing to gender differences, particularly norms and practices around economic decision-making and access to economic opportunities. Separate focus group discussions with young men and women aimed to explore differences in daily time use, local economic opportunities, and decisions surrounding family formation and the transition from school to work. Life story interviews with young men and women explored the socioeconomic factors that lead young people to be more or less successful in their labour force trajectories. Finally, a series of key informant interviews were held with community and religious leaders and with male and female elders. These aimed to explore the sociocultural factors that influence the successful labour force trajectories (or lack thereof) for young men and women in the community. The number of respondents per data collection tool and country are provided in Table 10.2.

While there were often significant differences in the findings for men and women across countries, and even within countries, in the following sections, we synthesise some of the commonalities pertaining to issues of education, family formation, and work, and their interactions.[4]

TABLE 10.2 Number of respondents per data collection tool and country

	Total focus groups		*Total focus group respondents*		*Total interviews*		*Total life stories*		*Total community questionnaires*	
	Men	*Women*	*Men*	*Women*	*Men*	*Women*	*Men*	*Women*	*Rural*	*Urban*
Tanzania	4	4	40	40	8	8	8	8	2	2
Burkina Faso	2	2	22	18	12	4	3	8	1	1
Uganda	3	3	45	36	1	2	1	3	2	1
Kenya	3	3	34	33	2	3	8	16	2	1
Ethiopia	1	1	12	10	3	1			1	0
Ghana	2	2	23	19	2	2	4	4	1	1

Source: Authors

Findings on education

In every study country, the level and quality of education that a young person is able to achieve is strongly related to the age of marriage and childbirth, as well as their work opportunities. As previously noted, in every study community, basic education facilities are available for children up until the level of primary education. Yet a number of issues emerged from respondents' views on education, including problems related to high dropout rates, education quality, and the utility of education for obtaining decent work. We will now consider these issues in turn.

Dropout rates

The data shows that dropping out of school is quite common for young people in the study countries. This is corroborated by the quantitative DHS data in Table 10.1 earlier in this chapter, showing that many young people fail to attend school beyond the primary level. Girls are more likely to drop out than boys, especially at the secondary level. Several explanations for the high dropout rates were offered by respondents. The most common ones were lack of motivation to study, economic hardship, early pregnancy, and migration to urban areas.

The lack of motivation to study often affects girls disproportionately. Data from all six countries show that most girls must allocate more time for unpaid domestic work and childcare than boys, meaning girls have less time available for studying, rest, and leisure. In addition, some schools are far from households, meaning it takes significant time to travel to and from school, leaving girls physically depleted and time constrained. The following quote from a young female respondent in Tanzania captures how an unequal gender division of labour and the distance to and from school combine to shape girls' everyday experiences:

> I did not go to the school close by here. My parents thought that it was a poor school. So, I had to travel for like an hour and a half to go to school. In the evening, I would do the same to get back home.... But before I went to school, I had to clean the house and the compound; I had to make sure that there was warm water for my parents to bathe and I had to leave tea in the thermos.... Coming back from school, I had to hurry up because there was cooking waiting for me.... When I went to bed, I was completely tired and could hardly touch my books anymore when at home.

The consequence of this dynamic is that girls often do not perform well at school, a situation that can negatively impact their sense of belonging at school and their motivation to study, sometimes causing them to drop out.

A second widely reported reason for high dropout rates in the study countries is poverty, with many students dropping out because they could not afford to pay for school fees or materials. When households struggling with economic hardship face a choice between keeping a boy child or a girl child in school, the boys stand a better chance. This is partly attributed to the fact that girls are less likely to complete their education and obtain well-paying jobs in the future and, as a result, their schooling would see less economic returns.

Some boys and girls have dropped out of school due to involvement in paid work, household production, or other economic activities. Once again, combining work and school can prove difficult as this quote from a young woman in urban Uganda illustrates:

> I wished to study and complete at least senior four; but, as an orphan, my mother did not have enough money to support me in school and I used to work (fishing) while studying in order to support my mother. While this worked fine while I was still in a nearby primary school, it became much harder to combine work and school at secondary level since the school was a bit far away from home. I eventually gave up and resorted to full time fishing and business (saloon).

There is a large-scale migration of Ethiopian girls to the Middle East in desperate search of low-skilled jobs, which of course means dropping out of school. In Kenya, young people often seek casual employment, influenced partly by peer pressure. Parents rarely seem to object to their children engaging in paid work. In some ways, children's education is burdensome for parents, particularly given the need to pay school fees. Once a child drops out, some parents may even be relieved and have no real incentive to ensure that child returns to school.

A third factor that contributes to dropout rates among girls is early pregnancy and childbirth. Pregnancy and motherhood almost always mark the end of a girl's education. There is a lack of social support for pregnant girls wishing to remain in school and, upon giving birth, many young mothers can develop an inferiority complex and feel like outsiders, choosing never to return to school. In many of the study countries, there is also the expectation that a girl who becomes pregnant must marry the father of her child. The following quote is from a 19-year-old girl in Burkina Faso who dropped out of high school. Similar experiences were also reported in other countries:

> *On peut dire c'est ma grossesse qui a bouleversé mes études quoi, on peut dire que ça bouleversé mes rêves. Vraiment ça eu un impact parce qu'après ça les parents ne veulent plus s'occuper de nous, parce qu'avec la grossesse, on se dit que le responsable doit tenir ses responsabilités.*
>
> [You can say it was my pregnancy that turned my studies upside down, we can say that it turned my dreams upside down. It really had an impact because after that the parents no longer want to take care of us, because with pregnancy, we tell ourselves that the person responsible has to take responsibility.]

A fourth common factor leading to high dropout rates, especially in rural areas, is migration brought on by the perceived attractiveness of urban living. The idea of being able to have a 'good life' in town—to enjoy cinemas, nightclubs, karaoke, and greater economic opportunities—is attracting more young men and women to drop out of school and migrate to urban areas. Those who move from rural to urban areas also play a role, by example or word of mouth, in influencing their peers back home to join them. Once migrated, young men and women can make a living by engaging in activities not available to them in rural areas, such as selling food, working as house-girls or house-boys, hawking, or working in the transport sector—some girls engage in prostitution.

In summary, there are many reasons that young men and women in the study countries may drop out of school, and this decision impacts the types of economic opportunities available to them, for better or for worse.

Education quality

There are several practical problems impacting the delivery of quality education in the study countries. The first problem, already mentioned above, is that not all schools are located near where young men and women live. In Kenya for example, the survey data show that some live as close as 50 to 500 metres from school in urban areas, but as far as one to six kilometres away in rural areas. This is a clear indication of the disproportionate lack of access to schools in rural areas.

A second commonly reported problem in relation to the delivery of quality education is teachers' lack of professionalism in the study countries. In several countries, teachers were reported to be frequently absent because they were working other jobs outside of school. In one community in Ghana, some teachers were reported to have drinking problems. They appeared drunk at school and were unable to attend to their students properly. In Ghana and in Tanzania, there were also troubling reports of sexual misconduct among teachers. Some teachers had sexual affairs with their students, at times in exchange for better marks. This affects girls disproportionately.

Lack of physical access to schools and lack of professionalism on the part of teachers both adversely impact the quality of education that young people receive in the study countries.

The utility of education for obtaining decent work

Across the study countries, the utility of education was viewed in conflicting ways. On the one hand, both male and female respondents believed that education can expand an individual's worldview and opportunities, command respect in the community, and act as a bridge to accessing more formal, stable, and better paying employment. As one young woman from rural Ghana stated during a focus group discussion:

> It's important [education], because, apart from getting work, now the world is about reading and writing. So, if you can't read or write, then you'll remain in this village for your lifetime.

The study documented different examples of community initiatives designed to create opportunities and help young men and women stay in school, reflecting the value placed on education within communities. For example, in most study countries, governments, private sector organisations, and non-governmental organisations provide scholarships and cover the cost of materials for poorer students, such as uniforms and books. In Tanzania and Kenya, there are also free school feeding programmes. Also, in Kenya, there are programmes in place to promote education of girls specifically, such as the Shoffco and Marie Stopes initiatives, which offer sexual and reproductive healthcare including sanitary pads and cancer-screening for girls. The Kenyan government also provides girls with one packet of sanitary pads each month.

On the other hand, with so many educated young people unable to find work, there is a perception among some individuals in the study countries that education is useless or irrelevant for obtaining decent and quality work in the formal sector. A limited number of jobs have resulted in high unemployment levels, even among educated youth. Sometimes individuals with low educational attainment fare better in terms of income when compared to those who have graduated from upper levels. For this reason, some young men and women no longer think education is a worthwhile investment. Focus group respondents in Uganda were quick to mention, "that rich man did not even go to school, yet he owns cars and many other assets", pointing to a rich man nearby that was driving off in his car. Some individuals who stay in school may later come to find their peers who dropped out are now far ahead of them economically, as this quote from a young man in urban Uganda describes:

> You leave your friends in the villages fishing or trading, and you go to school. After completing senior four or six you come back to the village without a job. Only to be employed by the illiterates to clean and arrange their fishing gear. Why did I go to school, one wonders! This is frustrating and as a result many youths in this village shun education and look at it as a useless venture.

For girls, education can seem particularly useless or irrelevant because they are more likely to get married at a young age and be taken care of economically by their husbands. This is unlike the situation for boys, who must fend for themselves and face pressure to provide for their families.

Findings on early marriage and childbirth

Early marriage

In all six study countries, the law prohibits marriage below the age of 18, and that was well known to most respondents. However, not all communities agree in practice about the age at which marriage should take place. Study findings reveal the prevalence of early marriages in all six countries, with girls often getting married between the age of 16 and 17 in rural areas and between the age of 18 and 20 in urban areas. This is consistent with the DHS data presented in Table 10.1. Early marriage is also clearly linked to dropping out of school since it is much more prevalent among out-of-school girls. Among boys, the age at first marriage is slightly higher, ranging between 18 and 20 years of age in both urban and rural areas. Boys tend to marry at a later age compared to girls because of social expectations, such as having a house or room that is furnished and liveable before they can marry. Where there is still the practice of bride price, the burden of payment can also deter young men from early marriage.

Several interrelated factors underlie the prevalence of early marriages in the study communities, including poverty, early exit from school, early pregnancy, cultural norms, and weak legal institutions.

Poverty is a major driver of early marriage, especially in rural areas where the bride price is considered a source of income. In some parts of Uganda, for example, the bride price has increased significantly and parents are more enticed to marry off school-aged children. With the frequently high number of children per household, some parents will look to marry off their daughters in order to ease their economic strain by having fewer people in the household to feed and care for.

Dropping out of school is also linked to early marriage for girls. Without an education or the skills to earn a living, marriage is seen as a way for girls to get ahead in life. In addition, when a girl leaves school, whether it is through dropping out or graduation, her parents begin thinking of marrying her off to minimise the risk of pre-marital sexual relations and pregnancy, which are considered to bring dishonour to the family. If a girl becomes pregnant, her parents will push her to marry the father of her child as a way to avoid stigma and create social and economic stability for all involved. In cases where pregnancy does not lead to marriage, cultural norms dictate that girls are often outcasts and abandoned by their families. To prevent sexual relationships between unmarried young people, in some cultures, boys are not supposed to be seen talking to girls in the evening. Once this happens, it is believed that the two are engaging in sexual relations and the parents arrange for their marriage.

The following quote from a key informant in Ethiopia illustrates the intricate relationship between early marriage, early pregnancy, and school dropout rates:

> My eldest daughter dropped out of school at grade seven due to teenage pregnancy; she gave birth and stopped going to school. The other four boys are going to school. I myself was an outstanding student but my parents forced me to quit schooling and married me when I was in grade six.

Cultural norms and beliefs about when a child becomes an adult can also lead to early marriages.[5] In some rural communities, girls grow up knowing that when they are close to finishing primary school, they are considered mature enough to find a husband and get married.

Finally, early marriage is only possible because of the lack of enforcement of laws meant to prevent it. In some communities, there are no effective sanctions against early marriages and normally no legal action is taken. It is difficult to enforce laws against early marriage because some parents support non-formal marriages; for instance, girls will disguise themselves as domestic workers or maids for households when they are actually the wife of a man who lives there. Even if a legal claim does get to court, technicalities can prevent a guilty verdict. It is difficult to prove a victim's age with certainty in absence of a birth certificate, which is more common among poor and rural households.

Early childbirth

In addition to early marriage, and sometimes related to it, is the issue of early childbirth. In each of the study countries, the qualitative interviews show that the ages of first birth for both boys and girls range between 12 and 22 years old, with boys tending to be slightly older than girls. This was also documented in Table 10.1. According to study respondents, the ideal ages for giving birth are between 20 and 35 years old for both men and women, with educated individuals believing a more appropriate age to give birth is above 25 years old.

Respondents' views on the preferred number of children a woman should give birth to vary, but between four and seven children was the average response. In rare cases, respondents argued that a woman should give birth continually because not all children survive. Individuals' views on the preferred number of children are based on economic and cultural considerations. Economically, fewer children are easier to manage and it is possible to give them the best quality of life. Conversely, there is also the thinking that a large number of children can boost a household's economic potential because children can support each other when they are younger and contribute financially once they are adults. Culturally, there is a belief that children are a blessing from God and families should have as many as possible.

Early pregnancy can be the result of different factors including early sexual initiation, peer pressure, sex for material gain, child marriage, or weak legal systems. Girls as young as 12 can physically become pregnant, and, at that age, most will not have received proper (or any) sexual education. They do not understand their bodies, such as the implications of the onset of menstruation on their ability to conceive. These young girls will also typically have little to no knowledge of or access to contraceptives. As a key informant from Burkina Faso put it:

> *Avec la honte de ne pas aller vers les agents de santé pour avoir des méthodes contraceptives, elles restent dans l'ignorance et tombent dans le piège.*
>
> [With the shame of not approaching health workers about contraceptive methods, they remain in ignorance and fall into the trap.]

Pressure to conform and be more like their peers can be another factor in early pregnancy. At puberty, young girls become aware of their sexuality and begin thinking that they are old enough to engage in sexual relationships. If their peers are engaged in romantic or sexual relationships, girls are more likely to seek out the same.

The study also documented cases where poverty compelled girls to have sex for material gain and led to early pregnancies. Some girls engaged in early sexual activity so they could afford school fees and materials or other items like clothing and cosmetics. Young girls can also be lured into sexual activity by men who offer them material goods.

Child marriage is a major cause of early childbirth in the study countries. When a girl is married, even if before the age of 18, she is no longer looked at as a child but rather a woman who is someone's wife. In principle, she is then supposed to engage in child-bearing. It is for this reason that early and child marriages result in early pregnancies and motherhood. The weakness of the legal system in the study countries is a major issue. The legal system fails to sanction or punish men who impregnate young girls, leading to the perpetuation of the practice. Even when there is a desire to pursue justice, families often prefer to maintain a harmonious environment by trying to reach an agreement outside the legal system.

Limited and poor-quality sex education is a major factor contributing to early marriage and especially early childbirth in the study countries. This was reported most in Burkina Faso. In most countries, respondents stated that talking about sex is a taboo and it is a topic for adults only. It is frequently believed that any sex education can lead to sexual activities by young men and women. It is for this reason that in families, and even in educational institutions such as schools, churches, and mosques, discussions about sex are avoided; it is a topic of shame and perceived risk. In most study communities, sex education was customarily left to specific individuals such as the *Ssenga*, an aunt who has the task of teaching young girls about sex, among the Baganda people in Uganda. In most cases, however, communities had no sex educators for men because of the assumption and expectation that they will discover issues of sex on their own.

Findings on early work experiences

A key focus of the research is the type of work that young people can obtain, especially for their first or early jobs. Across all the study countries, youth unemployment is a major problem, and, even among youth who have jobs, most are engaged in insecure work for survival purposes. In rural areas, young boys and girls are predominantly engaged in the agricultural sector, mainly in subsistence farming and animal husbandry, but this work is not economically lucrative.

In most of the study countries, education or training is regarded as an important enabler for young people to access better work opportunities as these quotes from respondents in Kenya and Tanzania illustrate:

> There are very many opportunities here in this community as long as you have education certificates. Especially for a Maasai girl who is educated, opportunities are many.
>
> I never looked for work; I just finished Vocational Education Training Authority (VETA) and I got a machine and started working as a tailor.

For many individuals, the challenge of finding decent and well-paying work is the limited number of jobs available, combined with low skill and education levels. Most formal sector jobs impose minimum educational requirements and past work experience as do some informal sector jobs. While some young men and women possess the entrepreneurial spirit and skillset needed to initiate their own income-generating activities, they still face real challenges accessing credit and start-up capital. Business workspaces are also hard to locate and very expensive in terms of rent and utilities. In rural areas, entrepreneurs face additional barriers to running a business, including limited access to power, piped water, and roads.

Youth in the study countries tend to be engaged in low quality informal work, characterised by long hours, unfavourable locations and working conditions, irregular payments, and job insecurity. Under these circumstances, youth will frequently change jobs in search of better pay and improved working conditions or because they are primarily engaged in temporary seasonal or contract work.

Migration is one of the responses to unemployment or poor-quality work. Most migrants in the study countries travel from rural areas to towns or bigger cities in the same country; but, in some cases, migrants will travel to other countries in search of work. For example, in this study, we documented cases of young men and women in Ghana migrating to Nigeria and Libya for work, and of young men and women in Uganda, Tanzania, and Ethiopia, migrating as far as the Middle East. Once migrated, these individuals frequently support their families back home by sending remittances.

There are some additional restrictions in place on the movement of young women compared to young men. In Uganda, Tanzania, and Ghana, for example, relatively few females move out of rural areas because they lack information about where to go and the types of opportunities available outside their community. They also lack the basic education required for formal employment. Respondents in all six of the study countries reported restrictions on the movement of young women due to their responsibility for domestic work and childcare. In Ethiopia, for example, young women will only go against social norms and resort to migration when they have failed in marriage as reported by one respondent: "the difficult circumstances that divorced and separated women find themselves in lead them to take desperate measures such as migrating to major urban centres or to the Middle East to be domestic workers".

For young women who can migrate for work, they are often offered opportunities in the care or services sectors, working as domestic workers, maids, nannies, bar staff, or salon attendants. Unfortunately, due in part to the predominance of women in these sectors, these tend to be low-paying jobs. For example, a young Ethiopian woman in the study reported that, even after migrating to Lebanon, she did not generate sufficient income to lead a better life because she was only able to find employment as a domestic worker.

Young women who migrate for work can also be subject to gender discrimination, harassment, and violence. Some study respondents reported instances where people did not pay after receiving their services or they paid late or only in part. Others deliberately refused to pay knowing that there are no chances for a young woman to hold them accountable. In the most serious cases, young women reported that they had been sexually harassed or physically assaulted at their jobs.

To add to all this, there is a widespread gender wage gap between young boys and girls in the study countries, which stems from women's and girls' disproportionate responsibility for unpaid care and domestic work. For example, in Ghana, we found that male poultry farm workers earn GHS 150–200 (USD26–34) a month. Females in the same position earn just GHS 100–120 (USD17–20) a month. In Uganda, while the average nominal wage for males in employment was UGX 110,000 (USD29), for females it is UGX 88,000 (USD23). And, in Ethiopia, we found that women earn on average 20% less than men for the same work. Similar gender wage gaps were also observed in the other three study countries.

Conclusions and policy implications

The results of this research indicate a very strong pattern of interaction between young people's transition from school to work and key family formation events like marriage and childbirth. And, while it is true that both girls and boys face difficulties in the school-to-work transition, the study data shows that the situation for girls is much worse.

For young girls, there is a strong relationship between dropping out of school and early marriage and childbirth, both of which are widespread in the study countries. Girls may drop out of school for a range of personal, economic, or cultural reasons. Having done so and with limited work options available to them, they may marry and/or become pregnant at a young age. In other cases, early pregnancy for girls who are still in school almost always forces them to drop out.

The negative health consequences of early marriage and early pregnancy can also be very serious for young women and their babies. Strong laws exist against child marriage in all six countries, but the legal framework is weak and not implemented. Many families continue with these practices because there can be strong cultural and economic incentives.

Early marriage and pregnancy also significantly restrict young women's work options. Early pregnancy implies the need for childcare, a responsibility which almost always falls on women and girls. Additionally, in cases of early marriage, husbands frequently will not allow their wives to work outside of the home due to social norms, which further restrict women's employment options.

If they are able to find employment in their own communities or by migrating for work, young women face the added disadvantage of a gender wage gap and are vulnerable to gender-based discrimination, harassment, and violence.

Four key policy priorities emerge from the research on improving school-to-work transition rates for young females in sub-Saharan Africa.

1 Invest strongly in education quality and in keeping girls in school

Access to quality education is key for a successful school-to-work transition, but too often the education available for young people is neither easily accessible nor high quality. Critical in this is ensuring teachers meet professional standards and having processes in place to monitor and evaluate their performance. This should include student evaluations and other feedback mechanisms where students can report issues and make suggestions without fear of negative repercussions.

A key component of quality education is sex education. Even though sex education is a controversial topic, opposed by both religious and cultural norms in the study countries, it needs to be part of the education that young people receive to ensure they engage in safe sexual practices and avoid unplanned pregnancy.

Critical to girls' employment outcomes are measures to keep them in school. More time spent on quality formal education can help socialise girls to resist the social, cultural, and religious norms that promote early marriage and result in early pregnancy. More formal education will also improve the chances of these girls entering the labour market, where they can earn their own income and not be dependent on finding a husband to make their way in the world.

2 Challenge misconceptions and discriminatory social and gender norms

While it may seem straightforward that high quality education leads to more positive employment outcomes, the high number of educated youths who are unemployed has caused some individuals in the study countries to perceive education as useless or irrelevant for finding decent work. Media campaigns on the importance of education, targeting young people and their parents as well as local government and religious leaders, are necessary to combat these perceptions that drive young men and women to drop out of school. They can also help combat the social, cultural, and religious norms that contribute to girls' early exit from school, including the practices of early marriage and early pregnancy that are still commonplace in the study communities. If young girls do get pregnant, the priority must be to facilitate their re-enrolment in school as opposed to forcing them into marriage.

The disproportionate burden of domestic work and childcare that falls on women and young girls is also a barrier to their completing school and finding work outside the home. The promotion of basic infrastructure (piped water, electricity) and time-saving technologies (lanterns, cook stoves) can reduce the burden and the drudgery of unpaid domestic work, and potentially encourage greater male participation in these tasks.

3 Adopt measures to broaden employment opportunities

The school-to-work transition is very difficult for many young people, especially girls, because of the limited number and quality of work opportunities that are available. This can be a major disincentive for families to invest in their children's education, and, faced with such decisions, investment in girls' education often takes a secondary priority. Policies that aim to create an enabling environment for business and support the expansion of the private sector to create the much-needed opportunities are necessary. Rural development programmes, such as public works programmes, can also be implemented to support young people who are out of work. Since many young people in sub-Saharan Africa will continue to work in agriculture, measures to modernise and update the agriculture sector are critical.

4 Enhance young people's opportunities and skillsets

A critical problem for young people in accessing decent and formal work opportunities is their lack of requisite skills and experience. This must be addressed to enable young men and women to take advantage of potential employment opportunities and/or create their own businesses through self-employment. Where employment opportunities are available, higher levels of education are associated with easier transitions to better paid jobs and occupational mobility. Hence, there is a need to not only focus on enrolment in education, but also on retention, completion, and quality. Furthermore, expanding access to and opportunities for quality vocational and technical training is central to helping youth find work in different sectors. Supporting opportunities to help young people migrate to find work, which is particularly difficult for young women, could also be useful.

Notes

1 See www.ilo.org/employment/areas/youth-employment/work-for-youth/WCMS_191853/lang--en/index.htm.
2 For further analysis of the relationship between paid work and childcare, see Chapters 4 and 8 in this volume.
3 A *kebele* is the smallest administrative unit in Ethiopia. It is similar to a ward or a neighbourhood.
4 A richer description of the research conducted in each country is presented in a series of working papers published about the project by Kibora (2018); Belay et al. (2018); Dankyi et al. (2017); Kabubo-Mariara et al. (2017); Kamanzi (2018); and Economic Policy Research Centre (2017).
5 For an in-depth review of the literature on social norms, gender, and women's economic empowerment, see Chapter 5 in this volume.

References

Alam, Andaleeb, and Maria Eugenia de Diego (2019). Unpacking school-to-work transition: Data and evidence synthesis. UNICEF Scoping Paper No. 02. New York: UNICEF. https://data.unicef.org/wp-content/uploads/2020/01/Unpacking-School-to-Work-Transition-Scoping-Paper_2019.pdf.

Belay, Moges, Addisu Meseret, Abbi Kedir, and Seid Nuru (2018). Early labour market transitions for women: Qualitative evidence from Kormaragefiya Village in Ethiopia. GrOW project on Women's Early Labour Market Transitions in Sub-Saharan Africa. Working paper, mimeo.

Dankyi, Ernestina, Louis Boakye-Yiadom, Monica Lambon-Quayefio, and Kwame Adjei-Mantey (2017). The gender dimension of early labour market transitions: Some qualitative evidence from Ghana. GrOW project on Women's Early Labour Market Transitions in Sub-Saharan Africa Working paper, mimeo.

Economic Policy Research Centre (2017). Education, marriage, fertility and labour market experiences of young women in Uganda: A qualitative approach. GrOW project on Women's Early Labour Market Transitions in Sub-Saharan Africa. EPRC Working Paper. Kampala: EPRC, mimeo.

Elder, Sara, and Sriani Kring (2016). Young and female—a double strike? Gender analysis of school-to-work transition surveys in 32 developing countries. ILO Work4Youth Publication Series No. 32. Geneva: International Labour Organization. https://www.ilo.org/wcmsp5/groups/public/---ed_emp/documents/publication/wcms_447495.pdf.

Elder, Sara, Hein de Haas, Marco Principi, and Kerilyn Schewel (2015). Youth and rural development: Evidence from 25 school-to-work transition surveys. ILO Work4Youth Publication Series No. 29. Geneva: International Labour Organization. https://www.skillsforemployment.org/KSP/en/Details/?dn=WCMSTEST4_141854.

ILO and MasterCard Foundation (2016). Can we measure the school-to-work transition of young persons with labour force surveys? A feasibility study. ILO Technical Brief No. 8. Geneva: International Labour Organization. https://www.ilo.org/employment/areas/youth-employment/work-for-youth/publications/technical-briefs/WCMS_535222/lang--en/index.htm.

Kabubo-Mariara, Jane, Mark Kamui, Phyllis Machio, and Anthony Wambugu (2017). The link between education, fertility, marriage and labour market transitions among youth in Kenya. Evidence from qualitative data. GrOW project on Women's Early Labour Market Transitions in Sub-Saharan Africa. Working Paper, mimeo.

Kamanzi, Adalbertus (2018). Qualitative description of selected factors influencing early labor experiences for young women and men in Tanzania. GrOW project on Women's Early Labour Market Transitions in Sub-Saharan Africa. Working Paper, mimeo.

Kibora, Ludovic (2018). Les premières transitions sur le marché du travail des femmes dans les pays africains à faible revenue: Cas du Burkina Faso [Women's first transitions to the labor market in low-income African countries: Case of Burkina Faso]. GrOW project on Women's Early Labour Market Transitions in Sub-Saharan Africa. Working Paper, mimeo.

Manacorda, Marco, Furio Rosati, Marco Ranzani, and Guiseppe Dachile (2017). Pathways from school to work in the developing world. *IZA Journal of Labor Development* 6(1). https://doi.org/10.1186/s40175-016-0067-5.

Matsumoto, Makiko, and Sara Elder (2010). Characterizing the school-to-work transitions of young men and women: Evidence from the ILO School-to-work transition surveys. ILO Employment Working Paper 51. Geneva: International Labour Organization. www.ilo.org/employment/Whatwedo/Publications/working-papers/WCMS_141016/lang--en/index.htm.

Nilsson, Björn (2019). The school-to-work transition in developing countries. *The Journal of Development Studies* 55(5): 745–764.

Sparreboom, Theo, and Anita Staneva (2014). Is education the solution to decent work for youth in developing economies? Identifying qualifications mismatch from 28 school-to-work transition surveys. ILO Work4Youth Publication Series No. 23. Geneva: International Labour Organization. https://www.ilo.org/employment/areas/youth-employment/work-for-youth/publications/thematic-reports/WCMS_326260/lang--en/index.htm.

CONCLUSION

Programming and policy lessons and future research priorities for women's economic empowerment

Gillian Dowie, Arjan de Haan, and Kate Grantham

Introduction

The contributors to this volume demonstrate two clear dynamics regarding the relationship between women's economic empowerment (WEE) and economic growth. First, economic growth alone is not sufficient to bring about WEE, even in the labour market. Factors such as the quality of work, job security, gender pay gaps, occupational and sectoral segregation, macroeconomic trends, social norms, and care responsibilities, all interact to shape women's experiences in the labour market and determine its empowerment potential.

Second, normative and structural barriers to WEE are deeply entrenched. While there are regional differences in how these barriers manifest—for example, female labour force participation (FLFP) in sub-Saharan Africa is extremely high, while in India it is low and declining—their existence is systemic and works to limit women's choices and opportunities globally. By exploring the role of institutions and macroeconomic growth, unpacking the constraints to women's labour market engagement, and examining the impact of social norms and women's care responsibilities, this volume demonstrates the deeply rooted and interlinked nature of barriers to WEE, with a focus on developing country contexts.

The collection of research in this volume, and in the GrOW programme more widely, has helped to build the evidence base on these dynamics and contribute to the development of policies and programmes that promote WEE and gender transformative change (as detailed in a GrOW programme report, de Haan and Melesse 2018). This chapter sums up the main lessons from the GrOW-funded research featured in this volume and identifies future research priorities for WEE and gender equality.

Ways forward: policy and programming lessons

A main thread throughout this volume centres around the systemic nature of constraints to WEE, and how macroeconomic factors, labour market structures, unpaid care, and social norms can coalesce to hinder or stall progress on gender equality. To move the needle forward, policies and programmes need to target these deeper structural issues that prevent women from achieving economic and social equality.

Labour markets

Gender differences and constraints in labour markets are extremely persistent. After seeing global progress in labour market opportunities for women in developing countries since the 1980s, expansion appears to have stalled since the 2000s. Women continue to grapple with the systemic barriers that prevent their transition into better jobs, and they remain overrepresented in informal and precarious work. There is clear evidence of progress on gender equality in education, but it has not sufficiently translated into labour market opportunities.

In Chapter 2, Heintz points to a number of key barriers that prevent continued advancement toward gender equality: labour market segregation; fertility, marriage, and unpaid care work; social norms; and gender-based violence (GBV). These issues are explored throughout this volume, and below in the various sub-themes, demonstrating that these underlying factors work together to constrain women's opportunities and choices.

Chapter 10 by Kabubo-Mariara, Kamanzi, and McKay finds that girls and their families can undervalue education because of the perceived lack of decent opportunities that await them. Promoting the quality of jobs and ensuring that workers in informal occupations have decent working conditions and social protection will be equally key to changing perceptions and realities for women's employment.

Policies and programmes designed to achieve the gender equality goals of the international community require a combination of supply- and demand-side approaches that take gendered structural barriers into account. Economic policies will be crucial to promote employment, particularly in Africa and other contexts where the growth of the working-age population continues to outpace the growth in demand for labour, for both young women and men. Evidence to identify what sets of policies can promote these objectives can play a very important role, and gender analysis is needed to ensure that broader policies address gender barriers and create inclusive opportunities.

Macroeconomics

Progress on gender equality remains slow, even at a time when gender-sensitive policies in developing countries are advancing. This is despite global commitments to the Sustainable Development Goals (SDGs) and evidence that lowering gender gaps—particularly in education—contributes to economic growth. The evidence in this volume shows that economic growth alone does not have a robust effect on women's employment. Women do enter the labour market when more and better jobs exist, but there is evidence of women leaving the labour market during those transitions as well—and of declining labour force participation notably in India—and, as mentioned, many of the jobs are of poor quality and unprotected.

The review of evidence of these links in Chapter 3 by Kan and Klasen highlights that the use of FLFP itself is an inadequate indication of the links between growth and WEE. It does not reflect the quality of jobs available to women and does not explain the transitions that take place as women move in and out of the labour market. The authors find that economic growth has little impact on gender occupational and sectoral segregation. There is some evidence that promoting trade in female-dominated industries, such as garment manufacturing and certain services, can create opportunities for women, though there is also evidence of overall job losses as a result of trade liberalisation.

As a result of the way that economic growth and WEE are (dis)connected, reliance on growth or trade alone will do little to promote WEE. Instead, more targeted and context-specific policies that take women's economic and social circumstances into account and focus on removing specific barriers to their empowerment are required. Gender equality should be the central goal in and of itself. More generalisable evidence is needed on specific macroeconomic policies and WEE, as well as other enabling factors such as childcare, affirmative action policies, financial inclusion, and investments in public infrastructure.

Social norms

Despite global commitments to gender equality, and progress in areas like health and education, the uneven progress toward WEE and equality in the world of work demonstrates the complex dynamics of women's opportunities, challenges, and choices. As Marcus lays out in Chapter 5 of this volume, and as is highlighted again across all the case studies, social and gender norms influence all aspects of women's lives, particularly adult women and girls transitioning into young adulthood.

Policies and programmes aimed at increasing women's access to opportunities have often failed because they do not adequately consider the underlying constraints on women imposed by social norms. Norms play an important role in explaining many labour market phenomena, such as persistent gender segregation, low or declining FLFP, women's double burden of paid and unpaid work, household decision-making, and the aspirations of women and girls.

In Chapter 8, Chopra highlights the example of women participating in programmes specifically designed to provide them with paid work, resulting in their mental and physical depletion as they struggle to combine this work with their unpaid domestic and care responsibilities. Similarly, a training programme in rural Pakistan, cited in Chapter 5, saw high attrition rates among women because of their inability to leave the boundaries of their village (Cheema et al. 2019, cited in Chapter 5). Even where women have managed to enter white-collar, higher paying jobs, research has found that these women typically have higher literacy levels than their male colleagues, pointing to discriminatory norms that may require women to achieve more than their male counterparts for the same outcomes (Mariara et al. 2018, cited in Chapter 5).

Norms are held and enforced by individuals, communities, families, and society, but, as Chapter 6 by Buss et al. highlights, formal institutions also reflect and often reproduce these norms. Women working in artisanal mining were found to be segregated in less lucrative roles on the periphery of digging. Some women were able to secure better positions as gold sellers or team supervisors, but these were reported to become even more challenging when local chiefs and mining associations/cooperatives added formal structures. The structures appear to have increased women's exclusion, formally putting control of the mines into the hands of men, pointing to the challenges of WEE initiatives in places where norms are reinforced by institutions.

Even in a post-conflict setting where one might expect a shifting of norms to allow women to work outside the home and access different opportunities, the study in Sri Lanka by Gunatilaka and Vithanagama in Chapter 9 suggests otherwise. Women are driven to engage in paid work out of poverty, but those who can live in a household with other men or who have access to programmes like cash transfers are much more likely to stay home. Women who work outside the home also remain limited to low-quality work and lack access to training and finance that could help them improve their income-earning activities.

Norms are deeply entrenched, but they are also changeable with time and intentional effort. Chapter 5 highlights evidence in some of the GrOW-supported research of shifting norms over long periods of time, particularly resulting from programmes on women's collectivisation and empowerment, improving access to childcare and incentives for training, education, and delaying marriage. Transformative change is slow, and research can support this process. It requires researchers to develop and utilise more qualitative and subjective indicators for WEE that are often hard to measure. Mixed-methods research in the GrOW programme provided insight into how norms impact women's lives and choices, but deeper exploration of the subject of changing norms, and capacities for providing local evidence are needed.

Unpaid care work

Norms around women's care responsibilities appear to be some of the most persistent and perhaps have the strongest role in shaping women's choices. In low-income contexts, women often seek paid work that is flexible and closer to home in order to balance that work with their unpaid care responsibilities, limiting their choices to low-wage and low-quality opportunities.

Several chapters in this volume show the role of unpaid care and domestic work in determining the quantity and quality of women's paid work. Chapter 7 by Nyariro et al. brings in the critical perspectives of women who had access to a daycare facility, which they report has very positive impacts on their children's welfare, and, subsequently, their own mental health and ability to concentrate at work. In Chapter 8, time-use surveys and qualitative interviews paint a picture of women's time being constantly consumed by some form of work, with additional hours of unpaid care work at home after their paid workday is complete. Chapter 10 looks at adolescent girls in their transition to adulthood, and finds that, as they get older, they take on more unpaid work around the family home, and a large number of them are likely to be married and begin having children early, making care their primary responsibility.

The absence of nearby infrastructure that would ease the burden of care—from water and fuel, to decent roads and safe transportation, to health centres and schools, and even quality childcare facilities—makes care responsibilities more time consuming and physically burdensome. Access to better services and facilities combined with decent work opportunities may go a long way in improving women's quality of life, their time poverty, and their mental and physical well-being. Many of these recommendations for advancing the care policy agenda are detailed in Chapter 4 by Folbre.

Future research priorities

Since the GrOW programme launched in 2013, the focus on WEE by researchers, governments, and multilateral institutions has grown. The international development landscape shifted during this period from the Millennium Development Goals to the SDGs, bringing with it an expanded and cross-cutting focus on gender equality and increased attention to research, data, and evidence on WEE itself. As we enter the final decade for delivering on the SDGs (including SDG 5 to achieve gender equality and empower all women and girls), research and investment on WEE should focus on delivering transformative impacts that address entrenched social norms, attitudes, behaviours, and systems that disadvantage women. The following are some emerging and future research priorities for WEE that build on the evidence generated from the GrOW programme.

Entrepreneurship

Women's entrepreneurship is believed to be a key enabler of WEE, and, though it was not a specific focus of the GrOW programme, several studies identified barriers to women's entrepreneurship stemming from discriminatory social norms or women's responsibility for unpaid care. More research is needed to flesh out other aspects of the relationship between entrepreneurship and WEE in specific contexts.

While some details and outcomes of women-owned and women-led businesses are documented by enterprise surveys like the World Bank Enterprise Surveys and the Global Entrepreneurship Monitor, they do not capture women's subjective experiences of entrepreneurship nor do they explore the full range of issues and what specifically is needed to create an enabling environment for women entrepreneurs (Joekes and Kaminski 2017; ICRW 2019; Data2X and Grantham 2020). On women's subjective experiences of entrepreneurship, research is needed to understand the school-to-work transition for women in different contexts and to document whether women are motivated by desire or necessity to engage in self-employed work. On barriers and enablers for women's entrepreneurship, we need international and comparative research on the impact of government regulations and tax regimes, social protection policies, market access, connectivity, access to safe public transportation, access to quality and affordable childcare, ownership of government issued identification, and gender discrimination in the labour market (ICRW 2019; Data2X and Grantham 2020).

Financial inclusion

Women's access to financial markets and opportunities was a key focus of the GrOW programme, but this did not extend to addressing women's financial inclusion specifically. This is despite the facts that women face unique and disproportionate barriers to accessing and using financial products and services and are often the targets of financial inclusion schemes, such as microfinance, savings accounts, insurance, digital finance, and, increasingly, gender lens investing. Recent research by Data2X at the UN Foundation finds that the

> growth in initiatives like the World Bank's Global Findex, the IMF's Financial Access Survey, and other surveys has increased the availability and use of sex-disaggregated data on access to financial services … however, data on women's use of and benefit from financial inclusion remains limited and fragmented.
>
> *(Data2X and Grantham 2020: 4).*

As a result, we cannot yet distinguish which design features and practices of financial inclusion are the most beneficial for WEE and gender equality (e.g. decision-making power, control over resources, access to market opportunities, etc.) (Vossenberg, Rappoldt, and D'Anjou 2018). More research is needed to determine the WEE potential of financial inclusion, and this should be a priority going forward.

Women's collectives, cooperatives, and self-help groups

Around the world and in many developing country contexts, women's collectives, cooperatives, and self-help groups are the foundation for WEE initiatives and for women's collective action against social and legal discrimination. Several GrOW-supported studies focused on programmes or policies that relied on women's collectives but did not specifically draw on findings about their role for WEE. Women's participation in different forms of collectives has been shown to improve income and working conditions, shift restrictive social norms and attitudes, and boost members' self-esteem and sense of identity, improving their position at home and in the community (Hunt and Samman 2016). A recent review of evidence on the impact of women's group interventions finds that they are effective as a platform for an intervention or for information to reach a large number of women and leverage supportive interactions among members (Dìaz-Martin et al. 2020).

Evidence on the drivers of collective agency, on building sustainable groups, and on the mechanisms behind the positive impacts remain a priority. Key questions include how to package and design interventions that promote positive spillovers, such as shifting norms and greater local political representation of women, and how group dynamics and factors such as size and meeting frequency can create positive results. Recent questions around collectives in a digital era in developing country contexts may open new programming avenues.

Measurement

A synthesis paper on the measurement of WEE in GrOW-supported research found that most studies used quantitative and objective measures for WEE (e.g. income, loan use, etc.), due in part to data limitations and the methodological complexity of capturing more qualitative and context-specific information (Laszlo and Grantham 2017). The same is true for the wider body of research on WEE (Laszlo et al. 2020). More methodological work is needed to develop robust and internationally standardised measures for the subjective dimensions of WEE—that is, measures which are centred on a respondent's own beliefs, experiences, and perspectives (Kabeer 1999, 2001; Quisumbing, Rubin, and Sproule 2016). This includes psychosocial and decision-making measures around agency, self-esteem, and stress, as well as attitudes toward discrimination and GBV. To capture women's own voices, understandings, and definitions of WEE in a given context, we emphasise the importance of mixed-methods and participatory research.

Interdisciplinary research positioned to make a difference

Each chapter in this volume documents the systemic nature of constraints on WEE, and the ways that multiple barriers interact to prevent women from achieving equality. The depth of understanding of women's experiences emerging from the GrOW programme can at least partly be attributed to the interdisciplinarity of the teams and the mixed methods that they employed. For example, the case study on artisanal mining in Chapter 6 was led by a team of legal experts, anthropologists, statisticians, and activists. In Chapter 7, the benefits of combining traditional economic methods such as randomised control trials with the qualitative and participatory approach of PhotoVoice are extolled. The combination of different disciplines and methods within the GrOW programme not only enhances the academic insights but also often leads to better positioning of the research to influence policy and practice (de Haan, Dowie, and Mariara 2020).

This highlights an important priority for the international development community—supporting local capacity for interdisciplinary research is critical to further progress on SDG 5. The GrOW programme demonstrated the need to support such capacity across academic disciplines; that collaborative research programmes can make significant contributions to promote local research leadership, to ensure the research is valid in specific contexts; and that recommendations are likely to lead to transformative and sustained progress toward gender equality.

Concluding remarks

We have been preparing this volume during the onset of the COVID-19 pandemic, and while it features research from the years prior to publication and hopes to inform scholars and practitioners for many years after, we must mention that this is a time when women's inequality in social and economic spheres is particularly visible and risks are becoming more entrenched. The discussion at the time of writing is on the serious potential for long-term setbacks in advancing gender equality. COVID-19 is expected to have devastating consequences for women and girls, reversing the limited progress toward gender equality achieved in recent decades (United Nations 2020). Hard won gains for women and girls in the areas of health (including sexual and reproductive health), education, food security, public participation, and more, are all at risk of deteriorating.

The impacts of the pandemic on women's labour force participation and responsibility for unpaid care are front and centre. Worldwide, the sudden closure of schools and childcare facilities, combined with restrictions around individual movement and social distancing requirements, has removed institutional and community support for parents, including during their own normal working hours. School closures have also meant that parents—and mostly the women—are being asked to take on the added responsibility for educating their children at home. The burden of care for people infected by the virus is also likely to fall on women.

As lockdowns result in workplace closures and decreased economic activity, many industries will contract and some businesses will not survive. Workers will be competing for fewer jobs, and women workers will be at a greater disadvantage if the burden for household care and domestic work is not shared. This may drive down wages, widen gender gaps in earnings and savings, and decrease women's labour force participation for a generation or more.

Yet there is also optimism during this crisis, with renewed calls to rebuild economies and societies to be more just, equal, and inclusive, and place greater value on workers, human wellbeing, health, and environmental sustainability. Conversations on care responsibilities have become mainstream, as women across industries feel the burden more directly than they had when a supportive infrastructure existed. Research will play an important role in addressing the COVID-19 pandemic and its aftermath. We need to gather disaggregated data and have gender analyses on the impact of the pandemic, as well as the recovery efforts, in order to understand the immediate and long-term losses and impacts on gender equality and WEE, and to develop evidence-informed programmes and policymaking.

There is a real risk that the COVID-19 pandemic makes achieving the global goals for gender equality even harder to achieve. Before the crisis hit, the World Economic Forum estimated that it would take more than 250 years for gender gaps in economic participation and opportunities to close (World Economic Forum 2019). The rise of populism and nationalism in countries around the world was already threatening to derail progress on gender equality. Growing evidence also indicates that women disproportionately bear the burden of the climate crisis and extreme weather events (Aguilar, Granat, and Owren 2015) with specific impacts on their economic empowerment (Patel et al. 2018).

To maintain and promote past progress, and address current threats, will require a renewed commitment to gender equality. We believe, and hope, this volume has demonstrated that locally embedded research has a role to play in advancing strategies and policies to promote equality and inclusion, and to support women's voice and leadership in navigating these crises. In particular, research can build the recognition of the systemic and complex nature of the barriers that women face and support commitments from across a range of stakeholders to deliver transformative change.

References

Aguilar, Lorena, Margaux Granat, and Cate Owren (2015). Roots for the future: The landscape and way forward on gender and climate change. Washington, DC: International Union for Conservation and Global Gender and Climate Alliance. https://portals.iucn.org/library/sites/library/files/documents/2015-039.pdf.

Cheema, Ali, Asim I. Khwaja, Farooq Naseer, and Jacob Shapiro (2019). Glass walls: Experimental evidence on access constraints faced by women. Working Paper. https://khwaja.scholar.harvard.edu/files/asimkhwaja/files/glass_walls_draft_november_draft.pdf.

Data2X, and Kathleen Grantham (2020). Mapping gender data gaps in economic opportunities. Washington, DC: UN Foundation. https://data2x.org/wp-content/uploads/2020/03/MappingGenderDataGaps_Economic.pdf.

de Haan, Arjan, and Martha Melesse (2018). Promoting women's economic empowerment: Emerging insights from a 5-year policy research program. GrOW Program Report 3. Ottawa: IDRC. https://idl-bnc-idrc.dspacedirect.org/bitstream/handle/10625/56980/IDL-56980.pdf?sequence=2&isAllowed=y.

de Haan, Arjan, Gillian Dowie, and Jane Mariara (2020). To RCT or not, is not the question: Methods for policy-relevant research on gender equality. *World Development* 127.

Dìaz-Martin, Lucìa, Akshara Gopalan, Eleonora Guarnieri, and Seema Jayachandran (2020). Greater than the sum of the parts? Evidence on mechanisms operating in women's groups. Working paper. Evanston, IL: Northwestern University. https://faculty.wcas.northwestern.edu/~sjv340/womens_groups.pdf.

Hunt, Abigail, and Emma Samman (2016). Women's economic empowerment: Navigating enablers and constraints. Research Report. London: Overseas Development Institute. www.peacewomen.org/sites/default/files/Womens%20Economic%20Empowerment.pdf.

ICRW (2019). Women entrepreneurs need more than capital: What do women's businesses really need to grow and thrive? Washington, DC: International Centre for Research on Women. www.icrw.org/wp-content/uploads/2019/10/Women-Entrepreneurship-Beyond-Capital_final.pdf.

Joekes, Susan, and Jonathan Kaminski (2017). Scoping study on gender differences in enterprise surveys. London: Business Environment Reform Facility. https://assets.publishing.service.gov.uk/media/5c791d60e5274a0ec9a1dc27/BERF-Scoping-Study-Gender-Differences-in-Enterprise-Surveys-April-2017.pdf.

Kabeer, Naila (1999). Resources, agency and achievements: Reflections on the measurement of women's economic empowerment. *Development and Change* 30(3): 435–464. www.utsc.utoronto.ca/~kmacd/IDSC10/Readings/research%20design/empowerment.pdf.

Kabeer, Naila (2001). Reflections on the measurement of women's empowerment. In Anne Sisask (Ed.), *Discussing Women's Empowerment: Theory and Practice* (17–57). Stockholm: Swedish International Development Cooperation Agency.

Laszlo, Sonia, and Kate Grantham (2017). Measurement of women's economic empowerment in GrOW projects: Inventory and user guide. GrOW Working Paper Series, GWP-2017–08. Montreal: Institute for the Study of International Development, McGill University. http://grow.research.mcgill.ca/publications/working-papers/gwp-2017-08.pdf.

Laszlo, Sonia, Kate Grantham, Ecem Oskay, and Tingting Zhang (2020). Grappling with the challenges of measuring women's economic empowerment in intrahousehold settings. *World Development* 132: 1–13.

Mariara, Jane, Andy McKay, Andy Newell, and Cinzia Rienzo. (2018). Gender gaps in the path to adulthood for young females and males in six African countries from the 1990s to the 2010s. *IZA Journal of Development and Migrations* 8(16): 1–19. https://izajodm.springeropen.com/track/pdf/10.1186/s40176-018-0124-8.

Patel, Amit, Marcia D. Mundt, Hyunjung Lee, Hina Loita, Muhammad Arshed Rafiq, and Ammar A. Malik (2018). Empowering women in South Asia's slums: The challenges of environmental degradation. GrOW Working Paper Series, GWP-2018–17. Montreal: Institute for the Study of International Development, McGill University. http://grow.research.mcgill.ca/publications/working-papers/gwp-2018-17.pdf.

Quisumbing, Agnes, Deborah Rubin, and Katie Sproule (2016). Subjective measures of women's economic empowerment. Unpublished manuscript. www.womeneconroadmap.org/sites/default/files/Wms Entrepreneurship_rev_clean.pdf.

United Nations (2020). The impact of COVID-19 on women. United Nations Policy Brief. New York: United Nations. www.un.org/sites/un2.un.org/files/policy_brief_on_covid_impact_on_women_9_apr_2020_updated.pdf.

Vossenberg, Saskia, Anne Rappoldt, and Jesse D'Anjou (2018). *Beyond Access: Exploring Gender-Transformative Approaches to Financial Inclusion*. Ottawa: IDRC. https://idl-bnc-idrc.dspacedirect.org/handle/10625/57156.

World Economic Forum (2019). *Global Gender Gap Report 2020*. Geneva: World Economic Forum. www3.weforum.org/docs/WEF_GGGR_2020.pdf.

INDEX

Page numbers in **bold** refer to figures, page numbers in *italic* refer to tables.

www.ingramcontent.com/pod-product-compliance
Lightning Source LLC
LaVergne TN
LVHW021120300926
849160LV00010B/802
* 9 7 8 0 3 6 7 6 9 4 7 9 1 *